EXPLORING the SPIRITUAL

Paths for Counselors and Psychotherapists

EXPLORING the SPIRITUAL

Paths for Counselors and Psychotherapists

David R. Matteson

Routledge
Taylor & Francis Group

Routledge
Taylor & Francis Group
270 Madison Avenue
New York, NY 10016

Routledge
Taylor & Francis Group
2 Park Square
Milton Park, Abingdon
Oxon OX14 4RN

Routledge is an imprint of Taylor & Francis Group, an Informa business

Printed in the United States of America on acid-free paper
10 9 8 7 6 5 4 3 2 1

International Standard Book Number-13: 978-0-7890-3673-5 (Softcover) 978-0-7890-3672-8 (Hardcover)

Library of Congress Cataloging-in-Publication Data

Matteson, David R.
Exploring the spiritual: paths for counselors and psychotherapists / David R. Matteson.
p. cm.
Includes bibliographical references.
ISBN: 978-0-7890-3672-8 (hard : alk. paper)
ISBN: 978-0-7890-3673-5 (soft : alk. paper)
1. Counseling—Religious aspects. 2. Psychotherapy–Religious aspects. 3. Counselors—Religious life. 4. Psychotherapists—Religious life. 5. Psychology and religion. I. Title.

BF636.6.M38 2007
158'.3–dc22 2007046185

Visit the Taylor & Francis Web site at
http://www.taylorandfrancis.com

and the Routledge Web site at
http://www.routledge.com

To Sandy, my beloved wife,
for forty-eight years of enriching my life
and keeping me grounded.

CONTENTS

Foreword

There was a time when counseling and psychotherapy were suggested to be "value-free." Most of us no longer subscribe to this idea. We know that therapists have their own value systems; ideals are built into the theories that they choose. Freudians espouse a notion of compromise among impulses, mechanisms of delay, and moral sanctions; Jungians center their approach on the primacy of the spiritual; Rogerians see their clients as essentially good and growing; and cognitive-behavioral therapists value efficacy and clear thinking. Whether or not these value positions are communicated to patients, they must be clear to counselors, otherwise we may find ourselves acting irresponsibly to influence clients in ways we are unaware. One of the admirable qualities of this book is that it is clear in its emphasis on the importance of spirituality in counseling—whatever various forms that may take.

In this introduction, it is not my intention to furnish an alternative to a spiritual approach, but rather to describe a set of naturally derived values that might provide a developmental foundation for spiritual experience. My own therapeutic goals are Freud's modest "love and work." *Love* refers to meaningful and mutually enriching connection with others; *work* means relatively conflict-free labor based upon one's abilities. My theoretical base for understanding human development is Erikson's psychosocial approach, which provides a blueprint for human growth that is both expectable and achievable.

Erikson posited eight life-cycle stages of ego development. These developmental periods and their associated ego strengths are the following:

- Infancy: basic trust versus mistrust
- Toddler: autonomy versus shame, doubt
- Early childhood: initiative versus guilt
- School age: industry versus inferiority

- Adolescence: identity versus identity diffusion
- Young adulthood: intimacy versus isolation
- Adulthood: generativity versus stagnation
- Old age: integrity versus despair

Each of these stages has its chronological period of ascendancy, but each one also occurs during the period of ascendancy of every other stage; that is, each psychosocial developmental issue occurs at every age. Therefore, there are not just the 8 major periods of growth, but 64 total stages. For example, an identity issue occurs at adulthood, and a generativity issue occurs during adolescence. Every age, then, has a major developmental crisis as well as legacies from previous stages and forerunners to succeeding ones. This theoretical configuration is important because it suggests that previously unresolved crises (e.g., trust during young adulthood) can be resolved at later ages. For example, what appears to be an intimacy problem at young adulthood may, in fact, have its origin in the basic trust versus mistrust crisis of infancy. The structure of the theory also allows for the precocious resolution of stages (e.g., generativity at adolescence). One might think of teenage pregnancies wherein the adolescent is confronted not only with the expectable issue of identity, but with "future" questions of intimacy and generativity as well.

Our research has established empirical validity for five of the eight stages: industry, identity, intimacy, generativity, and integrity. To accomplish this, we have expanded Erikson's theory to include not just the polar alternatives (e.g., generativity versus stagnation), but also the intermediate styles of resolving the crises (e.g., generativity, pseudo-generative, agentic and communal, conventional, and stagnant). The most extensive work has been done on identity, for which we have identified and established characteristics of four identity statuses or outcomes. We have labeled these outcomes achievement, moratorium, foreclosure, and identity diffusion.

Achievement persons have undergone exploration periods in such life areas as occupation, ideology, and relationships, and have made commitments. *Moratorium* individuals are still struggling to make such commitments; they can be said to be in an "identity crisis." *Foreclosures* are committed, but they have not done any significant exploring; the content of their commitments remaining at, say, age 22 much the same as they were at age 12. *Identity diffusions* have neither explored seriously nor are they committed.

Different therapeutic approaches are suggested for the different identity statuses. *Achievements* usually need only information and perhaps some advice. *Moratoriums* need to have their struggle validated, without the counselor taking sides with any alternatives presented. *Foreclosures,* because they will appear for therapy only when their rather rigid structure has been shattered, must be treated gently and "companionably" while new values are being established. *Identity diffusions* often require the therapist to become a primary object with whom the client can identify, similar to reparenting.

Embedded in the foregoing brief excursion into theory, research, and therapy are my own values. Because I am a therapist and teacher, I require a theory that provides a broad overview of the human condition and suggests realizable developmental possibilities. I do not need a theory that tells me, technically, what to *do,* but one that tells me where my patients may have *come from* and where I might expect them to *go*. I am willing to employ a variety of techniques to enable them to make the important developmental transitions. As a scientist, I require a theory that can be empirically validated, albeit sometimes with great effort because of my chosen theory's inherent nonspecificity. Although I recognize that questions can be answered in many ways, I prefer the scientific method, warts and all. To believe, I must see.

With respect to spirituality, the previous discussion may seem remote. However, the development of basic trust, autonomy, initiative, industry, identity, intimacy, generativity, and integrity furnishes both the foundation for spiritual experience and the capacity for integrating that experience into one's ongoing life. I do not think that a person can reason his or her way into the spiritual. It is more a question of feeling, of experience. The question then arises: "What are the psychological conditions that increase the probability of such an experience?" I think that they consist of a consciousness relatively free from the negative Eriksonian alternatives of mistrust, shame/doubt, guilt, inferiority, diffusion, isolation, and despair.

Is the experience of the spiritual something that should be sought? I think that people who actively seek it out are those who have already happened upon such an experience or who see it as a remedy for the feelings arising from the negative developmental positions mentioned previously. Certainly, the spiritual feeling-state can be achieved in many ways: meditation, drugs, selective brain stimulation, as well as other means outlined in this book. I cannot say that it is my goal in psychotherapy to serve as a spiritual guide. For patients seeking this, I make a referral to a good Jungian friend. My goal is to clear the ground (clean up the muck, if you will) to allow for the possibility and integration of such an experience. Rarely do I deal (at least consciously) with aspects of the Jungian Self. Primarily, I work with the Freudian/Eriksonian ego.

However, is the experience of the spiritual something that should be sought? Certainly, as a dear colleague, Janet Strayer, has suggested, most people in this state "do no harm." And from my modest therapeutic perspective, that is saying a lot. Most people, having had such an experience, want to repeat it. (Although I think that Jung is right when he says that such experiences can be terrifying, too.) I tend to listen respectfully to such experiences related by my patients. I confess to sometimes using my patients' religious beliefs (not necessarily the same thing as spiritual experience) in the service of therapy. Almost all major religions have precepts that can be therapeutically useful if reframed in psychological/developmental terms. I have also used patients' spiritual experiences to acquaint them with the vastness of their internal lives.

Still, is the experience of the spiritual something that should be sought? The most authentic answer I can make is that I don't know. For myself, and, yes, for my patients, too, I would like to have us both in some kind of psychological "state of grace" wherein such experiences are possible. If I can clear up the psychological impediments to a spiritual experience, then I shall have enabled my patients to get on productively, lovingly, humorously, sometimes joyously, with their lives in *this* world. This is sufficient for me. For those wanting to go further (or elsewhere), and even for those who would like a greater appreciation for the spiritual in counseling, I commend this book, which provides such a well-reasoned and highly useful guide.

James E. Marcia, PhD
Professor Emeritus
Developmental/Clinical Psychology
Simon Fraser University
Burnaby, British Columbia

Acknowledgments

The staff at The Haworth Press have been a joy to work with. I am especially grateful to Tara Barnes for her skillful and thoughtful suggestions in improving the manuscript.

I am deeply grateful to two persons who have carefully read and commented on most of this manuscript: my longtime friend George Banziger has been especially helpful in suggesting material in the social sciences that is relevant to the theme of each chapter, and my brother-in-law Monty Cox has provided insightful suggestions on spiritual and theological issues in the text, and frankly shared his perceptions when some of my opinions or conclusions needed rethinking. I also want to thank George Ochsenfeld, Darrell Lance, and James Harrison for their comments and input on specific chapters.

Many students in my teaching career have taught me much as much as I have taught them. I am particularly grateful for the students in three classes I taught in spirituality and counseling, whose personal involvement in the courses helped to shape this book. I have also been extremely fortunate to have a number of wonderful spiritual mentors in my life: Rev. Elmer Beacom, Professor Melvin Bernstein, Dr. William Hamilton, and Dr. James Ashbrook come to mind.

Finally, I want to thank my mother, whose openness both spiritually and intellectually has been an inspiration throughout my life.

Introduction

Spirituality and the Counselor's Connection with the Client

This book is intended for spiritual and religious seekers regardless of their particular tradition or faith. The book will help counselors explore their own experience of the spiritual and set it in the context of relevant material from the social sciences. My hope is that this combination of experiential and evidential material will lead the reader to a more grounded and vital spiritual life and practice.

The simplest profound definition of spirituality I have seen is this: "That which connects one to all that is" (Griffith & Griffith, 2001). Spirituality always involves a concern with more than just oneself; it involves transcending oneself, being open to an experience that is greater than the present self. Though spiritual growth includes care for self, it cannot be separated from care for others, including caring for our clients.

Counseling is a special connection to another human being. As therapists, we seek to connect to our clients' mental and emotional processes in order to help them make decisions, make changes, and live more fruitful and satisfying lives. We try to connect in ways that are fully respectful of clients' own goals and strengths. If clients see their own spirituality as a source of strength, it makes sense to connect with clients' spirituality. We must do so from our own spirituality, yet it is important that we do so in a way that does not impose or exploit or attempt to proselytize the client. We must use our spirituality to connect with, not violate, the client's spirituality.

The counselor's connection—both with the client, and with "all that is"—involves much more than just the beliefs and theories the counselor holds. Becoming a spiritually sensitive counselor cannot be done simply through reading books and thinking through one's spirituality, though this is important. In the cognitive section of this book (Parts I, II, and III), material will be presented to help the counselor deal with the cognitive aspects of becoming a spiritually sensitive counselor, including looking at belief systems and information from the social sciences that may be relevant. The professional counselor or psychotherapist (I will use these words interchangeably) must be a responsible scholar. However, even the most academically rigorous training programs for psychotherapists recognize that counselors need more than cognitive knowledge—they also need skills. Numerous texts and skill workshops assist in the training of counselor skills, and the present book will not focus on this. In addition to having cognitive learning and relationship skills, spiritually sensitive counselors need to be grounded in their own ethical and spiritual experience. The crucial learning in the intersection of spirituality and counseling concerns process, not content, and it can be learned only experientially. Thus Part IV of this book consists of a series of experiments intended to help the reader structure her or his experiential learning. Most of the experiments will focus on the exploration of the counselor's inner experience or on the counselor experimenting with new behaviors. The intent is to help you, as counselor, expand your own spiritual experience and become comfortable with the sort of process that will allow you to work more deeply with clients. As you become grounded in your own spiritual experience, I believe you will be less likely to shy away from the spiritual experiences and conceptualizations or beliefs of your clients, and less likely to impose your own views on them.

The first part of the book consists of essays on key conceptual issues in the interface of psychotherapy and psychology with spirituality and religion. Though these cognitive chapters present important factual and conceptual material, they are not "academic" in the sense of being totally analytical. I have tried to synthesize important themes in the fields of theology, history of religions, and social science, and to suggest some integration. I have taken a position (as openly as possible) on some of the issues, and I have shared personal experiences to illustrate what some of these themes have meant in my own life.

These two sections of the book, Parts I through III, and Part IV, are not intended to be read in sequence. Rather, it is expected that you, the reader, will move back and forth between the cognitive and the experiential material, gathering cognitive knowledge, and working on experiments to assist you in your own personal development. In the process, I hope you will draw some tentative conclusions, attempt your own integration, and find your own center.

How do you feel about reading a book from which you can both learn cognitively and try to apply it by doing some experiments? This might be a good time to take a look at one or two of the first experiments—turn to Chapter 10. You may want to use two bookmarks, or Post-its, so you can easily move back and forth as it fits your own desires to read or to experiment.

HOW TO USE THIS BOOK

This book has been written primarily for counselors and counselors in training, though it may be useful to others who have explored their own personal dynamics and feel a longing to move beyond this pursuit to a broader involvement with life. The book is geared for persons who have already invested significant time and energy in "finding themselves." However, it would be possible for someone who is still in the process of self-discovery to use this book. If you are a person who has not had the opportunity to form a firm identity, if you feel you do not yet have a solid autonomous self, you may be particularly conscious that *this book is not balanced.*

If you feel you do not have a firm sense of self, I would recommend that you use this book simultaneously with other works that emphasize the development of self. A pioneering work, Integrating Spirituality in Counseling, *by Elfie Hinterkopf (1998), is an especially useful companion.*

This book is an attempt to redress an imbalance I have experienced in my long career of counseling and teaching counseling. I believe, in the practice of psychotherapy and counseling in the West, we have maintained a focus on "self" that is in fact a distortion of life. It is as if counseling/psychotherapy has gotten stuck in an adolescent identity crisis and has failed to move on to other stages of development.

Much of my life's work has focused on identity issues. This book is not intended to deny the importance of these issues. It is intended to help us move beyond identity—at least for brief moments to transcend self-centeredness. However, because the material in Chapters 10 through 12 is experiential and uses grounding methods, I anticipate it will be fairly easy for most readers to avoid flying off into intellectualized speculations, or getting overwhelmed with emotional material. This is why I encourage you to move back and forth between the cognitive section (Chapters 1-9) and the experiments (Chapters 10-12). My hope is not to encourage a denial of self, but to help you move beyond self.

WHO'S WRITING? THE AUTHOR'S BACKGROUND

As will become obvious, this work is in part autobiographical. I think it is preferable to be explicit about some of my background that influences my perspective in this work. My early vocational decisions led me into the Christian ministry, expecting to become a college chaplain; I served a small rural church as minister for a few years, but discovered that my real gifts and talents were in counseling, especially group, couple, and family counseling. I have spent most of the subsequent years ministering in secular institutions. I became a counselor at a coed liberal arts campus, teaching psychology courses and researching identity formation. I then worked as clinical director of a public mental health center. However, despite choosing secular settings for my work, my spiritual concerns—though no longer exclusively Christian—have not abated. For the past 30 years my career has centered on counselor education, though my research and work with students has also included AIDS prevention programming, anti-oppression work, and pure and applied social science research. Teaching an elective graduate course on spirituality and experiential approaches to counseling has convinced me that many counselors and counselors in training share a longing for a more expansive view of life. My own attempt to integrate my spiritual and my psychological work was a major incentive for offering this course, and motivates my writing this book.

Two other attempts at integration in my own life deserve mention. The first concerns masculinity and femininity as they have been constructed in much of Western culture, and in American culture in particular. I have written in detail on this issue elsewhere (see especially Matteson, 1993a). Suffice it to say that our culture has split crucial components of the self along gender lines, encouraging women to develop a connected self while encouraging men to develop an autonomous, instrumental self. Despite the remarkable changes due to the recent wave of the women's movement and the important conceptual corrections feminism has promoted, as a society we continue to treat the connected self as inferior to the autonomous self. We do so not only in our allocation of resources as a society, but in our child-rearing methods as parents. If anything, we are upsetting the balance further as many women move into the "masculine" world while few men learn the nurturing skills of the "feminine" world. Counselors must heal the split within themselves between being "masculine" or "feminine," or they haven't a chance of healing others. It seems to me that the integration of "masculine" and "feminine" has both ethical and political implications. However, my purpose here is to introduce you to this assumption; it is not necessary for you to agree with my gender politics in order to pursue a deeper integration and to benefit from the text and experiments in this work.

Second, since my childhood days I have had a fascination with Asia, especially India. My mother developed an interest in India in third grade, and planned to become a missionary to India. In her college years she read Rabindranath Tagore, Swami Vivekananda, and Mahatma Gandhi, recognized their spiritual depth, and decided against imposing Western Christianity on this richly spiritual culture. As I write these words, I am working on the campus of Visva-Bharati, which is situated northwest of Calcutta, and was founded by Tagore. I am temporarily living in a nation facing incredible problems as it enters the new millennium. Indian culture is steeped in traditions, some going back at least five millennium. Most important, it is a culture that emphasizes the connected self and the spiritual self rather than the autonomous or individuated self. In ways that parallel the gender split, East and West have developed in different directions and with very different emphases concerning the meaning of life and the development of the self. Others have written on this subject—see especially Alan Roland (1988). As we move toward increasing globalization we are in danger of seeing not a genuine dialogue between East and West but instead the West dominating the East in much the way males have dominated females in Western social structures.[1] I believe we need an integration of this split as well.

In this introduction, I have shared two of the splits that I have felt in my own development. I have noted that at this stage in its development the field of counseling seems to be poised between focusing on its own identity and being ready to immerse itself in a larger Self, an identity that transcends our own.

I suspect most of us, at our best, will shuttle back and forth between involvement in concerns greater than ourselves, and reexamination and nurturing of our selves. I am not arguing here for a selfless life, only for a life that is concerned with more than self.

PART I: ASSESSING SPIRITUAL HEALTH AND DEVELOPMENT

Chapter 1

What is Health Spirituality? An Overview

The term *mental health* is a slippery one. The word *healthy* is commonly used in terms of physical health, and it is relatively simple to observe when a part of the body is functioning properly and making its contribution to the whole system. Psychological or spiritual health is not so simple. If we ask, for example, "What is the function of the stomach?" the answer is pretty straightforward. Conversely, it is fairly clear when the stomach is not functioning properly. When this is the case, we usually assume an illness. But how do we determine if a part of the psyche is functioning properly? How do we determine when it is ill and the system is not in synch?

If we as counselors and therapists are going to encourage our clients to bring their spiritual strengths and concerns into our sessions together, we need to take some care that the spirituality we are encouraging is promoting a more healthy life. The great spiritual leaders of the past have consistently recognized that we need to discern between genuine spiritual experiences and those that mask as spiritual but are in fact destructive. Jesus, for example, was highly critical of the religious leaders of his times, stating, "You shall know them by their fruits" (Matthew 7:16, 20, Revised Standard Version). If the desired outcome of spiritual experience is deeper connections with self, with others, and with life itself, then it is the experiences that produce these connections that are authentic spiritual experiences.

It is important to have a solid understanding of what we mean by healthy spirituality and by mental health, and to be clear discerning these. This chapter seeks such an understanding by reviewing the various models that have been used to define mental and spiritual health and by critically evaluating them. (For a more extensive historical review, see Oltmanns & Emery, 2001.)

In the second section of this chapter we will survey the vast differences in religious beliefs and in values across cultures, and see if common ground exists from which to base spiritually sensitive counseling. In the third section I will review the issue of positive thinking in order to illustrate how empirical social science can help us discriminate between healthy spirituality and a superficial or unauthentic spirituality. The focus of this research concerns principles of *consonance* (in social psychology), or *congruity* (in psychotherapy).

In the fourth section I return to some of the wisdom of traditional religion and present some integration of the material. Later, in Chapter 9, I more completely flesh out the process model; my view of how the counselor best relates to the client in regard to healthy spirituality will be presented.

MODELS CRITERIA FOR DETERMINING MENTAL HEALTH

In this section we will review and evaluate the medical model, and three psychological and social models: the normative or statistical model, the adaptation model, and the growth or developmental model. The purpose is to reveal the problems with some of the most used models of psychosocial health, and propose more fruitful ways to conceptualize healthy spirituality.

The Medical Model

At the beginning of the twentieth century, psychotherapy emerged primarily from the medical field of psychiatry. Since then, the medical model has had, and continues to have, an important influence on views of mental health and illness. This model is based on the metaphor of biological disease, and can be summarized as having three elements:

1. Specific symptoms are indications of dysfunction.
2. These symptoms cluster in patterns that can be diagnosed as diseases.

3. The occurrence of disease indicates that the system is out of balance, and homeostasis needs to be restored.

Symptom

An example of a symptom is a hallucination, seeing or hearing something that other people don't hear or see. Symptoms such as hallucinations and delusions (thought disorders) are thought of as occurring in clusters, which characterize particular syndromes. The combination of hallucinations and delusions most commonly occur in the syndrome that is labeled paranoid schizophrenia.

In many areas of biological medicine, specialists can test for specific disease mechanisms and determine, for example, the presence of a viral infection or a genetic defect to confirm a diagnosis. This is not yet possible in psychiatric medicine. However, in recent decades psychiatry has learned to use psychotropic drugs for their pragmatic effects in relieving symptoms, without a necessary correlation to diagnosis. Symptoms such as hallucinations or delusions are likely to diminish strikingly when certain drugs are used, which provides some evidence for a biological root for these symptoms, at least in some patients (Oltmanns & Emery, 2001). A biochemical imbalance or a neurological dysfunction may exist. These can appropriately be treated biologically, though the mechanisms of the disease process may be unknown, and these symptoms may not necessarily be part of a full syndrome or "disease" classification. In short, the effectiveness of a biological treatment such as a psychotropic drug does not necessarily imply the correctness of the whole medical model.

The model has no clear criteria for determining whether or not a particular behavior or experience is a symptom. Some of the symptoms listed in the American Psychiatric Association's *Diagnostic and Statistical Manual of Mental Disorders* (DSM) are dysfunctional in certain contexts, but are not so in other societies or social settings. A specific behavior, such as seeing a vision, in a particular cultural context may not indicate dysfunction. In some Native American cultures, a youth who has not yet found his life direction is *expected* to go on a "vision quest," and that journey often includes experiences that traditional Western psychiatry would call hallucinations. In these instances the assumption that the behavior is a symptom seems culturally inappropriate.

A further criticism of the medical model is that some behaviors have been labeled "symptoms" simply because they are statistically rare or uncommon behavior, not because they are either dysfunctional or part of a syndrome. They are abnormal in the sense of falling at one extreme on a normal curve. For decades psychiatry treated homosexual behavior as pathological, though no evidence proved it caused harm or that it was associated with other symptoms of mental disorder (Hooker, 1957, 1972). If we think of sexual orientation as a range from totally heterosexual to totally homosexual, the latter was labeled pathological solely because it was less common. Logically, bisexuality would seem to be the most flexible orientation, and either extreme (totally heterosexual, for example) might be seen as fetishistic! In short, the biological metaphor of medical diagnosis has been used in ways that, intentionally or not, masked the value judgments and the cultural ethnocentricity which led to the diagnosis. Objectively, neither homosexual acts nor visions confirming an identity are necessarily "dysfunctional."

Diagnosis

Though the diagnosis of biological diseases in terms of clusters of symptoms has proved a fruitful approach, its application in the mental health field has not been as successful from the point of view of scientific data. Beginning with Emil Kraepelin's (1923) *Textbook of Psychiatry,* followers of the medical model have assumed that a fixed set of mental disorders exists, and that their obvious manifestations cut across cultures. This assumption is called *cultural universality* (Sue, Sue, & Sue, 2000, p. 9). The medical concept that a series of symptoms form clusters that can be appropriately labeled "syndromes" or diseases has wide prevalence, and undergirds the major diagnostic categories used to provide insurance coverage (the DSM), but has little empirical validation. Studies for decades have shown little consistency in the use of diagnoses such as schizophrenia. Even the symptoms that are assumed to be defining are not the same between cultures. For example, a key symptom in defining schizophrenia in Germany, labeled *Gedankenentzug,* is not noted as a defining symptom in either British or American textbooks (Marsella, 1979). (*Gedankenentzug* refers to a patient's experiencing the loss of thoughts but believing the thought has been taken away from him or her by someone or something outside of him or her [Ute Binder, 2001, personal communication; Marlis Pörtner, 2002, personal communication].)

> Other symptoms or behaviors would be labeled disordered or dysfunctional in many cultures, both Western and Eastern. But the grouping of symptoms according to the patterns that Western psychiatrists have traditionally used . . . are not universally found. (Marsella, 1979, p. 247)

> The pattern of symptoms thought of as depression in Western society does not have an equivalent in many non-Western cultures (Marsella, 1979, p. 247).

The primary empirical bases for the clusters that have been called "syndromes" are statistical procedures (factor analyses) based on data limited to American and British cultures. By insisting on the use of the DSM, medical insurance companies have reinforced the perception that these categories are scientific, when in fact they are culturally biased. An additional factor in the failure of researchers and practitioners to recognize the cultural bias of these concepts is the increasing specialization in practitioner training. Persons trained in psychology or medical psychiatry are likely to have little awareness of anthropology. Yet the relativity of normal behavior was emphasized as early as 1934 by anthropologist A. Hallowell. He stated that the cross-cultural investigator:

> must develop a standard of normality with reference to the culture itself, as a means of controlling an uncritical application of the criteria that he brings with him from our civilization. (Hallowell, 1934, p. 2; cited in Marsella, 1979, p. 240).

As the training of practitioner counselors increasingly includes courses in multiculturalism, the recognition of the role of culture is increasing, but it has yet to fully permeate the mental health field at the level of training and research. In research, the official diagnostic systems of the medical model continue to serve as the constructs for most empirical studies in psychopathology, regardless of culture. And in clinical practice, official diagnostic systems of the medical model provide the definitions of mental illness (Oltmanns & Emery,

2001). This is "an unfortunate commentary on the ethnocentricity of [Western researchers and] practitioners." (Marsella, 1979, p. 244).

Homeostasis

The third element of the medical model is the belief that the system is out of balance. The concept of balance within a system is one of the more useful contributions of the medical model. It was originally applied at the biological level. At the biological level, it isn't important that two bodies have the same quantity of H_20 or of potassium, as long as the amount of water and potassium are in balance with the other elements in a particular person's system. Health implies that everyone should have the opportunity to achieve their individual optimal condition biologically, not that everyone fit a uniform and absolute standard of biological performance or measurement (as the World Health Organization [WHO] definition of health clarifies) (World Health Organization, 1958).

The concept of homeostasis can also be applied at the intrapsychic level, and at the social level (e.g., family systems). Intrapsychically, one person need not have the same way of treating work and play as another person, but they must achieve some balance. The whole mechanics of the id, ego, and superego in Freudian theory can be seen as a physical metaphor for the individual's attempt to achieve homeostasis. The cognitive parallel to homeostasis is called the principle of consonance (in social psychology), or congruity (in client-centered and self-theories of psychotherapy). We will examine this in more detail in the next section of this chapter.

Homeostasis as a definition of mental health ran into trouble because it gave the false impression that successful functioning is primarily a matter of stability, of staying the same. It suggests the image of the healthy person as standing still, standing in one place. But a healthy person, biologically, is not only capable of standing, but of moving and developing. To continue with the metaphor of balance, it would seem more accurate to define health as the ability to risk a temporary imbalance, then to regain balance, risk and regain again. This is, after all, what we do in walking. Moving through life is like moving through space: it demands a dynamic balance, not a static sameness. This leads us to a model that emphasizes growth and with it an openness to new experience. Developmental or growth models have been proposed by learning and developmental theorists as well as by "third force" therapists, and contrast to the symptom and disease emphasis of traditional psychoanalytic and behavioral therapists. This type of model will be discussed more fully. But first we will look at earlier psychological models that parallel the medical model.

How do you respond to the metaphor of balance and movement as a way of thinking about mental health? Does it fit for you, or is some other metaphor or image a better fit?

Psychological and Social Models

In both the medical and the psychological models it is important to clarify the criteria for assessing a behavior as pathological or dysfunctional. The early psychological models, parallel to the medical model, tried to avoid value issues and claim objectivity. The normative or statistical model of abnormality focused on particular behaviors and whether these behaviors were common and accepted in the society.

This attempt failed once we recognized that a behavior is not dysfunctional simply because it deviates from the norm. Some "abnormalities" are highly functional. For example, a very intelligent person who is at the extreme end of the normal curve of IQ scores is likely to be more capable of adapting than is a "normal" person (Sue, Sue & Sue, 2000). Thus the adaptation model gradually supplanted the normative model. A behavior was judged in terms of whether it was functional in adapting to the social setting; it allowed that some statistically uncommon behaviors or abilities are functional. Second, unlike the statistical model, the adaptation model recognized that behaviors that seem dysfunctional in one setting may be functional in another. For example, a Plains youth seeing flying objects in the sky during a vision-quest may be functional, whereas an urban Caucasian youth seeing UFOs would likely be viewed as having dysfunctional hallucinations.

The major problem with the adaptation model is that it assumes that mental health is defined by conformity to the norms of society. This value functions at two levels. First, it is assumed that to adapt to a society a person must perceive reality in much the same way as those around him or her. At the perceptual level, a person who sees or hears things that those in his or her own culture do not hear or see is considered "crazy"; it is assumed the person is hallucinating. Whether the treatment is a form of psychotherapy or the use of psychotropic drugs or a combination, one's goal is to get the patient back to normal perceptions.

Second, by allowing each culture to be the determinant of its own moral norms, we are left with no basis for determining whether the culture itself is good or bad. Though this cultural relativism avoids the ethnocentrism of cultural universality, it raises its own problems. Clearly, when we look back on the German Third Reich and the atrocities of the Nazis, we would not claim that someone who easily adapted to that society was "healthy." Most of us view as heroes those such as the theologian Bonhoeffer who worked in the underground to undermine Nazi society and are ashamed of the cowardice and complicity of the clergypersons and teachers and government officials who tried to ignore what was happening. The point is that adaptation to society avoids the issue of evaluating the society. Any mental health or counseling ethic that accepts this criterion alone risks complicity.

A less extreme example of the adaptation view of "normal" comes from the typical grade school classroom, where an extremely high percentage of boys who show a higher activity level and a different pattern of attending are labeled "hyperactive" or as having attention deficit disorder (ADD). Like most controversial issues, this one is complex. A concept of adapting and normalcy may preclude looking at other issues. Is ADD functional in other settings, as some of the leading experts on ADD and attention deficit/hyperactivity disorder (ADHD) have argued (Irick, 1996; Pellegrine & Horvat, 1995; Pfeiffer & Stocking, 2000)? And is it partially the teaching environment, not the boy, that is the problem? That is, does the typical classroom require a passive and highly focused, less creative learning style? The frequent *mis*diagnosis of gifted children as ADHD lends weight to the latter interpretation (Cooper, 2001).

The Growth Model

As the first section of this chapter has stressed, much of the mental health field has moved beyond the adaptation model to the growth model in order to describe mental health. In the cross-cultural context, this could be seen as a move from a social definition of mental health to a social-psychological definition. The criterion of growth implies that both the process of the individual and the "fit" with the society are considered. At an abstract level, it seems apparent that growth and development are themes of every and all cultures, and a growth model might avoid the ethnocentrism of the medical model.

In the history of psychology, some useful attempts have been made to clarify mental health in ways that did not impose one's own values. The metaphor of whether a person's life is "in balance" is one such example. And the shift to the concept of growth was another such attempt. Though the concept of growth sounds neutral and may even seem subject to empirical validation, this perception is probably based on the objectivity of physical growth. As has been previously noted, applying a biological metaphor to personal and interpersonal behavior often masks the value issues that are involved. Similarly, when the metaphor of physical growth is applied to psychological development and is articulated in concrete detail, two implicit assumptions often become evident: that growth has a clear direction and that it unfolds in a particular sequence.

The first assumption, that healthy growth has a clear direction, is exemplified in the classic theory of family therapy developed by Murray Bowen (1976), which focuses on differentiation of self, the capacity for autonomous functioning. Healthy growth is viewed as the move from dependence to independence and from emotional reactivity to the ability to separate and balance thinking and feeling.

Other theories that conceptualize growth as a move toward an ideal, with life development attaining a particular positive goal, include those articulated by humanistic psychologists such as Carl Rogers (1961) and Abraham Maslow (1954). These approaches have the advantage of stressing the strengths of human personality, in contrast to focusing on pathology and symptoms as the medical model has done. Maslow proposed that self-actualization, creativity, and self-transcendence were final goals of development (Maslow, 1954). Other social scientists have proposed competence, or resistance to stress, as the goals or directions of healthy development.

Unfortunately, the perception of a particular direction or goal is largely in the eye of the beholder, depending on the culture and values of the theorist making the proposal (Sue, Sue & Sue, 2000). A risk in using the growth model as a criterion for mental health is that one may impose one abstract goal on all human development, regardless of the culture. Thus used, the model may be as ethnocentric as the medical model.

The second assumption in much of the writing on psychological development is that a clear developmental sequence unfolds regardless of culture. Yet the schemas for psychological growth have typically been shown to be permeated with cultural assumptions. For example, Erikson's assumption (Erikson, 1968, p. 135ff) that identity, Stage 5 in his schema, must precede intimacy, Stage 6, has been shown to be rooted in masculine and Western biases (Matteson, 1993a). Even in Western cultures it fails to fit the data on the typical sequence of female development.

At this point I do not wish to totally discard the value of viewing development as having some universal directions, nor do I wish to invalidate the usefulness of stage theories. We will return to both issues in more detail in the discussions of spiritual development in Chapter 2 and moral development in Chapter 3. I merely want to caution that it is easy to miss the cultural assumptions and the conceptual oversimplifications involved in stage theory.

Let us turn now to my impressions of some to common values or intuitions that can be gleaned from the fields of mental health, comparative religion, and anthropology. Perhaps these can form the basis for assessing spiritual and mental health. This material will provide a context for the final model, the process model, which will be briefly sketched at the end of this chapter, and developed in Chapter 9.

DO ETHICS AND SPIRITUALITY HAVE COMMON GROUND ACROSS CULTURES?

Counseling Ethics and the Consensus of the Field

Are the criteria that emerge from consensus in the field of mental health an adequate basis for our work as spiritually sensitive counselors? The divisions or associations within the professional mental health organizations have defined standards of conduct for their profession. For the most part, however, these have been limited to issues of professional integrity, protection of client confidentiality, etc. They have not tackled the criteria of mental health itself.

Across professions, probably the two most commonly agreed on criteria for mental health have been (1) the absence of clear psychiatric symptoms and (2) the developmental move from dependence to increased differentiation and interdependence. The reader can probably recognize that these reflect, respectively, the influence of the medical model and the developmental or growth model. As already noted, the traditional psychiatric symptoms (criterion 1), such as hallucinations, are culturally biased. The medical model gives no basis for discerning the difference between the function of "hallucinations" versus "visions."

As noted earlier, the clearest exponents of differentiation (criterion 2) have been the intergenerational family therapists of the Bowen school who have defined the functional family as one that led to individuation of its members. In fairness, some mental health professionals have attempted to clarify the difference between individuation and the American emphasis on the "self-made" individual. Nonetheless, until the feminist critique and the examination of gender issues, counseling's cultural bias toward individual achievement and development, often at the expense of intimacy and interpersonal connectedness, was often overlooked.

One very encouraging aspect of the current consensus in mental health and counseling is the increased awareness that value-free counseling is impossible. Interest in the importance of values in psychotherapy has resurged, at least since the late 1980s (Bergin, 1991). With this awareness has come an attempt to be more forthright about our own evaluative process, and to work collaboratively to understand the values and cultural context, of our clients. The professional associations have also been responsible in recommending appropriate safeguards in the education of counselors and psychotherapists, an issue to which we will return in Chapter 9.

It should come as no surprise that value issues are involved in any counseling approach, since mankind is basically "an evaluating animal" (Kluckhohn, 1964, p. 292). Recent work in psychology has attempted to articulate the values implied in each of four psychological approaches (Prilleltensky, 1997). Once we recognize that value issues are involved, and that dangers exist in simply accepting the norms and values of a particular society, we are left with the puzzling issue of how to determine what criteria and values to use. Can some common ground among religions provide the criteria? Can some basic and universal values be the basis for assessment?

The Values Propagated By the World's Major Religions and Belief Systems

The attempt to isolate the common elements of the world's great religions and articulate the values they have in common is relatively new in the mental health field, though it has over a century of history in the field of interreligious dialogue. To engage in this search it is important to get beyond the false commonalities that are held up in our culture's usual approach to differences: an attempt to deny the existence of important differences. Just as the race issue is often swept under the rug with statements such as "we all have the same feelings; color doesn't matter," religious differences can be ignored in ways that actually perpetuate misunderstanding, such as saying "we all believe in the same God." Several of the world's largest religions do not have a defined position on belief in God or gods (e.g., Buddhism) or are not monotheistic in the sense of one God manifested in only one way (e.g., Hinduism). Some religions advocate a way of life more than a belief system (Taoism and Confucianism). In terms of beliefs, very real differences exist among the world religions. What is universal is that some form of religion or ideology (a system of beliefs and ceremonial observances concerning the sacred or the ultimate) is present in every one of the nearly 7,000 distinct cultures that are extant (Sponsel, 2000; Hammond, 1971). It would be closer to the facts to say that most cultures have been spiritual than to say they share a belief in God.

If you haven't already done so, this might be a good place to begin the experiential component of this book, reading the introduction to Part II, and going through Experiments 1 and 2.

Surveying Religious Differences

Even the word *spiritual* has its problems, because its use in modern societies is rather different than its earlier meaning, which referred to the belief that different spirits inhabited most living and even most inanimate things. Some form of "animism" or "animalism" is characteristic of the belief systems of most indigenous and preliterate people. The rituals of such cultures often included making particular offerings that were believed to ensure a good harvest, or good hunting, or human fertility. From the point of view of empirical science, we critique such beliefs as magical. But this spirituality has a profound beauty in that it does not split the natural world from the supernatural world. Native American spirituality, for example, is likely to be more reverent toward the natural world, and often more likely to protect the natural ecology, than the monotheistic religions have been. The latter have tended to see humans as "having dominion" over nature, and interpreted this as a right to exploit nature. (For a fuller discussion of the ecological implications of various religious points of view, see Sponsel, 2000).

The concept of "gods" or "God" emerged with a conceptual split between earth (creation) and "heaven" or "sky gods" (e.g., a creator God). Historically, most cultures at first believed in many gods (pantheism). Pantheism is not limited to ancient societies such as classical Greece. A pantheon of gods and goddesses represent the different aspects of the divine, different ways the holy becomes manifest to humans. Sometimes (usually later in history) one of those gods becomes dominant, the highest god, such as Zeus in Greek mythology, or Lord God in the Old Testament creation story. However, pantheism is not just an ancient form of thinking. Most of Hinduism as it is understood by the common people in India today, and most of Buddhism as it's expressed in Tibetan Buddhism, honor many forms of divinity, many gods and goddesses. The devout and the philosophical talk of a "spirit" or "divine presence" that is the source of all of the gods and goddesses. The source is seen as difficult or impossible to describe, which is why it must come to us in more concrete forms. In some cultures the dominant god eventually is seen as the only true God, and other manifestations are rejected; monotheism becomes the orthodoxy. However, the view that the highest divinity is a personal god who interacts directly with humans is not clear in Hinduism or Buddhism. The concept that god is a person is more likely to apply to the lesser divinities, with the Source or the Whole being conceived as closer to Tillich's (1955) concept of "The Ground of all Being," or "Being itself" (p. 58). These terms attempt to express "the ultimate ground and meaning of all reality," the God beyond gods (p. 58).

Within any of these conceptualizations of the holy may be an emphasis on a direct personal connection with the spirit or the divine presence. This brings us to mysticism, which some believe is the experiential center of all belief—the sense of the divine presence, but the awareness that it is a mystery that cannot be named or described. None of the religions of the world began with a scripture; first was some experience, some special person who was deeply connected to the holy. Then this was passed on by word of mouth. Only later did it get written down and become called a holy text. Groups in both the Eastern and the Western religions have felt that the experience, rather than beliefs or rituals, is the central concern. For example, it was in the mystical community of Hasidic Judaism that one of the most important Jewish theologians of the twentieth century, Martin Buber, was raised. Within Christianity, the Religious Society of Friends (also known as the Quakers) emphasize silent services in which they simply open themselves and wait to experience the inner light that will guide them. Both Hinduism (in bhakti Yoga, the path of devotion) and Buddhism (in Zen) have traditions that focus on the experience of the holy rather than on beliefs and doctrines.

Since the emergence of the scientific worldview, many have felt a conflict between the rational-empirical knowledge of science and the expectation from institutional religions that one should believe solely on the basis of authority and/or blind faith. In addition to this intellectual crisis, the modern world has brought on a moral crisis, in part because of the plurality of moralities, but also because of the atrocities of the holocaust, of Hiroshima, and of subsequent reigns of terror. This moral crisis has led some to a rejection of the belief in God, or to at least an agnosticism about the existence of a supreme being. Yet many have retained a spiritual orientation. This has usually taken one of two forms: a spiritual atheism, or a secular humanism. For readers who have always thought of spirituality in the context of belief in God, spiritual atheism sounds like a contradiction in terms. Certainly much of Western atheism has involved a passionate belief that the material world is all that exists—as expressed in Marxist economic materialism. But Buddhist atheism has been a prominent religious position in the East since philosophic discussions about the Buddha were first written down roughly two or three centuries before the Christian era. In protestant Christianity, a nontheist tradition of theology began with Tillich in the 1950s, and in about 1970 a clear atheist

Christianity emerged with the "death of God" theologians who argued that the concept of God in this period of history bore too much metaphysical baggage and required more belief than modern intellectuals could muster. Atheist Christian scholars continued to turn to the historic person Jesus of Nazareth to derive their ethics and religious symbols. The dramatic phrase "death of God" was embraced by a minority of seminary professors and students and soon went out of fashion, but the work of Tillich remains influential, and some liberal churches (such as Unitarian Universalist) have a high percentage of members who consider themselves atheists yet are connected to Christian and other religious traditions.

Those who identify with secular humanism are likely to be uncomfortable with the word *spirituality,* yet they believe strongly in moral values, in "individual autonomy that does not violate the spirit of social responsibility." They view "critical intelligence, infused by a sense of human caring" as "the best method that humanity has for resolving problems." Yet reason "must be tempered by humility, since no group has a monopoly of wisdom or virtue." They "believe in cultural diversity and encourage racial and ethnic pride" but "reject separations that promote alienation and set people and groups against each other" (Zorn, 2001, p. A12).

Within Group Differences

The values affirmed within any particular religion or ideology are varied. The beliefs of members of a particular faith do not necessarily follow the official positions of that group or the statements of institutional authorities (priests, ministers, rabbis, imams, and other religious leaders). For example, the majority of American Roman Catholics do not agree with the teachings of the Pope on issues of birth control, and the better educated they are, the more likely they are to disagree. On the other hand, in many of the mainstream protestant denominations, the educated clergy hold more liberal views about the authority of certain verses in the Bible than do the average parishioners. And protestant Christians in mainstream denominations may have very different views than those in denominations that have broken away from the mainstream, in "free" churches that are not part of any denomination. Fundamentalists (those who hold to literal interpretation of their particular scriptures) tend to be similar in their claims of having the final truth and in their hatred and persecution of other groups, regardless of whether these fundamentalists are Islamic, Christian, or Hindu. Within most of the world religions are some groups who use religion to defend their own superiority. Socially, they bond in a tribal manner with others who hold the same opinions, seeking to maintain their own purity and avoid learning about or being influenced by those who are different from themselves. The values of persons who join religious groups that view differences and change as threatening and seek security or a return to the past are likely to be rather different than the values of persons who join groups that encourage personal exploration and think of the spiritual voyage as a quest. These are differences within a particular religious tradition, and the span from defensiveness to open search exists within many, if not most, of the religious traditions.

If a counselor is going to incorporate spiritual issues in his or her work, it is important that the counselor not only recognize but respect this incredible array of belief systems. The first and probably the most important lesson that the counselor might take away from surveying the variety of patterns of belief is the recognition that a client may have a very different way of perceiving and expressing the holy than does any particular counselor. As counselors, it is our responsibility to honor these differences.

Approaches to Finding Common Ground

To return to the issue of common ground, recent scholarship includes a number of very different approaches in seeking some common ground given the variety of religious expression. These include Joseph Campbell's (1968, 1979, 1988, 1990) attempts to uncover the meaning beneath the literal content of religious myths, stories, and symbols; the work of anthropologists (Kluckhorn, 1964; Boyer, 2001) to find common values or intuitions; and the scriptural search for the historical persons who originated the great religions prior to the institutionalizing of the religion.

Anthropology and the Common Ground

A Basis for Spirituality in the Evolution of the Brain

So far, this discussion has focused primarily on institutionalized religion. Anthropology tends to focus more on the beliefs and values of people in a particular culture, which may or may not be the official beliefs of institutional religion. Some recent work in anthropology has been influenced by the development of new methods in neuropsychology that provide clues to the functions of specific portions of the brain, and complement the speculations of evolutionary biology. The human brain sorts the objects we encounter into categories, with particular inferences arising from the way the object is categorized (Boyer, 2001). Considerable evidence suggests that infants and young children are particularly interested in facial stimuli, and eventually become very sophisticated in differentiating among individual human faces. They categorize most other "faces" by species (cats, giraffes, etc.), rarely differentiating individual faces within a species other than humans. Human face recognition is handled by a special area of the brain separate from the areas that generally interpret complex visual shapes (Boyer, 2001), though faces of pets thought of as persons are also treated in this special area. "Persons" becomes a crucial human category. Boyer (2001) argues that the religious beliefs that really matter in any society concern beings that are perceived as having personlike qualities, including an ability to gather strategic information about us and an interest in our moral decisions. However, these spiritual beings are not thought of as similar persons in other respects. This process of applying only some of the criteria of a category (such as the category "persons") and not others is called *decoupling*. So spiritual beings are called persons, yet are not persons, much like imaginary playmates are playmates but not really playmates.

This capacity to believe in a paradoxical category of beings is available to children, of course. Children ages 3 to 10 often have imaginary playmates, and are capable of stable relationships with these playmates even though they can articulate or respond in ways that show that they know these "playmates" don't really exist. (Boyer, 2001). This illustrates the ability to take seriously a "person" who is decoupled from some of the usual expectations of "person." Spiritual beings may be seen as different (decoupled) from the category "persons" in that they are invisible or are able to know our thoughts even when they are not expressed, etc.

Of particular importance is children's ability to intuit the feelings and mental states of other people. Studies of neural activation in normal subjects show that when we see someone making particular gestures, we generally imagine making the same gestures ourselves. A part of the brain is imagining performing the action witnessed, but the motor sequence is inhibited—except in infants, who actually imitate other people's gestures.

Apparently this ability to inwardly experience the actions of others evolves or combines with other mental abilities, leading to empathy or intuitive understanding of others. Some comparative psychologists now believe that the ability to understand another's perspective is uniquely human (Povinelli, 2001). Evidence in the studies of primates (de Waal, 1996) suggests chimpanzees are capable of taking another individual's perspective and acting altruistically, as will be described in Chapter 3. In any case, Boyer (2001) believes the human brain contains a system that produces a description of how events affect other persons.

A collection of subdomains of the brain account for "intuitive psychology" (Boyer, 2001, pp. 104-105). In my earlier discussion of developmental stages, I noted Kohlberg's theory, which views moral development in terms of increased cognitive abilities to reason based on principles. As Boyer (2001) points out, an alternative account of moral judgment (developed by Hoffman 1977, 1983; see Gibbs, 1991) is based on feelings and the gradual development of specific emotional reactions as children increase in their capacity to represent the thoughts and feelings of others. This capacity for empathy gradually extends to others, and the norms become internal to the child's mind (Boyer, 2001).

The growing field of social cognitive neuroscience clearly supports Boyer's contention that person perception, "the human ability to assess the thoughts, beliefs and desires of other people on the basis of behaviors, [expressions], and vocal utterances" is adaptive, and is based on "a multi-step process" related to very specific parts of the brain (Ochsner & Lieberman, 2001, p. 725). Furthermore, damage of certain parts of the brain makes it clear that "certain types of reasoning" are dependent on emotional involvement. Without emotion, they do not occur (Ochsner & Lieberman, 2001, p. 725).

Experimental studies suggest that both emotional and cognitive factors are at play in moral development, but that a specific inference system, a specialized moral sense underlying ethical intuitions, is present very early in development. Ethical intuitions that are not easily revised by social situations occur in some three- and four-year-olds (Boyer 2001, citing Turiel, 1983). Moral imperatives are distinct from other aspects of social interaction; children do not see them as simply social conventions. Though other areas of reasoning are modified as persons mature, the view that something is wrong because it is wrong, not because of what people say (called "moral realism"), does not usually change. These moral dispositions, expressed as moral feelings, reflect the evolutionary need for human cooperation; purely rationally motivated values would likely not be able to sustain cooperative behavior in situations in which one's actions are not seen. The biological and evolutionary basis of morality relies on "abundant evidence of history that cooperative individuals generally survive longer and leave more offspring" (Wilson, 1998, p. 59). Though a particular individual may die from altruistic actions, the continuation of altruistic genes is guaranteed by the increased probability of the survival of the group (Wilson, 1998). Thus moral dispositions (or "moral instincts," as Wilson terms them) emerge because of the evolutionary value of cooperation.

In Boyer's theory, these moral dispositions develop early in children and are predecessors to religious or spiritual beliefs. Most people feel guilt when acting in a way they suspect is immoral. Rationally, they can develop self-serving justifications, but they may intuit that someone with full knowledge of the facts would classify their behavior as wrong. Since this intuition does not come from conscious thought, it is easy for people to understand these intuitions as coming from the viewpoint of a spiritual being. This experience of inner moral responses is the seedbed for religious ideas, projecting the inner "voice" outward to "spirits" or "gods" who observe us. People in different cultures have very different concepts concerning religion or the supernatural, but their moral concepts are remarkably similar. These moral intuitions are the common ground from which different views of the supernatural develop (Boyer, 2001).

These lines of research (both evolutionary anthropology and social cognitive neuroscience) suggest that cognition as tested in most psychology experiments is too removed from actual cognition embedded in the motivationally charged stream of everyday life (Ochsner & Lieberman, 2001). That the development of empathy and morals are dependent on brain structures that have emerged across humankind suggests that some aspects of human values, and possibly of spirituality, could be universal. This inference leads to a review of some earlier data from cross-cultural anthropology.

As a counselor, how does it affect you to think of spiritual tendencies, based on intuition and empathy, as built into the brain and neurological system of humans?

Do Universal Values Exist?

Some anthropologists have argued that a basic ethical standard emerges in any society as people have to learn to live together, and that this results in certain rules or commandments that, with minor variations, become part of the code of civilization regardless of culture. This was articulated most clearly by anthropologist Clyde Kluckhohn (1964) more four decades ago, who stated that "despite all the influences that predispose toward cultural variation. . . all of the very many different cultures known to us have converged upon these universals" (p. 295).

> No culture tolerates indiscriminate lying, stealing, or violence within the in group . . . No culture places a value upon suffering as an end in itself—as a means to the ends of the society (punishment, discipline, etc.) yes; as a means to the ends of the individual (purification, mystical exaltation, etc.) yes; but of and for itself, never. We know of no culture—[not even] the Soviet Russian where the official ideology denies afterlife—where the fact of death is not ceremonialized . . . [And] all cultures define as abnormal individuals who are permanently inaccessible to communication or who consistently fail to maintain some degree of control over their impulse life. . ..The mere existence of universals after so many millennia of culture history and in such diverse environments suggests that they correspond to something extremely deep in man's nature and/or [that they] are necessary conditions to social life. .. The phrase "a common humanity" is in no sense meaningless." The facts of anthropology attest to it. (pp. 294-297)

The Case of the Stranger and the Limits of the Tribe

Returning to current evolutionary anthropology and social cognitive neuroscience, it would seem that these universal values reflect the nature of human learning, given the structures of the evolved human brain and the general social conditions of normal development (such as infant interaction with nurturing adults). What emerges are intuitive criteria for evaluation of one's own and others' behaviors, such as a sense of fairness, by which people of all cultures generally evaluate transactions with others (Boyer, 2001). "Specific moral prescriptions vary a lot from culture to culture, but their connection to social interaction does not" (Boyer, 2001, p. 187). These intuitive criteria do not seem to match rational economic models, but they pay off in terms of the evolution of humans under certain conditions—namely, when persons are with others whose habits and language are similar. Then they can read the cues that tell them whether a person, on the whole, is a good cooperator or not. But when with strangers whose habits and language are different, the cues may fail. Thus, not surprisingly, "the history of tribal mankind is also the history of solidarity within tribes and warfare between tribes" (Boyer, 2001, pp. 187-188).

Joseph Campbell's work on the similarity of stories and myths across cultures has inspired many who are not interested in the details and complications of careful cultural anthropology (see Campbell, 1987/1997). Scholars in anthropology may find fault with his emphasis on similarities. However, it is noteworthy that, despite his bias toward similarities, Campbell clearly recognized that in most cultures these myths and stories have been used to affirm the connection within a tribe or "in group" and to set themselves apart from other groups. The heroes he describes are usually heroes of one single tribe or single religion—for example, Moses for the Jews. He argued that, at this point in history, as our world has shrunk with global communication and economic inter-dependence, we need a mythology that can unite all people, and heroes who bring all people together. In one of Campbell's last radio interviews with Michael Thoms he noted that all people in the world today share the same problem, the ecological problem, and he expressed the hope that this may be enough to unite us. (Campbell, 1970-1980, Tape 4).

Common Ground in the Great Religions

The Spirituality of the Originators of Two Great Religions

The "common ground" we can discover from anthropology and sociology demonstrates concern for others, but this concern is often limited to the particular social or tribal group. Thus it does not provide a satisfactory ethic for today's pluralistic cultures and global problems. Similarly, institutional religions often fail to transcend their particular cultural and historical constraints. What would we find if we studied the teachings and life experiences of those spiritual leaders whose lives inspired some of the world religions? Did they somehow manage to transcend the tribes in which they were raised?

Such an approach seeks common ground by uncovering the central values of the founders of the different religious traditions. It steps outside the institutional forms of the religion and examines the lives and teachings of these founders in their historic context. Probably the most familiar explorations in this vein are the comparisons of Jesus and Buddha (Borg, 1999; Hanh, 1995). In his preface to *Jesus and Buddha: The Parallel Sayings,* Borg (1999) describes five striking similarities that can be summarized as follows:

1. Both the particular and the general ethical principles taught by Buddha and Jesus are similar, e.g., the love of enemies and the primacy of compassion.
2. Both Buddha and Jesus underwent a spiritual quest, had life-transforming experiences at around age 30, and afterward began their public activity.
3. Both initiated renewal or reform movements within the religious tradition they grew up in, Judaism and Hinduism respectively. Neither saw himself as the founder of a new religion.
4. Both were later perceived as more than human, and given exalted—even divine—status, though their humanity continued to be affirmed. Both rejected even mild forms of this deification [especially in the earliest writings about them].
5. Both were teachers of wisdom. Wisdom consists of fundamental changes in ways of seeing and being. "Wisdom is not just about moral behavior, but about the 'center,' the place from which moral perception and moral behavior flow." (Borg, 1999, p. *viii*).

Hanh (1995) points out still another aspect that the lives of Buddha and Jesus shared:

> both spent time socializing and eating with persons their societies considered "sinners." They were not afraid of contamination or guilt by association (pp. 93, 96-97).

Thich Naht Hanh (1995), though raised in the Zen Buddhist tradition, developed a connection to Christianity through working with Christians in the peace movement during the war in his native Vietnam. He bases his devotion to both the Buddha and the Christ on their common emphasis on love, understanding, and acceptance. But, more important, he points to the living presence of the Buddha or the Christ within us. In contrast to fundamentalists, he points out the scriptures that stress a universalism beyond any one religion: "All those who are led by the Spirit of God are [children] of God" (Romans 8:14, RSV). In his view, the experience of a relationship with the sacred, of the presence of the holy, is more important than the way it gets expressed in words or formulated as religious belief. Beliefs and dogmas are secondary; it is the transforming experience that is central. The living Buddha and the living Christ portray the ways persons raised in two different traditions experience the presence of Spirit, but the experience is basically the same.

Common Ground in the Mystic Traditions within the Religions

Another way to observe the similarities among religions is to examine the mystic traditions within each of the major religions. Thich Naht Hanh's emphasis on direct experience rather than on belief or words or formulations is close to what was described previously as *mysticism.* The search for a common ground in experience among the different religions is not simply a result of our pluralistic world situation in recent centuries. Persons from different religious traditions in earlier periods met and recognized in each other a common experience, and worked together in a common intellectual and spiritual search. Thirteenth century Spain was a such a period; leaders of mystical spirituality in Christian, Jewish, and Islamic traditions cultivated a personal religious experience that seemed to lead to a mutual respect between persons of these different faith traditions.

Unfortunately, mystical experiences are often perceived by religious authorities as a threat to their power, and thus as threats to the organized church, or mosque, or similar institution. For if we can experience the holy directly, what need is there for priests or others to mediate for us? Only two centuries later in Spain the exciting intellectual climate and the openness across faiths to the mystic presence was replaced with the most bloody and repressive inquisition in Europe, defending the "one true Church."

The similarity in the teachings and lives of the founders of the great religions and the similarity of the mystic experience that may lie behind the words and doctrines of a religion provide some clues that an ethical and spiritual base may exist that is common to humankind despite the vast cultural differences in the ways it is expressed. However, the common ground found among these selected inward-looking spiritual leaders is not the same as the common ground of values and religious instincts demonstrated in anthropology.

Contrasting Great Spiritual Leaders and the Brain of Evolution

A crucial difference exists between the universals that some anthropologists posit and the ethics proclaimed by the founders of Buddhism and Christianity and implied in the mystic tradition. The responsibility of the person, in the ethics Kluckhohn (1964) describes, is only to the in-group. Each culture expects its members to restrain from violence, dishonesty, and failure to respect the property of their own community or tribe. Similarly, the cognitive dispositions of the evolved brain as described by Boyer (2001), which incline all humans toward spiritual thinking, are adaptive to our tribal origins, and serve to enhance chances of the survival of the tribe. They encourage loyalty to the group—our own group—but are not necessarily adaptive in a globalized and multicultural world.

In contrast, what the great religious leaders suggest is that we have a responsibility to all humankind. The moral imperative is not simply some common ground in which we all share the same moral standard; it is a valuing that applies universally to all humankind. It is not enough to love those in your own house, or your own clan. We are enjoined to love our enemies.

Persons who have reached very high levels of spiritual development (persons such as the Buddha, and the historic Jesus) have moved from acceptance and love of themselves to acceptance and love of their own community, to embracing and loving those outside their community, and finally to loving their enemies. The process involves an increasingly expanding circle of caring. At least two modern heroes have demonstrated inclusiveness that transcends tribal boundaries. Mahatma Gandhi and Martin Luther King, in their teachings and in their work, sought to embrace all humankind.

The professional ethics of counselors expects that they embrace multiculturalism. The implication for the spiritually sensitive counselor is that he or she develop a value stance and a spiritual orientation that is not "tribal," but is open to clients of all cultures and creeds. In this sense, the spiritually sensitive counselor comes from a different perspective than the religious counselor who understands his or her role as representing a specific faith position.

This has been studied with psychologists, and according to Bergin (1991), "psychologists' understanding and support of cultural diversity has been exemplary with respect to race, gender, and ethnicity" (p. 399), but in the area of religion, psychologists have been less tolerant and empathic. Clinicians often do not understand the cultural content of their clients' religious worldviews, but instead deny its importance and end up coercing clients into values and concepts that are alien to the clients' culture (Bergin, 1983; Lovinger 1984). It would seem that the criteria for counselors' ethics—to truly embrace multiculturalism—must include being accepting of different faith perspectives. This does not mean that the counselor needs to believe as the client does. Nor does it mean the counselor cannot be aware of, and when sufficient rapport is established, confront the limits of the client's openness. Where the client's perspective limits the client's move toward a more inclusive spirituality, it may be appropriate to confront, but the counselor must also be open to growth in the direction of increasingly wider circles of compassion. At least the ideal of an ethics of universal compassion seems necessary for the spiritually sensitive counselor. Returning to the counselor's evaluation of the client and the theme of this chapter: the criterion of health is not a certain stage, or a specific level of love, but whether the person is open to that process of expanding—whether she or he is growing in acceptance and love.

The search for a common ground of ethics that is similar regardless of culture or creed comes from our wish, as counselors, to avoid imposing something on our clients that is simply our point of view. Avoid approaching others' traditions and beliefs by reducing them to the lowest common denominator, thus removing their distinctive perspective. For example, we may claim that "all religions are merely variations on the golden rule" (Church, 2001, p. 25). This attempts to formulate the "common ground," and in doing so shapes it to look like our own creed or central value. In the concepts of Boyer's neuroanthropology, the common ground is the intuitive level that is preverbal and prerational. In the poetry of the mystics, the common source of the experience is beyond words and concepts. In either case, as soon as we try to express it, we have moved away from the common experience to shaping and distorting it with culture and words. Not that we can do without words, but that the attempt to find an all-embracing ideology or metaphysics that incorporates both the client's viewpoint and our own is doomed to failure since it is our own construction.

We stand with our clients, not by building some cognitive superstructure that resolves our differences but by recognizing that both their "truths" and our own "truths" are only fragments of the mystery, only perspectives on the whole story, and only limited colors in the multihued band of the light (Church, 2001).

Moving Beyond a Common Ground to a Culture-Free Process of Evaluation of Individual Spiritual Growth

It is possible that the models examined earlier in this chapter come from formulating the question incorrectly. Behind the question "what is healthy spirituality?" is the desire to provide clients with counseling that honors their own development, to guard clients from counselors imposing their values or beliefs on them. Another way to look at the question, at least as it concerns our relationship with clients, is to ask, "What is a healthy process for promoting spiritual growth in our clients?" This moves the issue from the content level to the process. (By remaining open to the client's content and cultural context, counseling can be less culturally biased. This is not to say that it is value-free, only that it is multiculturally open).

Some recent research in psychotherapy supports the move from content to process in a very specific way that reminds us of the anthropologists' material on moral development described previously. Recall that Boyer (2001) emphasized that morals emerge from an intuitive process. Rea's (2001) review of research suggests that the best psychotherapy is done by clinicians who respond intuitively, in contrast to those who focus on deductive reasoning to guide their interaction with clients. Rea's review indicates that intuitive therapists can be effective in fewer sessions than those who rely on standardized treatments. Intuition may sound like a fuzzy or vague construct, but it can be measured through lab experiments such as asking subjects to read a nonsense language with undisclosed grammatical rules. Intuitive respondents are able to compose their own "sentences" using the rules of the nonsense language, though they cannot explain the rules. In fact, when they are told the rules, they are slower in developing grammatically correct nonsense; it appears their rational deductive knowledge slows them down. Counselors interested in refining their use of intuition are referred to his guidelines (Rea, 2001). Much of what we have in common with others, including our clients, is at the intuitive, preverbal level. It is important that we do our counseling work at this level. This will be examined in more detail in Chapter 9.

Intuitive counseling alone is not sufficient. The educated professional counselor has a responsibility to check his or her practice against the results of empirical research. The intelligent spiritual seeker has a responsibility to be sure that his or her "core beliefs are consistent with known facts" (Keen, 1994, p. 104). The topic of positive thinking provides an example of how empirical research can bear directly on key issues in our work. Can we avoid the "dark," the "negative" in our work? Or is it crucial that we and our clients encounter our "shadow" and face it directly? Does it help our clients grow spiritually when we encourage them to think positively?

POSITIVE THINKING RELATED RESEARCH FROM SOCIAL PSYCHOLOGY

Many aspects of healthy spirituality can be illuminated by a more detailed examination of the data of social sciences. The issue of positive thinking has been chosen as an illustration because considerable relevant research exists, and because it is an issue shared by persons trying to develop their own spiritual potentials (such as our clients) and persons trying to learn what therapeutic approaches are effective (such as therapists and counselors in training).

The Case of Positive Thinking

One of the most common ways popular psychology has tried to combine psychology and spirituality is in advocating positive thinking. A very popular book called *The Power of Positive Thinking* was written by a pastoral psychologist half a century ago (Peale, 1952) and is still popular in audio format and in a revised version (Peale & Peale, 2000). A recent search of an online book retailer for books with the words "positive" and "thinking" in the title produced 102 available matches!

Clearly, negative thinking can be dysfunctional. Studies of depressed clients and persons with low self-esteem demonstrate this, but an illustration directly concerning counselors may be more poignant. Evidence shows that for counselors in training, high negative self-talk and low positive self-talk are related to increased anxiety, which results in poorer performance in video recordings of counseling skills. If negative self-talk declines over time, the skills improve (Hiebert, Uhlemann, Marshall, & Lee, 1998).

Persons who do not have much training in either psychology or theology may falsely assume that both disciplines view positive thinking as unambiguously constructive. In fact, both the effectiveness of positive thinking in human interpersonal relationships and the integrity of positive thinking in human/divine relationships have been questioned. When is positive thinking an indication of solid contact with reality, and when is it a sign of denial? The empirical question is this: when does affirming a positive view of self result in better functioning, and when does it fail?

The Theory of Self-Affirmation

Extensive literature of psychological research examines the effectiveness of "self-affirmation statements." Most of this experimentation has been conducted to test cognitive dissonance theory (Festinger, 1957). In the first section of this chapter we discussed homeostasis and the metaphor of growth as models for mental health.

The principle of cognitive dissonance parallels the biological principal of an upset in homeostasis. Out of the social-psychological research on cognitive dissonance has come a theory of self-affirmation that claims to be a more encompassing theory about human thought and action than Festinger's original theory. (See Steele, 1988; Steele, Spencer, & Lynch, 1993). To quote an excellent review of research on self-affirmation theory (Aronson et al., 1999):

> According to self-affirmation theory, thought and action are guided by a strong motivation to maintain an overall self-image of moral and adaptive adequacy. We want to see ourselves as good, capable, and able to predict and control outcomes in areas that matter. Awareness of information that threatens this image motivates us to restore it to a state of integrity. Like dissonance motivation (in Festinger's theory), the self-affirmation drive can be strong or weak, depending on the size of the threat to the self-image. But because the objective is global self-worth, and not cognitive consistency, we have tremendous flexibility in satisfying the need to restore a sense of general goodness . . . For instance, a person does not have to rationalize a regrettable decision at work if his or her global sense of self-worth is secured by being a good parent or community member. (pp. 128-129)

According to this theory, people with high self-esteem should be less inclined to rationalize in dissonance-inducing situations than people with low self-esteem (Aronson et al, 1999). *Dissonance-inducing situations* refers to (experimental) situations in which persons are given information (sometimes false) about themselves that contradicts their own view of themselves. Studies have shown that if subjects have a chance to affirm some important strength about themselves, or some other resource, or if they are reminded of their high self-esteem, they have no need to rationalize when they are given information that might threaten their self-esteem. This supports the theory that resources of self-esteem are more important than self-consistency in predicting reactions to threatening situations. In lab experiments, it appears that it is self-affirmation, not self-consistency, that motivates responses to information that might be perceived as threatening.

Applications

These findings might lead us to believe that the popular psychology approach of thinking positively about oneself is valid. When people are depressed, or have negative thoughts about themselves, counselors could try to "build up their resources" by having them repeat "self-affirmations." This has been widely encouraged—and it does work in some cases. For example, undergraduate college students who scored low in self-esteem were instructed to read 15 positive self-statements to themselves 3 times a day. In only 2 weeks their depression scores had declined and self-esteem scores increased (Philpot & Bamburg, 1996). The problem of application is the temptation to use positive thinking indiscriminately, so that positive thinking becomes impractical in the face of real-life problems.

It would be nice to believe that the more one practices positive thinking the better. And it is common to assume that any increase in self-esteem will result in more functional behavior. Both assumptions are incorrect. One area in which research results have received fairly wide coverage in the mainstream media concerns the ineffectiveness of the most commonly used high school program for prevention of alcohol and substance use, D.A.R.E (Drug Abuse Resistance Education). Addressing self-esteem appears to have less payoff than other mediating variables such as personal commitment. Increases in a student's self-esteem does *not* result in less use of illegal drugs. Even when prevention programs lead to an increase in the students' "commitment" not to use drugs, this has no bearing on students' *actual* use of alcohol or illicit drugs (Hansen & McNeal, 1997). Programs that use more interactive teaching methods are far more effective than D.A.R.E (Ennet Tobler, Ringwalt, & Flewelling, 1994).[1]

Moving back to laboratory research, some studies have shown that self-affirmation, under certain circumstances, can backfire (Aronson et al., 1999; Galinsky, Stone, & Cooper, 2000). If students are induced to do something that goes against their view of themselves as compassionate, for example, to write an essay arguing that the university should stop funding for disabled students, and then are given feedback exaggerating their scores on a scale of compassion, thus affirming that they are, in fact, very compassionate, it results in the students becoming less compassionate (exhibited by shifting to actually believing the negative essay they had written). In contrast, students who wrote similar essays but were not given phony affirmation regarding their compassion, but instead were affirmed for their creativity, did not rationalize the essay they had written (Blanton, Cooper, Skurnik, & Aronson, 1997). Feedback on self-affirmation needs to be realistic enough to be plausible in the client's mind in order to genuinely reinforce the client's self-concept.

Effective self-affirmations are usually those that are compensatory ("I may have done bad in the math test, but I'm good at English"), not direct attempts to rebut an area of personal failure. If the self-affirmation is in the same area of the self that is threatened, instead of increased self-esteem, the result is likely to be increased defensiveness. I notice this phenomenon in my supervision of counseling students. Novice counselors are likely to try to reassure clients who are feeling inadequate and making self-disparaging statements about some area of their (in)competence. A student counselor's statement such as, "Oh, I'm sure you really didn't do that bad," minimizing the negative, is likely to lead the client to emphasize all the more how poorly he or she did.

In those cases in which self-affirmation is effective, it is usually an affirmation that comes from the reservoir of positive feelings and evaluations a person has about himself or herself. Thus Aronson and colleagues (1995) and other experimental psychologists prefer to think of their theory as self-resource theory. Positive conceptions of the self are not only resources, Aronson and colleagues (1995) note; they can also function as standards of conduct. When a counselor or teacher points out an area of strength, intending to affirm it as a positive resource, the recipient (the client or student) is likely to invoke a self-critical standard of conduct in that area. For example, if a student having trouble with spelling is reminded that he has a good memory when it comes to vocabulary, the student may point out an incident in which he couldn't remember a new vocabulary word.

Furthermore, a counselor's use of self-affirmation had best not be a phony attempt to try to persuade the client to "feel good" in opposition to the evidence. Such attempts backfire. With genuine strengthening of self-affirmation, a client can be prepared for stressors in the future, for personal threats and occasional inconsistencies in his or her own behavior. The client can be open and supportive of the incredible diversity that surrounds him or her, and not experience this diversity as a threat but as an opportunity for further growth. But "feel good" feedback is not specific enough to provide this kind of inner strength.

To put this another way, if a person is focusing on one area for her or his self-esteem, then threats in that area are very damaging and the person may dig in his heels and refuse to change his mind because it is self-threatening or dissonant to do so. Take, for example, persons who are pro-choice or advocates of capital punishment. If directly presented with material opposing their viewpoints, they become entrenched. But if before hearing the alternative viewpoints they receive affirmations of their social perceptiveness skills (another area of their self-esteem), they are more likely to be open to other views (Cohen, Aronson, & Steele, 1997). The self-affirmations that reduce defensiveness are not denials of the recipient's areas of limitations, but resonate with their other resources.

Discussion of Positive Thinking

The cognitive dissonance research is complex, but fairly comprehensive, and seems to fit well with clinical experience. A simple attempt to convince a person that they are okay in an area in which they do not feel okay is likely to backfire. It simply draws attention to a personal standard that they have failed to live up to, and thus increases dissonance and defense (Blanton et al., 1997). What *is* effective is helping people bring to the foreground the areas of their personality and behavior that they do feel good about (resources). When this is done, they are less likely to rationalize negative feedback or defend against new information. Again, this fits with research on self-efficacy; when people are led to bring their resources to the foreground, they can address specific behavior problems and make changes. Counselor guidance in developing a specific plan of change, with realistically achievable goals, moving through graduated improvements in behavior, is more effective than blind optimism.

This parallels health-related studies that show that positive experiences and positive beliefs (optimism) may serve as resources for processing negative information. They "may shield people from the fear that may accompany attention to potentially negative outcomes, fear that might otherwise interfere with subsequent processing and effective action" (Reed & Aspinwall, 1998, p. 127, citing Aspinwall & Taylor, 1997; Jepson & Chaiken, 1990; Levanthal, 1970). However, false optimism that involves self-deception turns out to be unrealistic and can be dysfunctional and even dangerous—for example, when an individual seriously underestimates the physical risks involved in his or her behavior (see Schneider's [2001] excellent discussion of "realistic optimism"). A number of studies have been done with children and young adults that suggest that a pessimistic style of explaining life events may feed into depression.

Very little study has been done with older people; one study gives evidence that elderly persons who have a pessimistic explanatory style are likely to have lower immunity to diseases (Kamen-Siegel, Rodin, Seligman, & Dwyer, 1991). However, being overly optimistic can also be dysfunctional. A study of noninstitutionalized, non-assisted older adults showed that extreme optimists may be more at risk for depressive symptoms when they actually face negative life events such as losses or failures in achievement.

A shield of positive beliefs can be functional in that it keeps the self from being overwhelmed. Similarly, it may be functional to minimize the importance of certain negative information, at least until the person has rebounded from its impact (Simon, Greenberg, & Brehm, 1995). Thus the person can digest new information rather than defend against it and go into denial. This is the context in which positive thinking is useful—but when it becomes denial, a blanket whitewashing of the self or of life, it can fail to prepare one for life's adversities. It is self-affirmation as a grounding in the broader sense of self that reduces defensiveness—not the commitment to a particular belief or stance. Thus, self-affirmations are functional when they lead to openness. But they fail when they attempt to deny, and are phony.

Limited evidence supports that such openness to new information can affect health-related behavioral changes as well (Reed & Aspinwall, 1998). The health effect of positive thinking does not appear to be a matter of positive thoughts, or mood effects alone. These conventional explanations were ruled out in a study in which two different methods of reviewing the day's events were used (Keough, Garcia, & Steele, 1997). Some subjects used an exercise of consciously integrating daily experiences into a personally important value through journal writing; others simply reflected on the happy events of the day. Only the first condition led to improved health (cited in Aronson, Cohen, & Nail, 1999).

Another experimental study suggested that a positive relationship between self-affirmation and better health may be elicited by using the conscious accessing of resources as the context in which to digest unpleasant information (Reed & Aspinwall, 1998). Both of these controlled studies showed some changes toward more healthy behavior in the self-affirmed groups. The changes were not simply due to stress reduction. In fact, the self-affirmed respondents in the Reed and Aspinwall (1998) study chose to read and process a higher proportion of *negative* or challenging information than did the non-affirmed respondents. The context of positive resources allows them to digest more negative information.

This ability to handle negative input if realistic positive affirmation is received leaves persons more ready to make personal changes, as is demonstrated by a large body of research on sense of self-efficacy (Bandura, 1997) and on internal locus of control (Rotter, 1971; Rotter, Chance, & Phares, 1972). Obviously, this reduction of defensiveness and the willingness to make personal changes is directly relevant to the therapeutic process. An appropriate goal of spiritually sensitive counseling is to prepare the client to withstand future assaults on self-confidence, such as personal threats from others, or occasional failures to live out one's value system. This preparation involves learning to face negatives rather than deny them.

A slightly different model from Aronson and colleauges' (1995) model of self-affirmation is Tesser and colleagues' concept of "satisficing, rather than maximizing, self-esteem." (Tesser, Chen, Collins, Cornell, & Beach, 1997). In this view, once self-esteem reaches or exceeds a certain threshold, people do not need to engage in defensive or self-enhancing behavior. Though not explicit, this model suggests a spiritual view of self, in the sense that a person comes to value not just self-growth, but openness or transcendence, getting beyond self (ego) to "truth" rather than defending one's present position. As previously noted, neither Buddha nor Jesus felt a need to defend their own righteousness. Both were comfortable being seen socializing and eating with persons their societies considered "sinners" (Hanh, 1995).

Other Research Strategies

The progression of theoretical frameworks discussed (Festinger's [1957] cognitive dissonance model, Aronson and colleaugs' [1995] model of self-affirmation, and Tesser and colleagues' [1997] "satisficing" model that moves beyond self-esteem) developed out of attempts to understand the experimental data. They lead us away from a simplistic view of "positive thinking" toward a view of a resourceful self that can tolerate threatening information about the world (e.g., causes of cancer) and about one's own personality (e.g., insensitivity to others).

Other models can be used for researching the issue of positive thinking and the principle of consonance (in social psychology), or congruity (in psychotherapy). Some findings from these other models will be presented, recognizing that far more extensive research has been done using these models will be presented here.

Risks of "Feeling Good" Approaches

That behavioral changes are not due to "mood effects" alone argues against a "feel good" popular psychology. It is not just that simplistically applying positive thinking doesn't work; the wish for people to "feel good" and the reinforcement of a constantly "positive attitude" can actually be harmful. Thanks to physiological instruments, psychologists in the past few decades have been able to measure biological responses that are indications of emotions even when the respondent is unaware of or denies having the emotions. It is now possible to test some aspects of the theory of repression of emotions. Using electromyogram (EMG) readings of the muscles of the face and forehead to measure anxiety, experimenters observed a group of college students who appeared almost "supernormal" and reported they had very little anxiety and that "nothing really was bothering them." The readings showed that this group, in fact, had the highest EMGs as compared to other students who were more open about their anxieties (DeAngelis, 1990). Studies of "repressors" (as persons with the psychological traits of the "supernormal" were later labeled) are most trustworthy when they include physiological or behavioral measures in addition to paper/pencil tests. People who seem super-positive (claiming to feel good even though they have recently experienced a serious problem, for example) are more likely to exhibit hypertension and, among females, are more susceptible to breast cancer. Some evidence exists that repressors are more rigid in their cardiovascular responses (responding to all emotions in the same way), and less able to remember childhood events (DeAngelis, 1990). Another study followed breast cancer patients from shortly after their diagnosis over a period of eight months, and assessed their desire for control. Women who had a high degree of "fighting spirit," an assertive mode of control, but were low on positive yielding attitudes showed the worst adjustment after eight months. In contrast, those who were high in *both* desire for control and yielding attitudes evidenced the best adjustment. (Astin et al., 1999). An overly positive and determined approach was less productive than a balance of control and yielding.

In this section, we have reviewed empirical data bearing on the issue of positive thinking. Though we have concentrated on the research that grew out of cognitive dissonance theory, it is clear that several lines of research, including not only laboratory simulations but data from physiological responses and from personality tests, argue against the simplistic use of positive thinking.

INTEGRATION AND TENTATIVE CONCLUSIONS

One issue with which the spiritually sensitive counselor must grapple in his or her practice is the tension between accepting the client as is, and challenging the client to change. This is especially salient in instances when the client's emotional conflict involves guilt or shame. The counselor may be tempted to help the client overcome a negative view of self too quickly, when what is needed is for the client to "sit with" some of the harm his or her behaviors have caused both to himself or herself and to others. Facile reassurance or minimizing the guilt is not likely to help the client reorganize and affirm himself or herself.

Several concepts within the field of spiritually based counseling try to address the problem of the misuse of positive thinking. The first is a pragmatic one: the recognition that if the counselor minimizes the client's presenting problem, the client is likely not to feel understood, and therefore may drop out of counseling. When novice counselors move too fast to try to solve a problem without entering more deeply into the experience of the clients' conflict, clients may sense that the counselor is not really with them. Much as clients would like easy relief, the quality of the relationship with the counselor may be even more important to them than a solution, at least during early sessions.

A Buddhist Perspective

Clinical psychologist and psychotherapist John Welwood (2000) has sought to integrate the Buddhist psychology of awakening (or enlightenment) into his counseling orientation. He has written cogently on a spiritual phenomenon that directly parallels the risks of positive thinking that have been described. He calls this phenomenon "spiritual bypassing." He started to notice this phenomenon among members of spiritual communities in the early 1970s:

> a widespread tendency to use spiritual practice to avoid dealing with certain personal or emotional "unfinished business." This desire to find release from certain earthly structures that seem to entrap us. . . has been a central motive in the spiritual search for thousands of years. So there is often a tendency to try to rise above our emotional and personal issues—all those messy, unresolved issues that weigh us down. (Welwood, 2000, pp. 11-12)

Individuals are particularly at risk when they are struggling with developmental transitions that require an expansion of their current identity. While still struggling to find themselves they

> are introduced to spiritual teachings and practices that urge them to give themselves up. As a result, they wind up using spiritual practices to create a new "spiritual" identity, which is actually an old dysfunctional identity—based on avoidance of unresolved psychological issues—packaged in a new guise. (Welwood, 2000, p. 12)

Spiritual approaches that stress surrendering one's identity instead of expanding it may lead clients toward retrogression rather than growth because the clients are shifted to a new form of greater dependency rather than an openness to diversity and a larger view of the holy.

A Christian Perspective

The words of the poet Wallace Stevens (1950) are relevant in the context of spiritual bypassing. He wrote: "The way through the world is more difficult to find than the way beyond it" (p. 67). Thomas

Moore (1997), the great contemporary Catholic mystic, has urged the teaching of "natural spirituality" because "it has in it no elements of superficial sentimentality and no signs of escapism" (p. 67).

The theological concept of "cheap grace" in protestant Christianity is relevant here. The phrase was coined by Dietrich Bonhoeffer, a leading pastor and professor of theology in Germany during the Nazi regime (Bonhoeffer, 2000). His courageous life story is worth summarizing because it bears directly on the spiritual necessity of facing the dark aspects of life.

Raised in the theological tradition of Martin Luther, which emphasizes salvation through God's loving grace, not through human efforts (de Gruchy, 1999), Bonhoeffer insisted the churches had corrupted the meaning of grace when they used it as an excuse not to confront and "change the things that can be changed." Bonhoeffer courageously confronted the Christian churches during the ascendance of Nazi power. The context was social ethics, and the way protestant churches used the doctrine of forgiveness to excuse the horrible atrocities of the Nazi holocaust.

Bonhoeffer's brother-in-law was a leading member of the Nazi army counterintelligence agency, so Bonhoeffer almost certainly knew more about the mass deaths of Jewish citizens than most (Nelson, 1999). However, enough public information about the persecution of Jews was available to make it clear that the Christian churches were in denial. Bonhoeffer insisted that, as a Christian, he must speak out against the intolerance and persecution of Jews in his native Germany. Eventually, with his brother-in-law's help, Bonhoeffer became a double-agent and a leader in the underground resistance, believing that, as a Christian, he must do what he could to stop the Nazis persecution of Jews. Among German pastors and theologians, Bonhoeffer was

> almost alone in his opinions; he was the only one who considered solidarity with the Jews, especially non-Christian Jews, to be a matter of such importance as to obligate the Christian churches to risk a massive conflict with the state—a conflict which could threaten [the Church's] very existence. (Heinz Eduard Todt, cited in Bethge, 1979, p. 55).

Though Bonhoeffer's position makes no bones that we are called to a very demanding ethical stance, it also acknowledges that the ethical choices we make, no matter how well intentioned, often turn out to be a mixture of good and evil. This is well expressed in an essay titled "Grace: More than Forgiveness of Sins."

> The moral situation of human beings is complex. Sometimes it is not enough to say that an act is right or wrong. It may be ambiguous, meaning that the best decision possible may cause harm [as well as doing] good. . . . Good and evil, right and wrong, may be involved, but [they] do not exhaust the reality. In these cases we must refer to the tragic. . . .
>
> . . . by the tragic we mean a situation that involves suffering to the extent that it is (1) unavoidable and/or (2) pointless and irredeemable. (Cauthen, 2006)

In these two important ways, the recognition of the serious demands of discipleship and the ambiguity of ethical decisions, we must not minimize the power of the dark side in daily living.

The research in cognitive dissonance theory reviewed in the previous section focuses on changes in self-perception and the perception of consequences to self. Bonhoeffer's analysis went beyond focus on self to examine the ways we avoid change in our social behavior—we become complicit with evil by minimizing the destructive consequences of our denial on the lives of others. He pointed out how our failure to see what is happening around us leads to the dissolution of humane society.

Bonhoeffer insisted that "grace" be seen in the context of Jesus' radical call to abandon security and follow him as a disciple, even to the cross. Thus, the doctrine of grace could not be used to excuse the church or the individual Christian from responsibility in the real world of relationships. Valid spiritual experiences are those that open the person to act with empathy and compassion, even if this requires great personal risk. Grace is tested by its fruits. (Matthew 7:16, 20, RSV). Jesus appears to interpret "fruits" as ethical, interpersonal, and social actions, in line with the values of the prophetic Jewish tradition. In fact, Borg (1999), whom I cited earlier for describing the similarities of Jesus and Buddha, believes one major difference existed between the two: Jesus was a social prophet and challenged the system of oppression of his day and its ruling elites (p. *xi*). Borg may be exaggerating this contrast. Some Buddhist scholars believe that Buddha intended his teaching—especially his focus on the "nonself" in contrast to Hinduism's focus on the "self"—to be a criticism of the Hindu caste system and thus an indirect appeal for social reform. The difference between Jesus' direct style and the Buddha's more indirect critique of society may simply reflect a difference in their cultures. In any case, Jesus likely thought of his ministry as directly challenging both the institutional religion and the government of his day.

In his faithfulness to Jesus, Bonhoeffer spoke of discipleship even to the death, and he "walked his talk." He was imprisoned in 1943 (Bonhoeffer, 1997) and executed in 1945 for being part of the group that tried to organize the assassination of Hitler and the overthrow of the Third Reich.

Martin Luther King Jr.'s life and death paralleled Bonhoeffer's in that he too taught a level of love and acceptance that transcended the usual barriers of in-group/out-group. He affirmed an ethic that united belief and action rather than "cheap grace" that excused inaction. He embraced persons in spite of race, but also in spite of sexual orientation and theistic or nontheistic religious point of view (see his eulogy of Unitarian minister James Reeb in King, 2001).

Convergence of Perspectives

The psychological critique of superficial positive thinking, Welwood's (2000) Buddhist critique of spiritual bypassing, and the Christian critique of "cheap grace" all point to the need for the spiritually sensitive counselor to be prepared, inwardly and in relation to clients, to face the negative, dark facts of human existence. The counselor needs to confront both the existence of evil in human society and the possibility of destructive thoughts and behavior in herself or himself.

Tentative Conclusions

Let's briefly review the criteria that have been suggested for assessing whether the counselor's and the client's spirituality is healthy.

Spiritual health is not static; it involves growth. The metaphor of balance in life is useful, but spiritual growth also involves risking temporary imbalance to move forward. The forward movement is not so much to achieve a goal, but to encounter the sacred in new experiences. The counselor needs to focus on the process of the client's openness to the sacred, not on belief or dogma. The process of spiritual growth involves openness to new data and experience, including negative experience. Solid grounding in the realities of life require wrestling with uncomfortable and tragic events, not simply "thinking positively."

Openness also entails continually expanding the boundaries of caring—moving beyond the limits of one's own group or tribe—and inclusiveness of justice and compassion. But the counselor's focus is on the process, the way in which the client is expanding, not on a particular stage or endpoint that the client has achieved or will achieve. Expending the boundaries also includes a move beyond individual ethics to social ethics. We have surveyed concepts such as cognitive dissonance, self-affirmation, spiritual short circuiting, and cheap grace. All of these concepts point to the risks of seeking easy answers to the human struggle to deal with one's own "dark side." The Christian perspective on cheap grace goes a step further, and forces us to look not just at our own "dark side" but to face the dark side of society. I have noted earlier that the growth model suggests that the mental health practitioner must transcend the judgments of society. The example I gave was of a boy labeled by the school system as having ADD. We must not just assess the boy, but assess the school system. It may be that the "dysfunction" lies in the school's false expectations of passivity and compliance. The social roots of our constructs of meaning suggest that the practitioner needs not only to transcend society's judgments, but to critique the society from a higher value perspective.

To propose that the focus of spiritually sensitive counseling is on process, openness, and inclusiveness seems to me the healthiest integration of social science and values that we can make at this point—but it is clearly a position based on certain values. As pointed out in the second section, One very encouraging aspect of the current consensus in mental health and counseling is the increased awareness that value-free counseling is impossible. We need safeguards in spiritual counseling to ensure that neither our beliefs nor our values are imposed on the client. In Chapter 3, I include a section on safeguards against imposing values. In Chapter 4 I make suggestions concerning safeguards that reduce that risk that the counselor's beliefs will be imposed on the client.

But first let's examine spiritual and value development, and explore the concrete crises and conflicts that bring clients into spiritual counseling. The next chapter will present three different models of spiritual development, which will give more substance to discussion of the kinds of growth that may occur.

Chapter 2

Models of Spiritual Development

The process of spiritual development may sometimes be incremental, but it does not necessarily occur simply by gradual and additive growth. Often it involves crucial periods in which previous frames of reference are challenged by some very fulfilling "peak" experiences, or by experiences of suffering, grief, or crisis. In the previous chapter several models of psychological health were examined (the medical, adaptation, and growth models), and several models of human development were referred to (Kohlberg's moral development stage model, Erikson's model of life "crises," and Marcia's identity status model). In this chapter we will examine three models that directly look at spiritual or religious development: Fowler's "stages of faith," Wilber's "stages of spiritual development," and Washburn's "dynamic of dialectic development." These three models provide an overview of the developmental view of spirituality, and have prompted more research or analysis than other existing theories of spiritual development. I present these models despite my criticisms of stage models of development (see Chapter 1) because they provide a useful introduction to the issues of crisis and exploration, which are central to ensuing chapters. As you read these models, keep in mind the limitations of step-by-step stage theories. The focus with the client is on the process or growth and inclusiveness, not on whether a particular stage has been reached. The first is a model that emerges out of the major religious traditions. The second and third are more secular models that emerge from the field of transpersonal psychology.

FOWLER'S MODEL

This model is built on the foundation of three better known developmental models—those of Piaget (1965), Kohlberg, and Erikson. James Fowler (1981) has explicated and researched what he calls the "stages of faith." It is important to understand Fowler's choice of the word *faith* in his theory of spiritual development.

Faith As a Universal Human Process

First, faith does not mean the same thing as *belief,* although the word is commonly used in that way today. To believe is to assent to a set of propositions, or to commit to a system of thought (Fowler, 1981). The words of sacred scriptures that have been translated as "believe" would more accurately be translated "to set one's heart on" or "to be loyal or committed to." The English use of the word *belief* changed from the sixteenth century to the nineteenth century, and has come to mean primarily an intellectual or theoretical act. Its original meaning was "to hold dear" or "to love" (Fowler, 1981).

Second, this act of holding dear, setting one's heart, is a central part of Buddhist, Hindu, Hebrew, Greek, and Latin religious scriptures and writing, and in each of the relevant languages (Hindi, Hebrew, Greek, and Latin) the key words translated "faith" are verbs, and do not refer to acts of the mind alone (ideas) but to acts of the whole person. Unfortunately, in English, *faith* is not a verb, so it easily gets misinterpreted as a static mental act rather than a dynamic and holistic process. Given this ecumenical definition of faith, the development of faith is not unique to Western religions; it appears to be a universal human concern regarding the act of orienting one's life.[1] Fowler intends his stages to be universal, regardless of religious tradition or culture. For that reason, they are focused on the "structures" of faith rather than on the specific content. We will return to the issue of content later in the description of his model. He conceptualizes the following five dimensions of faith:

1. Faith is a universal human phenomenon, the process of making meaning out of life experience.
2. It is a way of interpreting or construing human experience, a way of moving into and giving form and coherence to life.

3. It is relational, a mode of being in relation to another or others in which we invest commitment. It is triadic, involving self, others, and shared causes and values.
4. Knowing through faith is cognition inextricably fused with passion or valuing in regard to the transcendent. "There are both negative and positive moments of being in faith" (Furushima, 1983, p. 13, citing Fowler, 1974); one may fear, mistrust or revolt against it—or trust, give loyalty, have love or admiration (citing Fowler, 1976).
5. Faith is a "primary motivating power in the journey of self" (Furushima, 1983, p. 13, citing Fowler and Keen, 1978); "the basic focus upon which a person makes, maintains, or transforms meaning in one's life" (Furushima, 1983, p. 14, citing Fowler and Vergote, 1980).

Fowler's Six Stages

Fowler assumes a prestage of undifferentiated trust in the parent-child relationship during infancy that sets the stage for later faith development. The development of certain cognitive processes are a prerequisite for the emergence of each level of faith development However, as Fowler's discussion of the meaning of faith implies, the commitments that a person makes at each level are not simply cognitive judgments but are decisions made in relationships and involve the emotional maturation of the person as well as one's intellectual development. In describing each stage, Fowler attempts to incorporate the dynamics of interpersonal development, relying heavily on Erik Erikson's psychosocial theory.

Stage One: Intuitive-Projective Faith

The child of ages two to six or seven, using the new skills of speech and the ability to symbolize and to organize experience into meaningful clusters, develops an intuitive-projective faith. At this stage the child can understand only from the point of view of his or her own perceptions; he or she cannot yet coordinate and compare two perspectives of the same object (perceptually) or two personal points of view (in relationships); the child exhibits cognitive egocentrism, in Piaget's sense. The images children develop influence their thinking more strongly than any logical process; their thinking is fluid, magical, and imaginative, without the ability or need to resolve illogical or contradictory elements. A sample from Fowler's research interviews with four-year olds illustrates:

INTERVIEWER: When you do something bad, does God know?

FREDDY: Yes. He spreads all around the world in one day.

INTERVIEWER: He does? How does he do that?

FREDDY: He does 'cause he's smart.

INTERVIEWER: He's smart? How does he get all around the world in one day?

FREDDY: Uh—he can split or he can be like a god.

INTERVIEWER: He can split into lots of things?

FREDDY: Yeah.

INTERVIEWER: Can he do anything he wants to?

FREDDY: Yeah.

INTERVIEWER: Is there anything he can't do?

FREDDY: He can do things, things that are good, not bad. God never tells a lie in his life.

INTERVIEWEr: Never?

FREDDY: Nope. (Fowler, 1981, p. 128)

Concrete stories and images typify this level of development, though precursors of conceptual abstractions are present, for example, in Freddy's statement that God "spreads all around the world in one day." The power of the imagination at this age provides opportunities for images of sustaining love, but also at this age the child can be vulnerable if overexposed to frightening images, such as of fiery torments of punishment (Fowler, 1981, citing Helfaer, 1972). Fowler (1981) theorizes that the contribution of faith development at this stage is "the rise of images of (the) Numinous" (p. 290). This would seem to provide an experiential base for faith.

Stage Two: Mythic-Literal Faith

Ten-year-olds were interviewed for this stage. They constructed more orderly, linear, and dependable worldviews in contrast to the imaginative ones of the preschoolers. By then children have the ability to take another's perspective, and they also project God's perspective, resulting in full-fledged anthropomorphic images of God. For Millie, God has the capacity to take another's perspective. Millie's anthropomorphic God-image seems filled with the contents of Millie's perspective taking with her parents as decision makers.

INTERVIEWER: Does God care when you do something wrong?

MILLIE: Sure he—he cares. And he knows that you're—he knows that you are sorry about it. And he always tries—he always forgives you, usually.

INTERVIEWER: What if you're not sorry about it?

MILLIE: Then he knows, probably. He probably will still forgive you probably because he knows that you're probably going through a rough time. And I think that probably like some people who don't even believe in God. God still probably believes—uh, forgives them, because he knows that, you know, people have their own ideas and beliefs. (Fowler, 1981, p. 140)

Stage two faith is also characterized by a sense of reciprocal fairness and lawfulness, with God treating individuals as they treat God, tit for tat. Beliefs are appropriated with literal interpretations, less imaginatively and egocentrically than in the previous stage. Story becomes the main method of connecting and unifying experience. The constructive result of this stage is the "rise of narrative and the forming of stories of faith" (Fowler, 1981, p. 290). But meaning is "trapped" in the stories. At the cognitive level of mythic-literal faith, the believer cannot step back from the story and reflect on it or conceptualize it.

Stage Three: Synthetic-Conventional Faith

With early adolescence comes an ability to notice contradictions in stories and to seek points of view from outside the home and outside the flow of experience. The adolescent is now able to formulate alternative views and hypotheses and to make judgments from abstract ideals. Most important, the adolescent is now cognitively able to see himself or herself "from outside," as others may see him or her. This interpersonal perspective taking often leads to self-consciousness, but it is essential to the forming of a conscious identity. Though a danger arises of "the tyranny of the they" from the adolescent's focus on other's expectations (Parks, 1980), the adolescent hungers for "a God who knows, accepts, and confirms the self deeply" (Fowler, 1981, p. 153).

Linda, 15, illustrates this stage. She speaks of God's talking to her in the form of feelings she gets when she has really struggled with a problem.

> Once when one of her friends had turned against her she went into her bedroom, thought about her situations and cried. She said, "Then I remembered that, you know, there was *God,* and I just asked him to tell me something, tell me what I could do. . . ." Linda's dominant images of God have the Stage 3 qualities of companionship, guidance, support, and of God's knowing and loving her.
>
> Her beliefs are grounded in both what she feels and what she has been taught, primarily by her parents. (Fowler, 1981, p. 156)

For some adolescents, the forming of identity and faith in stage three is open-ended and clearly anticipates a transition to stage four (some years hence). For many, though, this becomes a stable identity and they never move beyond it. In either case, the system of informing images and values through which they are committed is a tacit system, a kind of "knowing" that they do not examine, which functions similar to basic assumptions (Fowler, 1981). It is "conventional" in that the person "dwells" in this meaning world and has not stepped outside it to examine it. Yet these beliefs and values are deeply felt. This stage leads to a personal "myth" of one's own growing identity and faith. Typically, some form of crisis is needed for the individual to move on to stage four. We shall review the types of crises later.

Stage Four: Individuative-Reflective Faith

A genuine move to stage four requires an interruption of reliance on external sources of authority. Instead of the conventional acceptance of other persons' views, authority is relocated inside the self. A critical stepping outside of one's own previous assumptions or tacit values occurs. Essential features of this stage are a distancing from one's previous assumptions, and the emergence of an "executive ego," a part of the self that can consciously be a spectator and get perspective from which to make life decisions. The person who has achieved this stage knows that he or she has an ideology, that this worldview has changed over time, and that it is situated in one's culture and social systems. Often this ideology affects the person's occupational decisions, and a sense of a vocational dream or mission emerges. For some, the transition to this stage comes around the mid-twenties (as part of identity and intimacy development). But others don't undergo the transition until the thirties or forties, resulting in greater disruption of their established relationships and roles. And for still others it never emerges.

To illustrate this stage, Fowler (1981) presents a case study of Jack, a young man of Irish and Italian Catholic descent who attended a Catholic parochial school from seventh grade through high school, and was a very committed Catholic until bullies in his class tormented him for his religiosity. At that point Jack believed God had failed an agreement with him. In his early twenties, Jack went into service and "identified himself with a group of black soldiers, held together by their commitment to soul music and the Panther ideology" (Fowler, 1981, p. 173). He burned his bridges with the past and began to shape a new identity and faith. His identity had previously derived from the groups he grew up in, not groups he had consciously chosen. But his identifications in his twenties led him to choose a new reference group. As a genuine stage-four youth, his choice of groups, with the ideological perspectives they bear, became a function of the identity he was crafting.

Stage Five: Conjunctive Faith

Stage five rarely emerges before midlife. This stage has been hard to describe, even for Fowler himself (Fowler, 1981). Most important, it is a move beyond the logical and dichotomizing conceptions of stage four to affirm a more paradoxical, organic, or complex view of life. It is an attempt to open oneself to experience, to the cosmos, without imposing on it one's own categories. It involves "going beyond the explicit ideological system and clear boundaries of identity that Stage Four worked so hard to construct . . . " (Fowler, 1981, p. 186). This letting go of ego often involves interfaith conversations that are receptive to the truth of the person with whom one is in dialogue—a genuinely mutual ecumenism. A trust exists that reality is bigger than any one tradition's mediation of it, a radical openness to the truth of other's traditions. "The strength that emerges from this stage is a sense of paradox, depth and intergenerational responsibility for the world" (p. 290)

Fowler (1981) illustrates stage five with an interview with a 78-year-old single woman who rented rooms to graduate students. She had identified with both Unitarian and Quaker traditions, had taught art and music in mental hospitals (also caring for a younger half-brother who had been institutionalized for 30 years), and had written two small books. In the interview she was asked if there are beliefs and values everyone should hold:

> Miss T cites the founder of Quakerism, George Fox: "There is that of God in every man." If you really believe that . . . it would change your relationships with people . . . It's far reaching. It applies nationally and individually, and class-wise; it reaches the whole. To anyone that I loved dearly I would say, "Put that in your little invisible locket and keep it forever."

Interviewer, mindful of her suffering, and her devotion to other sufferers, asks how, if at all, she makes sense of the unfair suffering in the world.

> MISS T: Take my brother R. If there ever was a pure, sinless, human soul, it's my brother R. Why did he have to have a life like this? I said to myself. I've got to solve it if I am going to believe in a good God . . . I came out of it more or less this way: human life is a moment in eternity. (Astronomy and anthropology) meant more to me . . . than any other (courses). Your perspective opens out to an absolutely incredible degree . . .
>
> It may be that R's . . . in the cocoon stage . . . I have a sense that I should somewhere someday, along the pathways of God, meet R. when he is come into his own, and he comes with rushing wings . . . I can't help but feel that all the suffering of all these people, all the people that are starving to death, that their time will come.

Interviewer (late in the interview) asks her about her understanding of sin.

> MISS T: Sin!? I don't use the word sin, ever. I think on the whole people are doing the best they can with what light they have. And I think more in terms of mistakes than . . . of deliberate sin . . . (there are) gigantic blunderings . . . It's past belief the stupidity of the world today. The American people are shipping arms to the whole world because the industry has to make money . . . You really have to have a deep faith in Almighty God and the power of good not to just go down under that gigantic stupidity and say it's hopeless. So I think sin, in one sentence, is the result of being cut off from God.
>
> INTERVIEWER: . . . Do you feel you are changing or growing now in your life as a religious person?
>
> MISS T: . . . One of the things that has come to me in . . . the last few days is that this Cosmic Flow, which is God, call it what you will, is the life back of every cell in the body. It's a nice metaphor, the river is the flow, because it has come to me more deeply that I am just sort of porous; That this refreshing healing love of God is flowing through me, and that's a very marvelous thing to believe, if you are 78 and you've got arthritis, and . . . burdened with . . . old age . . . that this Reality, of this actual life . . . Life flows through you at every moment of your waking-sleeping experience. Consequently you can be creative till your last breath. (Fowler, 1981, p. 197)

Persons in stage five know the sacrament of defeat and the reality of irrevocable commitments and acts. The boundaries of self and outlook, which were important to clarify in stage four can now be loosened, can become porous and permeable. This stage tries to unify opposites in mind and experience, to be vulnerable to the strange truths of those who are very different from oneself, ready for closeness to that which is strange or threatening to oneself and one's outlook. In this stage one becomes freed from the confines of tribe, class, religious community, or nation. A person can both appreciate symbols and critique them, secure that he or she has been grasped by the depth and reality to which they refer (Fowler, 1981).

Can you think of an example in your own life of when you have affirmed the value of an old stance and at the same time realized the importance of moving on, being reopened? The Buddhist refer to this opening up as having a "beginner's mind."

Stage Six: Universalizing Faith

In spite of its depth, persons in stage five remain divided between an untransformed world and a transforming vision. In some few cases, this vision leads to the call of radical actualization that typifies stage six.

Persons in stage six typically exhibit qualities that upset our usual standards of normalcy. Their vivid sense of transcendent moral and religious actuality make what they say and do somewhat unpredictable—they don't value our more mundane reality. Life is both loved and held to loosely. Their selfless passion for a transformed world leads them to live a life of inclusiveness of community and radical commitment to justice and love, which is experienced as subversive to the accommodations and compromises that people of goodwill make in situations of social tension.

Representatives include Gandhi, Martin Luther King Jr., and Mother Teresa, and also possibly Dag Hammarskjöld, Dietrich Bonhoeffer, Abraham Heschel, and Thomas Merton. Such persons are not perfect, or even necessarily "self-actualized" (in Rogers's or Maslow's sense). Fowler (1981) notes that "greatness of commitment and vision often coexists with great blind spots and limitations" (p. 204). My favorite example of this concerns Ghandi. Erik Erikson's recognition that the Gandhi he idolized, in the midst of his exemplifying a method of humble nonviolence, could be psychologically violent and arrogant in his relationship with his wife, and on top of it, rationalized [these outbursts] with ambivalent phrases and principles" (see Erikson, 1969, p. 243).

Fowler seeks, in his discussion of stage six, to make a place for persons of different faith traditions to make a radical commitment to the transcendent as it is revealed in their particular faith tradition, and yet to affirm that the "absoluteness" of their commitment should not involve exclusivity. He tries to avoid a secular relativism in which traditions are eroded rather than transcended (Fowler, 1981). And he recognizes that his descriptions of stage six come from his Judeo-Christian tradition and are offered as "a faithful effort" rather than a final statement (Fowler, 1981). I quote his concluding description:

> The bearers of Stage Six faith, whether they stand in the Jewish, Christian, or other traditions, embody in radical ways this leaning into the future of God for all being . . . What is it about these persons that both condemns our obsessions with our own security and awakens our taste and sense for the promise of human futurity? . . . . These persons embody costly openness to the power of the future. They actualize its promise, creating zones of liberation and sending shock waves to rattle the cages that we allow to constrict human futurity. Their trust in the power of that future and their trans-narcissistic love of human futurity account for their readiness to spend and be spent in making the Kingdom (of God) actual. (Fowler, 1981, pp. 210-211)

A Summary of the Development of Faith

Fowler posits a development of faith from the fluid, imaginative, and contradictory ideas of a child through the development of perspective and logic leading to a somewhat ego-bound defense of the conventional faith of one's own subculture. In early adulthood, a critical evaluation of one's own and one's culture's assumptions may result in a more personal view of a God who confirms and accepts the self, but also in a sense of one's own worldview and ideology as changing, developing. For those who remain open to change, with more life experience the logical and dichotomizing aspects of one's worldview may give way to greater acceptance of paradox and complexity. The specialness of an individual's own view is less likely to be used to build walls within himself or herself and between self and others who have different views. For an incredible few, mature faith becomes a selfless passion for a transformed and united world; such people do not lose focus in the dualities of life. Faith matures into an inclusive belief that is still a powerful activator in their own lives.

Critique of Fowler's Stages of Faith

Structure and Content

Has Fowler's focus on the structure of faith development and his wish to develop a universal stage theory led to an inability to distinguish the development of a destructive faith stance from a mature and humane one? In a critical interdisciplinary examination of Fowler's work, deLaurentis (1985) argues that the humane content of faith does not enter the theory until stage five. A stage-four individuating-reflexive Nazi with genocidal intentions is considered more developed in faith than a stage three (conventional or conforming), because of the former's self-aware adherence to his chosen (Nazi) norms and his translation of conventional symbol into ideas. Thus deLaurentis (1985) argues for integrating both form and content issues in the assignment of categories.

Fowler (1981) seems to recognize this issue, and writes:

> The tricky thing, however, is that an intrinsically motivated Marxist, an intrinsically motivated individualist follower of Ayn Rand, and an intrinsically motivated Orthodox Jew may all be best described (as Stage 4) . . . Individual-Reflective faith. . . . Their faith can be said to be more adequate structurally than that of their co-religionists . . . in the Synthetic stage. Evaluations . . . (of) truth, ethical adequacy, or the humanizing power of their faith . . . would have to be based on criteria that included both structural and content . . . dimensions. (p. 301)

DeLaurentis (1985) criticizes Fowler for limiting his model to the structure of faith development and not sufficiently elaborating the content of faith. Fowler acknowledges the danger of cognitive structure alone as a criterion of faith, and later comments that his stage theory "in its highly formal stage descriptions, [has] no religious richness of sufficiency to offer" (p. 293). He concludes that it needs the content of a particular religion to be constructive—the "stories, the images of power, and the centers of value that particular faith traditions can offer." Without these, the stages of faith are "mere scaffolding" (p. 293).

This use of the word *contents* (by both Fowler and DeLaurentis) needs a bit of explanation, since neither author seems to intend it to refer to the cognitive belief system of faith. Rather, Fowler indicates three contents of faith that shape its development:

1. The centers of value
2. The images of power we hold, and how these support us or constrain us
3. The "master stories," the characterizations of patterns of power in action, which are central to a person's meaning (similar to what some counseling theories call "narratives" or "scripts")

DeLaurentis's criticism assumes Fowler's own polarity between cognition and particularity. Fowler views the structure of faith as cognitive, but its particularity is religious. But in a pluralistic culture, ethics and ideology need not be based on particular religious tradition.

Does the Model Have Hidden Cultural Biases?

By incorporating dynamic psychosocial theory in his description of stages, Fowler escapes the criticism leveled at Kohlberg's (1969) work, that (moral or religious) decisions in real life are not made on the basis of cognitive processes alone. However, Fowler's stage model has both empirical and conceptual problems. A full review of these is not possible here, and in contrast to some of his theological critics (see especially Furushima, 1983, Chapter 2) I appreciate his effort to create ways to observe and measure the development of faith, even if it does not fully describe the transcendent aspects of faith.

Limits of Empirical Data

In contrast to research on Piaget's theory, very little cross-cultural research has been done on Fowler's stages. One such study, Furushima's (1983) thoughtful exploratory study in Hawaii, suggests that the rational-cognitive criteria involved in defining stages three through six do not work particularly well with Japanese-Buddhist subjects. At least three of Furushima's twelve subjects seem to use an intuitive and artistic style of faith, which can be equally well categorized as stage three or stage six. For most of the subjects, the transition from stage five to six does not appear to be hierarchical or invariant, which led Furushima to question the stages in general and most clearly the "arbitrary indicators" in these last two stages (Furushima, 1983). This raises serious questions both about the accuracy of the sequence of stages Fowler theorizes and about whether the rational-cognitive criteria are in fact an imposition from Western culture and masculine style.

Conceptual Problems

Several problems need to be addressed concerning conceptualizing development in terms of stages. First, any stage theory assumes that a linear progression occurs from the first to the second to the third stage and so on. Assuming such a progression in a purely cognitive system such as Piaget's is logical: certain thought processes are not possible without certain other, more basic, cognitive operations.

I have already argued that some of Erikson's later stages seem to occur in different sequence for women than for men, and that the progression is changing for women; in short, at least parts of the sequence appear to be cultural rather than inevitable (see Matteson, 1993a). Both Kohlberg's and Erikson's schemas have been criticized for making assumptions that better fit Western male development than other populations. Since Fowler's stages build on Kohlberg's and Erikson's, are they vulnerable to the same criticism?

Kohlberg's and Erikson's stages have each received considerable psychological attention and research beginning in the mid-1960s. Partly because Fowler's stage theory emerged roughly 25 years later than the others, and partly because the psychology of religious development has to some extent been relegated to the fringes of mainstream psychology, Fowler's theory has not received as much empirical testing.

The elegance of the Piaget cognitive stage theory is that each stage can be clearly assigned through a series of experiments with the subject. The sequence of stages is not just logical; we can test empirically whether it is possible for a subject to move from stage one to stage three without going through stage two. Though cross-cultural research suggests that, in some traditional cultures, it is rare for anyone to reach the highest stages, this does not challenge the idea that higher stages may exist or that the sequence of the early stages exists for most people.

Fowler's early stages of faith are somewhat parallel to Piaget's cognitive theory: stage one interviews can be seen as eliciting the kind of faith statements that can be made given the child's cognitive egocentrism, in Piaget's sense. Fowler's stage two is similar to Piaget's second level: it is assessed in terms of whether the child has developed the ability to take another's perspective and applies this to his or her religious concepts, for example, the concept of God. Stage three includes a cognitive criterion, the ability to take a perspective outside the flow of one's own experience, again parallel to Piaget's cognitive theory, and adds the influence of peer culture and the ability to critique authority, which are observable and testable aspects of identity formation (using, for example, Marcia's interviews and categories of identity formation [Marcia, Waterman, Matteson, Archer, & Orlofsky, 1993]). Stage four takes the ability to get perspective one step further from the original egocentrism. It is as if the individual can step outside his or her own culture enough to examine his or her assumptions, to look at the "tacit values" that underlie his or her worldview.

These first four stages involve a logical sequence of greater and greater cognitive decentering, in direct parallel with Piaget's stages. The latter two stages, even concerning the aspect of cognitive decentering, involve a criterion of the size of the reference group, thus having more to do with the degree of inclusiveness than the level of cognitive structuring.

Overall, however, Fowler's stage theory seems more similar to Erikson's than to Piaget's. Fowler recognizes that the criteria for assessing a stage involve not just descriptive material but normative judgments. This is especially true of the later stages of faith (stages five and six), and these seem to me more problematic. When I look at the examples Fowler chooses for his final stage of religious development—Gandhi, Martin Luther King, Jr., Mother Teresa, Dag Hammarskjöld, Dietrich Bonhoeffer, Abraham Heschel, and Thomas Merton—they include all four of my most important contemporary spiritual heroes or models. So my intuitive response is that Fowler and I agree on what the highest stage of spiritual development looks like. But when I step back and take perspective and try to discern the "tacit" values and assumptions, it appears that stages three through six involve a dialectic between

- analytic or Western logical-deductive skills, in which "objects" are analyzed and looked at with perspective, and
- synthetic, intuitive, prehensions in which the self and the other, the object and the subject, dissolve into an "I-Thou" or even into an awesome and full nondualsim.

It is not clear to me that a particular conclusion to this dialectic is a "higher stage." Perhaps keeping the dialogue alive, the *process* of being open to both ways of apprehending Truth is the central cognitive issue, and later stages of that process may take many forms.

What I would suggest is a reformulation of the stage theory into one or more processes, which are not easily assigned stages, much like what has emerged in research on the later stages of Erikson's theory. I will return to that parallel in the following sections.

Ages and Stages: Rethinking Fowler's Model

As one would expect in a developmental theory, the examples given for the first five stages in Fowler's book are progressively older. The earliest age of transition illustrated for each stage is the following:

- Stage one, age 4
- Stage two, age 10
- Stage three, age 15
- Stage four, age 18
- Stage five, midlife.

For stage six, though the two examples were more than 61 years old when interviewed, one gets the sense that they reached the final stage long before that. This is also true of some the well known historical figures Fowler cites to illustrate stage six: Mahatma Gandhi, Martin Luther King Jr., Mother Teresa, Dag Hammarskjöld, Dietrich Bonhoeffer, Abraham Heschel, and Thomas Merton. All seven of these spiritual leaders were well on their life path by midlife. At least three of them seem to have reached stage six fairly early in life, certainly before middle age. Mahatma Gandhi was 25 when he was living in South Africa, and he led a political protest in response to the government passing a bill depriving Indians in South Africa of their rights; Bonhoeffer at age 27 fought the non-Aryan paragraph supporting Nazi racism his German church denomination passed; Martin Luther King Jr. was also only 27 when he led the Montgomery bus boycott. These are, of course, rare people. It is certainly arguable that they moved through the stages faster than is possible for most. It is also possible that stage six, as Fowler describes it, has more to do with personality variables than with structural development of one's ethics or spirituality. I have no doubt that developmental antecedents to the emergence of these two strengths exist. But is the transition to spiritual maturity (stages five and six) as personified in these seven spiritual giants truly a natural progression from the previous stages in the same sense as is the move from conventional (stage three) to individual-reflective (stage four)?

Who Can Reach the Final Stage?

The personality variables that seem to be involved in the personalities Fowler admires and chooses for his highest level include the ability to commit one's whole self to a single purpose and cause, and putting one's values into action.

The first concerns the kind of purity of heart that Kierkegaard equated with the ability to "will one thing." The high value Fowler places on this variable is revealed in his early discussion of faith; he speaks of "radical monotheism" in which all values and priorities, everything, is relativized and ordered in relationship to one "transcendent . . . principle of being" (Fowler, 1981, pp. 22-23). Though he claims that this singularity (this ability to will only one thing) is "not limited to Western culture of predominately Western religion," it is noteworthy that every one of his exemplars were highly influenced by the West. Only Gandhi among them spent his childhood in a non-Western culture, and even he, during his young adulthood before the emergence of his stage six "faith," was educated in England. If I were asked to list persons from the past who reached stage six of spiritual development, I would certainly include Jesus and Buddha. In that regard, I think it could be argued that Jesus, coming from the monotheistic tradition of Judaism, indeed developed a "radical monotheism" close to that which Fowler describes. It is harder, I think, to fit Buddha into this schema. Buddha in his early adulthood attempted a radical asceticism, but he later moved to "the middle way," which balances full affirmation of pleasure and sensory delights with "detachment" from making them goals in themselves. It is not accurate to see this "middle way" as a single principal of being, since he also advocates detachment from any belief, including belief in any one god. Remember that his tradition was Hindu; Buddhism can be interpreted as the Protestant Reformation within Hinduism. A reflection on my experience in Hindu India may be relevant. In India, young adults who had been raised to offer morning devotions to a particular god or goddess but in their youth find another avatar or symbol of god more meaningful may shift their devotion to that god *for that stage of their life.* I was told that this was not seen, in any sense, as a refutation of their Hindu background but as a natural process. At any particular period in life a different way of expressing or symbolizing one's faithfulness may be appropriate, and the deeper faith is that all of these lead to the "same" transcendent reference.

In short, I think that the ability to totally focus on one center, one "cause," and to subject all other values to its absolute priority is a Western ideal for identity. Furthermore, Fowler's concrete symbol of "radical monotheism" is indeed a Western image of total submission to the transcendent, which was probably most fully expressed in Islam. The Eastern religions are both more inclusive and less "singular."

I am not arguing that radical monotheism is a false symbol, but that it is clearly a culturally bound symbol, and is not necessarily the only way to live a "fully faithful" life. Thus it seems to me that the paths of legitimate spiritual development may be sequential in the early phases of development, at least through stage three or four. But different styles of faithful identity may emerge after these stages.

This reconceptualizing of Fowler's stages parallels the reconceptualizing of Erikson's stages in the research on identity formation. (This is examined in more detail in Chapter 9.) A shift has occurred in the theory of adolescent development from viewing identity process as ending in a particular status to a sense that the mature result is an openness to an ongoing process. As Sam Keen (1994) puts it, "I have no identity that will not be lost and found and lost again" (p. 149). It is not, however, a fluidity that is totally molded by the social environment without the individual's power to participate in and shape that environment. Integration of the various parts of self occurs, as does integrity in relation to the outside "realities" and the outside social context. A center of values exists, but those values include a recognition of indefiniteness and uncertainty, and a willingness to resume exploration.

Fowler's valuing of a firmness of commitment, a centering on "one thing," is similar to Erikson's search for a firm identity. The shift that has occurred in identity theory suggests that such an end point in "stages of faith" may be too closely bound with twentieth century Western culture. The importance of living faith in the concrete, practical world is stressed in all the major religious traditions, and was emphasized by both Jesus and Buddha; I am not arguing for a nebulous process that does not engage the current situation. I am arguing that a fully mature spiritual life may not be as "fixed" on one belief, or as certain about its direction as Fowler's model implies. The direction of greater inclusiveness, of openness to an unpredictable future and its claim on one's life, may be "radical" not because of its pureness or certainty, but because of its willingness to risk uncertainty, even in the area of belief.

WILBER'S CONTRIBUTION

I will be much briefer in my summary and comments on Ken Wilber's contribution to the issue of stage theory and spiritual development. In Wilber's work, "Spirituality and Developmental Lines: Are There Stages?" (Wilber, 1999) he makes the important observation that "most people, even if they are in fact progressing through stages of competence, rarely experience anything that feels or looks like a stage" (p. 3). The construct of stages is not an experiential one, and is observable only when someone (either the person himself or herself, or a counselor or researcher) stands outside the experience and looks at it from an external perspective. Wilber illustrates this with Piaget's cognitive stages. He claims that children, in a later stage of cognitive development, if shown videotapes of themselves prior to achieving that stage, "will accuse you of doctoring the videotape, because nobody could be that stupid, and certainly not them" (Wilber, 2000, p. 132). This does not mean that stage theories cannot be helpful to the observer in assessing development, but it suggests that clients themselves are unlikely to understand their own development in this way.

Wilber views the role of cognitive development as "necessary, but not sufficient" for psychological, moral, or spiritual development.

Most of the changes in thought patterns that are encouraged for spiritual development (thinking holistically instead of just analytically) require the ability to access what he calls "vision-logic." But access to holistic apprehension may change our belief systems, but do nothing to develop our emotional, moral, or spiritual maturity. "You can have full access to vision-logic, and still be at moral stage one, with safety needs, egocentric drives, and narcissistic inclinations" (Wilber, 2000, p. 137). These paradigm shifts do not necessarily transform our interior consciousness. It is the movement through these "interior stages of the growth of consciousness" that Wilber believes is crucial, which involves "going through at least a half-dozen major interior transformations, ranging from egocentric to ethnocentric to worldcentric, at which point, and not before, (human beings) can awaken to a deep and authentic concern . . . an actual embrace of global consciousness" (Wilber, 2000, pp. 137-138). The interior growth in consciousness comes from an inner practice, not simply a cognitive shift, Wilber argues. The stages that interest him have to do with "unfolding waves of subtler and subtler experiences." Wilber believes that "when you compare these experiences over a large number of people" or across different meditative traditions, certain similarities in unfolding, and in levels, occur. His conclusion is that spiritual stages exist.

At first, in his earlier work (1990), he formulated six stages that closely parallel the stages of Piaget, the sixth including formal hypothetical thinking and the ability to assume perspective of others. These are similar to Kohlberg's and Fowler's stages and won't be described here. Later he outlined four additional stages:

Stage seven (ages 21 and up), a stage of "vision-logic" or holistic-synthetic thinking, integrating feeling and thought, allowing for wholeness and authenticity. He compares this stage to Abram Maslow's stage of "self-actualization" (Maslow, 1968).

Stage eight (28 years and up), the "subtle" stage, with visionary intuition, and spontaneous altruistic and devotional feelings. Wilber believes paranormal psychic abilities may also be present at this stage. He sees the last three stages as levels of Maslow's final stage, "self-transcendence" (Maslow, 1971).

Stage nine (35 years and up), involves a unitized consciousness—the contemplation of unity of the human and the divine, with radiant absorption in the godhead.

Stage ten, "ultimate unity" is, theoretically, the final and highest possible stage, and is attained only in exceptional cases; it is not given an age period. It is marked by unity beyond all division and duality—complete psychic integration and coincidence of the individual with reality.

In Wilber's (2000) work on the stages he continues to argue that a specific progression of interior development of consciousness occurs. Stated differently, a process of movement in a clear direction occurs. The unfolding is more and more subtle, and more and more inclusive. However, he does not list the stages (though he states "there are stages") except in his chart, and there he substitutes for the last stages four forms of mysticism.

In his discussion of the moral development, he is a bit more concrete. He states his interest not only in the principles of moral judgment—that is, how one reaches a moral decision—but also the "moral span," the span of those "deemed worthy to be included in the decision in the first place." This is the dimension I refer to as "inclusiveness." The progression is from egocentric (includes just oneself) to ethnocentric (including the tribe or clan) to "worldcentric" to "theocrentric." The last should not be confused with mythic theism; it is the transpersonal realm, and so may be more accurately called "pneumocentric," or spirit-centered (Wilber, 2000).

This same progression in the span of concern, or empathic identification, is implied in Wilber's view of spiritual development. The stage theories of Piaget, Kohlberg, Erikson, and Fowler suggest a series of steps, and an assumption that one cannot hop over any particular step but must build each on the previous. The image Wilber presents is one of concentric circles, moving outward to larger, more inclusive circles. At least for the earlier stages he implies "necessary, but not sufficient" prerequisite stages, which suggests steplike growth. The later stages are experienced in the sense of an inclined plane, or spiral, moving upward, rather than a series of defined steps or levels. If this interpretation is correct, his conceptualization is closer to what I have called "process" than it is to the steps or stages of Piaget, Kohlberg, and Fowler.

Though Wilber attempts to convey his stage theory in highly rational and abstract writing, he is clear that the learning needed to move through these stages is experiential, not just cognitive. The progression of spiritual consciousness might be thought of as an empathic embracing, a caring or mindfulness toward a wider and wider circle of beings and being. It requires not simply a wider worldview (the cognitive prerequisite), but a bigger and bigger heart.

WASHBURN'S MODEL

Michael Washburn (1995) developed the other leading developmental theory in transpersonal psychology, elaborated in his book *The Ego and the Dynamic Ground.* At least in its earlier articulations, Ken Wilber's theory appeared to be structural and hierarchical (closer to the metaphor of steps). In contrast, Washburn's theory is dynamic and dialectical (Washburn, 1995). He specifically uses the image of "spiral," an image also used in Fowler's later writing, and in my description of Wilber's last stages. Washburn sees the purpose of transpersonal theory as "to integrate spiritual experience within a larger understanding of human nature and human development." Similar to Carl Jung, he maintains that "the drama of human development becomes fully intelligible only when seen in the light of spiritual symbols." These symbols are "understood experientially rather than doctrinally or historically" (Washburn, 1995, p. 1). His beginning point is experiential and transcendent, as suggested by his consistently capitalizing the term *Dynamic Ground,* which seems to carry meanings similar to Tillich's "Being Itself" or "Ground of Being," pointing to the reality that precedes and is superior to individual experience. Washburn conceptualizes human spiritual development as a psychic interplay between the "ego" and the "dynamic ground."

He sees the psyche has having a bipolar construction: the "egoic pole" is the seat of "rational cognition and volition, discursive thought and deliberative will." The "nonegoic pole" (or the "seat of the dynamic ground") is the source of "upwelling dynamism, spontaneous impulse, feeling, and creatively forged images" (Washburn, 1995, p. 11). The interplay between these two psychic poles processes through five stages of development in which the individual human's consciousness first emerges as preegoic (or unified, not split into subject and object) gradually becomes differentiated (egoic, a departure from the ground) and then returns to the ground in a "higher synthesis."

The five stages articulated in this theory, in Washburn's words, are:

1. The ego initially emerges from the Ground (the preegoic of body-egoic stage)
2. The ego asserts its independence and develops itself in repressive disconnection from the Ground (the egoic or mental-egoic stage)
3. The ego undergoes a regressive return to the Ground (regression in the service of transcendence)
4. The ego in touch with the Ground, is spiritually transformed by the power of the Ground (regeneration in spirit)
5. The ego is wedded to the Ground in a higher ego-Ground synthesis (the transegoic stage). . . . Development is thus a departure-and-higher-return, negation-and-higher-integration interplay between the ego and the Dynamic Ground. (Washburn, 1995, p. 10)

This dynamic interplay can be better understood by thinking of the ego as having two modes (or types of processing)—it either "asserts itself by exercising ego functions (active mode) or 'lets go' and opens itself to nonegoic influences (receptive mode)." (Washburn, 1995, p. 14). Usually the ego switches back and forth between these two modes, though possibly a "completely integrated psyche can exercise ego functions effectively while at the same time being open to the full range of nonegoic potentials" (Washburn, 1995, pp. 14-15). But this possibility is dependent on prior bipolar integration, on both having developed a differentiated self and having become rooted in the nonegoic pole (the dynamic ground).

Washburn's book includes a careful description of how his view differs from his understanding of Wilber's (1995) view. Some of the differences have to do with Washburn's acceptance of Freudian and neo-Freudian dynamics: his theory sees conflict between the two psychic poles as essential to development, and repression as necessary to the progression to higher stages. Counselors who work largely out of psychodynamics theory may appreciate this aspect of Washburn's work. A more important difference may be the view of self. Washburn sees the self as a "real thing," one pole of the bipolar experience, "that needs to be transformed and reunited with a large-S

Self" (the power of the Ground as spirit). In contrast, according to Washburn, Wilber "conceives of this small-s self as an illusion that needs to be dispelled (a transitional structure that needs to be dissolved)" (Washburn, 1995, p. 43). In this respect, Washburn seems closer to Western psychology, and Wilber closer to Eastern, especially Buddhist, psychology.

COMPARING THE THREE THEORIES

All three of these stage theories have two things in common: (1) they assume that cognitive development is crucial to higher levels of spiritual development, and (2) they recognize that emotional or motivational and other aspects of personal dynamics are also crucial to spiritual development. The three theories also share two weaknesses: (1) They demonstrate greater clarity about the characteristics of the early stages of development and the differences among these early stages. The final stages are less clear, partially because such a small portion of humanity actually attains these higher stages, and partly because the particular point of view of the each theorist seems to bias their descriptions of what the ultimate stages are like. (2) It is not altogether clear what factors, other than cognitive development, contribute to a hierarchical or steplike formulation. Stated another way, it is not clear that some of the other facets of spiritual development progress in a systematic, steplike manner.

All of these theories value an openness to growth or progress (a thrust forward or upward), yet they recognize a need for grounding (or stabilizing or rooted dimension). The specifics of this dynamic are the least agreed upon: Washburn attributes to imagery and feelings the creative thrust of spirituality, and connects these with "the dynamic ground." Thus spirituality and grounding are linked. (Stanislof Grof's holotropic breathwork makes a similar connection and develops a methodology for exploring it [Grof, 1988, see Chapter 12].) Fowler suggests a different dynamic, a dialectic between cognition and the concrete tradition or religious community one is anchored in. Fowler also describes growth from egocentrism to "other" relatedness and increasing inclusiveness.

Comments

My own attempt to understand the developmental dynamic of spiritual maturation would incorporate the recognition of connectedness and empathy as basic to human neurological development, rooted in the evolutionary success of cooperation. When I use Washburn's image of poles, I identify with his attributing spiritual power to both the upward, creative thrust and to the rooted, downward groundedness. I do not see tradition as "concrete" in the way Fowler seems to—I see it as an ego-identification that both defines identity and must be transcended, never taken as spirit itself. In a pluralistic society, it is possible to be connected to many people, and many traditions, and even to experience times in which communion occurs despite the lack of a common tradition or community. At the highest levels of spiritual maturation, the particular tradition or heritage may be a vehicle for the transcendent, but it never "contains" it. If I understand Wilber correctly, I share his view that the higher levels are mystic, and that this should not be confused with mythic, since mythic symbols are only vehicles. It is possible that Fowler has not clearly articulated his fifth and sixth stages—they seem like the articulations of someone still in stage four—because Fowler has not fully assimilated the implications of pluralism, though he recognizes its importance. His view of incarnation and of community is still rooted in traditional society rather than in pluralistic society. It may be true, as George Santayana is supposed to have said, that "No person can be religious in general." But this has to do with the specificity of living out one's spirituality, not with the particularity of its experience or conceptualization. I believe Fowler is wrong, in a pluralistic age, to assume that the most mature stages of faith must "take essentially religious forms" (Fowler, 1981, p. 293). We will return to the issue of grounding spirituality in Chapters 3 and 6.

WHAT IS USEFUL TO COUNSELORS IN THESE MODELS?

To Assess Is to Intervene

Stage theories have been very popular among students of social sciences and among clinicians despite being highly criticized by experts in the particular research areas and by academicians. I think this is because a sequence of stages provides a simple cognitive outline on which to order the confusing and complex data of human life. Perhaps it is better for a counselor to have an overly simple developmental model than it is to ignore development altogether. The least we must demand of such a model is that it directs clinicians' attention to gradual growth and alerts them to tailor their interventions to the client's age or stage. Counselors are not wrong to have some sort of assessment tool in their heads, first to make some sense of the material a client provides, and second to guide the them in asking appropriate questions. Even if the clients themselves do not experience their progression as a movement through stages and are unaware of the cognitive restructuring they undergo (as Wilber suggests), it may help counselors to have a conceptual overview that allows them to sense where clients are on their journey. Given these heuristic values of a developmental schema, I would conclude with words of caution for counselors: don't let a "universal" cognitive schema keep you from seeing clearly the client's unique worldview, and don't trust that any of these models will work well with persons from cultures very different from our own.

It is more important to use interventions that help clients move forward in their unique path than it is to assess precisely where they are on the path. One advantage of the types of interviews done in these studies is that the questions seem to help the client clarify his or her experience. In at least two types of research—studies using Fowler's stage interviews (Nooneman & Holcomb 2002), and those using Marcia, Matteson, or Waterman's identity interviews (Marcia et al., 1993)—researchers have discovered that the data collection is, in fact, an intervention. Remember that the questions encourage self-reflection; e.g. in the Fowler interview, respondents are asked such questions as "how, if at all do you make sense of the unfair suffering in the world?" "Do you feel you are changing or growing now in your life as a religious person?"

The clearest empirical evidence that the interviews themselves facilitate growth is Nooneman and Holcomb's (2002) study of college students graduating in 2002, half of whom had been interviewed each year for the four years of their undergraduate program, and half of whom were first interviewed in their final year. Many in the first group spoke about having realized, after the interview, that it was the first time they had ever attempted to address these issues for themselves. Many pondered the issues after the interview. Some noted that, knowing the interview was coming up each spring, they thought about the issues periodically during the course of the study. At the time of Nooneman and Holcomb's (2002) presentation, the final interviews had not been transcribed, so measurable effects weren't clear, but Nooneman "had no doubt" that the interview also had the effect of an intervention (Nooneman, 2002, personal correspondence). This parallels the experience of researchers in identity; the identity status interviews used in studies by Marcia (Marcia 1966; Marcia et al., 1993), Matteson (1977a,b), Waterman (1985), and others appeared to encourage their subjects' own process of self-exploration. Here's an example from a recorded interview on gender roles with a high school girl:

INTERVIEWER: Can you picture a situation where you'd continue working and he [future husband] would quit?

RESPONDENT: Well, if I were making more money! [She laughs heartily.]

INTERVIEWER: Really?! [Mild surprise because of the contrast to previous statements.] If you were making more then you'd keep working?

RESPONDENT: Yes. [Softly, sounding doubtful.]

INTERVIEWER: Are you sure about that?

RESPONDENT: [More firmly.] I would think so. Because if I . . . [Pause.], but I can't really imagine him earning less money.

INTERVIEWER: So you think it's unlikely?

RESPONDENT: I can't picture a man doing that.

INTERVIEWER: [Surprised.] You can't picture a guy wanting to do that? [Pushing her to imagine it.]

RESPONDENT: Not any guy I would marry!

INTERVIEWER: Can you say what your picture is of a guy who might do that?

RESPONDENT: It just seems like he's . . . he's just living off me. I don't like that. [She then recognizes that the reverse might be true of the traditional woman, and discusses this possibility.]

INTERVIEWER: You seem to be saying—I'm not sure—are you saying it's better for the wife than for the husband to stay home, but it might not be good for either one?

RESPONDENT: [More clearly.] Yeah.

INTERVIEWER: But you are saying it's better for the wife than for the husband—is that right?

RESPONDENT: Yeah. [Sheepishly sensing the conflict with her own previous egalitarian statements.] I think so. [Stressing that the personal value isn't absolute.]

INTERVIEWER: That's fine. I just wanted to be clear. [Accepting her present position.] (Matteson, 1993b, pp. 150-151)

The interviewer uses humor and challenge to bring out the inconsistencies, but provides acceptance of the respondent's present state of incongruity and makes no attempt to reach a resolution. The intent is to get a clear picture of the respondent's present status, not to produce consistency that does not presently exist.

Since the topics of the identity status interviews are varied, and differ from those in the Fowler interview formats, it seems unlikely that any particular questions are behind this developmental process. Rather, we can hypothesize that youths' experience of repeatedly reflecting on their own development, getting perspective on their own process, and observing their own changes encourages them to view their own life in a larger perspective; this may precipitate a movement into a higher stage or status.

The research interviews are done one on one, so the respondents may feel them as highly personalized attention. It may not be the interview alone, but the dynamics of a youth having to describe his or her development to an interested and nonjudgmental adult that gives the experience its potency. But these same factors are present in a counselor-client relationship. So it seems likely that the counselors' attempts to get clients to articulate their path of spiritual development may have a positive effect on the continuation of that spiritual process. As long as the counselor is not judging the inconsistencies, it can be appropriate to respond in ways that make them more obvious. For example, the interviewer's question, "You can't picture a guy wanting to do that?" is posed with humor,[2] somewhat similar to the way an adult asks a child, "You don't like ice cream, do you?" This type of closed question can be useful when a response is unclear. The slant of the question is so obvious that it is easy for the respondent to rebut it. Yet it pushes the respondent to picture the concrete scene and share her deeper response to it.

Where to Begin?

It would not be appropriate with clients to conduct the standardized interview formats used by Fowler or Marcia (1964). However, some structure in counseling interviews can be helpful, especially in the early sessions. I typically structure my first interview with a client in a way that discourages the client from devoting the whole session to a recital of weaknesses and failures. In the first session, clients tend to dwell on their problems. I make sure that I have adequate time for that, and for responding empathically. But I prefer to start in a way that places problems in the context of a full person, so I deliberately limit my early questions to ones about their strengths, and in that context, I ask whether their spiritual or religious life is a strength they can draw on. In later sessions, when appropriate, I ask them to relate some of their most memorable experiences that they would call "spiritual" or "sacred." (Chapter 10 provides information on how to follow up on these experiences.)

Peak Experiences and Experiences of Crisis or Searching

Kohlberg and his followers had previously noted that a crisis of some sort could propel a person into the next level of cognitive functioning. Similarly, Fowler and those who have pursued his schema of stages of faith suggested that two different types of events can facilitate movement from one level to a higher level of faith development or spiritual development: "peak" experiences of great fulfillment, or experiences of crises. Either type of experience is an entry point for the sacred. The spiritually sensitive counselor, by careful listening and following and by making the client aware that spiritual issues are legitimate areas for exploration, can open the way for clients who are interested in their spiritual development to make that part of the counseling process.

Since clients typically come to us because of crises or events that have led them to focus on their inadequacies and deficits, it seems useful first to discuss the connections between crisis and exploration and its importance to spiritually sensitive counseling.

I have deferred until Chapter 10 reviewing with clients their experiences of the sacred. After all, it is rare that persons seek out counseling because they are undergoing a period of great fulfillment. But in reality this organization of material is somewhat arbitrary. As I have stated, I structure the first interview to emphasize the clients' areas of strengths and competence, and if clients spontaneously bring up spiritual experiences, or mention them in response to the counselors' questions about their strengths, I don't delay their discussion.

Think about ways to increase your sensitivity to a client's discussions of periods of great fulfillment. If you step outside the model of client's initiating counseling, what would be a way to reach out to people when they are undergoing periods of high productivity and fulfillment?

Returning to Crises

For counselors, one of the important contributions of these developmental theories is the recognition that a period of crisis can be a period of transformation, an opportunity for deep and important positive movement. A crisis may open the person up to a larger awareness, a realization that their previous stages of caring and comprehension were too limited.

Erikson's stages of development are perhaps the best known of all the developmental schemas. He called each stage a life crisis. However, his use of the word *crisis* creates some confusion, and needs clarification. A crisis period is a phase in which the organization of the person's cognitive and emotional structure that has functioned for them up until then is now challenged. The word does not indicate a negative or destructive event or period, except in the sense that an old system of thinking or behaving is destabilized and begins to fall apart to allow a more comprehensive structure to emerge. Though not entirely correct, many have translated the two Chinese characters used to denote the word *crisis* as *danger* and *opportunity.* (The second character is more correctly translated as "incipient moment" or "crucial point" [Kessler, 2007], but this doesn't mean you can't interpret *crisis* to mean danger and opportunity.) Similarly, in Hindu mythology, Shiva is often referred to as the god of destruction, but it would be more accurate to think of Shiva as the force that breaks down the old structures so the new can emerge. Erikson recognized that for a person to move forward in personal-social development a transition was needed that involved some challenge to the old. When James Marcia (1966) attempted to develop systematic interviews to operationalize Erikson's concept of the identity process, the scoring system assessed whether the youth were considering a variety of alternatives in a particular life arena (vocation, values, politics, and others). Later, in my identity studies, I substituted the phrase *search among alternatives* for the word *crisis* (Matteson, 1975). The phrase has the advantage of operational clarity, and focuses on the reconstruction process—though it may minimize the importance of deconstruction.

Fowler's view of the role of crisis in developmental change regarding faith or spirituality has been summarized by Backlund (1990):

> Fowler suggests there are three major kinds of life changes which influence faith stage development: (a) developmental, (b) reconstructive, and (c) what he calls intrusive marker events. Under developmental change, he notes the following aspects: (a) biological or bodily maturation, (b) perceptual and cognitive development, (c) emotional and affective maturation, (d) capacities for moral and social responsibility, and (e) development in faith. (Fowler, 1978, pp. 101-102)

Reconstructive change is seen in a breakdown and rebuilding of one's understanding of life. Here, "Deep going change in our lives usually comes in response to some experience of shipwreck, of failure in love or work, or of spiritual struggle or illumination" (Fowler, 1978, p. 103).

Intrusive marker events are those life events after which one's life can never be the same. Some of these events are of the expectable variety, such as "graduations, leaving home, marriage, the birth of children, certain kinds of successes and achievements, our children's marriages, their home leavings, our retirements, etc." (Fowler, 1978 p. 106, cited in Backlund, 1990, p. 31)

Paralleling the experience with identity development, evidence from studies of spiritual development suggests that personal engagement with new and different viewpoints plays an important role in maturation. Empirical support comes from four studies: a sample of persons in midlife transition (Bassett, 1985), a sample of persons living with AIDS (Backlund, 1990), a study of Canadian college students (Mischey, 1981), and a longitudinal study of some U.S. college students (Edwards, Hall, & Slater, 2002; Edwards & Hall, 2003). Crisis does not seem to be a factor in the movement between earlier stages (between stages one to two or two to three). However, the move away from conventional to individuative-reflective faith (stage four) does seem to be prompted by crisis, at least in the limited sample in the study conducted by Bassett (1985). Forty-two professional male and female adults, ages 35 to 45, drawn from a health care system and a local school system were given the Fowler faith development interview and a series of psychological tests. The great majority of subjects were rated as stage three or stage three transitioning to stage four. Of interest was the finding that stage four respondents seemed to have moved to this higher stage after some sort of major midlife crisis, such as divorce, emigrating to a new country, a change of vocation, or marriage to a person outside one's race or family religious tradition (Bassett, 1985).

Using interviews with self-identified gay men, 20 who were HIV positive and 20 who were HIV negative, Backlund (1990) found that the Fowler protocol for analyzing the faith-development interviews was not particularly sensitive to assessing transition. Backlund developed a more intensive assessment of the interview content, and this measure did show significantly more transitions in faith development for the HIV positive sample. Having experienced the death of a friend during the previous year was also highly correlated with undergoing transitions in faith development for both the HIV positive and HIV negative samples.

Among college-age adolescents in a Canadian population, Mischey (1981) found that significant life challenges were a factor in stage development. Such events as death of a friend or relative, family poverty, emigration, serious ailments, failure and defeat, and major responsibilities early in life were more prominent among those in the higher levels of this group (stages three and four) (Mischey, 1981).

Longitudinal data from a study of religious and spiritual development during the college years at several American colleges (using the Fowler stage interviews) suggested that three types of life events stimulate spiritual maturation: a developmental crisis (in Erikson's sense) that involves engagement in an emotional or intellectual challenge; some form of cross-cultural exposure, through living abroad or in a different subculture of United States than the student's family background; and/or giving service to others that leads the student to "walk in the other's shoes" and see the "God image" in the other (Edwards et al., 2002; Edwards & Hall, 2003). These data also suggested three factors that encourage spiritual development. One is a personality factor: when the student has a sense of humility in relation to experience, a recognition of her or his own ignorance, in contrast a prideful stance of already possessing the truth. The other facilitating factors have to do with the educational setting: an environment that encourages free inquiry rather than teaching through indoctrination, and a curriculum that fosters seamless learning through interdisciplinary studies rather than the compartmentalization of knowledge. Growing in spiritual maturity is thus associated with an opening up rather than with a self assuredness about having or getting "the truth." It requires both an encouraging environment, and new stimulation.

The importance of crises in spiritual development will be apparent in several of the chapters that follow, in which we will look at the crises of values, the crisis in beliefs, and the crisis of body changes (Chapters 3, 4, and 5). These chapters will provide concreteness now that we have a sense of the process of development through crises and exploration.

PART II: AREAS OF CRISIS

Chapter 3

The Crisis in Values

PERSONAL INTRODUCTION, VALUE CRISIS, AND PSYCHOSOCIAL DEVELOPMENT

After almost eighteen years of living in a family that, for me, was very warm, supportive, and loving, I went off to college. My dormitory room seemed cold and impersonal. I loved the intellectual excitement of the liberal arts college and the lively discussions with my new acquaintances, but when I'd wake in the morning and look beyond the boring brown window drapes toward the sky, I no longer felt sure that a personal God was looking down on me. The frightening thought struck me: *if no God exists, then maybe nothing matters.* My plans to become a minister, my passion about racial equality, my longing to marry and raise kids—all of this might be baseless, without foundation. Years later when I heard the great modern protestant theologian Paul Tillich speak about "the shaking of the foundations," I immediately knew I had already experienced it.

More fed into this experience than simple homesickness. Most of my new friends were from New York City and were Jewish. I was from a small, rural town; all of my classmates except one had been Christian. I felt I had more in common with these new friends and their passion for learning and exploring than I'd had with almost any of my high school classmates, so I couldn't easily dismiss them. Neither could I continue to assume that all people who were good must share my Christian beliefs and assumptions.

The crisis of faith and values that I experienced was not unique to me. Many people, when placed in a social environment that is markedly different from their previous experience undergo a personal crisis and reassessment. As we experience increasing interaction in multicultural situations we realize that many of the values we hold and assumptions we make are not shared by others around us. New peers, a new culture, or simply a powerful new experience (such as a deep awareness of suffering) can initiate a sense that the foundations are shaking. It's not that the reality around us has really changed. The shock waves are not from a change in the foundations; the shock comes from our recognition of what's been true all along—that what we assumed to be "foundation" was actually a construct from our very limited knowledge of life, our false generalization from our tiny sample of humanity. Now we realize that it was not the foundation, but just one island of "truth."

That's how I look at it now. But as a college freshman away from home that shaking up of my life was real. I had already begun to attend some meetings led by the college chaplain, and felt he was a person of depth and of intellectual integrity, so I confided in him my fears and doubts. I know that the personal contact of that meeting was very valuable to me, and that I left feeling much more steady and calm. The only words I can recall from our conversation was a homework assignment the chaplain gave me: "It's okay to continue listing the things that you doubt, that you aren't sure you can still believe in. But I also want you to try to sense, if all these beliefs and opinions do fall away, what is the one thing you will still hold to? What one thing do you feel sure of, even if all the rest goes?"

Love. That was the answer that kept coming over the weeks. Sometimes it was "I am loved." Sometimes it was "I will be loving," a commitment to the ethic of love. As I write this, almost 50 years later, I still feel grounded in love. What fear is still present comes not so much from the shaking of the foundations but from recognizing the implications of living out that radical love. By radical love I mean much more than the romantic love our culture idolizes; I mean the love that cares deeply about those who are different from oneself, love that is willing to maintain human respect even for one's enemies.

I don't question that love is the path I should follow, but I often question my ability to live in a radically loving way, and my courage to stake my life on it. I believe I am a loving person, and sometimes I am courageous in the sense of being authentic and open, but I'm not physically courageous—I don't know how much discomfort I could handle and still be faithful to the love I believe in. What would the real thing do? At some points in my younger life I was tempted to charge off toward some dramatic fulfillment—perhaps to prove that I could be courageous. But now I'm usually content to wait for opportunities to come, and to be open to each particular challenge or ministry. Yet, though I question my courage, I never question that love is my highest value.

Returning to my college chaplain's question: "What one thing do you feel sure of, even if all the rest goes?" Whenever I'm aware of facing a value decision, two pieces of sacred writing come immediately to mind: The first is "the two great commandments" taught by the Jewish Rabbi Hillel (first century BCE) and later by Jesus: "You shall love the Lord the God with all you heart, and with all your soul, and with all your mind" (Deuteronomy 6:5, RSV) and "You shall love your neighbor as your self" (Matthew 22:37, 39, RSV). The second is the serenity prayer: "Lord, Grant me the courage to change the things that I can change, the serenity to accept the things I cannot change, and the wisdom to know the difference."[1]

How has your own experience with the church of your childhood affected your view of the "authority" of the church? Do you take the church's positions into consideration for some concerns, and for others consider the church to be unqualified as an authority?

The crises that lead to spiritual searching can be individual, but they can also be social crises. A culture-wide crisis in Catholic Ireland provides an example, and parallels more recent events in Catholicism in United States. Beginning in 1996, a pedophilia scandal involving Catholic priests galvanized Irish society in a way that previous clerical scandals had not. Pedophile priests went on being priests, were moved from parish to parish, went on preying on children, and were protected by the hierarchy. The national radio broadcasting company of Ireland conducted a national survey to determine the emotional responses of the overwhelmingly Catholic audience. When asked, "Has this scandal affected your faith?" a shocking 97 percent said no. But when asked, "Has this scandal affected your relationship with the church?" 97 percent said yes (Chittister, 2002b). Follow-up questions found that one after another the Irish asserted "Jesus and the sacraments mean everything to me; there's nothing wrong with them." In that sense their faith was not challenged. But their relationship with the church was altered. As one respondent bluntly put it, "They're not going to tell us again what's right and what's wrong. . . . From now on, we'll be figuring those things out for ourselves" (Chittister, 2002a,b). They were not giving up their spiritual tradition or practice, but they were no longer going to accept the church as an authority concerning their ethical standards.

Social changes need not take the form of dramatic headlines to have a powerful impact on persons' spiritual development. In recent decades, as women have taken more control over their own bodies, the majority of American Roman Catholics (both men and women) make a distinction between their practice of the faith and their ethics concerning sexual and reproductive issues. Similar to the Irish, they don't let the Church tell them what's right and wrong, at least in this area of concern.

In an earlier book on adolescence (Matteson, 1975), I discussed five sites where the battle of late adolescent identity crisis is waged: the body, sex, work, values, and authority. The previous chapter on the development of mature faith has made it clear that the crises and stages are not restricted to the periods of late adolescence and youth but extend well past middle age. This is true in the area of values, as well. Though an individual may have specific periods in his or her life in which the reassessment of values is most prominent, the first crisis does not always occur in adolescence or youth, and later shifts and crises may follow even when a person seems to have done considerable exploration of values at an earlier stage. A lot has to do with the social environments in which a person is living; when a person is put in a setting that challenges previous decisions about values, a new assessment may not only result as a reaction, it may be healthy and appropriate.

Thus it is helpful for both counselors and clients alike to realize that their own crises in values are not just individual crises, but are at least in part a reflection of a crisis in values and beliefs throughout modern civilization. The historical roots of that crisis include:

- The scientific worldview, which emerges from the Renaissance into the Enlightenment, challenges traditional religious authority.
- The Copernican revolution challenges the cosmology that is assumed in the scriptures of Judaism and Christianity

- The view of mankind as "created in the image of God" is brought into question by the data that leads to Darwin's theory of evolution.
- The view of humans as a conscious decision makers exercising free choice is challenged by Freud's evidence for unconscious or subconscious motivations.
- The approach to understanding classical and ancient texts, historical and structural "higher criticism," is applied to sacred texts (the Bible) as well.
- The recognition of the variety of human cultures leads to pluralism or relativism about values.
- The injustice of slavery and apartheid uncover the issues of dominance and oppression, defended by viewing some races as biologically inferior. In the United States, black men were emancipated and given the vote before women were allowed to vote, which exacerbated consciousness of the oppression of women. Early feminism—with women demanding control of their own bodies, including birth control—challenged the male hierarchy and the sexual ethics of the religious institutions
- Consumerism and unfettered capitalism undermined communal and personal values.

These historical changes continue to impinge on our individual lives. I shared at the beginning of this chapter how my own move from small-town culture to the university campus brought me in contact with many people with very different worldviews and with academic knowledge that was somewhat new to me; these precipitated a crisis in values, a "shaking of the foundations." More recent social science, especially the study of human development, clarifies the process we go through as we mature in our development of values. As you read the follow section, consider your own personal changes in values as you have matured. Historically, it was the scientific tradition that ushered in the crisis in values in Western culture. That tradition can also provide us with the most extensive research on how values develop and mature, and provide the empirical grounding for the counselor's work with values. A review of its results follows.

EMPIRICAL RESEARCH ON VALUE DEVELOPMENT

Before we immerse ourselves in a series of studies that try to unravel some of the complexities of value development it is useful to spell out some of the questions such research helps us answer. Stage models of human development, though immensely popular, are fraught with difficulties (as has been noted in Chapters 1 and 2). They may suggest more order in the sequence of development than actually exists. On the other hand, a purely relativistic stance on values—the idea that one set of values is as valid as another, and that all value learning is simply a consequence of the particular cultural indoctrination—leaves the counselor with no way to assess whether a client has matured during the counseling process. The importance of the extensive research program on the development of values (described in this section) is that it provides evidence for a direction of maturation of values that is not simply a cultural preference, but exists across a huge range of cultures. The limits of this assertion are noted near the end of this section. A central thesis of this chapter is that a similar sequence of values development occurs in almost all cultures. Unlike Fowler's stages of faith development described in Chapter 2, the progression of value development is not different between Eastern and Western cultures. Neither is it different between men and women. Nor does it seem to be limited to a particular social-economic class.

The series of empirical studies to be presented in this section clarifies the developmental aspects of moral thinking, based on the model of Kohlberg (1969), and tests whether or not clear stages exist. These studies, led by James Rest, have been the focus of research at the Center for the Study of Ethical Development at the University of Minnesota for several decades. Though the theoretical foundation is similar to Kohlberg's, the contributions and critiques of Gilligan (1982), Hoffman (1983), and Gibbs (1991) are integrated into this approach.

Most of the studies have used the Defining Issues Test (DIT) (Rest, 1979), an instrument designed to build on the interview techniques of Lawrence Kohlberg. This instrument presents dilemmas and has the subject rank standard items in order of importance in an attempt to elicit the respondents' implicit process (schema) for making moral judgments (Rest, Narvaez, Bebeau, & Thoma, 1999). After reviewing more than 400 published studies, Rest's team has reformulated Kohlberg's six stages into three basic schemas, because the empirical findings from the DIT clearly support these three—though more refined instruments may eventually support more (Rest et al., 1999). The three "schemas" of moral development that the Rest team believes are empirically supported are:

1. Personal interest (parallel to Kohlberg's stages one, two, and three)
2. Maintaining norms (derived from Kohlberg's stage four)
3. Postconventional (refined from stages five and six and proposed later stages) (Rest et al., 1999, p. 36)

Rest and colleagues (1999) do not assume these three schemas enable us to describe *all* of the cognitive skills necessary to make decisions about real-life moral issues; they do claim that they enable us to describe the *developmental aspects* of moral judgment, and the individual's construction of basic moral concepts.

They acknowledge some important limitations to their focus on moral thinking, or "moral judgment" as they prefer to call it; moral sensitivity, motivation, and character also play important roles in moral behavior (Rest et al., 1999), and moral judgment alone predicts less than 20 percent of the variance in behavior measures. Nonetheless, it is a key to understanding moral decisions and especially to understanding higher levels of morality.

Conventional morality (schema one and two), a morality of being good, of friendships and personal obligations in relationships within one's own group of people, requires empathy and caring. In contrast to Kohlberg, Rest's team recognize that face-to-face ethics emerge in young children; children are not limited to egocentric responses or to deference to authority (Rest et al., 1999). In fact, as early as 26 months of age children know the difference between moral issues conforming to social conventions or authority, and will argue for defying authority when another person would be directly hurt by compliance (Tisak, 1995). The development of the morality of friendship has been usefully explicated by Lawrence Blum (1980). Rest's team acknowledges the contribution of this work and consider the development of ethical face to face relationships "one of life's greatest social goods" (Rest et al., 1999, p. 15).

However, *post*conventional morality (schema 3) requires more than empathy and caring for ones own; it requires a higher level of care, a concern for strangers, for persons outside ones group, and a sense of impartiality and justice. Justice requires certain cognitive operations, which do emerge sequentially (Rest et al., 1999). The research of Rest's team undertakes a different task than that of Blum's research:

> The possibility of establishing a system of cooperation at a society wide level (among strangers and competitors, not just among kin and friends) calls for impartiality, generalizable norms, and "a level playing field" among diverse ethnic, religious, and racial groups. (Rest et al., 1999, p. 15)

Rest and his team study this macrolevel of morality, and recognize that their Kohlbergian approach does *not* illuminate the development of the other domain, the morality of friendship, which they call "micro-morality" (Rest et al., 1999, p. 15). I will come back to some problems in this conception of two domains, and the role of empathy, in my critique that follows.

Though Kohlberg, following Piaget, believed that every individual would follow "a stepwise, irreversible, upward progression in the stage sequence . . . with no stage skipping or reversals [one moves up the staircase one step at a time, and always forward]" (Rest et al., 1999, p. 16), Rest's team do not claim the data fit this. "Rather, children in all stages of development typically show multiple ways of thinking about a phenomena (such as a moral dilemma), but as they mature they *shift in the frequency* with which they rely on particular 'schemas' or ways of thinking" (Rest et al., 1999, p. 19, citing Siegler, 1997. Emphasis mine). Rest and colleagues affirms this "soft stage" or "schema" model of development.

The direction of development can be conceptualized as a move from making moral judgments on the basis of "What is good for me?" or "What's good for me and those close to me?" to "What maintains order in society?" The shift in focus during the preconventional stages (between schema one and two) is from self to society, from doing what pleases me to doing one's duty to others, following the laws or rules. The authority of the rules or laws themselves are not questioned.

The next shift, to postconventional morality, uses the criterion "What creates a society with universal values and rights?"—a morality of impartiality (Rest et al., 1999, p. 14). The focus is on creating a society based on moral ideals, or "What promotes a fair and just society?" Any particular law or rule can be questioned on the basis of a projected higher ideal that could better serve the people. This is not simply a critical view of authority, or a negative attitude toward the establishment (Rest et al., 1999). In postconventional judgments, authority is replaced by sharable ideals. Since these levels are cognitive schema rather than hard stages, an individual may use processes involving any or all of the three levels of development, but the preponderance of which processes are used changes with development, so those who reach postconventional morality more frequently use the later types of schemas or criteria. The DIT scoring system rates which of the three types of schemas or criteria are used for making judgments on each of the "defining issues" presented, and gives higher ratings to issues that are processed using the second criterion, and still higher ratings to issues using the third type of criterion. More than 30 longitudinal studies have been published using the DIT and following individuals over the years; these studies consistently show increases in the DIT scores (Rest et al., 1999). Both longitudinal and cross-sectional studies, about 800 studies, show that each higher level of education is accompanied by an increase of about 10 points in the DIT score (Rest et al., 1999).

However, it is not enough that the research indicates that moral judgment includes a developmental sequence. It is important to ask if a higher score on the DIT is really better. Four types of studies provide an overwhelming yes to that question:

1. Persons with higher DIT scores also demonstrate a higher comprehension of moral concepts.
2. Higher development on the DIT is associated with higher scores on such developmental instruments as tests of ego development, reflective judgment, and Piagetian formal operations.
3. Higher performance on the DIT is linked to more "prosocial behavior" and more highly valued job performance.
4. Respondents who score high on the DIT are more able to recall and reconstruct moral arguments in narratives (Rest et al., 1999, p. 76).

It seems fair to say that the three "schemas" are not simply three different ways of thinking about morals but that they indicate an increasing quality of moral judgment, and an increasing ability to understand others. Postconventional respondents can easily understand the thought process of those who use personal gains, or social order, as their criteria; the reverse is not true—those using personal gains or social order thinking are unable to comprehend postconventional judgments. It is similar to other areas of cognitive development. The person who can understand the basic ideas of modern theories of relativity can easily comprehend Newtonian physics, but the reverse is not true. And the person who can grasp algebra can easily comprehend basic arithmetic, but not vice versa. In short, it is descriptive to say that the third type of "moral schema" is a "higher" level of moral development.

Some Limits of Rest and Colleagues' Assertion of Cross-Cultural Applicability

Postconventional morality involves more than reasoning, however. It is possible to comprehend higher moral concepts but not use them in one's judgments. An interesting study by Lawrence (1987) found that radically fundamentalist seminarians could understand moral judgment concepts at a much higher level than those they actually used in their own moral decisions. These seminarians reasoned that making moral decisions was not up to their own mortal judgments; rather, God has told people in the Bible what moral values to have. Even though they understood concepts of higher justice, they reverted to basing their decisions on the authority of scriptures (Rest et al., 1999). A measurement of "utilizing" the concepts in actual moral judgments increases the strength of predictions of moral behavior, but research using the utilizer score is relatively new and just beginning to untangle the links and the failures to link moral judgment to moral action (Thoma, 1994).

Another example of a cultural factor that can inhibit the development of higher levels of morality was demonstrated in a region in southern Italy, Lucania, in which cooperation among people is so meager and solidarity so weak that people there rarely rise above the personal interest schema (Banfield, 1958). The great majority of cultures, however, are "collective" rather than individualistic; such societies strongly support persons moving beyond pure self interest to caring about the good of the group. They can be seen as supporting a move from Rest and colleagues' first schema, personal interest, to the second, maintaining norms. However, as Turiel's (1978, 1983) studies point out, even young (Western) children distinguish between moral issues and issues of social convention. They do not see the moral domain as simply a matter of what authorities say is "right." They intuit that a transgression such as deliberately injuring another child is wrong in itself regardless of social rules (see Helwig, Tisak, & Turiel, 1990, for a review 48 studies showing this distinction in children in various countries). The difference between Turiel's and Kohlberg's use of the concept of *conventional* is carefully described in Rest and colleauges' (1999) work, but the issue of whether the second schema, maintaining norms, concerns simply social norms or norms based on some "higher" duty, becomes confounded when we look at cultures such as the Hindu temple town of Bhubaneswar, India, in which transgressions of social conventions are considered *more* serious than transgressions of moral rules. Furthermore, these Hindus believe their social conventions should be universal. In short, this particular subculture gives social conventions the status that Western children give only to moral conventions (Shweder, Mahapatra, & Miller, 1987, 1990).

It appears that, in some cultures, when a person is functioning at the conventional level, they do *not* make the distinction between social and "higher" norms that is common to Western children. For example, a violation of social norms, such as an eldest son getting a haircut on the day after his father's death may be seen in this Hindu culture as just as serious as violating an ethical norm such as ignoring an accident victim (Shweder et al., 1987). Nonetheless, when postconventional morality develops in an individual, fundamental differences from the person's previous worldview emerge, both in the Indian and in the Westerner. The worldviews of preconventional individuals are similar and the worldviews of the postconventional individuals similar regardless of culture (Jensen, 1996).

It appears that the ability to move to the fourth or fifth Kohlberg stages requires a sense of perspective beyond social conventions, and depends on some recognition of the plurality of life experience. A review of 54 cross-cultural studies based on the Kohlberg interview approach shows that, while Kohlberg stages one to four are found in virtually all cultures, stage four is most likely to appear in the more educated, cosmopolitan areas of the world (Snarey & Keljo, 1991).

The postconventional stages (stages five and six) occur even more rarely, but the studies using the DIT demonstrate that postconventional moral thinking does exist across cultures as a developmental shift connected with increased age and education (Moon, 1985). The main dividing line is not between Eastern and Western cultures, but between industrialized nations with demanding educational systems and less-industrialized (third world) countries with less-demanding educational systems (Gielen & Markoulis, 1994; Roetz, 1996; Rest et al., 1999).

At least three societal factors are involved in whether the postconventional stages are reached (using either Kohlberg or Rest instruments):

1. As already noted, postconventional thinking may exist, but postconventional moral decisions may be suppressed, even in a society that is supportive of higher levels of moral thinking, if that individual subscribes to fundamentalist or authoritarian view of faith that considers it sinful or heretical to question and scrutinize morality.

2. Certain cultures may not provide the experiences, or may suppress the decisions, that allow research subjects to be classified as postconventional. In a DIT study conducted in 15 nations, 3 nations did not portray clear developmental trends: Egypt, Kuwait, and Sudan. What is the common factor among these three nations? They are all Middle Eastern. But we must note that each of these nations has a different system of government; this suggests that totalitarian society is not the common thread.[2] Though all three countries are Muslim, the impact of Muslim culture on moral development is harder to determine. Some respondents in another Muslim population (a portion of Nigeria) showed the typical developmental trend, which suggests that the suppression of higher moral development cannot be generalized to Islamic cultures. Yet the low percentages of Nigerian Muslims in the postconventional levels leads the experimenters to question whether "the strict socialization practices prevailing in Muslim society, combined with the politico-social restrictions of Nigerian society, prevent role-taking opportunities" (Markoulis & Valanides, 1997, p. 312; they also cite another Nigerian study, Maqsud, 1977, as supportive of this interpretation). Problems with the instrument for gathering the data cannot be ruled out; "There are signs in these studies that the DIT may not be a satisfactory test of moral reasoning in Arab societies" (Gielen, Ahmed, & Avellani, 1992, p. 25). One

hypothesis, then, is that postconventional morality does not emerge when a culture does not provide sufficient role-taking opportunities.

I have noted that the Nigerian sample did show developmental trends, but had low percentages of subjects in the postconventional levels of moral development (Markoulis & Valanides, 1997). This same pattern was true for the samples from the two Caribbean countries studied, Belize and Trinidad and Tobago (Gielen & Markoulis, 1994). Students from these three cultures, all third world countries,

> endorse principled moral arguments much less frequently than the students from industrialized East Asian and Western countries . . . The moral ethos of Caribbean societies appear to depend on conventional, role-oriented, interpersonal yet individualistic expectations which are frequently reflected in [Kolberg] Stage 3 moral reasoning. (Gielen & Markoulis, 1994, p. 98)

Unfortunately, their report doesn't clarify whether these Caribbean cultures provide many role-taking opportunities. Hopefully future studies in Muslim cultures, and in third world societies, will be designed to test the role-taking hypothesis.

3. Some evidence suggests that alternative forms of postconventional moral thinking may exist that don't fit the "rights" and "principles" standard of the scoring guides, but that contain more "communitarian" themes (Snarey & Keljo, 1991; Snarey, 1985). For a more careful analysis of the results and the limitations of these cross-cultural studies, see Rest and colleagues (1999).

In sum, the results concerning the three Arab nations and the three third world nations studied are ambiguous, but the results from European, North American, and East Asian societies clearly support Rest and colleagues' hypothesis of moral development to postconventional levels. The three developmental levels posited do not seem to be gender specific (gender differences tend to be small across all studies; female students from collectivistic East Asian societies such as Taiwan or South Korea are especially likely to prefer principled moral arguments). Nor do social class differences have much effect. "Given these findings it must be concluded that the DIT is not biased in favor of individualistic, male-oriented, upper-class, Western conceptions of morality" (Gielen & Markoulis, 1994, p. 98).

This is an important finding, since many measures from Western psychology are biased in that way. Moral autonomy as understood by

Kohlberg and Rest should not be thought of as rugged, rule-oriented individualism. Rather, it refers to "an orientation toward internalized, *sharable,* moral principles," that "reflect schemes of cooperation rather than the arbitrary preoccupation with self-expression in the service of individualism" (Gielen & Markoulis, 1994, p. 99).

Recognizing the social influences on the development of morality does not lead Rest or Kohlberg to moral relativism. Anthropologists have discovered many moral orientations in the world, some of which are incompatible with one another. But to conclude that morality is whatever the norms of the group happen to be and that no grounds exist for selecting one moral order over another leaves us with no grounds for tolerance or for human rights, and no rationale for organizing cooperation in a pluralistic society (Rest et al., 1999). Moral respect for diversity entails a higher cognitive construction of morality than simple relativism. The relationship of culture and moral judgment is viewed by Rest and his colleagues as a reciprocal one, not simply one of culture filling in the content for the Kohlbergian structure; moral judgment is shaped by cultural ideology, but it also selects and interprets the cultural ideology. There is more to the psychology of morality than just moral judgment (Rest et al., 1999).

Many people have the perception that social science leads to ethical relativism. Notice that Rest and colleagues' data does not support such an interpretation. Would you question Rest's interpretation? If it is correct that the higher levels of morality are based on principles rather than on social conformity, is this the morality taught by most churches, mosques, temples, and synagogues?

Critique of Rest and Colleagues' Conceptualization

Rest and colleagues acknowledge that postconventional morality involves more than reasoning, and that it is possible to comprehend higher moral concepts but not use them in one's judgments. Unfortunately, by focusing the research project primarily on "moral reasoning," the conclusions give the impression that the emotional factors in moral development operate primarily in the early period of life and in the development of conventional morality (face-to-face ethics), a morality of being good, of friendships and personal obligations in relationships within one's own group of people. Individual thinking that fosters the ability to "de-center" and gain perspective ushers in the possibility for postconventional morality. Cognitive ability to perform logico-physical operations of a Piagetian nature seem to be a prerequisite for higher moral development (Markoulis & Valanides, 1997). But more is required. A sense of caring that encourages an ethic that is universal, that moves beyond tribe, and that applies the ethic even to those not personally known requires an ability to imagine the needs of a stranger; opportunities to take on various roles in different social settings, if not a prerequisite, are at least an important factor in enhancing this ability. Thus empathy seems to be an important component of postconventional morality as well.

The most important researcher in the role of empathy in moral development is Martin L. Hoffman (1983). John C. Gibbs (1991), in a valuable attempt to integrate Kohlberg's and Hoffman's theories, states:

> Although cognition plays and important role in the motivation to correct an injustice, empathy for the distressed victim of the injustice may play a critical role in the intensity and persistence of the effort on behalf of the victim. (p. 97)

Hoffman (1977) cites an excellent illustration of the importance of empathy in the shift to postconventional morality, taken from an interview (by Coles, 1986) with a 14-year-old Southern male "redneck":

> After several weeks of joining his friends in harassing black children trying to integrate his school, this boy, a popular athlete, states that he . . . began to see a kid, not a nigger—a guy who knew how to smile when it was rough going, and who walked straight and tall, and was polite. I told my parents, "It's a real shame that someone like him has to pay for the trouble caused by all those federal judges." (Coles, 1986, p. 27f, cited in Hoffman, 1977, p. 56f, and also in Gibbs, 1991, p. 98).)

Repeatedly, the boy sees "that kid behaved himself, no matter what we called him, and seeing him insulted so bad, so real bad."

> Then it happened. I saw a few people cuss at him. "The dirty nigger," they kept on calling him and soon they were pushing

> him in a corner, and it looked like trouble, bad trouble. I went over and broke it up. . . . They all looked at me as if I was crazy. . . . Before (everyone) left I spoke to the nigger. . . . I didn't mean to . . . It just came out of my mouth. I was surprised to hear the words myself: "I'm sorry." (Coles, 1986, p. 27f, cited in Hoffman, 1977, p. 56f, and also in Gibbs, 1991, p. 98)

As Piagetian theory would predict, Gibbs (1991) points out that cognitive sources were involved, specifically the cognitive construction of the injustice to the black youth ("It's a real shame that someone like him has to pay. . .," someone mature enough to refrain from reciprocating insults and physical harassment). But the surprising action to protect the black youth and to apologize to him seems to have involved empathy for the youth's plight, as well as some empathy-based guilt. As Hoffman's theory would predict (Gibbs, 1991), I think that the development of a morality that moves beyond one's own tribe or race, though it certainly has cognitive prerequisites, is likely to be primarily motivated by empathy rather than by cognitive issues alone.

To conclude, though certain cultural contexts are required for the highest levels of moral development to emerge, the preponderance of data does suggest morality is not simply an arbitrary and relative cultural construct. Some forms are morality are clearly "higher" and preferable to others.

INTERNALIZATION OF EMPATHY AND VALUES

The fact that the 14-year-old southern boy was surprised to hear the words "I'm sorry" coming out of his mouth points out the experiential side of the process of internalizing a sense of justice, an empathy that calls us to stand against suffering or injustice even when the victim is not "one of us." Even though taking this stand with the black child was unfamiliar and new to him, he did not doubt its correctness. The experience is strikingly different than assimilating conventional standards—often it is almost the opposite, a standing in opposition to convention for a higher "good." Yet the inner experience is frequently one of deep assurance that this stance is the only authentic place one can stand. One thinks of Martin Luther's words when he, as an ordained priest in the Catholic Church, was pushed to the point of having to reject the authority of the Pope himself: "Here I stand. I can do no other."

This inner certainty reflects what I would call the transcendent dimension of postconventional values, a sense that one's stance is not simply a response out of one's own identity (though it certainly reflects an identity struggle) but that it is rooted in one's connection to, not conformity with, the whole human community, that it draws its power from some universal oneness, something beyond self and others.

When I was about ten years of age, I went with my whole family to Sunday school prior to the church service. Usually the junior high Sunday school class in our church was led by a layman who was in his early thirties, younger than our parents yet old enough (and in communication with youth enough) that we respected him and enjoyed his teaching. But he was sick that Sunday, and the minister of the church took over his class. The scripture we studied that morning was from 1 Chronicles 13, the story of when the original tablets containing the Ten Commandments, which Moses had brought down from the mountain, were put in a coffinlike box called the "ark of the covenant." This ark was considered so sacred that no one dare touch it. The future king David was leading a joyful procession, and two men, Uzzah and Ahio, were driving the oxen that were pulling a new cart holding the ark. They were pulling this heavy ark across rough terrain toward where the temple would be built to house it when the oxen stumbled. Uzzah instinctively put out his hand to steady the ark. But the Lord was so angry that Uzzah had touched the ark (so the story reads) that He immediately struck Uzzah dead.

As the minister solemnly read this story, and stated the man was struck dead, I blurted out, "God wouldn't do that!" The minister glared at me in judgment.

"David," he intoned, "it's in The Book."

"I don't care," I responded, "it's not fair and God wouldn't do that."

Our family custom was to have a big dinner after the church service. We would have a leisurely discussion about what had gone on in Sunday school and in the service. So I told about this interchange, and asked my parents if they believed God would do that. My mother was the one to respond—but she didn't answer the question by stating her opinion on the issue. Instead, she explored my opinion, and then stated, "whatever happened back then, it's okay for you to think about it, and ask questions, and disagree." It was clear that the issue to her wasn't that particular scripture. And it wasn't that I had challenged two authorities: the Bible and the minister. The issue for her was educational, and she clearly wanted to support my thinking independently. I can't recall Dad saying anything, but I could see that he was not upset, and that he was comfortable with Mom's response.

In this illustration, an inner sense of justice that went beyond legalism or rules was so deeply rooted in me that it had far greater authority for me than did the minister and his literal interpretation of the biblical story.

SOCIAL AND HISTORICAL ROOTS OF POSTCONVENTIONAL VALUES

Just as certain developmental achievements are necessary before an individual can move to postconventional morality, certain advances in the organization of cultures and civilizations are prerequisites to the emergence of the postconventional values.

It can be argued that the basis of tribal values, a sense of caring and even of sacrifice for others in one's own group, is a development of biological evolution. A Dutch biologist who studies primates makes a convincing case that a number of the elements of ethical behavior have their origins in the other (nonhuman) primates. The natural conditions for the development of values exist in chimpanzee colonies. Only the higher apes and man have been observed not only to empathize with another individual, but to *take the other's perspective*—they realize what the other individual wants, and they offer it. This is "altruism with the other's interests explicitly in mind" (de Waal, 1996, p. 830). Furthermore, while many animal species will not share food—macaques, for example, when presented with attractive food, move into a competitive mode—chimps, when special food arrives, exhibit what the Buddhists call "sympathetic joy." They throw themselves into each other's arms with obvious delight (de Waal, 1996).

Chimpanzees are also capable of *actions of impartiality;* a quarrel between two individual chimps may escalate into a brawl with numerous chimps taking sides and joining in the fray, but the alpha males have been known to break up the fray by stopping all the fighting without taking either side (de Waal, 1982). *Peacemaking functions* ameliorate social relationships to the advantage of the intervener. These represent "a first step toward a system such as human morality that actually elevates community concern above individual interests" (de Waal, 1996, p. 33).

Evidence suggests a neurological basis for empathy in both monkeys and humans. In the early 1990s a team of Italian researchers working with macaque monkeys discovered individual neurons in the monkeys' brains that fired both when the monkeys grabbed an object and when the monkeys watched another primate grab the same object. These have been dubbed "mirror neurons" since these nerve cells respond equally when we perform an action and when we witness someone else perform it. Neuropsychologists cannot perform the same types of intrusive wiring to the premotor cortex in humans as di Pellegrino, Fadiga, Fogassi, Gallese, and Rizzolatti (1992) and Gallese, Fadiga, Fogassi, and Rizzolatti (1996) did with the monkeys, but they have shown, using recordings of motor-evoked muscle potentials, that humans have a more general mirror system (Fadiga et al., 1996). The recordings from the muscles and nerves of human hands showing that the human is getting ready to move are the same for preparing to grasp an object, and for witnessing someone else grasping that object. These neuroimaging techniques provoked a series of experiments in which empathy in observing another's actions or responses mirrors the neurological responses that occur when the person himself or herself carries out the action or has those responses. For example, Wicker et al. (2003) used neuroimaging to look at human responses of disgust and found that a person viewing a film of an actor wrinkling up his face into a disgusted look produces the same neurological pattern as when a subject himself or herself directly inhales a disgusting odor.

As one of the neurologist of the University of Parma (Italy) group puts it: "It seems we're wired to see other people as similar to us, rather than different. At the root, as humans we identify the person we're facing as someone like ourselves" (Gallese, 2005, p. 49, cited in Winerman, 2005). Though earlier studies of the origins of morality in early childhood relationships preceded knowledge of this neurological basis for empathy, they were congruent with this research in emphasizing that "a perspective on relationships underlies any conception of morality" (Gilligan & Wiggins, 1987). Certain dimensions of human experience are universal across cultures. Two that are crucial to moral development are the child's awareness of inequality, of being smaller and less capable than adults and older children, and the experience of attachment, which includes being capable of having an effect on others, of being moved by others, and also of moving others. These two dimensions "lay the groundwork for two moral visions, one of justice and one of care. Since everyone is vulnerable both to oppression [inequality] and abandonment [versus attachment], two stories about morality recur in [all] human experience" (Gilligan & Wiggins, 1987, p. 281). Children know both stories, and test them in a variety of ways. American children appeal to justice in the face of unequal power by claiming "it is not fair" or "you have no right"; they assess the strength of a case by stating "you do not care" or "I do not love you anymore" (Gilligan & Wiggins, 1987, p. 281). Two key moral injunctions—not to treat others unfairly and not to turn away from someone in need—emerge in early childhood and provide the roots for justice and caring.

The key point here is that face-to-face relationships form the foundation *not only* of childhood (conventional) morality, but of principled morality as well. To state this personally, my crisis in values my freshman year of college was not simply a reaction to the intellectual climate around me, but was precipitated primarily because of the friendships I had developed with Jewish classmates. My worldview was changing, partly because I was trying to include new data about the world. But the real issue concerned whether I could genuinely include these new people who were outside my Christian "tribe." Now that I cared about these individuals, I could not accept as fair any theology or social contract that excluded them.

> A principled morality that extends caring or concern or justice to individuals outside one's own tribe or social group seems to be a much later human development. That is, in the history of primate development empathy and mirroring occur in primates that precede the human species. And in individual development, empathy and mirroring occur in early childhood. But principled morality comes much later, both historically and individually. There appears to have been a point in the development of human civilizations at which some spiritual/moral individuals attained a breakthrough in human thought, and proclaimed an ethic of higher morality, a principled level of moral reasoning in which self-chosen, abstract moral principles focus on respect for individual dignity, benevolence, liberty, equality, humanity, and the

> maintenance of interpersonal trust. The person is able to take an outside-of-society perspective: that is, the person decides moral dilemmas from a point of view that could, ideally speaking, be adopted by any rational and impartial person in a given situation. Moral decision making is expected to be shareable or universalizable, representing . . . a consensus based on non-arbitrary social cooperation" (Gielen & Markoulis, 1994, p. 87).

This breakthough appears to have occurred in many cultures, perhaps first in the golden age of Chinese philosophy, in the principled emphasis on moral autonomy and "human-heartedness"—*jen* or *ren* (Gielen & Markoulis, 1994). But within a 600 year span (from 800 to 200 BCE) this same breakthrough in human thought—though set in very different metaphysical contexts—occurs in India (the basic metaphysical writings leading to Hinduism, Buddhism, and Jainism), in Classical Greek philosophy, and in the sayings of many of the Hebrew prophets (Jaspers, 1949).

For the first time, highly reflective philosophies of human destiny begin to endorse and share an emphasis on universal human meaning; the replacement of myth by rational thought; a new conception of history; a pervasive questioning of traditional custom and traditional thought; the transcendence of traditional life and its customs, values, and norms; and new and much more reflective and interiorized conceptions of what humans are about, their inner nature, and their spiritual potentialities. Interwoven with these new philosophical and religious conceptions come higher, more abstract, and more differentiated levels of moral-ethical reflection (Gielen & Markoulis, 1994).

The historical evidence that spokespersons for a higher morality occur only when the civilization has reached a certain level of maturity is intriguing; it adds weight to the argument that postconventional values are not simply ones of many value positions, but constitute a higher level of moral development.

MULTICULTURAL COUNSELING AND THE RISE OF VALUE CONSCIOUSNESS IN THE COUNSELING PROFESSION

Within the professions in which psychotherapy and counseling are practiced an evolution in the attitudes toward dealing with value issues has occurred. Near the end of the nineteenth century and the beginning of the twentieth century the scientific method began to be applied to the fields of mental illness, most notably by Sigmund Freud. At roughly the same time, the social sciences, especially psychology, began to emerge as distinct from both philosophy and the physical sciences. In both cases, the model for what was considered scientific was that of the objective, dispassionate observer standing in neutral relationship with the object of study. Psychological laboratories mimicked the laboratories of physics and chemistry, and psychiatric diagnostic classifications mimicked the verifiable disease entities of biological illness. Freud considered psychotherapy "a technical procedure, like surgery, that does not involve the values or life-style of the treatment agent" (Bergin, 1991, p. 396).

One the one hand, Freud courageously challenged the taboos of sex and aggression. On the other, he helped to instate taboos against open discussion with clients of issues of religion and values. When these topics were initiated by the client, they tended to be interpreted as expressions of their pathology. When the psychiatrist in training (or later, the student counselor or the psychology intern) expressed any of their own values, it was likely to be considered a violation of the dispassionate role the therapist was supposed to assume.

What followed was precisely what Freudian theory would have predicted: the value issues were driven underground, and became inarticulate and outside of awareness. Yet values continued to be constantly at play in psychotherapy, as research has demonstrated (Bergin, 1980; London, 1986; Lowe, 1976; Strup & Hadley, 1977). For understandable reasons, the helping professions failed to acknowledge the role of values in the therapeutic relationship. Perhaps most important was the fear that if the role of counselors' values were normalized, counselors might be encouraged to more actively advocate for their own value position and risk imposing their values on the clients.

In the second half of the twentieth century, following the civil rights movements of the 1950s and 1960s, the fields of psychotherapy and counseling were increasingly reexamined in light of multicultural perspectives. The multicultural emphasis helped to uncover the hidden values that were operating in the teaching and practice of counseling and psychotherapy. It is beyond the scope of this section to analyze the complexity of these historical events (and the three previous paragraphs are simplistic and broadly generalized indications of the shift). A consensus has now developed that value-free counseling is impossible.

Perhaps the most influential work encouraging the paradigm shift toward acknowledging the important role our own values play in our therapy was *Soul Searching: Why Psychotherapy Must Promote Moral Responsibility* (Doherty, 1995). Doherty opened his book with an interaction from his own clinical practice that led him to challenge the client in moral terms. "Bruce," a 40-year-old client whose wife has just left him, is overwhelmed and depressed, and tells Doherty that he is considering packing up and moving far away. He rationalizes that "maybe the kids would be better off if I just stayed away." Doherty recognizes that the man is acting out of hurt and anger, but decides to approach the issue as an ethical issue concerning his responsibility to his children rather than simply as an issue of the client's own psychological state. Doherty (1995) writes, "I gently but forcefully told him I was concerned that his children would be damaged if he abandoned them" (p. 22).

For the most part, Doherty, as therapist, was using the client's own value system as the basis for his challenge. But the main thrust of his book is to clarify that when we approach clients simply in terms of their own needs, desires, and psychological dynamics, and ignore their interpersonal involvement and the value issues in which their decisions are imbedded, we do them a disservice. We are not, in fact, working scientifically—we are remaining blind to important aspects of their lives and the narratives they tell us. The previous paradigm in psychotherapy assumed that the counselor was responsible only for the client's self interest and pleasure; now Doherty and others in the profession are arguing that the counselor has an obligation to be concerned for the client's moral and spiritual self, and even for others affected by the client.

Those of us who approach counseling from a family systems perspective may have been flirting with this shift in paradigms as part of our move away from a focus only on the dynamics of the individual. It is helpful to read Doherty's work to clarify that the shift is not simply from individual needs to the needs of others but from understanding the issue as a *psychological* one to viewing it also as a *moral* one.

Some of the value issues implicit in counseling are illustrated by a composite case from my practice. Dan (not his real name) is a married man of about 40 who has recognized over that past several years that he is sexually attracted to men as well as to women. Recently he has begun to explore the "gay side" of his identity, but he does not want to risk telling his wife about this exploration as he believes that she will be very hurt, and that she does not have the background and education to understand his bisexuality. The discovery of the "gay world" has been very exciting to him, and in some ways a spiritual experience. "I feel like I've finally come home—I've found my own kind—when I'm dancing at a gay bistro and all that gay energy is accepted; it's such a relief to be myself there, to be horny and feel it's okay." This letting down of his guard has spilled over into several spontaneous incidents in which he has had unprotected sex with another man. Each of these incidents has been extremely gratifying in terms of his increased acceptance of himself as bisexual.

I have deliberately chosen this case because it is hard to miss some of the questions it raises: what is the counselor's responsibility as far as addressing the risks that the client is taking concerning his own health? What is the counselor's obligation concerning the client's wife being put at risk for contracting AIDS? Legal issues exist (in some states) concerning the "duty to warn," since the client's behavior puts a specific person in danger. As counselor, do I concern myself solely with my client's satisfaction and growth, or do I try to persuade him to consider others' needs as well as his own? In previous sessions I had supported his need to explore and discover his own full sexuality—but had I failed to balance this with sufficient concerns about risks? Since I encourage personal (in this case sexual) growth, how can I fail to encourage moral and spiritual growth? As a spiritually sensitive person, I can identify with the metaphor of "coming home" and the sense that a deep acceptance from others and from self is occurring in these encounters, and I do not want to objectify and minimize this experience, yet the client, and his wife, are real persons in mortal bodies who can pick up real viruses.

When I have presented this case to graduate students in counseling, it has usually provoked a lively discussion of the variety of ways in which the counselor might make the ethical challenge to the client. How a counselor makes that challenge will depend on what degree of rapport and how much "leverage" the counselor has.

The counselor might first ask Dan for his own evaluation of the risks he's taking, both physically and in terms of his relationship with his wife. This could lead to exploring the need for safer sex, but also to a discussion of the effects of deceit on the intimacy he longs for. Certainly I would comment positively on how his understanding of his sexual identity has expanded, and on how he has dared to explore new things. Then I might ask, along with his exploring a new identity, is he ready to do some exploring in terms of his moral development? Is he willing to consider trying new things such as risking disagreement or rejection in order to show caring and to be authentic?

The shift that Doherty (1995) advocates, toward a counseling relationship in which the counselor encourages the exploration of value issues in the client, need not mean a move to a judgmental stance in which the counselor assumes a position of moral superiority. The spiritually sensitive counselor may directly address the ethical dimensions of the client's behavior, but this can be done in a way that assumes the client has potential for growth, not in ways that subtly berate the client.

In the 1990s, counselor educators began stressing the importance of counselors recognizing their own values and examining them—and clients were actually being encouraged to articulate their own value orientation as part of their therapeutic work. In the case of Dan, the counselor's attempt to be more forthright about his own evaluative process can be paired with an attempt to work collaboratively to understand the values and the cultural context of the client, thus avoiding the imposition of the counselor's values on the client.

Safeguards against imposing values: several strategies exist for handling the ethical and therapeutic dilemma of readmitting value issues into the counseling room yet protecting the client from our prejudices and biases and the limits of our personal and cultural experience. One I have already mentioned is training in multicultural issues. Openness to the client's point of view and the client's heritage is another. Value issues may emerge from the client laying out a personal dilemma or concern and beginning to explain the "solutions" that he or she has already tried. Usually the client is dissatisfied with the outcome of these attempts, though he or she may also be defensive, justifying them. The counselor can use the dissatisfaction to motivate an exploration of the personal and cultural heritage that has led to these "solutions." This exploration can include both the client's degree of comfort with these received values and the inner conflict the client already experiences that may lead him or her to question the adequacy or appropriateness of these values. Many if not most of our clients in this multicultural and fast-changing society experience conflicts of values within themselves, once we give them a chance to explore. Usually a conflict involves having at least two views of a situation or dilemma; this results in ambivalence. Thus it is not a case of the counselor having to impose an additional viewpoint—rather, it is a process of clarifying the client's own conflict and ambivalence. From there the counselor merely has to follow the accepted process for working with ambivalence, which is to avoid taking sides with either polarity. The counselor helps the client move back and forth between the conflicting "sides" until a new integration or new sense of self emerges.

Be alert to the next time you're with a client who is experiencing ambivalence. By now you have probably used "Experiment 3: Ambivalence and Shuttling," in Chapter 11. Review it now and be ready to use it with a client who is ambivalent, when it seems right for that client. I find it helpful when preparing to use something new in the course of an interview to prepare a card with some key "prompts" written on it to help me present the new experiment in the best sequence.

Openness to the client's cultural heritage necessitates a collaborative approach, regardless of the amount of training and knowledge a counselor has regarding the client's particular religion or ethnicity. A Lithuanian woman client of mine, "Mary," was struggling with her Catholic heritage. It was important when helping her explore her religious heritage to listen carefully for what Catholicism meant to her, which turned out to be quite different than the official doctrines of the church. Her view of Catholicism also proved to be much different from how I, coming from a different culture and different religious heritage, had understood (or misunderstood) Catholicism. An approach that is frequently helpful is to make the client the expert. "I know a bit about Catholicism, of course, but tell me what your belief is and how it impacts on your decisions on this issue."

Occasionally value conflicts emerge that at first do not seem to be noticed by the client. At first blush they do not appear to be "inner" conflicts. In Doherty's (1995) case of "Bruce," mentioned previously, the father is considering abandoning his kids, and only the counselor seems to see this as a moral issue. Doherty correctly points out that the assumptions of much of counseling history have been totally individualistic, leading to responses such as, "I wonder if you have considered the regret you will feel if you take yourself out of your children's lives?" or "You may not be in a healthy enough frame of mind right now to make long-term decisions." Such self-centered responses may be appropriate, but they are inadequate in that they totally fail to address the moral dimension. I agree with Doherty (1995) that, on moral issues, "it is generally a mistake to appeal only to a client's self-interest" (p. 23).

Where I disagree with Doherty (or at least with the way he summarizes the interaction in the case of Bruce) is that he "forcefully tells the client . . . " of the moral dimensions as he, the counselor, sees them. I believe it would be preferable to invite the client to examine his own moral stance (O'Hanlon, 2002). This might begin with a reflection and a statement such as, "so far, you've shared how devastating this has been for you. Are you able to observe how it's affecting your kids?" This might lead to "at the moment you're feeling so overwhelmed you don't believe you have much to give your kids—but what do you believe they need, and what do you wish you could give them?"

I accept Doherty's (1995) belief that by this point in the counseling he had "a bond of real trust with Bruce" (p. 23). But the moral dimension is presented as coming from the counselor, imposed on Bruce. Since we have every reason to believe Bruce is a person who has connected with his children in the past, in contrast to a person who is deficit in the ability to understand from another's point of view, "morality" does not need to be imposed on Bruce. It would be both more respectful and more effective to elicit the moral perspective by inviting the client to explore. It seems to me a collaborative approach, rather than a challenge, is needed.

In the situation with my Catholic/Lithuanian client "Mary," the counselor is facilitating the process within the client. In Doherty's counseling relationship with "Bruce," the counselor is facilitating the communication between the client and the client's perceptions of his children (object-relations). In neither case does the counselor need to impose his or her values.

If counselors work from a process model, these instances pose no worry that the counselors will make addressing moral issues an excuse to propagate their own religious opinions or beliefs or to "prey

. . . on the weak" (Kelter, 2001). In these two types of situations it is appropriate to keep the focus on the client. Work with either intrapersonal or interpersonal exploration of values has several components: first, helping the client develop his or her own stance on value issues begins with clarifying what is deeply meaningful for the client, and what the client feels most sure of. Second, it is important to help the client root his or her spirituality in her own direct experience. When a client focuses on what others say, or on authority, I typically ask, "Does that fit with your own experience?" The point is not to directly challenge the authority but to bring the experience with the authority into dialogue with the clients other experiences so it can be integrated. By *direct experience* I don't necessarily mean a clear sense of relationship with the holy, God, or the experience of nonordinary or mystical states of consciousness. Less dramatic but equally important may be specific experiences that remind a person of what is meaningful, of what brings a deep sense of peace and acceptance, of what restores our ability to take in and to give. These are not rooted in beliefs or concepts, but in direct experience.

The third step may be to clarify some axioms, or boundaries, of what defines whether an action is "good" or "bad," helpful or dysfunctional. So many opinions we've introjected as ethical issues are simply matters of taste, and judgments about them serve only to separate us from others who are different from us. What is really crucial? Who is really helped or hurt by a particular action? Is it a "victimless crime" that really hurts no one? Again, it isn't important that a clear formula emerge, but perhaps the client's discovery of a central principle, or a guiding light, will help the client feel more focused.

Though focus is important, recognize what must remain unknown, remain comfortable with ambiguity, a sense of awe and mystery and humility about questions that will remain unanswerable. Perhaps in simpler times when one culture was dominant and differences among humans were less in our face, many seekers felt that by midlife or before they had a clear map or formula by which to live their lives. This is not likely anymore, and it's not at all clear that it would be desirable. As Silone (1968) concludes in his essay "Choice of Companions," we no longer have a map—God simply provides enough light to see the next step we must take, and that is all we need.

Finally, with some clients it is helpful to clarify the next step in order to begin a concrete plan of action. This does not mean avoiding feelings or ambiguity, but it does mean connecting. Spiritual growth inevitably means facing difficult realities that don't fit our fantasies of what life should be like. However, the "dark night of the soul" does not need to be compounded with isolation or depression. Getting involved in issues in order to learn through experience, not just through thinking and rumination, is crucial to growth and identity development, and it reduces the likelihood of depression.

When the conflict the client experiences is within, among parts of his or her divided self, or when it is interpersonal, emerging in relationships that are close to the client and can be brought into the counseling room, the counselor can work with the system to some degree as an observer. However, in some counselor/client relationships, intrapersonal conflict or interpersonal conflict focused on the client's family or close others doesn't exist, and instead a direct conflict of values between the client and the counselor exists. In terms of professional ethics, this type of situation is the hardest the counselor may face in the attempt to openly address morals. An example from my own practice concerns the case of Dan, a bisexual married man I was seeing in a therapeutic men's group. My own values are that important information that impacts a significant relationship should be shared with the other person—in this case, Dan's wife. So when Dan disclosed that he was having a relationship with another man in order to explore the "gay" side of his bisexuality, I had no trouble empathizing with his need to explore an important area of his own identity. But I was very uneasy that he wasn't telling the truth to his wife, whom he claimed was his closest friend. In this particular case, the issue was confounded by Dan's disclosure putting Dan at risk for personal rejection both for his homosexual behavior and for his infidelity with his wife. It was particularly important that I not encourage shame in a client regarding issues that are genuinely identity issues.

In some settings, the counselor's attitude toward gays and bisexuals might easily have been suspect. In this case, the group I was leading and in which Dan was a participant was sponsored by a gay organization. Fortunately, the men in this group were already fully aware that I was not homophobic, so Dan would not likely have misinterpreted my addressing the "infidelity" issue as a criticism of his bisexuality.

One perspective is that Dan placed a higher value on sustaining the love relationship with his wife than he put on being truthful. But is it really a sign of love that he leaves his wife out of decision-making processes that directly affect her? The issue of including her is not a simple one, however—remember that earlier, when he had tried to include her, she had opted out. As in so many human ethical decisions, the ideals concerning "truth" and "love" are not sufficient for making the concrete real-life decisions when the two values seem to be in conflict.

In situations of a value difference between the client and the therapist, self-disclosure on the part of the therapist is often necessary. A particular type of self-disclosure is needed in which the therapist shares his or her own value stance in a way that does not imply that his or her way is "the right way" for everyone. However, as Doherty (1995) stresses, it does mean treating it as a moral issue, not just an issue of self-interest. This means standing beside the client as another human who sees the need to be clear about a moral issue, but realizes that the client will have to make his or her own decision on what is moral for the client.

I shared with Dan, in front of the group, that my own experience was that whenever I am dishonest on an important issue that affects both me and my significant partner, the dishonesty builds a barrier between us. Even if nothing is said, I believe that my partner experiences the barrier. It is as if we both sense that something stands between us, something unspoken, and it weakens the trust. So I have come to a decision not to keep such secrets, even if working through the issues is painful and frightening.

My disclosure deeply affected Dan. He stated that he longed to be more open with his wife, and that he had tried to share some of his feelings toward men with her, but that doing so had scared her and pushed her away. She had told him not to say any more. Dan stated that he envied me that my partner and I could be open on very difficult issues, but it seemed his wife could not tolerate this. It seemed a wall stood between them whichever way he handled it, honestly or dishonestly, so he chose not to risk losing her altogether. From his perspective, he loved her too much to insist on absolute integrity for himself.

Future sessions included some reassessment on Dan's part concerning whether he was underestimating his wife's ability to deal with the issue. However, the moral issue itself, the issue of his own honesty versus his holding on to the relationship was not reconsidered. I felt that Dan had heard my input as it was intended—as a concern for his own moral integrity as well as for his wife's well-being, but nothing in his own perception of the dilemma had changed. What had changed in me was that I developed a new respect for our differences. I became more humble about my "rules" for intimate relationships; perhaps they don't apply to every couple. At the very least, I was not in a position to judge Dan's marriage.

The issue I have tried to illustrate in this description of Dan and my relationship is a value clash. As a process therapist, I cannot know the ultimate moral truth for Dan. I need to work openly with a moral issue when it's what's occurring between me and my client. The way to do so, I believe, is through self-disclosure. However, a counselor can't expect that self-disclosure will function as persuasion. To the contrary, self-disclose as a peer, as a fellow-traveler in the identity search and the search for a moral path.

BEYOND THE HIERARCHY OF VALUES

Though postconventional values appear to be qualitatively "higher" than preconventional values, when one relates to a client and discloses a difference in values between the counselor and the client, the "status" on the hierarchy of values is not relevant. One is sharing person to person. Each person is simply who he or she is at the moment. Because no uniform value system exists from which to judge others, as spiritually sensitive counselors we must be especially client-centered and process orientated.

Dan longs for the openness that I can have with my wife; he recognizes that his wife's ignoring the importance of his identity as a bisexual creates some distance between them. But Dan listens to his wife and believes that, as she has told him, she does not want him to share his feelings toward men with her. Dan has chosen to live out his bisexuality, even though it means rejecting society's monogamous standard for marriage that he, at one time, had accepted. It is likely that Dan's wife knows this, but has chosen to ignore it as a means of coping. Dan is trying to respect her right to decide what she can and cannot face, even though he would feel better if they could openly talk about this aspect of his life. I connect with him as another human being who experiences longing and grief—not as a counselor who has achieved some sort of moral or psychological superiority. Whether or not we are at the same "stage" of moral development is not important, since, no matter what stage one is in:

> The line separating good and evil passes not through state, nor between classes nor between parties either—but right through the human heart. (Alexander Solzhenitzyn, 1973)

In a real sense, nothing separates one from the other when two persons confront their lives as ethical and spiritual creatures. This experience of a lack of separateness may be what several of the stage theorists have tried to express as a quality of transcending "beyond duality," a quality that emerges only in the last stages of moral or spiritual development. Fowler (1981) labels the highest stage of faith as "universalizing faith." In the previous stage, in spite of their depth, persons remain divided between an untransformed world and a transforming vision. For those rare persons who move to Fowler's stage six, however, a vivid sense of transcendent and moral "actuality" and a selfless passion for a transformed world leads them to live a life that is not experienced as divided. Similarly, in Wilbur's (1999, 2000) highest stage of spiritual development (stage ten) "ultimate unity" is attained and is marked by unity beyond all division and duality—complete psychic integration and coincidence of the individual with reality.[3] In the Buddhist tradition, one speaks of moving beyond duality, but all doctrines in Buddhism are stated with the recognition that words themselves divide things, and the state of being beyond duality is inexpressible. My sense is that Fowler and Wilbur would humbly admit that this quality of being cannot be adequately put into words.

To this point, we have talked about value conflicts and crises in terms of intrapersonal (and neurotic) conflict, and interpersonal or society-based conflict. Questions of value are also rooted in the human condition itself, sometimes called *existential* questions. A client's value crisis may be precipitated not just by the availability of so many options in a pluralistic, multicultural society, but by the pervasiveness of suffering. When a value struggle is based in an existential issue, such as suffering or the certainty of death, it can't authentically be resolved. Rather, a spiritual stance that stays with the experience without trying to remove it or fix it—a quality of just being present—is needed. Such a spiritual stance may make such a conflict easier to bear, though it will not eliminate the conflict.

I think I first learned this during a summer I spent working in rural Minnesota. A year or two earlier I had attended a national conference of college students involved in campus religious groups, and heard a preacher, Dr. George Buttrick, whom I found particularly insightful and challenging to my religious development. Buttrick had become the pastor of a large church in Minneapolis, and I went out of my way one weekend to participate in the worship service in that church. Very early in the service it became clear that this community of people had undergone a terrible tragedy the previous night—a group of teenagers from the church were in a vehicle together, going to some youth event, and were involved in a horrible accident in which five or six of the youth from this church were killed. The whole tenor of the worship service was affected by this, and Dr. Buttrick totally scrapped the sermon he had planned to preach, and spoke personally and humbly of his own reactions. What follows is my memory of the gist of what he said:

> In the midst of our deep sorrow and pain, we search to understand why such a horrible thing could happen. We scream out to God, asking why He didn't prevent it. We long for an answer. I do not find an answer to these questions. My faith does not provide one. The one thing I know is that God is here in our sorrow and pain—God suffers with us.

This sense of honest, humble presence rang true for me. It may involve the counselor simply being present, as another human, in the face of suffering and doubt. With some clients, it may be appropriate to witness to a sense of divine presence, if this fits the client's beliefs and openness, and it is done in a way that does not suppress the questions and doubts.

Before we can discuss more fully where this leads—the role of values in the process of commitment and trust—we first need to look at the crisis in beliefs, in Chapter 4, with particular attention to the possible role of doubt in developing a mature spirituality.

Chapter 4

The Crisis in Belief: Science, Spirituality, and Authority

From the cowardice that shrinks from the new truth,
From the laziness that is content with the half-truth,
From the arrogance that thinks it knows all truth,
O God of Truth, Deliver us.
Ancient Hebrew prayer

(Brown, 1953)

Holism is not possible when multiple points of view are denied.

(Markowitz & Ashkenazi, 1999, p. 20)

You can do anything if you want to bad enough. That is why we see so many people who can fly.

("Cynical Sayings," 2003)

ARE SCIENCE AND SPIRITUALITY IN CONFLICT?

Throughout childhood I loved the study of nature, and even had a "museum" in a section of our basement devoted to my collections. Natural science fascinated me. But it wasn't until junior high school that I learned about Darwin's theory of evolution. During my junior high school years, a man in his nineties regularly attended the Methodist church in my small hometown where my family and I were members. Decades earlier this man, Reverend Beacom, had been the minister at this church. By the time he entered my life he had retired, and with his wife had moved back to this town. Somehow he learned that I was interested in science; he encouraged me to drop by his home anytime after school. "I love science," he said, "and I'd like to have you tell me about what you're learning."

So when the material I was learning in school began to conflict with what I was learning in church, Reverend Beacom became a safe person in whom to confide. The two of us shared a love of science and a dedication to the ministry. He was a great listener, and on one visit he pulled from me what I understood about the theory of evolution. I blurted out the beginnings of a crisis in belief. "How can that be, if the world and animals and man were supposed to be created by God?" I asked in fear.

"Are you saying that evolution seems to be at odds with the creation story in the Bible?"

"Well, doesn't it?" I said with a bit more courage.

"Which creation story do you mean?" he asked with a twinkle in his eyes.

"The one in Genesis," I responded, knowing that he already knew this, and wondering what was going on.

"Let's take a look at it," he said, and he got out a Bible, the old King James Version, and opened it to the beginning. "Read this to me," he requested. He listened carefully as I read Genesis 1, and started to read Genesis 2. But when I finished the fourth verse, he stopped me suddenly. "Read that last phrase again, would you?"

I read it aloud: "in the day that the Lord God made the earth and the heavens."

"Who made them?" he asked.

"It says 'the Lord God,'" I responded, a little puzzled. Then Reverend Beacom had me go back to the beginning of Chapter 1, and count the times the word "God" appears. "The name 'God' is there thirty-four times," I stated, "and I just noticed something. Where you stopped me, that's the first time it says 'the Lord God'"

"Good," he said, "now you're beginning to pay attention."

Then he gave me a little lecture to explain the most likely theory of why the name for God changes. He pointed out that for the next three chapters it consistently refers to "Lord God" or just "Lord." The Hebrew name for God in one kingdom of the holy land was *Elohim;* the King James Bible translates this as "God." The name in the other kingdom was *Yahweh,* which translates as "Lord God." At the time Genesis was compiled, the two kingdoms were uniting, and they took the creation story of each kingdom and patched it into one story. So, as you can see, we really have two creation stories, and they don't match literally. The first starts with the lowest forms of life and works its way up to man and woman, the last living things created. But the second starts with man, then animals, then man's wife.

"So what does it mean?" I asked, both amazed and fascinated.

"Well, first of all, clearly it does *not* mean we are supposed to take it word for word as history. Obviously those editors knew these were two different stories, and they allowed them to both exist, side by side. They didn't say 'only ours is true' and try to stamp out the other one. So one thing it says is that they were trying to be accepting of each other's ways of expressing what is holy. I suspect they realized that there is deeper spiritual sense in this which both kingdoms understood, a sense of the holy behind all of this earth and its animals and man and woman."

I'm not sure I trusted it immediately—but gradually I realized that a third story of creation, Darwin's version, could stand beside the other two. The wonder and awe of this remarkable and beautiful creation is not limited to a particular story of how it happened.

On Whose Authority?

My own search to integrate scientific knowledge and my personal faith was by no means unique. It reflected a crisis in belief that has existed in Western culture at least since Galileo questioned the view of the earth as the center of the solar system and got himself in trouble with the authorities of institutional religion of his time. Just as Western culture is experiencing a crisis regarding moral authority (examined in the previous chapter), a crisis exists regarding the grounds for establishing what is true. A central issue concerns what authority one accepts as the basis for one's own beliefs. We will examine the different types of "truth" in the section on kinds of knowledge, but first, it is important for counselors to notice another aspect of the two biographical anecdotes I have shared in these two chapters: the difference between personal authorities and institutional authorities. In the incident that culminated in my declaring to the minister that "God wouldn't do that!" (Chapter 3), I rejected the sovereign authority of my minister's interpretation of the Bible, and later was reassured by my mother that it was okay to follow my own doubts and seek my own answers. In the anecdote just presented, Reverend Beacom became a trusted personal authority, allowing me to be open to the learnings of science and to see biblical truths in a new way, as references to a transcendent experience concerning nature and life, but not as a literal description of the way nature and life came into being.

Note that in each of these scenes from my own spiritual journey I was able to become more authentic and more integrated in my values and beliefs because of nonjudgmental acceptance from a trusted personal authority. My mother and Reverend Beacom each demonstrated their own deep spirituality *not* by trying to mold me to be like them, but by encouraging me to sort out my own conflicts and come to my own judgments. Niether of these trusted persons asked me to place their authority above that of the church or the Bible, substituting one external authority for another. Rather, they helped me to rely more on an inner conviction—my passionate concern for justice in the first incident, my consuming search for truth in the second.

A recent letter from a friend of mine refers to this type of awareness, this revelatory recognition of what is realized to be deeply true and important:

> There are times in your life that you have some experience, or witness some event, and sense that this is important and will stay with you the rest of your life. You realized then (or in some cases recognize later) that something important was happening; that what you were seeing was something you would need to remember. "Witnessing" may be a better word than "seeing," because the thing that tells you is inside—or at least you register it inside. It doesn't come from anything like "authority" or "nature." (Watt, 2002)

This use of personal authority, to encourage the growth process of the client by witnessing it rather than to advance the personal power of the authority, is precisely what is needed in counseling. It is important to recognize that each of our spiritual paths are different, and I would be remiss as a counselor to insist that a client replicate my own path. On the other hand, often the struggles clients are dealing with are not simply intrapersonal issues but reflect the path that society has taken, and it can be freeing for clients to learn from the counselor's disclosures that they are not alone in this experience. This helps clients to see their particular doubts and questions in the context of our culture's history.

COMPONENTS OF THE CRISIS IN BELIEF

Beliefs that are socially supported can have powerful effects, whether or not the beliefs are based on evidence. In the United States a superstition exists that the number 13 is unlucky; in China and Japan, the number 4 evokes fear. In the Japanese, Mandarin, and Cantonese languages the number 4 and the word *death* are pronounced nearly the same. Reactions to the number can actually affect the timing of person's death. A study of American death certificates found that Asian Americans were 13 percent more likely to die of heart failure on the fourth day of any month than were Caucasian Americans (Cooper, 2002).

Many modern spiritual seekers desire to move away from superstition to a belief system that is not at odds with the scientific knowledge of our day. It is worth noting, for historical perspective, that the ancient Jews or the ancient followers of Islam were not asked to believe doctrines that were contrary to the "known facts" or their day (Campbell, 1970-1980, Tape 1). The writings these traditions have called scriptures were congruent with the cosmologies of their day. They were not faced with a conflict between an evolutionary view of creation and the images of the Genesis stories, or between a universe with the earth as center and a view of the movement of planets around the sun—until the techniques for scientific observation were developed. A conflict between "scientific facts" and "faith" did not exist for them.[1] But for today's spiritual seekers, the crisis of "facts" and "faith" is not simply an individual crisis but a cultural one. I believe it is helpful for counselors to have at least a sketchy overview of this crisis, which I will break down into four components:

1. The split in types of knowledge, between objective and subjective truths
2. The impact of the physical sciences, including the exploration of astronomy and of biology and their impact on modern cosmology and the view of man

3. The scholarly understanding of scriptures: textual criticism and history.
4. The spread of the democratic ideal and its impact on authority

In what follows I will explore each of these aspects of the current crisis, then discuss the relevant data from the social sciences.

Kinds of Knowledge

As counselors, when we work with a fighting couple we recognize that who said what or who said it first—the facts—are not as important as the way it is said and the impact the statement has on the process. We distinguish between *report* and *command* (Watzlavick, Beavin, Helmick, & Jackson, 1967). For example, if a married couple sits down to begin their first interview with me, and the husband says to the wife "you can begin," on the surface (report) it is a statement of deference, politely allowing her to speak first, but at the process level (command), the husband has attempted to establish that he is the one who will make the decisions regarding who will speak. So the "command" effect of the statement is nearly the opposite of the literal meaning.

In the discussion of the Genesis creation stories I noted the difference between literal truth and the transcendent reference. Though one can not logically take both Genesis 1 and Genesis 2 as literally true, both are stories that point to a meaning or purpose beyond just the obvious existence of life on earth. It is appropriate to call these stories mythological, which means that they express a worldview, they point to some central values that help unify a particular culture. Calling a story a myth, in this sense, does not infer that it is false—it simply recognizes that it is one perspective on life, and that its central message is not at the literal level. However, typically a tribe or religious group does not recognize its own narratives as myths unless it is in contact with other tribes or religions with different assumptions and stories. Though common themes (such as the "hero") occur in many cultures (and thus has "a thousand faces"—Campbell, 1968), they are not labeled as myths until one has enough cross-cultural experience to see them in perspective. Yet, even within a unified and believing community, the stories that are told and retold, liturgically, are recognized as not literal descriptions of everyday time and real places. "Once upon a time, in a land far away. . ." sets the tone for the telling of a story—an important story, but not one to be taken literally. The stories are "believed" and the images are identified with and used as an orientation to everyday life, and yet are not totally of this world.

At least two levels of meaning exist in communication between couples (the report or literal level, and the process or command level), and at least two levels exist in religious cosmologies and mythologies: the literal or historical descriptive meaning, and the meanings that point to the transcendent. Language is always inadequate to describe the transcendent, as is recognized by such ancient customs as the Jewish taboo against writing out the full name of God. Even in some indigenous religions such as Shintoism, the spirits are represented only by the empty space in the center of the shrine; no sculptures or names can contain them. The phrase *not of this world* in the previous paragraph, at a pure descriptive level seems to suggest some other world. But the world that myths point to is not another world so much as a hidden dimension of the same world. The spirit that is in a living person is not separate from the body, but is seen as animating the body much like the breeze that is moving the trees, which is invisible and yet necessary to their movement. In the ancient Hebrew language, the word for *spirit* and for *breath* are the same. As discussed in Chapter 2, animism was one of the earliest spiritual schemas or belief systems. The aliveness, energy, movement of all that is—that is the holy.

As the tools of careful description and prediction emerged, what is *literally* true became clearer and more testable and definable. The language of articulate thought began to separate, roughly, into the discourses of expression (the arts) and discourses of description (the sciences). This distinction is suggested by Rheticus, in trying to defend Copernicus: "The Bible's purpose was not to present natural philosophy (i.e., science), but rather to lead to salvation." (Howell, 1997, p. 264). I think it is fair to say that when mythologies were developed and transmitted orally, no distinction was made between expression and description. Myths were powerful conveyors of the human experience.

As the sacred stories were written down and became formed into finalized cannons of scripture (especially in the Western religions of the Book—Judaism, Christianity, and Islam) these writings were treated as descriptions of reality. Meanwhile, when science first emerged, it sought to become a method of objective truth. The split between subjective experience (which can be expressed) and objective knowledge (to be described) became deeper and deeper—and the phenomenal success of the scientific method, and its spin-off in technology, led to more and more emphasis on the material.

But human experience is not limited to the material, and the focus just on the material fails to satisfy our deeper longings. Our lives today are too influenced by science and technology to try to deny their existence. But how do we reconcile our spiritual longings with the facts of science?

The Limits of Science

The conception of science as objective and material is not entirely accurate. First, it is important to note that science is *not* limited to a description of just matter, the material, but also of energy. It seeks to explain all that is observable, and not only modern physics, but pure science from its earliest days, was interested in "movement"—the movement of the heavenly bodies and the movement of falling objects, the use of pulleys and levers, etc. In this sense, the physical sciences do not accept the dualism that sees body and spirit, matter and movement, as separate entities. As we will see in Chapter 5 on the body, it does not make sense, in either science or Christianity, to think of the soul and the body as separate.

Second, as physical science has become more refined, the terms *subjective* and *objective* have proved to be inadequate. Experiential knowledge is often checked against a community experience, and thus is not simply subjective. Recall Sam Keen's (1983, 1994) warnings concerning the risks of not roping onto other climbers when navigating the higher altitudes of spiritual climbing (see Chapter 1). Scientific observation is always from a particular perspective in space and time, and is thus more accurately described as perspectivist than objective; this does not mean its knowledge is totally relative, but it does mean that any piece of data is "true" only in relation to the perspective from which it was gathered. All current scientific knowledge is limited by the methods used to gather it and the perspective from which it was observed. This provides science with a built-in openness to future findings and revision of its theories.

But even though science extends its descriptive domain to include energy and movement, and even though it takes more of a perspective view of truth than a purely objective one, science is still limited. It cannot provide the "truth" about value questions. And its methods do not express the deeper longings of humankind. The limits of scientific method, and it's resulting data, are not, of course, limits of the scientist as person.

One of the twentieth century's best-known scientists, Carl Sagan, known for his part in authoring the television series *Cosmos,* states that the two important attributes of the scientific method are skepticism and wonder (Sagan, 1997). His view of the scientific approach has a spiritual component, the sense of wonder that is reminiscent of the experience of awe that Otto (1970) considered the central component of religious or spiritual experience. The attitude of wonder includes both a profound sense of awe, and a curiosity that encourages exploration. Sagan also describes the scientist as having "a judicious mix of openness and skepticism." The latter involves demanding stringent standards of evidence (Sagan, 1997). However, that the scientist begins with wonder does not mean that the findings or facts of science express this sense of awe.

Appropriate Doubt

It *does* seem to make sense to talk about different types of "knowing," and to separate that which is apprehended through "gut experience" or "intuition" from that which can be known through the stringent standards of evidence required by science. If our worldview and our languaging were limited to the findings of science and the knowledge of pure facts it would be devoid of inner experience and values. But if our arts and our cosmology are based on outdated facts and a worldview that is incongruent with our contemporary experience, we are left struggling to believe that which is at odds with our intellectual honesty. Surely the saints of the past had a faith beyond facts. But should the believer of today be expected to have faith in something that contradicts the facts? Martin Luther trusted that humans are saved, not because we are good but because the God of grace forgives us in spite of our sins. Modern Christian theologians such as Paul Tillich have argued that in our modern scientific era, doubt is the parallel to sin in Luther's era. We are accepted, Tillich proclaims, not because we have reached the truth, but the God of truth accepts us in spite of our doubts. In both sin and doubt, the attitude a humility in the midst of our spiritual voyage is all that's expected of us. From this perspective, both the scientific method and the modern act of faith are rooted in awe and in openness to a process, not in a predetermined truth.

Doubt is not simply something to be put up with as part of the human condition. It is actually an aid in the search for truth. A parallel to this exists in developmental psychology. Erik Erikson in his popular theory of stages of life emphasized that the first stage of human development focused on the issue of trust versus mistrust. What is less widely recognized is that he stressed that the healthy resolution to this stage was not simply trust, but a mixture of trust and mistrust. A sense of doubt about one's own beliefs, rather than a closed faith, appears more developmentally mature (see the section in this chapter titled "The Understanding of Attitudes toward Authority in the Social Sciences").

This parallel between the method of science and faith, this sense of mystery and openness, are exemplified in the current Dalai Lama, who, as a child, was sequestered in his isolated quarters in a palace. One of his favorite pastimes was spying on the comings and goings of people in the city below using a telescope inherited from the previous Dalai Lama. At night he turned the telescope to the skies, studying the stars and the volcanic peaks and meteor craters on the moon. One night as he peered through the telescope he saw that the craters and peaks cast shadows. Surely, he suspected, this means the source of that light comes from somewhere outside the moon—not from inside the moon as he had been taught in his monastic studies (Dalai Lama & Goleman, 2003a,b).

The youthful Dalai Lama then tried to check his hunch by scrutinizing astronomical photos of the moon in a magazine. This independent evidence validated his own observation—they also showed a shadow to the side of the craters and peaks. His traditional Buddhist faith stated that the moon was illuminated by an intrinsic source of light, but his own systematic observations forced on him the "realization that the traditional description was not true." A 1,200-year-old teaching was being contradicted by his own observations. This led to "a principal which the Dalai Lama has repeated many times since: If science can prove that some tenet of Buddhism is untrue, then Buddhism will have to change accordingly" (Dalai Lama & Goleman, 2003, p. 33).

The scientific method does not result in a final truth, but rather in a current state of knowledge that is self-correcting and open to new information. In Buddhism, that attitude of openness to experiment and investigation has precedence over even the words of the Buddha himself. The practicing Buddhist is not expected to simply take the Buddha's word for something, but to test it out for himself or herself (Dalai Lama & Goleman, 2003)

A modern faith seems to me to be one that accepts "what is" in the sense that it does not suspend scientific method. Propositions that fly in the face of the scientific evidence can be rejected, and are not grounded. They do not really buttress a solid faith. Skepticism and doubt may be held within trust and affirmation, just as the negatives or shadow of oneself must be held within the positive, or the positive becomes phony and ineffective. Modern faith is not antiscientific, but it recognizes that science is limited—it cannot test a value, nor can it test the expressions of the soul.

Unfortunately, organized religion has often asked that its followers leave their brains in the foyer before entering the sanctuary or temple. Hopefully, if spirituality involves the integration of the whole person, a person is not expected to deny his or her intelligence in order to practice spirituality. Certainly rational-empirical thinking alone might not help a person develop deep empathy and intuition, but intuitive thinking alone can also be off balance, leading to superstition, and providing no way to distinguish spirituality from magic and hocus-pocus.

Some of the great spiritual leaders (Buddha, Jesus) have urged us to discern the spirits. If the problem of dogmatic religion is its being closed to the new truths of our time, including science, the inverse problem with some of new age spirituality is its being open to any belief or fashion, no matter how foolish.

Each counselor and each client will need to find his or her own way of integrating modern knowledge with the deep and intuitive spiritual truths. The conceptual scheme each adopts is less important than each remaining open to the different levels and kinds of knowledge so that they are not living with their head in the sand in terms of practical and scientific reality, and yet are guided by values and centered in a spiritual reality that is beyond the methods of science to grasp or express.

THE PHYSICAL SCIENCES, MODERN COSMOLOGY, AND THE VIEW OF MAN

If we raise the question of whether science and institutional religion are in conflict, the answer from much of the institutionalized Christian church is a resounding "Yes!" In the seventeenth century, when Galileo succeeded in collecting empirical data to prove Copernicus's theory that the earth revolves around the sun, the Roman Church declared:

> The doctrine that the earth is neither the center of the universe nor immovable, but moves even with a daily rotation, is absurd, and both philosophically and theologically false, and at the least an error of faith. (Roman Catholic Church declaration, 1633, de Santillana, 1955)

In the twentieth century, the Roman Catholic Church had the honesty to admit that it had been wrong to condemn Galileo (de Santillana, 1955). This example suggests that the positions of institutional religion can eventually become congruent with those of science, but it can take more than three centuries for this to occur.

This delay is not always the case. Darwin's observations and theory of the evolution of species, including humans, were at odds with the literal interpretation of the creation accounts in Genesis. When Darwin died, his

> family wished to bury him on their estate at Down, but twenty Members of Parliament, with the support of the Anglican Church, appealed to them to allow him to be interred at Westminster Abbey, a few feet away from Isaac Newton. You've got to hand it to the Church of England. It was an act of consummate grace. For you, they seemed to be saying, who have done the most to raise doubts about the truth of what we say, we reserve the highest honor—a respect for the correction of error that is, incidentally, characteristic of science when it is faithful to its ideals. (Sagan & Druyan, 1992, pp. 69)

Catholicism as well as some of the mainstream protestant denominations now claim that evolution is not incompatible with the doctrine of God's creation. This truce with Darwin is especially impressive when one considers that the theory of evolution more directly challenges the *literal* meaning of the Bible than does the view that the earth revolves around the sun. As Sagan & Druyan (1992) note:

> Evolution in no way *implies* atheism, although it is *consistent* with atheism. But evolution is clearly inconsistent with the literal truth of certain revered books. If we believe the Bible was written by people, and not dictated word-for-word to a flawless stenographer by the Creator of the Universe, or if we believe God might on occasion resort to metaphor for clarity, then evolution should pose no theological problem. (p. 67)

Sagan & Druyan (1992) go on to emphasize the importance of this theory to modern science:

> But whether it poses a problem or not, the evidence for evolution—*that* it happened, apart from the debate on whether uniformitarian natural selection fully explains *how* it happened—is overwhelming. (p. 66)

The Darwinian perspective is central to all of modern biology, from investigations of the molecular structure of DNA to studies of the behavior of apes and men (Sagan & Druyan, 1992). This should not imply that evolution has become a dogma in science. The theory of evolution, as with any scientific theory, is always open to new data.

What seems to be emerging in some parts of Christianity is a recognition of the limited authority of the Bible. The scriptures may be inspired and authoritative in issues of the spirit, but their revelations were received by men who were limited by the cosmologies and factual understandings (and misunderstandings) of their day, and these outdated conceptualizations are not of central importance to the biblical message.

Many believe it is possible to affirm the central messages of the Bible without accepting their literal interpretation. However, this reconciliation of science and religious authority requires further clarification. We need to distinguish between the authority of the scriptures and the authority of the Church as the interpreter of the scriptures. The authority of the Roman Church seems to be tarnished by its centuries long delay in acknowledging the evidence regarding the earth as the center of the solar system. But what about the authority of the Bible?

This leads us to another challenge to traditional religion: the tools of literary and historic criticism.

Textual Criticism and Scriptural Authority

If we hold that the writers of the scriptures were limited to the knowledge of their day as far as facts and cosmologies are concerned we begin to realize that the historical and cultural context in which these inspired authors were writing might also affect the meanings they placed on the words they used. It becomes important to understand the original context of the written words in order to discern and comprehend the central message. Some knowledge is gained directly from the text itself and in thinking about it rationally. The example at the beginning of this chapter concerned the use of two different names for God in the two creation stories at the beginning of Genesis. From the consistent use of two different names we infer two different authors. (For other, more complex reasons we may infer that the authors come from two different localities and cultures.) This approach is called *textual criticism,* and is applied to many types of ancient or historical texts. To give an overly simplified example, if we find that a particular Greek book consistently uses one word when talking about love, and we find another book consistently uses a different word for love we might begin to wonder if they were written by different people, though we would need more patterns of word usage to be sure of it. This type of analysis has been applied to some of the letters of the New Testament attributed to the apostle Paul. It is fairly widely agreed by New Testament scholars that only six of the nine books (in the New Testament canon) attributed to Paul were actually written by him (Ehrman, 2002).

The meaning we give a text is derived in part from our judgment of its literary form. The writings of Paul to the churches appear to be letters, each geared toward a specific group and culture. The Genesis creation stories are more difficult. They can be read as scientific history (though this was not a literary form at the time), or as allegory, or as myth (Achtemeier, 1996).

A more specific illustration concerns the narrative about the virgin birth of Jesus as it is written in the gospel of Matthew. The reason Matthew gives for this event is "so the prediction given by the prophet would come true" (Matthew 1:22, RSV). The quotation of the prophet follows, but it comes from a Greek mistranslation of Isaiah in the *Septuagint,* the Greek form of the Hebrew scriptures that Matthew apparently used (Miller, 1994). In the original Hebrew version, the word translated as *virgin* (*almah*) simply means a young woman. Another Hebrew word, *bethulah,* would have been used if the intent were to imply that no sexual intercourse occurred (Achtemeier, 1996). In the same chapter Matthew also lists 42 generations of the genealogy of Joseph, from Abraham through King David down to Jesus, in order to show that Jesus was a descendent of David. This implies that Joseph is the blood father.

Is Matthew to be taken literally? If so, what do we make of his error about what Isaiah said? Or perhaps Matthew's message is that Jesus is of royal descent, whether in terms of the political kingdom of David, the patriarchal lineage of Abraham, or the current emperors of Rome, the caesars, who were believed (by some) to be virgin born.

This chapter will not summarize the many areas in which understandings of scriptures are greatly changed when the specifics of the text and the cultural context of the author are known; I have focused on the Christian scriptures, because this is where my training lies.

Similar questions arise from textual criticism of the sacred scriptures of Islam, the Qu'ran, attributed to Mohammed. Guillaumo (1956) notes that the historic Hebrew figures (used in an attempt to link the origin of Islam to Abraham) are consistently referred to by Greek versions of their names. What does this pattern tell us about the author's understanding of Hebrew? I do not have sufficient knowledge of the Qu'ran to evaluate the conclusions Guillaumo (1956) reaches from this and related data. My point is simply that any text, scriptural or otherwise, can be analyzed in terms of its use of language, the cultures it borrowed from, the translations of texts the author was dependent on, and other historic factors. Knowing these data may affect our understanding and interpretation of the sacred texts, whether they are Jewish, Christian, Islamic, Hindu, or Buddhist scriptures.

The Process of Forming "The Canon"

Two additional developing fields of scholarship placed the scriptures under further scrutiny. One was the history of how the books were chosen, which became "the canon" (the standardized scriptures agreed upon by a particular religious group). I will focus on the canon of Western Christianity, since its history has undergone the most study.

Up until the fourth century after Jesus' death, numerous writings about his life and death and resurrection and about the early Christian communities circulated throughout the Near East and Europe. As late as 450 CE, one bishop counted at least 200 different gospels circulating in his diocese (Ellerbe, 1995). Once it became clear to the Roman empire that this sect (Christianity) was not going to be wiped out, Orthodox Christianity and the Roman government cooperated to encourage uniformity by prohibiting and burning gospels and other writings that were not on their approved lists. The Roman Emperor Constantine, who "saw in Christianity a pragmatic means of bolstering his own military power and uniting the vast and troubled Roman Empire" (Ellerbe, 1995, pp. 17-18), instated it as the official religion of the empire and joined with the church in suppressing dissension within the empire. It was in this spirit of suppressing dissension that the books of the canonized Bible were assembled.

Culture and Interpretation

The second area of scholarship concerns the effects of cultural influence on the person or group who are interpreting the scripture. (I am not referring here to the culture in which it was written, which is part of higher criticism as just discussed; the focus in this case is on the culture of the persons reading, or translating, or preaching from the scripture.) Abraham Lincoln, during the Civil War, commented that both sides "read the same Bible and pray to the same God, and each invokes His aid against the other" (cited by Harshbarger, 2002).

More recently, through the study of the history of oppression, we realize that interpretations of the Bible have regularly been used to justify prejudice and reinforce the self-righteousness or superiority of a particular group. A case can be made that the persecution or subjugation of left-handed people, witches, women, slaves, and gays were each justified by interpretations of the Bible. Two historic examples will suffice here, concerning women and slaves.

Gender

The Bible was used, in much of Judeo-Christian history, to justify the "inferior" status of women. Women were not allowed to be rabbis, could not be ordained in most protestant churches until the nineteenth century, and still are not allowed to be Catholic priests. One can argue that Jesus included women in leadership positions during his ministry, and that the gospel writers reported them as the first to witness Jesus' resurrection. But both the early history of Christianity as a branch of Judaism and the leadership of Paul in the development of the gentile churches led to a regression to sexism in the leadership. Whether or not one accepts this, it is clear that both the Old and New Testaments continue to be used to justify keeping women in inferior roles in the home and the church.

Race

The Bible was used to justify slavery—in fact, the word *slave* occurs about 250 times in the Revised Standard Version, and the word *servant* (which is usually the same word, deliberately mistranslated as *servant* in most English versions), occurs about 1,200 times. In these passages slavery usually is taken for granted. Yet few of us today would argue that slavery is justified for Christians. In Jesus' time slavery was not primarily based on racism or on economic enterprise; rather, slaves were the visible spoils of conquering. Capturing slaves was seen as more humane than murdering the conquered people. Later, the numerous biblical passages about slavery were certainly used to justify racism and to uphold an economic system in pre–Civil War America, as Lincoln (1865) noted.

First, we must ask whether these biblical writings are being used to justify current prejudices (e.g., racism, rather than spoils of war) that go far beyond the biases of the biblical authors. Even if these interpretations are justified, because of the central role of love and justice in the Judeo-Christian tradition we must consider whether we are compelled to rethink the views of some of the biblical writers, especially if the views are based on the writers' acceptance of the limited perspectives of their culture, such as male chauvinism or tribal superiority. Training in multiculturalism promotes the recognition of the role of culture in the development of a point of view; one of the principle values of counseling today is an acceptance of multiple points of view, and a reaching out with a special effort to those who are the strangers or the oppressed. Certainly the ethical teachings of many religions promote a special concern for the "stranger in your land" (as a basic tenet in Hinduism, for example, or as a corrective to the "specialness" of the particular chosen people in Judaism).

In what sense is Jesus an authority for you? Orthodox Christianity after the fourth century has stated that, as the Christ, he was both fully human and fully God. Does fully human mean that he changed his views with new experiences? Did he learn from experience, or was he all-knowing from the beginning? Is it possible that Jesus held some cultural biases, and then changed his mind?

The concern for overcoming barriers and reaching beyond one's own tribe is stressed in Jesus' interpretation of the "second" great commandment, "thou shalt love thy neighbor as thyself," which he illustrates with the story of the good Samaritan (Luke 10:13). It is not clear that Jesus held this view when he began his ministry. Because I love traveling in foreign lands, I am fascinated with the account of Jesus' first recorded travel outside the boundaries of the ancient tribes of Israel. Jesus, in an encounter with a pagan woman in the region of Tyre and Sidon, at first seems to respond with the prejudice of most Jews. She falls at his feet and begs his healing for her sick child. His response is brusque: "Let the children first be fed, for it is not right to take the children's bread and throw it to the dogs" (Mark 7:27, RSV)—implying that his ministry is intended only for the lost sheep of the house of Israel. Instead of responding defensively, this mother, in desperate need of saving her acutely ill child, responds in all humility and respect, "Yes, Lord; yet even the dogs under the table eat the children's crumbs" (Mark 7:28, RSV). At this point Jesus seems to change his mind. Just before this incident (in Mark's account), Jesus has been rebuking the legalism of the Pharisees focusing on rules of cleanliness while ignoring human needs; he argues that it is inner attitudes that really defile a person. Perhaps he remembers his own words.

Jesus sees that *his* attitude toward the woman has been exactly like the attitude of the Pharisees toward him, and he changes his mind. Immediately after the woman has said "even the dogs under the table eat the children's crumbs," Jesus responds, "For this saying, you may go your way; the demon has left your daughter" (Mark 7:29, RSV; Lance, 1992 citing Mark 7:24-30 and Matthew 15:21-28). Jesus stretches his own boundaries and heals her child.

If Jesus is a model for you, think about what his response to the foreign woman implies for your own spiritual growth.

It is this process of being open and stretching our boundaries that is so central to spiritual development. The apostle Paul recognizes it when he says that "there is neither Jew nor Greek, there is neither slave nor free, there is neither male nor female; for you are all one in Christ Jesus" (Galatians 3:28, RSV), and he goes about taking this loving and boundary-less good news to the "pagans." Of course, Paul too is a person in growth, and at times is inconsistent and fails to see his own prejudices.

Our task as counselors is not to judge our clients' levels of development but to foster their growth when they are moving toward opening up their boundaries. This is where belief can be so damaging. If Jesus had defended his belief that the children of Israel had priority, he would not have been able to respond to the human needs of the mother with a sick child. Beliefs can express values and process, but they cannot define them, and when made into dogmas, they can undermine them.

HISTORY AND THE DEMOCRATIC IDEAL

"We (in America) have a freedom to disbelieve in authority, and more importantly to declare our disbelief, a freedom unknown in the various fatherlands" (Sennett, 1981, p. 119). To understand the role of authority in human history and its connection to knowledge, a brief overview is necessary. This will lead to the explication of the democratic ideal.

One of the unique characteristics of humans is that we are able to learn not only from our own experience, but from the experience of others. Many animals can learn a new behavior by directly imitating a behavior they observed in another animal. Humans can learn by listening to or reading words about behaviors, thoughts, or attitudes. This passing down of information and experience is possible only because of the human ability to codify experience into language. Throughout all of prehistory, transmitting this experience was totally dependent on oral communication. The way humans learned from those who preceded them was primarily through the repetition of stories passed down from generation to generation—what we now refer to as oral history. These traditional stories, prior to written language, needed to be entertaining, and in forms (such as verse, or song) that made them easier to remember. Some people obviously had better memories, more ability to learn the stories, and more skill at telling them, and may have been invested with more authority. It was crucial that humans honored the memories and traditions of their ancestors; otherwise they would have been limited to what could be learned in one lifetime, similar to other animals. Tradition and oral history had power and authority because they were believed/recognized to have survival value. It is their survival value, of course, that makes such beliefs functional for the society as a whole, in accordance with the anthropological theory of social functionalism.

Since most human societies during the early economies of nomadic food gathering were quite small, the leaders were personally known, and authority was negotiated face to face. Furthermore, most tasks were shared—though some differentiation in tasks may have occurred as individuals' natural talents were recognized.

As groups learned to use seeds, to plant in particularly fertile areas, and to return there to harvest the growth, eventually agricultural societies emerged. Storing grain, possession of land, counting and measuring what is owned and stored and writing it down—written language and numbers—all followed, as did the domestication of animals. Controlling animals and defending territory increased gender specification of tasks because of the advantages of men's larger musculature. The tasks crucial to the nomadic gathering societies did not particularly favor either gender, but the emergence of agricultural economy seems to have favored males, and gradually the hierarchies of gods and goddesses seems to have reflected the increasingly male-dominant societies—though the evidence for exactly how the economic and gender changes were linked to the changes in the objects of worship is scanty and the connections are unclear (Fazel, 1999; Guerrero, 2003).

The emergence of the written word meant that those who were educated in writing—those who could inscribe (the "scribes")—became authorities in the keeping of the memories. Maintaining tradition shifted from being able to tell stories to being able to read and write them. Leadership shifted to the educated.

Routes of trade existed very early in human development, and trading centers gradually became cities. As larger social groups lived together (in cities), differentiation of jobs increased further. So did the hierarchy of leadership and the depersonalization of authority. Quite possibly one might be subject to a lord who one rarely saw, and certainly didn't know on a face-to-face basis. Thus, at the time agricultural economies were gaining power and the great traditions were being written down rather than passed down orally, the religious stories were changing from those that honored the fertility and creativity of the feminine, or of both men and women, to stories of male gods who became the highest in the pantheon of gods—in short, stories of male superiority and domination.

It is fascinating that the "religions of the Book" (the religions that placed the most authority in the *written* revelation of God: Judaism, then Christianity, and still later Islam) emerged along with the most absolute emphasis on monotheism—the supremacy of a male God. But the differentiation of roles between males and females occurs in almost all known societies. Furthermore, the development of male dominance seems to be present in almost all literate societies and is challenged only with the shift to technological and service economies.

The development of writing and of counting and then of more advanced mathematics, the valuing of learning and understanding, and most particularly the belief that more accurate understanding can emerge from logical consideration and discussion of ideas, can lead to a new kind of authority—the authority of consensual logic and group decision making, and the authority of counted votes. When we consider the emergence of democracy in classical Greece, we are at first struck by a contrast in the character of human shared learning. The emphasis in traditional religion seems to be on the passing down of knowledge from the ancestors, whereas in Greek democracy, the emphasis seems to be on the discovery of knowledge in the present interaction. Such a contrast is too bold, and fails to note the honoring of elders and of history in Greek society, just as it fails to note the element of immediate (present-oriented) revelation in the prophets of Israel, confronting both the authority of kings and the rigidity of past traditions.

Nonetheless, the roots of democracy, and to a lesser extent the roots of science, are present in ancient Greece, and they grow into a fruitful plant that spreads throughout the Western world and begins to supplant the authority of custom with the authority of law (Russell, 1968). In the late eighteenth century, the Age of Enlightenment, democratic ideals reemerge, especially in France and what became the United States. Simultaneously, nonhierarchical forms of religion begin to emerge, especially in the United States. Several of the best known signers of the Declaration of Independence came from religious traditions such as Unitarian and Deism, in which traditional authority and dogma were questioned. This, along with many of the colonies being founded by persons escaping religious persecution by established church hierarchies, may have been a factor in the establishment of a separation of church and state in the U.S. Constitution and Bill of Rights.

In the nineteenth century, the rise to affluence and power of new industrial magnates occurred without any traditional claim to superiority (Russell, 1968), which contributed to a love for equality of status irrespective of birth, and to an emphasis on authority based on merit.

Let us move now from this sweeping impression of the development of human civilizations to some clarification of the types of authority.

Issues of Authority

Distinctions in Types of Authority

It is a mistake to lump together all types of authority. We need to distinguish personal authority in primary face-to-face relationships (e.g., parents, teachers, sometimes ministers or priests) from impersonal or institutional authority. Persons holding institutional positions of authority may affect our daily lives, but we don't usually have face-to-face relationships with them (e.g., political leaders, those in the hierarchy of the church, police, etc.).

On another dimension, we need to distinguish traditional authority, where a role may be passed on by others without a screening for competence (e.g., royalty; in some cases religious leaders) from earned authority, where the status is based on knowledge, skill, or wisdom, and the person's authority is limited to the area in which they have special competence.

In addition to these (and overlapping with these) are legal-rational authority, in which a position is held based on rules or elections, and the "authority" is based on the position; and charismatic authority, in which the spiritual or heroic force of an individual results in esteem from the group (Max Weber, cited in Sennett, 1981). Examples are, respectively, the U.S. president, and Martin Luther King Jr. Authority is not simply set up by institutions and imposed on individuals. Rather, we choose our authorities; we give them allegiance in exchange for their meeting our needs (Sennett, 1981).

My dad was trained as an auto mechanic. As a young adult, when I was shopping for a used car I'd always take him with me. In my eyes he had earned authority in this particular area because he had knowledge and experience. This type of authority may include a surgeon, a professor who wins a Nobel prize, a general who has demonstrated his strategic skill, or a chef who reliably combines different ingredients to produce delicious meals.

One of the characteristics science and democracy hold in common is the valuing of earned authority. The scientist Darwin "hoped none of his children would believe something just because it was he who told it to them" (Sagan & Druyan, 1992, p. 69). He did not want his personal status to subvert the process of having to demonstrate any claim. Earned authority must be demonstrated. Similarly, the founders of democracy in United States did not want leadership to be accessible because one was a member of the aristocracy or nobility, and neither the presidency nor personal wealth should be inherited (the way the crown is inherited). It should be earned. The democratic ideal is that each person starts out as equal, both politically and economically, with all others. The scientific ideal is that each idea must "earn" allegiance by being demonstrated through experience and experimentation. Even religion, in the U.S. experiment, was not to have special aid from the government. The separation of church and state meant no particular religious institution or idea should be established by the government. The implication was that all religions were to be treated as equal, starting out with no advantage.

I take it as agreed on that a social system of any size cannot function without some persons assuming roles of leadership, and that some hierarchy of decision making will usually be needed for a social group to complete complex tasks. As long as leadership and hierarchy are based on merit and are task driven rather than power driven, they do not conflict with democratic ideals (see Kramer & Alstad, 1993). The real power of the ideal of democracy is that we begin to look at authority as something to be earned through demonstration of competence or objective knowledge. When citizens in a democracy are told to believe because the minister, priest, pope, Bible, or president says it's true, they are inclined to say, "show me!"

The Understanding of Attitudes toward Authority in the Social Sciences

The Contribution of Social Psychology

The surprising finding of social psychology is that a large portion of citizens in United States will obey the demands of an authority figure even when the results appear to be extremely harmful to someone. A famous series of experiments conducted by Milgram (1963, 1965, 1974) and associates (Milgram, Sabini, & Silver, 1992) at Yale University recruited volunteers through ads in newspapers to participate in memory experiments. To the surprise of experts, when an experimenter demanded it the recruits were willing to administer higher and higher voltages of shocks to a "learner" who made mistakes on a memory task. The recruits could not see the other person, but could hear over a speaker system the learner's pleas to stop the pain; yet recruits would continue. As the recruits continued to follow orders, the learner's appeals became more agonized—finally he or she would burst into shrieks, yelling, for example, "Let me out of here. My heart's bothering me. You have no right to hold me here. . . . Let me out!" Similar screams were heard for each of a series of increasing shocks, then nothing was heard, a deadly silence. The experimenter still urged the recruit to continue. Experts had predicted that only 4 percent of recruits would continue after the silence. In fact, more than 80 percent continued simply because the researcher insisted "the experiment requires that you continue." (Be assured that no shocks were really administered, and the cries were acted—but the recruits did not know that.)

A large body of social psychological research has attempted to unravel the many variables involved in such acquiescence to authority. Was it due to the prestige of Yale University? Milgram (1974) discovered that if the same procedure was conducted in a rundown section of a city disconnected from the university, an incredible 48 percent of recruits still obeyed the "experimenter" beyond the learner's silence. However, if the "boss" appeared to simply be a college student, only 20 percent would obey. So both prestige and credibility of the "boss" played a role in the compliance of recruits. However, in none of the variations of the experiment were the bosses known personally to the recruit—so as high as 80 percent of recruits will obey impersonal authority if the authority appears credible. This willingness to obey demands to the point of cruelty does not seem to be motivated by releasing aggression, for when it is the "learner" who requests that the recruit continue "to help me learn," but the "experimenter" tells the recruit not to do so, 100 percent of the recruits obey the authority and stop the shocks (Kenrick, Neuberg, & Cialdini, 1999).

It seems that most people are willing to cede responsibility for harming others to an arbitrary authority when conditions are arranged optimally (when the victim is somewhat remote, the authority is in the room with the respondent, etc.). These moral decisions are not simply a result of individual volition, but involve social constraints. When the authority is physically more remote (giving instructions by telephone rather than in person) compliance drops to 21 percent. When the victim is in the room with the respondent, and the respondent is told to hold the victim's hand on the shock plate, compliance drops to 30 percent. And when another person is in the room with the respondent, a "teacher," and this other defies the experimenter and refuses to give shocks, compliance by the respondent drops to only 10 percent (Kenrick, et al., 1999). When authorities are presumed to know best, then following their lead becomes a sensible response. We have suggested that it is functional and appropriate for children to follow the lead of persons they believe know more than they do. Less educated people tend to be more obedient to authority figures than better educated people, probably because they presume that the authorities know more than they do (Kenrick et al., 1999).

Again, authority is more likely to be obeyed if the person in authority appears credible, if she or he has knowledge or "expert power" (Kenrick et al., 1999, p. 206). Symbols and titles can be very powerful. The results of a study conducted by a team of physicians and nurses revealed the force of one important symbol, the word *doctor.* Hospital nurses received a phone call from a man they had never met but who identified himself as the doctor of a patient on their floor. He ordered them to deliver twice the maximum acceptable dosage of a drug to that patient. Ninety-five percent of the nurses obeyed! They had to be stopped on their way to the patient's room (Kenrich et al., 1999, citing Hofling, Brotzman, Dalrymple, Graves, & Pierce, 1966).

If the authority is not only credible and carries a title, but also has the power to reward or punish, it is even harder to resist. In such cases an obvious error by a person in authority often goes unnoticed—and even if noticed goes unchallenged, even when the consequences can be disastrous. For example, airplane crew members appear to assume that if their captain said it, it must be right, even when evidence indicates that the captain is wrong and the plane is headed for a crash (Foushee, 1984).

The characteristics of authority just noted—authority that appears credible, carries a title, or has symbolic power, and has the power to reward or punish—are all attributes of most religious authority. So these findings of social psychology help us understand the tendency of people to yield to the authority of a minister, priest, pope, or Bible even when one might expect, because of the democratic ideal, the influence of science and the findings of historical and textual criticism to incline modern Americans to question and possibly challenge the authority.

The Contribution of Developmental Psychology

While social psychology was assessing the social factors involved in a person's yielding to authority, developmental psychology sought to understand changes in attitudes toward authority within the individual as she or he moves toward maturity.

It is appropriate for a young child to be dependent on adults for guidance, since decisions as basic as what is safe to eat and where it is safe to walk require a level of knowledge and experience that can be attained only over a period of years. Children learn early the importance of pleasing their parents, since they are almost totally dependent on the actions of parents to meet their needs. Many psychologists and therapists continue to believe Freud's theory that the value of pleasing authority, learned in relation to parents, is later transferred to teachers and other nonparental authorities who also hold the power of praise and reproof (see for example Raven, 1999). However, the assumption that attitudes toward nonparental authorities are transferred from and are similar to attitudes toward parents is not validated by the best research on this issue. As early as 1957, Burwen & Campbell showed that a person's attitude toward his or her father were no more correlated with attitudes toward nonparental authority than with attitudes toward peers. Thus it would be more accurate to say that a generalized attitude toward other people exists rather than an attitude toward all authority. Evidence suggests a generalized response to *nonparental* authorities, but it appears to be distinguishable from both attitudes toward parents and attitudes toward peers.

In thinking about religious authority, then, it is important to note the legitimacy of roles of leadership in religious institutions as in any institutions. Is the authority claimed based on some competence or merit, or is it a claim for power that encourages the follower to maintain a childlike dependence? Intellectual maturation involves a gradual progression from accepting guidance to gathering information to learning to ask the right questions, analyze information, and solve one's own problems. Emotional maturation can be described as a gradual move from dependence on those who are older and more mature to interdependence on one's peers or equals. Wouldn't spiritual maturation also involve a gradual move away from dependence on powerful authorities to interdependence with other spiritual seekers?

To clarify, the issue of young adults who develop critical attitudes toward political or religious authorities will be examined. What is striking is that the critical attitudes appear to be part of the move toward a mature value system rather than a "transference" from negative attitudes toward parents. The Freudian assumption was that attitudes toward authority were a result of Oedipal conflict. This theory would predict that when a young person moves out of the parental home the conflict would be reduced and negative attitudes would decrease. However, research shows an *increase* in negative attitudes toward nonparental authority among students who leave home and move to college, whereas we do not see this pattern in those who continue to live at home while attending college (Matteson, 1974). It seems more accurate to describe the changes in attitudes, as youth mature, as a healthy increase in critical attitudes toward nonparental authority, since they do not necessarily reflect a negative view of the world. During the period of intense social activism in the 1960s and early 1970s, the press frequently echoed the views of Freudian writers (such as Bruno Bettleheim, 1970) who claimed that it was alienated youth who were most likely to become social reformers. Research showed, however, that it was the youth who were *closest* to their fathers rather than those alienated from their fathers who became young activists (Watts, Lynch, & Whitaker, 1969).

To extend this more generally to the youth of today, a developmental model for making identity decisions (Marcia et al., 1993) argues that youth need to move through a period of exploration (moratorium) before they can make sound life commitments. Identity research classifies youth in four categories on the basis of this move through exploration to commitment:

1. *Foreclosure* youth move directly into identities similar to those of their own parents or authorities with little sense of turmoil or confusion. Their path to identity does not involve much searching.
2. *Diffusion* youth experience the variety of options open in a pluralistic society, and become confused by the multiplicity of truths and voices they hear. Even after some years of search, they seem unable to take a personal stand, to form a personal identity.
3. *Moratorium* youth become deeply involved in the struggle among alternatives, exploring them not just cognitively but experientially, and are able to move forward to make decisions about their own lives, at least in such domains as occupation, and values.
4. *Identity achievement* is a state of commitment following a period of exploration.

Compare the two classifications of youth who fail to really engage in this process: diffusion and foreclosure. Youth with a diffuse status may consider alternatives but can't seem to make commitments. Foreclosure youth, in contrast, make commitments prematurely; they move easily into accepting the opinions and roles of their parents and other authorities. The foreclosure style may have worked well in traditional societies in which very little change occurred between generations and a single cultural style was almost universally accepted. In many such tribal settings the authorities were known face to face (Russell, 1968), and the community could reject leaders whose claim to authority seemed inauthentic. However, in the large social groups of fast-changing and multicultural societies, this style does not prepare the youth for the diversity of options and viewpoints they will encounter. Some ability to remain open and evaluate options before reaching a decision is needed, and this includes, at least temporarily, living with some uncertainty about "answers," accepting ambiguity without jumping to embrace a the pre-given conclusions of an outside authority. (For a more thorough review of these issues see Matteson [1975], especially Chapters 10, 13, and 14.)

Youth who move through an identity struggle and make real commitments to engage the world, not those who remain in alienated or diffuse patterns, come from homes in which the fathers are active participants in child rearing (Matteson, 1974). Critical attitudes toward nonparental authority are strongest in those youth who have positive relationships with their fathers (Keniston, 1968). Critical attitudes usually occur in youth who have removed themselves from the sphere of influence of (parental) authority and can reenter it with a sense of its limits (Sennett, 1981).

We hear much about the deterioration of American families. Among the *positive* changes that are occurring in the American family is the increase in fathers' involvement in child rearing, at least among educated families, as compared to very low father involvement in the decades of the 1950s through 1970s. The fathers of the most functional families, in both the studies of social activists in the 1960s and 1970s, and the more recent studies of identity development, were those who could accept their sons' challenging them directly.

An interaction I had with my dad when I was about 9 or 10 illustrates this. We were visiting my paternal grandparents' home; again the scene is sitting around the dinner table, this time with the extended family and some guests. My father was telling a story, and used an incorrect grammatical construction that is common among rural people—something such as "he don't do that sort of thing." I interrupted him and corrected his grammar: "Dad, it's 'He *doesn't* do that sort of thing." Grandma glared at me, then looked at Dad.

"Are you going to let your son speak to you like that?" she said critically. Dad thought a moment, seemed relaxed, smiled, and said calmly to his mother, "I expect he's right."

Notice that my dad did not put down his mother, but he certainly empowered *me*. Rather than squelch my criticism, he affirmed that it was probably correct. I'm fully aware that the great majority of American fathers at that time (about 1948) would see my father as not being strong enough with me in that incident. But I think my dad was wise, and knew exactly what would be useful to me at that point. He modeled polite disagreement with another adult without deliberately trying to embarrass her.

Often when we hear discussions concerning the relationship of youth to authority, we hear adults argue that it's "important to respect authority." Usually in this context the word *respect* involves fear, and it suggests that it is wrong to criticize. However, a major developmental task for youth is to make important life decisions, so we need to reframe the issue of authority—for example, "What institutional structures will help youth learn to make good decisions?" One of the best ways to learn to make good decisions is to make them with others, especially with more experienced mentors, rather than to try to be totally independent. (Realistically, none of us is totally independent. This is the myth of the American cowboy, but it's true only in the movies.) So I think the most fruitful answer to the issue of institutional authority is to encourage shared decision making, by which I mean that the process of making decisions is structured to involve more than one person, or more than one group, and encourages them to make the decision collaboratively. The great advantage of shared decision making is that people are less likely to feel abused, controlled, or put down. The great disadvantage is that shared decision making requires some rather difficult skills in communicating, which are not usually taught in school or in the home.

The jump from knowledge about what is good for the development of individuals to assumptions about what is good for society as a whole is a huge one. We can say that a foreclosed identity does not succeed as well in modern society, but we cannot be sure that the propensity of morally mature youth to criticize authority will necessarily change society for the better.

CONCLUDING THOUGHTS ON AUTHORITY AND GROWTH

> Science can destroy myth, but it cannot create personal meaning or values.
>
> (Kramer & Alstad, 1993, p. 27)

The social science data that has been presented may lead to the impression that compliance with authority is at best a necessary evil. Certainly this is not the case in regard to rational or earned authority. To repeat, authority and hierarchy are not destructive, and are probably necessary to social order, except when they are based on power rather than merit or competence. One danger lies in the propensity of institutions, including the institutions of religion, to perpetuate their own existence and point of view through coercive power. A second danger has to do with the tendency for individuals to act in harmful ways in compliance with arbitrary authority, as shown in the Milgram studies.

None of the challenges to traditional religion that have been summarized are of themselves threats to a deep spirituality, assuming that the spiritual perspective involves an openness to change and emerging truth rather than a static view of revelation. It seems clear, however, that human history is at a point where authoritarian institutions are not functional. Kramer and Alstad (1993) extend the argument to include all authoritarian moralities that minimize the valuing of present life (in contrast to a future life). "Fear is structured into all renunciate religions through proclaiming that some higher power is watching all actions . . . and will reward or punish them as deserved" (Kramer & Alstad, 1993, p. 30). The value of their analysis is the recognition that many factors, including the challenges we have already discussed, have resulted in "an erosion of religious certainty, which was the foundation and authority for morality . . . [This] is creating what we consider an inevitable rend or tear in the movement of history" (Kramer & Alstad, 1993, p. 29).

A polarization exists between those who believe that the current problems in the world come from straying from the traditional truths, and those who are reaching for something new, though experimental, and not yet fully understood. Kramer and Alstad (1993) seem to believe that these two directions, looking back and looking forward, are irreconcilable. Furthermore, if I interpret them correctly, they believe that traditional religion is inevitably authoritarian. I question both of these conclusions.

First, we must recognize that much of what has become "traditional religion" began as a challenge to the authoritarian institutions and beliefs at the time of that religion's beginnings. Both Buddha and Jesus sought to call Hindu authorities and Jewish leaders, respectively, to a more open and life-giving spiritual view and to a less rigid and stratified social structure. The same can be said of both earlier religious leaders such as the Hebrew prophets, and the Chinese writer Lao Tzu, as well as later religious leaders, including Martin Luther and Mahatma Gandhi. Experimentalism and an openness to the spirit are one aspect of the dialectic of religious history as well as secular history.

Second, cultural and personal changes seem to occur *both* by looking back and looking forward. I think Kramer and Alstad (1993) are correct that people are wistful for "certainty, for clear-cut rules and roles" and that science "has eroded the absoluteness of belief through valuing change and questioning over (blind) faith" (p. 27). However, few of us can handle uncertainty in several areas of our lives at once. I previously used walking as a metaphor for growth (Chapter 1). When we walk we lift one foot, but *keep the other on solid ground.* We also learn to trust a new balance, where the center of balance lies at a point in front of the center of gravity of the body. This kind of trust may be closer to what the word *faith* actually means.

Let me turn from metaphor back to social science. I think no one will disagree that this is a time of great uncertainty. The social psychological experiments on compliance (with both authorities and peers) suggest that increases in uncertainty motivate increased reliance on other people's judgments rather than on one's own judgment (see Kenrick et al., 1999). Cult group leaders often deliberately manipulate feelings of uncertainty and disorientation, which leads to greater deference to the group and the cult leader (Hassan, 1990).

Openness to change (again, either individual or societal) is most encouraged by a climate of personal trust. This is usually possible when certain limits and foundations are kept secure. In individual counseling, rules such as confidentiality, and experiences such as being unconditionally accepted by the counselor provide the grounding for accepting changes in thoughts and attitudes. Similarly, in group or societal settings, personal authority can provide the trust necessary to question. As Newcomb (1962) discovered decades ago, the greatest shifts away from authoritarian beliefs and values occur in college or university settings in which professors have enough personal contact with students to serve as mentors (Newcomb, 1962). This is congruent with the social factors that reduce compliance (in the Milgram experiments), such as touch, and having an ally in the room who defies the authority.

The task in our society is to develop a web of personal support that makes the rapid change in ideas and beliefs less of a personal threat. The overcoming of authoritarianism goes hand in hand with the sense of community. Any attempt to overcome inauthentic authority without this connectedness to others is likely to lead to cynicism.

Implications for Counselors and Clients

It is crucial to understand that the implications of the material presented in this chapter may be markedly different for the professional counselor than for the client. It is part of our professional responsibility and our training as counselors to be able to view beliefs, attitudes, and behavior from a multicultural perspective. In as much as we function professionally in the secular world, we are committed to a professional perspective that transcends the boundaries of a particular religion, sect, or tribe. Certainly we may affirm our own personal stance, which may remain connected to the religion and subculture of our roots, but we work from a broader perspective.

Evidence suggests personal engagement with new and different viewpoints plays an important role in spiritual development. Longitudinal data from a study of religious and spiritual development during the college years suggested that three types of life events stimulate spiritual maturation: a developmental crisis (in Erikson's sense), which involves engagement in an emotional or intellectual challenge; some form of cross-cultural exposure, through living abroad or in a different subculture than the student's family background; and/or giving service to others, which leads the student to "walk in the other's shoes" and see the "God image" in the other (Slater, Hall, & Edwards, 2003).

The data also suggested three factors that hindered spiritual development. One is a personality factor: a prideful stance of already possessing the truth, in contrast to the student's sense of humility in relation to experience, a recognition of her or his own ignorance. The other hindrances have to do with the educational setting: teaching through indoctrination rather than an educational environment that encourages free inquiry, and the compartmentalization of knowledge, in contrast to a curriculum that fosters seamless learning through interdisciplinary studies. Growing in spiritual maturity is thus associated with an opening up rather than with a self assuredness about having or getting "the truth." It requires both an encouraging environment and new stimulation. My hunch is that for many counselors, spiritual maturation requires a new attitude toward doubt. Traditional religion has often viewed doubt as an evil, a threat to faith. But the developmental data just presented, and the developmental approach suggested in this book (see Chapter 2) suggest that doubt may be a sign of the person's opening up, of letting go of a prideful stance and letting in a new and more integrated "truth." The most important spiritual act may not be to fight the doubt, but to surrender to the "shaking of the foundations," and accepting that we are not able to fully know (Tillich, 1958). Surrender to one's process is utterly different from compliance with one's authorities or traditions. Just as a youth's questioning of his or her parents does not imply a lack of respect, but instead suggests that he or she trusts them enough to dare to ask; deep spiritual questioning implies a sense that reality or God or the ultimate is not fragile, and is not offended by the questions.

As Weston (1993) elegantly put it:

> Cherish your doubts, for doubt is the attendant of truth. . . . A belief which may not be questioned binds us to error, for there is incompleteness and imperfection in every belief. Doubt is the touchstone of truth; it is an acid which eats away the false. Let no one fear for the truth, that doubt may consume it; for doubt is a testing of belief. The truth stands boldly and unafraid; it is not shaken by the testing.

Let us look first at what is needed in the spiritual growth of the counselor, and then at what is needed in the way the counselor facilitates the growth in the client.

The Spiritual Growth of the Counselor

The obvious question that follows this developmental view of spiritual growth is: how mature is my spiritual belief system? The corollary question is: how does this enhance, or detract from, my ability to be a spiritually sensitive counselor?

The counselor's search grows, at least partly, out of his or her education, including having been schooled in the social sciences. Often the counselor in training senses an incongruity between what was learned in Sunday school, Confirmation classes, and Confraternity of Christian Doctrine (CCD), and what is learned in the university. This may lead to a search to integrate scientific knowledge and personal faith.

It is not only the exposure to particular fields of knowledge that may result in an exploration of one's own beliefs. The whole process of intellectual pursuit of knowledge in a marketplace of ideas such as a liberal arts school may lead one to welcoming the challenge of weighing different hypotheses and alternatives, in contrast to accepting particular "truths" or "doctrines" on the basis of authority. This may lead to questioning what authority a person accepts as the basis for his or her own beliefs or spiritual ideas.

The intent of this chapter has been to affirm that a healthy spirituality involves the whole person, including the thinking brain. The integration of one's intellectual faculties with the articulation of one's spirituality is not just allowed, it is to be encouraged. Of course the process of exploration is not limited to cognitive development. Counselors, in their practice and field work, and later in their jobs, have the opportunity to develop deep relationships with people from very different backgrounds and walks of life than their own. Their work involves exploring with these people their intimate thoughts and feelings. Thus a day-to-day multicultural experience exists that is not available in the work lives of people in most other professions and occupations. These experiences may lead counselors to value their own openness to growth, challenges, and doubts. It may lead them to question and explore their own beliefs. The question counselors must ask themselves is whether they have had the opportunity to explore their beliefs, check them against the knowledge base of current times, and reformulate them to make them truly their own.

Beliefs are only one part of one's spiritual life. As has been stated earlier, beliefs and doctrines grow out of some direct experience, and are a later attempt to capture it in words and concepts. Beliefs are never synonymous with the experience itself. It is possible to have had significant religious experiences but not have developed mature beliefs about them. In addition to experiences and beliefs, a spiritual life usually includes a number of practices (prayer or meditation, acts of praise and gratitude, public worship, etc.), and a guiding ethic, a way of relating to other people. So if, in reading this chapter, you begin to question the maturity of your belief system, it does not necessarily mean you are immature in all these areas of spiritual development.

If much of what has been presented is quite new to you, congratulate yourself for having the courage and persistence to have read this far. Don't berate yourself for experiences you haven't had. If this kind of exploration is new to you, now is a good time to start it.

A person who is just learning to climb mountain paths should not try to lead others in climbing. The most important skills in spiritual counseling do not deal with leading the client, but with carefully following him or her. As I summarized in Chapter 1, from the best approach to spiritually sensitive counseling does not focus on the client's beliefs, but on the process. The real question for counselors who are wondering, after an assessment of their own maturity in beliefs, whether they should attempt counseling in this area is this: will your own inexperience with the process of exploration of beliefs make it hard for you to accept and attend to the client's process? For example, if the client is questioning the authority of the Bible, and you have not seriously questioned it, will you unwittingly try to suppress the client's doubts? If the client is moving away from belief in a doctrine that you still hold, will you try to protect him or her from some "error" rather than help to the client fully engage his or her mind in the search?

It may be helpful, at this point, to stop and ask yourself how you have reacted to the challenges of this chapter. Does it interest you to explore some of these ideas more? If so, chances are good that your interest and excitement would be sensed by a client who is beginning to explore, and that you could identify enough with his or her process to be helpful. If the topic of a crisis in belief primarily evokes fear in you, it might be better to refer such a client to another counselor.

Safeguards against Imposing Beliefs

I have previously noted the fear that practitioners will use the increasing interest in spirituality in the counseling professions as an excuse to propagate their own values or religious opinions and beliefs. In a Chapter 9, three approaches for safeguarding against imposing values will be described: eliciting the internal conflict of values, exposing the unexpressed conflict between self and object-relations, and directly addressing the value issue through self-disclosure on the part of the counselor. Each of these safeguards can also be used in issues of beliefs and opinions. However, an additional and more important safeguard against imposing beliefs exists: experiential counseling methods that do not encourage the counselor to focus on beliefs or opinions are preferred. Cognitive and analytic methods increase the risk of the counselor imposing his or her own belief structure on the client. Experiential methods decrease that risk.

Two cases using focusing work may be helpful to specifically illustrate work with areas of beliefs. Hinterkopf (1998) notes the importance of being sensitive to the terms that are used by the client. She gives an example of using nontheistic terms with "Mr. K.," who had

> said that he was spiritual but had difficulty relating to the term *God.* After discussing the issue involved, I asked him, "What is your experience of being related to something greater than yourself?" The client said "It feels like getting in touch with a larger background where you're aware of feeling connected to everyone and everything else." Then I asked him, "How does getting in touch with a larger background feel in your body right now?" He said, "It feels more relaxed. My body feels bigger and there is a quiet energy. My head feels clearer." Then the client said "I think I just had a spiritual experience!" I agreed.
>
> Had I insisted on using the term *God*, instead of affirming the client's words, I would have run the risk of hindering or negating the client's spiritual process. (p. 79)

Notice in this example that the counselor focuses on the client's felt experience, using his terms, but also checking out whether another phrase, "greater than yourself," fits the client's experience. The counselor does not attempt to persuade the client, only to find the language that fits the experience for the client.

Another example from focusing work further illustrates this focus on the client's process, without getting hung up on differences in beliefs. Hinterkopf (1998) advises:

> In supervising counselors I have sometimes heard counselors tell clients they cannot relate to the client's experience because it is unfamiliar to them. This unfortunate and unnecessary response usually stops the client's psycho-spiritual process and leaves the client feeling isolated. (p. 79)

Hinterkopf (1998) goes on to illustrate the handling of unfamiliar or unexpected spiritual content, without getting lost or distracted by differences in belief:

> A Chinese woman from a Buddhist background talked about feeling "very tired much of the time." At first she thought it was a physical tiredness from her busy schedule and not enough sleep. But then she realized that her tiredness was due to "too many reincarnations without enough enlightenment."

After the counselor reflected on her new realization, the client continued:

> "Life is getting old for me." She explained that she knew that she wasn't here to just live this life but that she was here to get enlightened. Again I responded empathically and reflected her felt sense words. I then suggested the question, "Perhaps you could ask yourself 'What does this whole thing need?'" After spending some time with her attention directed inside, she received the answer, "Light and love in the heart area." She realized that she was so tired because she wanted to achieve enlightenment by herself. She said, "Instead I now realize that I need to *receive* enlightenment—that enlightenment is a gift, a moment of grace when I remember to receive light and love from the universe. This is the only way to receive enlightenment." With this answer her tiredness disappeared. I suggested that she stay with her new feeling of easing." (pp. 79-80)

The change or "felt shift" that occurs for the client does not come from the counselor engaging in conversation about the beliefs, but from facilitating the experiential process. In this case, the new "insight" that is achieved is the client's own rewording of her experience.

In both of these cases, the client is encouraged to experience more deeply. In the first, the counselor's question about his "experience of being related to something greater than yourself" opens him to access an experience that he wasn't in touch with. In the second, the question about what the whole thing "needs" leads to the client's accessing her needs for love from others and the Other. In neither case do the questions or leads involve the counselor imposing her beliefs on the client. The questions are based on the process.

Facilitating the Client's Spiritual Growth

I have suggested that those of us privileged to engage in counseling or psychotherapy have the opportunity to directly witness deep experiences of other persons in a way that few other employment situations can offer. We need to recognize that our clients may not have had this variety and depth of vicarious experience. In some cases a particular client has undergone a search to integrate scientific knowledge and personal faith, or to resolve a conflict between the exclusive character of his or her faith and his or her own inclination toward tolerance. In others such a process is just now beginning, and may play a role in the client's current spiritual search. In still other cases, no sense of incongruity has emerged, and no experience of "crisis" regarding traditional beliefs has occurred. We cannot assume the client's educational or life experiences have led to an awareness of the discrepancies between traditional religious thought and contemporary scientific knowledge, or to an openness to the variety of views and opinions that are available.

It is easy for us when we meet others who are different from ourselves to focus on the content of the differences, and, for example, to try to persuade the other to accept the content of our own beliefs and opinions. Once we have formed opinions or points of view on a subject, we tend to focus on the content of those opinions rather than on the process that led us to these conclusions. It takes practice and skill as a counselor to avoid this inclination and to keep the attention on the process.

We may need to remind ourselves that what we want, as counselors, is not that clients replicate our viewpoints and behaviors, but that they come to an awareness of their own authentic viewpoints. As in many other areas of counselor-client interactions, we help our clients by encouraging them to sort out their own conflicts, to rely more on their own inner convictions, and to come to their own judgments.

Asking counselors to leave their own opinions behind and focus on the client's agenda, to work on the conflicts and incongruities the client experiences, is not a unique request. In the spiritual realm, however, where our opinions mean so much to us, we may find this harder to do.

Is Psychoeducation Useful?

The counseling process values the inner discovery. The counselor follows the client's agenda, yet the counselor may appropriately give the client feedback on the patterns he or she sees in the behaviors of the client, including "denial," a lack of realism, or lack of taking responsibility.

Just as with some couples I might explain the two types of messages (report and demand, discussed early in this chapter), in some situations the counselor might appropriately provide a brief description of the difference between literal and mythical truth. My own style is to ask, "would you be interested in doing some reading on this?" and to offer to provide some written information in the next session. Within a session it is more commonly appropriate to comment on different types of knowing and to separate what is apprehended through "gut experience" or "intuition" from what can be known through the stringent standards of evidence required by science. Different ways of knowing, and different ways of giving and receiving love, are often appropriate content in couples counseling. But, as with most psychoeducation, I am careful not to say more than a sentence or two without soliciting a response and returning to the process occurring within the individual client or between the partners in a couple. It is interesting how frequently in the gospel narratives Jesus responds to a question with another question—pushing the inquirer to explore rather than providing answers.

Dealing with Authority in the Client's Meaning System

Our clients must chose the authorities who meet their needs. If clients' needs are for dependence, subjecting themselves to the will of another, then we need to respect the clients' levels of development, at least as the starting point. An academic discussion of authority is likely to build defenses against exploration and growth rather than facilitate them.

What role does the counselor have in providing new experiences? The counseling relationship itself is a new experience. With most clients, it is not a place for describing new worldviews, but is the chance for clients to "test" their own conceptions of alternative worldviews against their real-life experience. I seldom work with clients without discussing experiences they may want to try between this and the next session (though I avoid the label "homework" since it suggests a purely cognitive or academic assignment). Most of the experiments between sessions are not just cognitive, nor are they assignments. They are designed through an interaction with the client, building on the specific learning or growth of that session.

As with all counseling, experiments must move a step at a time; the counselor must follow and follow some more before he or she can lead. Care must be taken to avoid overwhelming the client and setting up experiments in which the event may be experienced as a failure.

The question may arise concerning whether the counselor, in providing "informed consent," should state in the first session (or in written materials given to the client at the end of that session) that his or her approach to counseling assumes the client will be involved in trying new things. My own answer is "no," because such an expectation would be overwhelming for a highly anxious client. I don't want this to be an expectation coming from me as the authority. I want the exploration to be a careful pacing in the relationship between me and the client.

With a client who is coming specifically because he or she is experiencing some crisis of faith or values, it is appropriate to ask in the early sessions some of the foundational reasons for his or her coming, and to help the client formulate questions about testing what is helpful. The client may formulate questions about beliefs: How do I check whether my beliefs are helping me grow? or questions about process: How do I know what I know? How do I stay open to what I need to learn or unlearn? Questions about the interactions with the counselor are also appropriate: How can I tell the counselor when the counseling session is frightening or overwhelming? When will we evaluate whether this process is going okay?

Support During Exploration

The attitude of exploration stands in contrast to trying to be the client's authority. It implies encouraging the client to find other guides and resources.

Referrals to clergy in the client's tradition may be helpful, but I give such referrals only when I know the clergy are genuinely open to the issues the client is exploring. For example, if client is exploring gay issues, I am careful to refer only to clergy who are nonjudgmental on the issue. Similarly with clients who are questioning authority. If the client already has a clergy with whom he or she has decided to meet, it may be useful for the counselor to help the client construct the questions he or she wants to ask the clergy as they begin a discussion, choosing questions that will help the client feel out whether it is safe to go into the more sensitive issues with this person.

In a session following such a meeting, the counselor may suggest reviewing with the client how a meeting with a clergy went. My stance would be primarily a questioning one: "So when he said that, what did you feel?" "So that was *his* position. What position are *you* moving toward at this point?" It is especially important, when the client is dealing with issues of authority, to be sensitive to the client's level of anxiety, and to the interface issues between you and the client. The client is likely to feel "in the middle" between the religious authority and you as the counselor. It is important that the client senses that you don't need him or her to take a position that pleases either you or the clergy, but to find his or her own position. Perhaps even more crucial is that the client senses that you are intuitively following the conflicted feelings involved in his or her exploration and are willing to walk with him or her through the fire, at the client's pace, so that the fear and pain will not overwhelm the sense of shared joy, curiosity, and excitement that are part of all growth and exploration. Spiritual growth can be conceptualized in the context of the total developmental processes of the personality. This does not imply that all growth (spiritual or otherwise) is incremental and gradual; crisis may provide openings for major changes and for unpredictable leaps forward. Nonetheless, if the counselor sees the changes in the broader context of growth, he or she is less likely to subtley press for bigger steps than the client is ready for.

It is not uncommon for persons undergoing spiritual crisis to decide they have outgrown the particular religious group with which they have been affiliated. Sometimes a client needs help in developing new support groups. It is especially important with men to challenge the assumption that they should carry on their search by "going it alone." Finding small ongoing support groups, weekend labs, or conferences or retreats can help the client recognize that he or she is not alone in these doubts, explorations, and exciting discoveries, and may heighten growth and a sense of groundedness.

I have emphasized that the process of being open and stretching our boundaries is central to spiritual development. This process has the potential to connect us to a larger human community, but it may lead to our dissatisfaction with the more insular and dogmatic community that has been our spiritual home. It is unfortunate if we allow the move to a more expansive spiritual orientation to cut us off from human connectedness, when it is precisely that connectedness that calls us to burst out of our previous prejudices, and, similar to Jesus with the desperate mother, to "change our mind" and connect with persons we had previously seen as outside of our circle.

Chapter 5

The Body, Passion, and Spirituality

> There is one thing that, when cultivated and regularly practiced, leads to deep spiritual intention, to peace. . .and to the culmination of wisdom and awakening. And what is that one thing? It is mindfulness *centered on the body.*
>
> (The Buddha, from the Satipatthana Sutra, in Brach, 2003, p. 93, emphasis mine)

This chapter and the next concern the body and sexuality. This chapter is personal and focuses on the acceptance of one's own body as a path to deeper spirituality. Chapter 6 is social, and presents the key social issue that threatens to split much of institutional religion: homosexuality. The issue of whether or not the church can be inclusive depends largely, I believe, on whether the people in the church have learned to accept their own bodies.

THIS IS MY BODY

Embodiment

Throughout this chapter I will be developing an assertion that may not at first be obvious: that acceptance of one's body can enhance one's spirituality. My assertion runs against the common belief that spirituality and sensuality are in some sense opposites. If you, the reader, were raised in one of the Western religious traditions, you may have picked up the sense that the body is "material" and is in some way degraded compared to the "things of the spirit." On the other hand, if you have been trained as a counselor or have been influenced by pop American psychology, you have been told that it is important for a person to develop a positive body image. Given these two competing sources of influence, it would not be surprising if you, and most readers of this book, experience ambivalence about my asserting a positive link between the body and spirituality.

This ambivalence is not simply a personal response. Many of the great religious traditions, as well as much of the Western philosophic tradition, have held very ambivalent attitudes toward the body. Nelson (1978), in a rich and groundbreaking book on the significance of the sexual body to Christian theology, *Embodiment,* traces sex-negative religious attitudes to two kinds of dualism: spiritualistic dualism (a mind/soul split), and the patriarchal (male-dominate) gender dualism that pervaded Hebrew history. These two issues are intertwined throughout most of Judeo-Christian history, and affect attitudes toward the body, sex and gender, and sexual orientation.

Nelson's (1978) focus is on Christian tradition, since it has played the major role in shaping Western attitudes. But he also notes a shift that took placed in Greek tradition—the other major source of Western thought. During the Greek classical age—the Helenistic period from 332 to 63 BCE—Greek culture viewed erotic experience as a basic key to the eternal (Nelson, 1978). By the beginning of the Christian era, however, a body-spirit dichotomy was common in Greek philosophy and culture.

In short, both Judaism and early Greek thought tended to affirm the body and were relatively sex-positive, but around the time of the beginning of the Christian era, both of these strands of Western tradition became dualistic. Sexual alienation and rejection of the body are usually associated with a dualism in which the body or the material is viewed as evil or corrupt, and the spiritual is viewed as separate from the body. Much as we may want to think that contemporary culture has overcome this dualism between mind (or spirit, or soul) and body, Nelson's (1978) book is well worth reading today.

It is important to note that body-negative attitudes are not unique to Christianity. Buddhist practice emphasizes the use of the natural rhythms of breathing as a basic way to move out of words into a meditative state. Yet parts of Buddhism even more explicitly reject the body than do many strands of Christianity; the rejection of sex and bodily expressiveness is considered essential to the attainment of freedom—in contrast to the words of Buddha cited at the beginning of this chapter. For many centuries Hinduism made use of sexual yoga (tantric tradition) as a way of approaching the divine—the beautiful and explicitly sexual sculptures on the sides of some medieval Hindu temples attest to this practice (see the photo essay on Khajuraho by Narain, Arya, & Dube, 1986). Yet much of day-to-day Hindu life was regulated with strict, caste-based rules and prohibitions (Nelson, 1978). Even our views of "primitive cultures" as freer and more natural about sexuality express only one side of a complex ambivalence. Some indigenous groups were strongly antisexual; the people of Manus Island, New Guinea, for example, degraded sex and rigidly controlled its expression (Nelson, 1978; Mead, 1935, 1953).

Western Christian History

Returning to Western history, during the first centuries of the early Christian church many of the negative views of the body and sexuality became more and more institutionalized in the church, and eventually the whole hierarchy of the Roman Church mandated celibacy. Furthermore, only males were allowed to be in decision-making positions.

Though somewhat oversimplified, there is considerable truth in the summary "Christianity did not make the world ascetic: rather the world in which Christianity found itself strove to make Christianity ascetic" (Enslin, 1930, p. 180).

We have very few recorded comments from Jesus on matters of sex and gender. However, the few we do have are striking given the prevailing ethos of spiritualistic and patriarchal dualism (Nelson, 1978). Jesus explicitly condemned infidelity and divorce as violations of the creator's intended one-flesh union of woman and man. He insisted on the supreme importance of love and forgiveness in sexual matters as well as in every other area of life. And he insisted on the fundamental equality of the sexes (Nelson, 1978). His consistent concern for the oppressed included a rejection of oppressing women and treating them as property in divorce (Nelson, 1978).

The letters of Paul contain more explicit statements of sexuality and the body than those of Jesus; Paul presents a rather ambivalent view, seeing the body as leading us astray: "I pommel my body and subdue it" (I Corinthians 9:27, RSV). "While we are at home in the body we are away from the Lord" (II Corinthians 5:6b, RSV). Yet he also states that "your body is the temple of the Holy Spirit within you. . . . So glorify God in your body." (I Corinthians 6:19, 20, RSV).

But in the period after Paul, the first five centuries after the New Testament era, the church fathers were "far less ambivalent about the sexual body than was Paul. By and large, they were simply negative" (Nelson, 1978, p. 52). Unfortunately we have almost no writings from this period except those of the males at the top of the church's hierarchy, so we don't know if the ordinary priests or the laity or the women of the church shared these sex-negative views (Nelson, 1978). The church hierarchy, besides being totally male, also became restricted by a rule of celibacy, so that official Roman Catholic doctrine on sexuality was propagated totally by men who, in theory at least, were not having sexual experience.

The Protestant Reformation brought two changes in sexual attitudes. Marriage was lifted by Luther to a new level of affirmation, and virginity and celibacy were less valued. Calvin argued that companionship, rather than procreation, was God's chief intention for marriage (Nelson, 1978). Unfortunately, the combination of the emphasis on women being companions for men and the deemphasis on celibacy narrowed the options for women to have roles relatively independent of men (such as becoming nuns). Thus, though Protestantism began a return toward a more positive view of marriage and sex such as had pervaded Jewish culture, it did little to overcome the gender imbalance, and it did not bring about a move to sex-positive attitudes; ambivalence about sexuality remained.

Gradually a particular form of Protestantism emerged, Puritanism, which viewed all forms of physical pleasure as contrary to spiritual development. In its extreme forms, Puritanism taught that a person should not enjoy the taste of food while eating, nor the pleasure of sex while having intercourse, but should carry out these acts only because of their necessary function for life. Though this extreme form of Protestantism was never pervasive, it was the form of religion that the early colonizers of what is now the United States brought to America. The United States is the only country founded by Puritans, and thus has lived through some of the harshest of sex-negative views of spirituality.

The Body: A Positive View

The sex-negative view of the body is not necessarily a Christian view. The traditional church doctrines insist that Jesus was fully human, yet the church and countless Christians have trouble believing that Jesus was, therefore, a sexual being. The Vatican document on gender differences (Ratzinger, 2004) emphasized that God chose to be incarnated in the male form, in Christ, yet it implies that the normal functions of a Jewish male—marriage and procreation—were not part of Jesus' historical experience. In fact, the gospels[1] do not record Jesus ever claiming that he was born of a virgin, or that he was a virgin himself. Although he was sharply critical of certain aspects of Judaism, there's no evidence he criticized the Jewish faith-culture about its rejection of celibacy both in theory and in practice.

It seems likely that Jesus, during the period about which we have no written information (between his ages of 12 and 30) had followed the prevailing custom and married as a young man. Thus Phipps (1975) concludes that the notion of a celibate savior is a later outgrowth of Christianity's being influenced by Greek dualism. As Nelson (1978) points out, this is not simply a curious historical debate. If we are not really sure about the full humanity of the one we claim is "truly human," we can only be confused about what authentic humanity might mean for us. "If we retreat from thoughts of his sexuality . . . it is . . . likely that we shall either deny much of our own sexuality, or [have trouble] integrating our Christological beliefs into the reality of our lives . . . " (Nelson, 1978, p. 77).

Some of the early gospels that were suppressed at the time the Roman Empire and the Catholic Church established a canon (the Bible) have been rediscovered. In the period a century or so after Christianity emerged, many Christians were influenced by the philosophy of gnosticism, which taught that salvation comes from knowledge (or wisdom) of our true nature. For gnostics, our true nature is that we are "sparks of the divine" that have become entrapped in the body. The material world, including the body, was believed to be the result of a cosmic mistake. Many of the sayings of Jesus that appear in the (noncanonical) Gospel of Thomas reflect this gnostic view that the body is only a trap, and not part of our true essence. Some gnostic Christians believed Jesus was not really incarnated, but was a divine being who took on human appearance (Ehrman, 2002). This rejection of the full humanity of Christ was later called docetism, and both docetism and gnosticism were declared heresies by the fourth century Roman church (Nelson, 1978).

The classical doctrine of incarnation in Christianity points to a more basic sense that we are our bodies, and our bodies are not denigrated by God, but are accepted as a vehicle for God's grace.

What is your attitude toward your own body? Does this view seem congruent with your religious upbringing? Have you gone through a process of learning to affirm your body? What would you consider an appropriate process of rethinking the spiritual view of the body?

Gaining Knowledge through the Body Senses

In the period of early Christianity, the Greek Platonists thought of the soul as timeless and immaterial, and the senses were of no account in knowing the real world, the world of changeless truth. Pure contemplation and the ascetic ideal were celebrated, and marriage, family, and earthly ties were renounced (Nelson, 1978). By Jesus' time, Roman Stoicism had become the reigning ethical philosophy. Seneca (a Stoic philosopher and contemporary of Jesus) taught that the sign of true greatness was the achievement of a psychological state in which nothing could possibly disturb or excite one. This was not so much a rejection of the body itself as a rejection of passion.

We now know that our understanding of the natural world comes to us through our senses. "Truth" is not a pure idea floating in the air, but is our construction of concepts and perceptions that are based on the sounds and sights and other sensations that come through our bodies. The Platonists had a negative view of the emotions that emerge from the body, as these emotions hindered the development of a placid state that they believe allowed the pure ideas to more easily enter the mind. We now realize that learning is most likely to be retained if it occurs in conjunction with some emotional response. Knowledge and wisdom come to us through our bodies.

This is not to say that the science of classical Greece had it all wrong. This science acknowledges a kind of mindfulness, or opening the mind in a quiet state, that leads to wisdom. This is the process of awakening that is referred to in the opening quote attributed to the

Buddha. But even this type of wisdom comes through accepting the body.

The deeper wisdom of classical Greece, I believe, lies in the myths. The story of Narcissus is particularly relevant here, because it points out an error in modern pop psychology about "self-image." The story directly discusses self-love focused on the body. Narcissus looked into a spring pond, fell in love with himself, and stared longingly into ponds and lakes, feeling his love was unrequited. He pined away, died, and was transformed into the flower narcissus.

The obvious message of this ancient myth is that too much focus on one's own looks or one's self can be destructive. The development of mature self-love is not focused on how a person looks to others, or how a person looks in the mirror; rather, it is a celebration of the sensuous and feelings of the body and the world as they are directly experienced.

On the factual level, it is interesting to note that throughout human history few persons have had the opportunity to see themselves clearly reflected. The water in natural lakes and ponds is rarely still enough to see ones own reflection, and until recently, only the very rich could afford glass or metal mirrors with smooth enough surfaces to reflect an undistorted image. Staring into a mirror each morning to shave or apply makeup is a relatively modern convenience, but one that feeds into believing the media's stress on appearances.

It is interesting that only the highest primates (humans, chimpanzees, and bonobas [new world chimps]) are able to recognize that a reflected image is oneself. Other animals, looking at their own reflections, move around hunting for another animal behind the mirror (de Wall, 1996). A body of social science research on the phenomenon of "self-focused attention" involves the study of the behavioral effects when people are led to focus on an image of themselves projected by a mirror or video camera. These studies show that the ability to conceptualize or experience one's self separate from others is closely related to internalizing the values of one's social reference group, to noticing discrepancies between one's behavior and one's internalized values, to anxiety and alienation or loneliness. (See Samuel & Dollinger, 1989, and Schwartzer & Wicklund, 1991, for a review of research on self-focused attention.) Much of our looking at ourselves has to do with our perceptions of how we appear to perspective mates.

Thus we criticize our looks in terms of our idealized images of gender-appropriate looks.

For the most part, what we call *body image* is not naturally developed from an external perspective on oneself. It is a person's awareness of his or her own body sensations from *inside* that is most important to the development of the person's self, not the image in the mirror or imaginations. An acceptance of one's body involves a return to trusting the direct sensations rather than the image others see. It is the experiential knowledge of one's body that opens the gates to spirituality. (We will return to this assertion in a later section.)

Recent Scientific Evidence Refuting the Split of Mind and Body

As noted previously, a theological perspective need not be sex-negative. The dualistic view of "soul" (or mind) versus body no longer fits with current scientific information. For example, the development of medications that markedly change the mental processes (psychotropic drugs) demonstrates that biological processes undergird cognitive and emotional states. This is not a new discovery. Psychologists have known for more than a century that injuries to particular parts of the brain result in specific and sometimes irrevocable losses of mental functions. Anyone who has ever woken up with a hangover has some sense of how susceptible the brain is to poison. We now know that certain chemicals in the brain transmit messages from one brain cell to another. At least two of these, serotonin and norepinephrine, play a role in psychological depression. In ways not fully understood and too complex to detail here, medications that affect the levels of these chemicals can markedly improve sleep patterns, ability to work and concentrate, interest in food, and other behavior patterns related to depression. This does *not* prove that depression is simply a biological phenomenon; we know otherwise, since psychotherapy is as effective in relieving depression as are psychotropic drugs. (Psychotherapy is even *more* effective than drugs in some patients.) What is clear is that when depression occurs, so do changes in brain chemistry, and when the right corrections in brain chemistry occur, whether induced by drugs, aerobic exercise, or psychotherapy, depression is diminished. The mind and the body/brain are not independent entities.

Note that these facts do not imply a simple, unidirectional view of determinism. Another example of recent scientific learning involves new imaging techniques that allow neuropsychologists to observe the changes that take place in the brain when new learning occurs. Just as psychopharmacology makes it clear that the chemistry of the brain affects the processes of thinking and feeling, neurological imaging techniques make it clear that the processes of learning change the structure of the brain (Siegel, 2002).

> Everything we learn . . . causes millions of neurons to fire together, forming physical interconnections called neural maps or networks, the architecture of all our experiences. (Wylie & Simon, 2002, p. 28)

Though the details of the interaction are only beginning to be teased out, the Cartesian dualism of mind versus body, and the theological view that mind and body are opposite and conflicting aspects of humanity, do not fit with the now observable interactions and connections.

Another example of the unity of mind and body has to do with the emotions. At the level of self-reflection, this example may be the most obvious: the root of the word *emotion* has to do with what moves us, and most of us recognize that our emotions are a combination of our thoughts and our feelings. The conventional view is that information about the world is transmitted via our eyes, ears, and other senses to the thalamus, the brain's central relay station, which then ships it directly to the neocortex, the "thinking brain." There the incoming signals are recognized and assigned meaning, and then passed on to the limbic system (the "emotional brain"), which triggers the appropriate visceral response. Though this appears to be how the system usually works, important exceptions exist. Work at the Center for Neural Science at New York University has revealed a parallel pathway that acts as a supersonic express route to the limbic system. In emergencies, the neocortex is bypassed entirely, and the signals are routed directly to the amygdala, a tiny structure in the limbic system that scans the information for potential danger. The amygdala can be thought of as the brain's emotional alarm center. It broadcasts a distress signal to the entire brain, setting off all the physiological changes referred to as the "fight or flight" responses. "Within milliseconds, we explode with rage or freeze in fear, well before our conscious mind can even grasp what's happening" (Atkinson, 1999, p. 22). This piece of our neurological design has had enormous benefits for our survival as a species. However, in many a communication between spouses or partners, it is very damaging. As Atkinson puts it:

> Before you can say "reframe that thought," the amygdala is sounding its sirens and suddenly he's yelling that she's the slob, not him, in fact, she's let herself go big-time and is . . . damn fat. And as he's shouting all this, his face is turning the color of boiled lobster, his heart is practically leaping out of his chest and he's sweating gallons. Depending on your theoretical orientation, you might say this man had just contacted his "wounded child," or that he had been sabotaged by his "problem story" or that he was reenacting a hurtful, family-of-origin script. But at the level of brain wiring, his neocortex just got hijacked by his amygdala. (Atkinson, 1999, p. 22).

This response is not simply the result of early traumatic memories. Our memory bank of factual data, the hippocampus, doesn't fully develop until we are at least two years old—but the hardwiring of the amygdala is fully mature at birth.

It is important to note that not all emotions can "hijack" the neocortex. Usually it is the fear response that, once triggered, is very hard to "unlearn." This bypassing the neocortex in times of danger had important advantages for survival. (For a more thorough but readable discussion of the neuropsychology involved, see Johnson, 2004, especially pp. 61-70.)

The most persuasive example of the unity of mind and body, for me personally, is an experience I had in late 2000 with encephalitis. Although encephalitis usually begins with physical symptoms such as a high fever, in rare cases (about 50 have been documented) it begins with what appears to be a psychiatric disease. In my case, soon after I returned from an exhausting drive in hours of snow, followed by a flight back from New York to Chicago with my 91-year-old mother, my wife began observing that I was becoming more and more manic. Since my wife is a psychiatric nurse, and since I trust her deeply, I could not dismiss her observations, though it did not seem to me that I was behaving strangely, and if I was, I thought it was just my exhaustion. However, a day or two later I found myself screaming at my wife, and realized she was afraid of me—both of which are totally deviant from our normal interactions. She finally persuaded me that it wouldn't hurt to have an evaluation, though I had begun to have fantasies of being locked up for years on a psychiatric ward as a political prisoner. I was fearful that my objections to the future Bush government's (then delusional) plans of war would be used against me. Though one could argue that later events (such as the Patriot Act and the imprisoning of citizens without allowing access to lawyers) proved me somewhat prophetic, the fantasies grew to truly paranoid levels. I became suspicious of the equipment in the hospital room where I was examined, convinced the government was using it to spy on me. Fortunately, our family doctor had grown up in India, and he knew I had recently returned from teaching in India. He had known me for 25 years and was convinced of my emotional stability. With this context, and his experiences in India, he declared that my behavior was typical of the (rare) psychiatric-onset encephalitis, and persuaded the rest of the medical team. After heavy doses of antibiotics and antivirals, the manic and psychotic symptoms disappeared.

Clearly the sane functioning of my mind is dependent on my brain having the exact physical conditions it needs. When an infection produced swelling in parts of my brain (encephalitis) my mental and emotional functioning became as deranged as the most disturbed of my clients. Certainly psychological or social conditions can also affect mental and emotional functioning, but, at minimum, mental health requires a physically healthy brain.

It is important to face that who we are as humans is very much influenced by the wiring of our body/minds. At least, in certain abnormal conditions, e.g., clinical depression, "hardwiring" may determine behavior to a large extent. This does not mean that rage, for example, is usually a result of hardwiring in a normal person. Rage and aggression may be the result of general arousal, which can be modified, mitigated, and reinterpreted.

Our uniqueness is embedded in the fact that we are concrete, embodied selves. Stated another way, the scientific view is that "there must be some universal human traits that come with the equipment. . . . When I ask what humans are like deep down inside, I am asking what comes with our kind of body, or our kind of animal—(and) I do think of us as animals" (Flanigan, cited in Dalai Lama & Goleman, 2003, p. 59).

Check your own experience. When you are sick, or tired, what is your spirit like? When your body is up, is your spirit also up? Are there exceptions, times when your spirit is strong though the body is weak?

Spirit Affects Body, for Good and Bad

The interdependence of body and spirit does not mean simply that the spirit must operate through the body. The influence is two-way. Some spiritual practices seem to lead to a healthier body. The strongest evidence concerns the practice of mindfulness meditation and yoga relaxation meditation. Documented health benefits include lower blood pressure and less reactivity of blood pressure and of stress hormones under challenge conditions. Changes in breathing, relaxation, and stress all impact the autonomic nervous system, and meditation leads to changes that have salutary results. (See a review of research in Seeman, Dubin, & Seeman, 2003.)

The evidence of the physical value of some spiritual practices should not be taken for a generalized endorsement of religion and spirituality, however. Evidence suggests that certain religious beliefs can interfere with healing, particularly when the patient has been led to expect physical healing and then, in its absence, believes God has abandoned him or her, or when dependence on faith has led to neglecting medical treatment (Powell, Shahabi, & Thoresen, 2003).

Distinguishing the Physical from the Material

As stated, my declaration that affirming one's body can enhance spirituality is based on an experiential, rather than external, orientation to the body. It is important to distinguish the body, a living system, from the material. A life grounded in the body is very different from a life of striving to acquire material things. Sensing our own bodies from within is not easily learned in our culture.

> We Americans are a nation of compulsive workers who prefer activity with end products, like contracts or new cars, to activity that has no visible goal, like meditation or sitting in the sun. We admire and emulate people who are very good at producing a great deal of evidence of their efforts—such as corporation pres-

idents, sports figures, or movie producers. Since we evaluate people based on what they produce and consume, we all wish to prove our worth by showing how much we can do. We fill our days with tasks . . . we always have a feeling of racing against time. We wear watches on our wrists and constantly check them to see how we're doing. . . .

When you lead a goal-oriented life, you pay attention to your ideas, your plans, and your expectations rather than to your feelings and the sensations of your body. Your body becomes little more than the mobile equipment that gets you across the street and to your appointments. . . . Your body intrudes on your goal-oriented consciousness only to demand food or sleep and to register pain. In this situation, your body never gets a chance to relax, to be itself, to please itself; it is always at the disposal of your head-derived concepts and goals. . . .

In many other cultures it is commonplace to retreat from everyday life for a prescribed time and get in touch with the aspect of ourselves that is not goal-directed and time-oriented, that is not concerned with gaining or losing, but is boundless and infinite. I call this aspect The One Who Is Not Busy. (Cohen, 2002, p. 119-122).

TWO TYPES OF BODY-CENTERED SPIRITUALITY: MEDITATION AND PASSION

Meditation

The Body, Grounding, and Incarnational Spirituality

Cohen's (2002) portrayal of "The One Who is Not Busy" comes close to describing the body state of a practiced meditator: goal-less, relaxed, living in the present, centered. The importance of the body goes beyond the practical fact that if our lives are interrupted by physical difficulty or pain, sensation is where we need to go to find out how to remedy these (Cohen, 2002, p. 121). It even goes beyond the concern for pleasure and balance in living. It is the body that grounds us in the present experience. Our ideas, our plans, our expectations, all have their role, but they move us out of present experience to the past and the future. They move us to doing. The sensual presence keeps us grounded in the now, in just being.

A genuine incarnational spirituality affirms the embodied human spirit, and to recognize that it is possible to be "too spiritual." That is, when a human becomes too focused on emotions and/or spirit and loses touch with the present, concrete reality, it involves a form of pride, the "sin" of hubris, an attempt to be God. Hinterkopf (1998) defines a "spiritual emergency" as being "overwhelmed by distressing feelings and preoccupied with spiritual content to the detriment of other dimensions of wellness" (p. 30). She describes a patient, "Mr. R.," who came to her

> because he was preoccupied with thoughts that another soul had taken over his body. He felt overpowered by an overwhelming energy that he called Kundalini energy. He experienced [this]. . . energy in his penis and in his heart. When I asked him to describe [it]. . . he said it felt like he would burst with energy, and it caused extreme discomfort. [This] extreme discomfort indicated that he needed more distance. (Hinterkopf, 1998, pp. 30-31)

The focusing method of counseling, as Hinterkopf explains it, involves helping the client find the appropriate distance from which to approach their issue or problem. Being centered can be conceptualized as finding a midpoint between openness and groundedness. A person in spiritual crisis is open to the point of being overwhelmed, and needs grounding techniques. So Hinterkopf (1998) suggests to Mr. R.

> that he might imagine himself as a neutral reporter who could describe the energy to me. He said that the energy was so overpowering that it felt like another being had walked into his body. It felt and looked like a balloon ready to burst.
>
> At this point I thought he had enough distance, so I suggested that he ask, "What in my life feels like this uncomfortable energy?" After many moments of silence he said he was getting an image of sucking on another man's penis. He realized that this energy had to do with his bisexuality, a fact that he didn't like to admit. The energy in his heart had to do with his love for

> women. I then asked him how the whole thing felt in his body now, and he said that the energy had calmed down and he felt relaxed, as though he were in a bed of light. (pp. 31-32)

Hinterkopf explains her work as follows:

> In this example, finding more distance from his overpowering energy helped Mr. R. become more *centered.* This, along with describing the feeling in his body and asking the Focusing question "What in my life feels like this?" helped *ground* him. After finding *the right distance,* he could *realize new connections* between the . . .energy and his bisexuality. (Hinterkopf, 1998, p. 32. Emphasis mine)

Mr. R's bisexuality becomes more integrated through this process. It is *embodied, rather than disowned* as if "another being had walked into [his] body."

The therapist's ability to help the client become realistically grounded in his or her own body is important to spiritual work in counseling; it reduces the risk of the client being overwhelmed by outside pressures and stress, or by intense spiritual experiences. Body awareness is an antidote to the flooding of transcendent or mystical experiences. This is in contrast to the situation in which clients "are too distant from their feelings regarding spiritual content," which Hinterkopf labels "spiritual repression"; for those the mirror opposite approach is used: techniques to open up to feelings (Hinterkopf, 1998, pp. 30, 33).

It is worth noting that counselors who are not familiar with spiritual emergencies or crises are likely to mistake them for mental disorder. Certainly some of the symptoms are the same. The response needed in a spiritual emergency may involve some of the skills that are used with mental illness, such as more directive techniques, and setting boundaries to reduce anxiety and flooding. But antipsychotic medications are likely to do more harm than good by blunting the growth potential of the spiritual experience. Spiritual emergencies contrast with most mental illnesses in that they are more likely to have sudden onset, intense temporary distress, but limited duration. An assessment of the client's own spiritual development, and their perception of their life as "on a spiritual journey" are crucial to differentiation. (See Hinterkopf, 1998, pp. 233-248, on assessment of spiritual emergencies and psychopathology.)

Being present in your body during stressful situations is particularly helpful, and body awareness meditations are especially useful in cultivating the ability to return to your physical body (e.g., to ones breathing) again and again, in whatever situation you find yourself. Eventually you understand intuitively that your body is the ground of your consciousness. You are not just a mind. "Awareness of body, breath, or sense impressions is a very grounding and settling reference point for the attention because they are not involved in the . . . judgments [about gaining or losing] of our day-to-day lives" (Cohen, 2000, p. 209). Judgments come from the head, not from the direct sense experience.

It is not coincidental that the word in Hebrew for the spirit of God is *breath.* To stay spiritually alive, as well as biologically alive, we must keep breathing. The spiritual breathing practice of Buddhist and Hindu meditation begin with learning to follow our breath, and the top priority in overcoming the fear that inhibits our spiritual growth is to pause and breathe. This practice helps us remember who we really are (Kornfield, 1993), especially when flooded by fear or tension.

Sensory Experience, A Gateway to the Holy

It is important to note, at this point, that when I refer to sensory experience as a gateway to the holy I am not implying that entering the holy is experienced only by those of us who are schooled in the aesthetics of poetry and the fine arts. Though I believe that many of the readers of this book would find their spiritual experience enhanced if they more regularly read poetry, I also think that many "common men" (and women) experience the holy but do not label it as such, partly because both academic theology and the institutions of religion have become in some sense elitist.

One example is music. Anyone who has observed the growth of a child who is at all rhythmic will be convinced that music affects that child even before he or she is verbal. Some children love to move with a beat months before they are able to speak in sentences. Music is visceral; it pulls at body and soul—and the pull is unified. It animates us, enlivens us, fills us with spirit. Perhaps the most primary aspect of the spiritual life is that it is experienced as integration. I've struggled for decades with Kierkegaard's phrase "purity of heart is to will one thing" (Kierkegaard, 1938). Perhaps he was trying to express that integration is the primary experience of the spiritual. Music may express this even more fully than poetry, because music itself is preverbal.

It is clarifying to look at this from the negative perspective, from the opposite of wholeness, the perspective of alienation. If the mind is alienated from the body, so also is the body from the mind. The body becomes a physical object possessed and used by the self. A sense of unity with the spontaneous rhythms of the body is lacking, as is the sense of full participation in the body's stresses and pains, its joys and delights. The body is experienced as a machine (Nelson, 1978). Alienation from the body, as with all alienation, is the root experience of sin, and involves not only alienation from the self, but from others and from God (Nelson, 1978).

Notice also that music is not contrary to mind—and as the child grows, his or her musical "taste" integrates more and more "mental" aspects. Music may become more and more sophisticated; yet, when it is really experienced and integrated, sophisticated music does not enter us purely as an intellectual experience. It doesn't just inform us or educate us; it awakens us and moves us. (I have noticed how frequently the announcements and appeals from the Chicago Symphony Orchestra stress the power of symphonic music to "move" us.)

It is important to remember that this power is not restricted to highbrow music. Lovers of country, rock, or pop music, when they are not afraid that they will be denigrated for their taste, often speak of the power of their favorite music to move them, or to make them want to dance. This is clear across all age levels and all degrees of sophistication or "primitiveness." One of the most enjoyable aspects of travel in other civilizations is participating in the dancing (call it "folk dancing" if you like) of the particular culture.

The connection of music to the holy, the whole, has little to do with sophistication. As stated, music is preverbal. Music is so important to the structure of human thought and communication that one of the most prominent theories of the origin of language contends that in human development singing preceded talking and formed the basis of human language. Singing expresses the most primitive and essential aspects of human survival—for example, courtship and territoriality (Skoyles, 2000)—and the human brain seems to be hardwired to acquire language and to link it to music (McMullen, 2004). Modern humans have been described as "musical primates" (Vaneechoutte & Skoyles, 1998).

Spiritual experiences rooted in musical expression seem to reverberate with this primitive connection. The beauty and joy of song and dance are part of many of the sacred scriptures—most notably in the Psalms. The tradition of singing and chanting continues throughout the history of Judaism and most other ancient religions. It is hard to imagine a Jewish wedding without dancing. My guess is that Jesus participated in the dancing at the wedding in Cana, where the records state he performed a miracle to provide enough wine. It seems probable that the dancing was edited out of the story by the first century transcribers of the records because of their dualistic views regarding body and soul, just as twentieth century protestants who supported prohibition did their best to edit out the wine in that story. Similarly, in non-Western religions music plays an important part. Within the Hindu tradition is a section of scripture (a veda) devoted to music, the Sama Veda, as well as a science and art of music (Nritya Shastra). My point is to indicate that the aesthetic experience is a central pathway to the holy,[2] but *aesthetic experience* itself is too intellectualized a phrase; a more holistic way to state this would be to declare that "pleasure is a gateway to the spiritual," though this statement could be misconstrued to mean selfish or exploitive grasping, in contrast to an integrative experience of contact.

Pleasure is a Gateway to the Spiritual

Pleasure in particular seems to me a gateway to the spiritual because it is intrinsically tied to the process of letting go. Pleasure cannot be possessed. A person must give himself or herself over to the pleasure—that is, allow the pleasure to take possession of his or her being. Whereas the response of pain involves a heightening of self-consciousness, the response of pleasure entails and demands a decrease of self-consciousness. "Pleasure eludes . . . the egotist. To have pleasure one has to . . . allow the body to respond freely" (Lowen, 1975, p. 82).

Of course, a fear exists in traditional religion that if pleasure is boldly affirmed, it may lead to a self-indulgence that will be destructive of personal communion and love. Certainly, in everyday experience sexual desires often are not immediately felt as interpersonal.

> When I enjoy and love my bodily self, body and self are united. . . . It is precisely this momentarily-healed self who is able to experience the depth of communion with the partner. (Nelson, 1978, p. 89, citing Milhaven, 1974).

"Self-love is not erased, for it has positive worth" (Nelson, 1978, p. 99). The affirmation that life, or self, is not just a body, that in some experiences the "I" transcends the body, longs for expression. Nonetheless, the orthodox Christian view is that the body is not evil in itself, and that the Christ was fully human, God was incarnate, in a real material body. Similarly, the early Christians insisted (in contrast to the later gnostic and docetic views) that the resurrection of Christ was truly a physical resurrection. In short, despite its ambivalence about sexuality and gender, orthodox Christian doctrine went to some lengths to stress that the body is not alien to divinity.

To put this in experiential terms, I am more than my body, but that more is dependent on the body. We are alive because we are embodied; the body must not be denigrated or diminished. I don't become "more" by separating from my body, or dissociating, but by inhabiting my body. I know myself by accepting my body—not by viewing it as an entrapment. The logos is embodied.

Passion: Excitation As the Path to Involvement and Commitment

Another "common" example of the experience of the body as self-transcending or holy is that music is recognized by most persons as a unifying experience, but—because of elitist views—may not be acknowledged as a holy experience. This is even more the case for the experience of sexual orgasm. Though I believe many women in Westernized cultures still feel a deep sense of connectedness with other people, especially with their infants and children, many men in Western culture have their sense of connectedness deeply undermined by the masculine stress on objectification and competition.

For many men, the most powerful connectedness they experience occurs during sexual orgasm. Nelson (1978) points out that to deny the experience of orgasm's spiritual status is to alienate many persons from their most valuable and holy experience. The experience of sexual orgasm has at least three components that qualify it to be appropriately labeled a spiritual experience: First, the physical experience involves a form of surrender, a letting go, in contrast to the usual masculine attempt to control one's body. It involves relaxing into the experience rather than performing it. Second, sexual orgasm often occurs while embracing and entering another; it involves transcending self. This is not simply a physical experience; biologically, for the man, it involves the letting go of the ejaculate, but experientially, it is frequently experienced as a merging into the other, a letting go of the boundaries of the self. The orgasm itself is often felt as a self-surrender or transcendence, a feeling of vulnerability and relaxing into the other—a surrender not just of ejaculate, but of boundaries. Third, for many men it provides their deepest moment of serenity. Though that serenity includes a relaxation of muscle and mind, which leads many men into slumber (and may lead their partners to feel abandoned), the experience of serenity is, in itself, a holy moment.

Much of organized Western religion is afraid to talk about the mystical dimensions of sexual orgasm. This aversion is partly due to the sex-negative attitudes that have pervaded much of organized Christianity. However, another reason for the negative stance of institutional religion toward the body may exist: the implications that trusting a profound personal experience may have for submission to authority. To accept that the experience of "oneness" during sexual orgasm is a legitimate mystical experience involves the risk that individuals will come to believe that they do not need the church hierarchy to mediate between them and the divine. The very allure, power, and numinousness of sexuality makes it a threat to official religious authority. Thus fear of sexuality may be encouraged by institutional religious authority because numinous experiences, whether sensual or mystical, undermine the need for priests and shamans as mediators.

Consider the role of deep pleasure in your own life, as illustrated by music and sex. Have either or both of these been viewed as separate from, or inimical to, your spiritual life? How do you want to further explore the connections?

Passion As Connectedness

Nelson (1978), in his articulation of the implications of sex for religious experience, notes that knowing and motivation are not separated; feelings are responses springing from what we are, and they are neither antirational nor irrational. "The feeling response . . . is the willingness to respond with as much of the totality of the self as one is able . . . the capacity to be deeply aroused by what we are experiencing" (Nelson, 1978, p. 31-32). Nelson uses the term *desire* to denote the active longing that yearns to know. He points out that the Old Testament occasionally uses the verb *to know* (*yadáh*) as a synonym for sexual intercourse (Nelson, 1978). "In the union of desiring and knowing, the partner is treated as a self, the treasured participant in communion." "Desire is both an expression of the body, and an intrinsic element in our openness to God." The Hebrew scripture "Song of Songs" (sometimes called "Song of Solomon") is a love song; it celebrates the richly sensuous love between a woman and a man. Its inclusion in the Bible has embarrassed many Christians, but Dietrich Bonhoeffer (a theologian martyred by the Nazis) wrote, "It's a good thing that the book is included in the Bible as a protest against those who believe that Christianity stands for the restraint of passion" (Bonhoeffer, 1953, p. 131). The doctrine of incarnation implies that the body is not merely the necessary physical structure through which the spoken and written word must come, but the body can be the word itself, the "Word made flesh." (Nelson, 1978). The body is the way we know the world, the self, and the divine (Nelson, 1978).

DISCIPLINE AND SELF-CONTROL

Because of my emphasis on the experiential, the reader may assume that I view spirituality primarily as being receptive to certain experiences. Yet "genuine spiritual work is not about a single experience—or 100 experiences. It is a way of life. A path without end" (McCorkle, 1966, p. 89). It requires very hard discipline (or discipleship). Similar to any other bodily sport or art—such as basketball or ballet—it does not develop spontaneously out of experience; it is a practice. The key to practice is attention.

However, though discipline takes practice, spiritual discipline cannot simply be understood as self-control. Discipline involves remaining open to the experience rather than trying to force it to preconceived needs of the self. It is not "willful" in the sense of pushing against self or reality. Self-control, in contrast, involves behaviors that require willpower. Baumeister (2003) conducted a series of experiments with 800 participants to investigate the levels of energy required for exercising self-control and resisting temptation. He theorized that when willpower gets depleted a person can become vulnerable to impulsive behaviors such as overeating or abuse of alcohol. In one experiment, participants who had skipped a meal were tempted with freshly baked cookies and chocolates. Three groups of subjects were compared: those who were told to resist the treats and eat radishes instead, others who were left to make their own choices, and a third group who had not been exposed to the treats. Afterward all respondents were asked to complete an insolvable geometric puzzle. Those who had been presented with treats but resisted them tended to give up on the puzzle sooner than participants who had been allowed to indulge, or those who had not been presented with them. Baumeister (2003) interprets these results to support the notion of self-control as a process that consumes energy.

Another study involved two groups of participants who viewed an upsetting video. One group was asked to control their emotional responses by stifling them (*self-control*); a second group was told to amplify their reactions (*self-expressive*). (Italicized phrases are my additions, elaborated in the next paragraph.) The researchers then gauged their physical stamina by testing how long they could squeeze a handgrip device. The group who stifled their emotions tended to give up faster on the handgrip task than those who expressed their emotions—a pattern of results again suggesting that maintaining control depletes or tires one out. Baumeister (2003) is completing further analysis of the data, but the evidence so far suggests that depleted self-control can be restored through sleep and through positive emotional experiences such as humor and laughter (Dittman, 2003).

Clearly self-control that stifles expression uses more energy. It is a Spartan style of discipline that tries to manipulate the self to fit some ideal. In these two experiments, self-control is complying with the requests of the experimenter and the external "should." On the other hand, simply following the pleasure of each moment with no concern for the longer-term value (of eating or rejecting sweets, or of stifling or expressing feelings) amounts to action without awareness. I use the word *discipline* to refer to choices made with perspective, in response to more than the narrow "self."

From a spiritual perspective, it is instructive to notice the connection between discipline and having positive emotional experiences. An interplay exists between relaxing and getting energized, between letting go and being rejuvenated. These are not opposites, but part of one process, similar to breathing out and breathing in. If one imagines self-control to be some frozen posture, a military man with chest out and stomach in, one misses the dynamic process. Instead, maintaining discipline is similar to breathing; it respects the benefits of breathing out, and it recognizes that air is a resource that must be replenished, and takes care of self by breathing in again.

The spiritual practice of letting go, and it's connection with physical relaxation, is explored in Experiment 2, "Quiet Self"; Experiment 5, "Relaxing"; and Experiment 6, "Self Soothing" in Chapter 11. If you have not yet completed Chapter 11, now would be a good time to go back to it.

It is noteworthy that Nelson (1978), in his exploration of the role of feelings in self-transcendence, also takes note of the capacity to be deeply aroused. This theme is highlighted in the anthropological reports of psychologist Bradford Keeney, who has lived for many years with the Kalahari Bushman of southern Africa. Keeney believes that Western science and medicine have disproportionately emphasized the role of relaxation in healing, and have failed to balance it with the important role of energizing. Among the Kalahari Bushman, dancing and shaking (or vibrating) are viewed as evidence that a person is being aroused by the spirit. Both the relaxation response and the arousal response are involved in healing. And, rather than a practiced discipline of stillness through meditation, the Kalahari dance themselves into stillness—not an exhausted stillness, but stillness as a meditative or trancelike state.

In contrast to the seriousness and piousness that is often associated with Western religion, the Bushman consider joking and even silliness as appropriate preparation for the holiness of dancing. The spiritual is not expected in the sanctimonious, but in that which leads or inspires, that which breaks the heart and finds in the breaking an opening. This recognition is not limited to the Bushman. Within Native American tradition is an awareness of humor, as well as seriousness, as a path to the spiritual. Black Elk states that "Truth comes through two forms: tears, and laughter." (Keeney, 1994, 2002; Black & Neilhardt, 2000).

COMMITMENT: SEX, CONNECTEDNESS, AND EVOLUTION

One more example of research that refutes the dualistic body/soul split comes from the evolutionary study of the brain. The data suggest that moral dispositions develop early in children and are predecessors to religious or spiritual beliefs. Traits that we consider spiritual, such as empathy and connectedness to others, are also traits that have helped the human species survive. Through evolution, our "spiritual" nature appears to have become part of our biological heritage (See Chapter 1, section on "Anthropology and the Common Ground"). Furthermore, studies of the social behavior of the other primates (apes, baboons, gibbons, monkeys) show that empathy, cooperation, and altruism occur under many conditions, even when they do not necessarily benefit the individual displaying these prosocial behaviors. The earlier interpretation of biological evolution as dependent on individual competition for survival has had to be revised (de Wall, 1996). These prosocial responses go beyond tit-for-tat acts of grooming or affection, and occur in situations in which the giving is not reciprocated. Friendship relationships sometimes occur in ways that violate the hierarchies of dominance; sympathetic attachment extends far beyond parent-child bonds, sometimes including a whole group protecting and nurturing a wounded peer (de Wall, 1996).

Cooperative responses that involve individual sacrifice may result in a group competing more effectively against other groups, just as is the case in team sports. Such behaviors promote the survival of a group or species, which is the probable explanation for how altruistic behaviors seem to have been built into the biological structures—including the nervous system—of mammals, and most especially of the primates (See de Waal 1996). Ironically, instead of the material body being "evil," it seems to have embedded in it the predisposition to the spiritual, at least in the sense of altruistic or self-transcending behavior.

The Subjective Experience of the Body and the Self

It is not enough, of course, to make an argument for the dissolution of the mind/body split from the positions of objective science or intellectual reasoning alone. Experientially, I think most of us consider the body as both "me" and "not me" or "only a part of me." The conviction that I am not simply my body, that "I" can't be reduced to just the material me, may be part of what is expressed in the gnostic image of the self as a divine spark. Similarly, the awareness that when the physical body dies, all if the chemicals and cells and sinews that make life possible—the whole body—is still there but the life is gone, leads one to conceptualize that one more element is present (a "soul," or in Hebrew, the "breath") that is necessary to life and has now left.

The conceptual problem is to find ways to express the transcendence of humanness without formulating the human in dualistic terms. This is, at least in part, the problem of two aspects of language, the purely descriptive (which risks sounding reductionist) and the expressive. It may be that the most heuristic or practical solution is to distinguish expressive language from descriptive language; that is, to recognize the value of poetry and other expressive forms of language but to resist taking such expressions literally and (mis)interpreting them as descriptions. Transcendence can be "pointed to" only through myth or poetry. As soon as we try to describe the transcendent, we reduce it to another thing—"something more."

An essay "The Experience of Soul" (Ventura, 2003) provides one of the clearest examinations I've seen of the types of experiences that involve a sense of embodiment and yet evoke the expressions "soul" or "spirit." Michael Ventura describes an experience, when he was only five years old, of watching a group of boys his age kick another five-year-old almost into unconsciousness.

The victim, nicknamed "The Giant" because he was unnaturally large and looked like a ten-year-old, was excluded by the group and sulked about on his own—quiet, reserved, and frightened. "The Giant" was attacked by "Big Archie," a heavy vicious bully.

> On this day in 1950, the pack, with me trailing after it, approached The Giant. Big Archie started punching him on the arm. The Giant didn't respond. Big Archie kept punching, first on the arm and then in the Giant's stomach. The Giant kept repeating "I can't hit you, you're smaller than me." . . . The Giant

> repeated his mantra, even when doubled over by stomach punches: "I can't hit you, you're smaller than me."
>
> When he finally fell down, Big Archie took to kicking him. The others joined in. I remember clearly, but even now cannot fully describe, the depth of my horror as I watched. . . .
>
> It was the first time I can remember feeling viscerally, mentally, emotionally, and inescapably connected to everything and everyone around me—while feeling what I can only describe as a sense of privacy so deep and unassailable that "loneliness" doesn't begin to describe it. . . .
>
> My sense of helplessness made me equally aware of something inescapably vulnerable in myself. My shame was, I realize now, rooted in a sense of responsibility—for I was ashamed not only of the others but for the others: which meant they weren't Other: they were committing an action that (though I had no part in it but as a witness) was something that stained me, too, with a stain that I'd have to find a way to redeem by my own behavior. And I was proud of The Giant—his courage, his dedication to what can only be called a principle of fairness, his determination not to sink to Big Archie's level were beautiful to me. I remember that clearly, the feeling that he was beautiful, a beautiful being. . . .
>
> My sense of Self cohered for the first time through the experience of identifying so closely with these Others. And this is where I go for, not a definition, but a conception of that troubling, thrilling word "soul." (Ventura, 2003)

Ventura's article about Big Archie emphasizes that the word *soul* describes not an entity but an experience "private and personal . . . yet it connects us to everything and everyone around us."[3] Instead of trying to describe soul or spirit as a thing, the essayist Ventura points to the holiness of transcendence in the body itself.

Similarly, Mary Oliver (1994) evokes the naturalness of the spiritual in her poem "Wild Geese."

> You don't have to be good.
> You don't have to walk on your knees
> for a hundred miles through the desert, repenting.
> You only have to let the soft animal of your body
> love what it loves.

Tell me about despair, yours, and I will tell you mine.
Meanwhile the world goes on.
Meanwhile the sun and the clear pebbles of the rain
are moving across the landscapes,
over the prairies and the deep trees,
the mountains and the rivers.
Meanwhile the wild geese, high in the clean blue air,
are heading home again.
Whoever you are, no matter how lonely,
the world offers itself to your imagination,
calls you like the wild geese, harsh and exciting—
over and over announcing your place
in the family of things.

From *Dream Work* by Mary Oliver (1994)

INTEGRATING THE TWO BODILY APPROACHES TO SPIRITUALITY

In the previous material I have rejected the sex-negative and body-negative approach of much of historic and institutionalized Western religion. It seems to me, in my own spiritual life, that two crucial dimensions to a robust spirituality exist. The first is a passionate involvement in life—one's own life, and one's most intimate relationships. Here I am not using *passionate* in its directly sexual sense, but in the sense of caring deeply and passionately, and making commitments. This is an approach that was thoughtfully explored in Sam Keen's (1983) classic work *The Passionate Life*.

However, no particular activity or relationship can be taken as "god" in itself, and we are invariably called to "let go," to relax and just "let it be." This meditative, accepting what is, this surrender to the flow of life, is the second crucial element of a disciplined spiritual life. For me the two seem to form a pulse, a rhythm back and forth, between passionate investment, and letting go.

Though the metaphors of "alternation" and "pulse" seem right to me, they may not be the best metaphors for others. Some may be more attracted to a compromise or integration. Buddha called it "the middle way." The Buddhist affirmation of the sensory experience comes from the Buddha's own experience with desire and deprivation.

Having been raised in a very protective environment as a prince, Siddhartha Gautama (the Buddha) in his early twenties encountered the sad, hard facts of old age, disease, and death. Once faced with the suffering of others, Gautama Buddha at first followed a path of rejecting the pleasure of the senses. He left his father's palace, his beautiful wife, and his newborn son, and wandered into the forest to discover the essential and saving truth about life and death, sorrow and happiness. He spent seven years seeking, struggling, in relentless, torturing self-experiment. He tried ascetic denial of the body's demands in extreme form. He finally succumbed to the dull blankness of a starving swoon.

When he regained consciousness, he was convinced that the path of renunciation was not the way of enlightenment. This radical punishment of the body brought exhaustion, torpor, and impotence of mind, not spiritual illumination and peace. Gradually he found more successful clues to understanding and liberation. His quest reached its culmination in a long period of meditation. Finally, after a period of temptation, he resolved to meditate until he received enlightenment—which tradition states occurred in the full moon of May 544 BCE. Rather than keep this illumination to himself, he determined to attempt to communicate it, and spent the next forty-some years teaching and preaching (Burtt, 1955). The two contrasting periods in the life of the Buddha (the indulged youth and the period of renunciation of pleasure) led to his mature teaching of "the middle way," affirming the body but not becoming addicted to its desires.

Ministering to Others: The Counselor's Role

It is important for the therapist to learn how to help clients nurture their own bodies. Our bodies yearn to be taken care of, and if we are connected to "the One who is not busy" we will feel generous toward our bodies:

> We are aware when we want to rest, to eat, when we need stimulation, when we want to challenge ourselves. We are sometimes indulgent and sometimes firm with our bodies, as with a child. If our bodies disappoint us, as when we have lost functioning that we once had, or we feel impatient with our bodies because they no longer obey our commands like slaves, we can practice letting them have their way or gently directing them here or there

> . . . give them a posture they enjoy, a chance to relax, promising to bathe them in appreciation for what they can do. (Cohen, 2002, p. 126)

Cohen (2002) describes a situation in which it was the client who taught the therapist. Cohen's client was an elderly but very active Japanese tea teacher who came to her with complaints of pain and swelling in her knees. Tea teachers sit on their knees for the better part of the day, and this woman lived where she had to walk up three floors to her apartment, and was concerned about the comfort and functioning of her knees. Cohen taught her how to gently massage her knees and dissolve the arthritic swelling by coaxing it into the bloodstream with her fingers. In the following session a week later, Cohen asked the client to demonstrate the massage technique to be sure she was doing it correctly.

> She put her fingers on her knees, began massaging gently, then added in a tender voice, "Oh, little knees, all these seventy-three years you have helped me so much, supporting me when I walked, holding me when I taught tea, carrying me up all the stairs in my life. Now, little knees, I will take care of you!"

> (Cohen remarks) "I was stunned with admiration. Would that all my clients demonstrated such an attitude toward their ailing parts!" (Cohen, 2002, p. 127)

Spiritual Support for Dealing with Body Rejection

Because our pleasant or unpleasant sensations so quickly trigger a chain reaction of emotions and mental stories, a central part of our training is to recognize the arising of thoughts and return over and over to our immediate sensory experience (Brach, 2003).

With much practice in returning to the sensory experience, and becoming clear what is present and what is verbal commentary, one can recognize pain and suffering without judgment, as "simply another part of the natural world." In dealing with chronic illness, Tara Brach (2003) writes:

> As I continued paying attention I could feel the arising and passing aches and pressures inside me as no different from the firm-

ness of earth, the falling leaves. There was just pain . . . and it was the earth's pain" (pp. 121)

Both of these authors offer meditations and exercises for dealing with pain through sensory awareness of the body experienced from inside out (Brach, 2003; Cohen, 2002). This concluding case illustrates the importance of the body in our sense of self, and the support that spirituality can provide when a person undergoes severe physical losses.

A woman, I'll call her Eleanor, had recently had a mastectomy due to breast cancer. Her husband of more than 30 years moved out of the house soon after she returned from the hospital—he couldn't tolerate being in bed with her now as he saw her as "disfigured." Her mother, who had been her close friend throughout her adult life, had become senile in the past year or so and was no longer mentally capable of engaging in the type of supportive conversation that had meant so much to Eleanor most of her adult life.

Despite the sad, feelingful description of her losses, a caring, warm personality came through in this early interview, and the counselor commented, "Despite all you've lost, you seem so thoughtful, so forgiving." The client responded, "I haven't felt completely alone in this. I can feel that there's a divine presence that stands beside me and cares about me in my hurt."

Fortunately, the counselor recognized that this client already had deep spiritual resources available in her life, and responded to these strengths without trying to minimize her pain or "fix" her. The counselor also showed a willingness to enter the client's spirituality on the client's own terms, by picking up on the language that the client had used in expressing her spiritual trust and encouraging her to say more about this divine presence. Thus the counselor's own belief system was not imposed on the client (Hinterkopf, 1998).

Being solidly grounded in one's own body yet receptive to the client's longings and needs allows a spiritual connection that can affirm the client's physical needs yet transcend them and be healing. If the counselor has become comfortable with her or his own body and sexuality, then the "hot" issue of homosexuality is less likely to be threatening. In the next chapter we will examine that issue.

Chapter 6

Spiritual Implications of Sexual Orientation

Sometimes I get letters and other unsolicited advice from people who tell me I shouldn't speak out for the rights of gay and lesbian people. Somehow they can't make the connection between racism and the bigotry experienced by gays and lesbians. But there is a connection between racist, anti-Semitic, sexist and homophobic attitudes. All are based on a dehumanizing fear that prevents empathy for the suffering of others, a sick need to dehumanize some minority to feel more adequate.

Coretta Scott King (1996)

For many, the most difficult issue that confronts spiritual seekers today, both within the traditional institutions of religion and in secular society is the issue of homosexuality. Some church leaders claim the gay/lesbian issue has become the most divisive issue in protestantism since slavery (William Sloane Coffin, cited in Lance, 1989). And, as with the issue of slavery, this issue has become highly politicized and has been used as a wedge issue to divide Americans during recent political campaigns. Though homosexuality is the sharp tip of the wedge, the hottest aspect of the controversy, the homosexuality issue is actually part of broader social change that concerns gender issues and definitions—the cultural understanding of masculinity and femininity.

ROOTS OF THE GAY RIGHTS MOVEMENT

Gender Issues

Two social phenomena in the past 150 years have led to the movement for justice and acceptance among sexual minorities. The first is the broader minority rights movement spearheaded by the black civil rights movement. The second is the changes in views of gender that have emerged, in part because of the two waves of the women's movement over the past one and a half centuries. Though we will explore gender and race issues more fully in the next chapter, I have chosen to place the discussion of the gay issue first for two reasons: (1) because within the spiritual community it is currently the most conflictual of issues regarding human differences, and (2) because some of the themes in the debate are directly related to one's attitudes toward the body, toward sensuality and sexuality, and thus are closely related to the material in the previous chapter.

We need to remind ourselves that when the U.S. Constitution was written, the words "All men are created equal" were understood to mean all *white free men.* In practice, slaves (which meant almost all African Americans) and women were excluded in the rights enumerated in the Bill of Rights. Specifically, neither women nor slaves had the right to vote. In the efforts to free the slaves, many abolitionists recognized this incongruity and also fought for women's rights. But women's right to vote was not achieved until 1920, long after slavery was abolished. Even when suffrage was achieved, women's roles remained highly constricted by society. During World War II, women served their country by taking over jobs that had previously been "men's work," since so many men were serving on the war front. New areas of employment for women led to a rethinking of the social divisions of work and family along gender lines. At first the women's movement focused on equal pay for similar work, but in 1964 Betty Friedan's *The Feminine Mystique* initiated a stream of books, magazines, and other literature that helped change women's expectations in the realm of work as well as in the family. Research demonstrated that women typically did not have decision-making power in the family comparable to men's unless they had their own income. The inclusion of "sex" in the federal antidiscrimination laws created the legal structure for greater gender equality employment.

By the 1980s many protestant seminaries were taking seriously the feminist critique of society and the church, much as they had taken leadership in the black-white civil rights movement two decades earlier. More and more women began to enroll in seminaries and to seek ordination in the mainstream denominations. Scholars began to rethink both secular and religious history and to research the important roles women had taken, for example, in the New Testament church, and in the underground railroad during slavery. Women's roles, both in the past and in the present, became more visible, and women's influence in the organized churches became more direct. Just as the black-white civil rights movement involved a move to overcome racial oppression of African Americans, the women's movement sought to reveal the subtle and not so subtle oppression of women by the social norms and the institutional rules and laws enacted largely by men. As is usually the case with oppression, persons in the dominate social group (whites in the racial struggle, males in the gender issue) often are not conscious of being the oppressors. They are simply carrying on life as usual. Similarly, many in the oppressed groups (blacks during the civil rights movement, women during the women's movement) have internalized the oppression, and do not even recognize it as oppression. They simply accept it as normal. Once a person realizes the phenomena of internalized oppression, he or she can understand that many in the subservient group are afraid of change and actually side with the oppressors (see Exhibit 6.1).

FEMINISM AND THE CHURCH

Development of the technologies of birth control was a major factor in freeing woman to exercise power over their own bodies. Soon after the technology became available, parts of conservative Protestantism as well as the hierarchy of the Roman Catholic Church took stands against birth control. The contemporary Roman Catholic position denounces feminism, opposes same-sex marriage, and attempts to clearly differentiate the sexes in theological terms, defending the all-male priesthood. At the same time it affirms that women have certain rights: the right to vote and to work (Ratzinger, 2004). In short, parts of conservative Protestantism and official Catholicism accepted the social changes that had already occurred, but tried to inhibit further change. In reaction to this official stand, many Catholic laity, and

EXHIBIT 6.1.
Questions to Help Unravel Gender Oppression in Your Own Life

1. What do you think caused your heterosexuality?
2. When and how did you first decide you were a heterosexual?
3. Is it possible your heterosexuality is just a phase you may grow out of?
4. Is it possible your heterosexuality stems from a neurotic fear of others of the same sex?
5. If you've never slept with a person of the same sex, is it possible that all you need is a good gay lover?

[Note: By now it is probably clear that these questions are tongue-in-cheek, mocking the questions that are often posed to homosexuals. But they show the assumptions that heterosexuals often make. As you continue to read them, sense your own reaction, and try to empathize with persons of a different orientation than your own.]

6. Why do you heterosexuals feel compelled to seduce others into your lifestyle?
7. Why do you flaunt your heterosexuality? Can't you just be what you are and keep it to yourself?
8. A disproportionate majority of child molesters are heterosexuals. Do you consider it safe to expose your children to heterosexual teachers?
9. Could you trust a heterosexual therapist to be objective? Don't you fear he or she might be inclined to influence you in the direction of his or her own leanings?
10. How can you become a whole person if you limit yourself to compulsive, exclusive heterosexuality, and fail to develop your natural, healthy homosexual potential?

(Author unknown)

some Catholic priests (even in cultures that are predominately Catholic and sexually conservative) have seriously questioned the Pope's authority on such issues. Many Catholics have decided they will not let a group of celibate men determine their sex lives. Despite this break with official authority, the majority of Catholics who decide to disregard the church's rulings and to use birth control have no desire to leave the church, and still find the rituals, sacraments, and sense of community very important to them.

Though some of conservative protestant Christianity takes a similar stance, in many of the mainstream denominational organizations laywomen have a vote in decisions, and a larger and larger percent of new clergy now are women. With increased leadership from women, ethics have begun to shift to focusing on human connectedness rather than rules (see Chapter 3 on emotions and value development). In both Catholic and protestant Christianity, the increased belief in gender equality has led to demands for gender-inclusive language in worship, for making the sacrament of ordination available to persons regardless of their gender, and making the sacrament of marriage available regardless of sexual orientation. A more "feminine" ethics is emerging in Christian seminaries, and many local churches have become inclusive churches even though their denominations have not yet affirmed gay or lesbian ordination or marriage. Parallel to the dissenting Catholics, these Christians do not want to see the church split because of differences. Their very approach to differences is to be inclusive. They sense an inconsistency when the church speaks of love then rejects persons whose love is expressed toward someone else of the same gender.

Now that we have placed the gay issue in the context of the women's movement and the civil rights movement, let us try to clarify what is unique about the gay issue.

SEXUAL ORIENTATION: WHY IT'S SUCH A HOT ISSUE

Issues of discrimination almost always involve issues of prestige and power (domination). Whether focused on gender, race, socioeconomic class, or sexual orientation, these are issues of one group seeing itself as superior to another. The issue of sexual orientation, whether a person is straight or lesbian, gay, bisexual, or transgendered (LGBT), has some added factors:

- Homosexual behavior is not only seen as inferior, but as morally wrong; LGBT individuals are seen as sinful people.

- Because the basis for discrimination concerns sexuality, the rejected behaviors are perceived of as more personal and more directly threatening.
- It is generally easy, in public situations, to see who is male or female, black or white, or Asian or Hispanic. Unlike race or gender, sexual orientation is hidden, unless the person "comes out" and self-identifies. This hiddenness makes it feel more dangerous. Though some safety exists for LGBT persons in being a hidden minority, it also allows false stereotypes to remain unchallenged (Ackbar, 2005.)

In short, the gay issue is perceived as dangerous because it is personal, moral, and hidden.

Perceptions and Decisions

Decisions are being made throughout society regarding the rights of LGBT persons:

- Government bodies at state and national levels are deciding what rights gay people should have: the right to equal housing and employment? The right to free expression of their relationships? The right to be legally married and thus have hospital visiting privileges, tax advantages, inheritance, and support in raising children?
- Religious institutions are debating what types of participation in their rites, ceremonies, and activities they will sanction. Are open lesbians and gays welcomed as members? Are they allowed leadership roles? Can they be ordained? Should their commitments and unions be sanctified by rituals such as the sacrament of marriage?

Counselors as members of professional groups can participate in organizational decisions on what types of psychotherapeutic practices are ethical in our work with LGBT individuals. We can also make use of the research data that our disciplines generate. Counselors as individuals must decide to what degree they are comfortable with homosexual behavior and whether they believe attempts to change are ethical in their counseling methods. Most professional counseling organizations (e.g., American Psychological Association) consider attempts to change sexual orientation both fruitless and unethical.

It is important to differentiate how decisions in one realm impact others. If a state approves legal marriage for same-sex couples, it does not mean that a church or mosque or synagogue must perform the sacrament or ceremony of marriage. Some gay activists are working to change the state institutions of marriage to allow marriage licenses to be issued to couples of the same gender. They are not trying to pass laws to require religious organizations to perform the ceremony (which would clearly violate the Constitutional separation of church and state, undermine religious liberty, and be counterproductive for civil liberties). The practical result could be achieved by states legalizing civil unions, but this might undermine the social result. As the Supreme Court of Massachusetts affirmed (February 3, 2004), if same-sex couples are allowed civil unions but not marriages, a stigma against the civil unions will result, which will prevent these unions from being perceived as equal to marriage. This stigmatization would create a parallel to the so-called "separate but equal" school systems prior to federal Supreme Court Decision of 1954 (*Brown vs. Board of Education*) and thus, the court argued, would be a denial of equal rights.

Governments must decide what is fair for all of its citizens, not what is "right" based on a particular religion's point of view. Suppose, for example, a coalition of protestant evangelical churches in Indiana were to persuade the state board of education to require that Christian scriptures be read over the public address system each morning in the public schools. In concept, this violates the separation of church and state. In practice, since the majority of citizens in Indiana profess to be Christians, it is conceivable that the majority could pass such a law. Here is where the system of government devised in the U.S. Constitution is so remarkable; it includes important checks and balances that protect against a "tyranny of the majority." As long as the court systems are independent of the legislatures, they can exercise a check over the "will of the majority" when it infringes on the rights of the minorities. Presumably, if the courts of Indiana failed to do so, the minority would appeal to the federal courts, and this (imaginary) law requiring readings of scriptures would be overruled.

Historically, however, groups who believe they have the final truth on a subject have sometimes been able to destroy the balance of powers, usually by weakening the independence of the courts, or by amending the constitution. Legislative bodies have been persuaded to implement a "moral" code that is not sensitive to minority views. An example would be the prohibition of alcohol (1920-1933 in the United States). Certainly misuse of alcohol has consequences beyond the individual user. Plenty of evidence supports that persons already prone to violence or sexual abuse may be even more likely to commit such crimes when under the influence (Locke & Mahalik, 2005), and certainly automobile accidents are often precipitated by drunk drivers. The question is, should control of these behaviors be accomplished by prohibiting *all* brewing or drinking of alcohol, even by those whose use of alcohol doesn't endanger others?

I cite this example to illustrate that when the citizens feel threatened by behaviors they consider immoral, they may support the weakening of the checks and balances that protect minorities. The "defense of marriage" acts that have been passed by many states appear to fit this pattern. The assumptions that energize such legislation are that "gay marriages" threaten heterosexuality and the sanctity of heterosexual marriage, and that homosexual behavior is immoral. We need to examine these assumptions.

WHAT INFORMATION DO COUNSELORS NEED REGARDING LGBT INDIVIDUALS?

Assuming those reading this chapter fit the national average—somewhere between 5 and 10 percent of my readers are homosexual, and may already have considerable information about this issue. Furthermore, most of those who are straight are likely to endorse an ethic of tolerance. Tolerance is a hallmark of the great majority of Americans in our pluralistic culture. For example, the great majority of people in United States, though they are religious, do *not* believe that only persons of their own faith tradition will attain salvation or go to heaven ("Where we Stand on Faith," 2005). So I assume most of you reading this are honestly attempting to be open to new information, and to become more personally connected to individuals from this minority group. Nonetheless, if you haven't been privileged to have a gay man or lesbian disclose to you their own sexual orientation, LGBT individuals may be a group you know only in abstract. If your sources of information are largely the mainstream media, you may believe some of the stereotypes of lesbians and gays that continue to persist in the media and entertainment world.

If you don't have social contact with open gays and lesbians, it may help you to see the personal side if you view some movies or documentaries. One movie you can almost certainly access at the larger video rental stores is Kinsey *(November 2004, Fox Searchlight), the personal and professional biography of the man who headed the earliest scientific surveys of the sexual behavior of Americans. An excellent portrayal of counseling with a gay man is produced by American Psychological Association:* Psychotherapy with Gay & Lesbian Clients: Coming Out, *(APA & Buendia Productions, 1995), and is in many university libraries.*

Are the Stereotypes Based on Facts?

The rates of testosterone in gay men is as high as in straight men. In fact, no differences in any of the sex-related hormones have been found between gay and straight men. (Meyer-Bahlburg, 1982). The majority of gay men are *not* effeminate in looks or in nonverbal gestures. In a controlled study, subjects watched videos in which various persons were shown interacting with one other person. The subjects were asked to rate each of the men on a scale for how effeminate they appeared. About 5 percent of the straight men in the videos were rated as "effeminate," compared to 18 percent of the gay men. This means that 82 percent of the gay men were considered masculine. Furthermore, since a larger percentage of men in the general population are straight, out of 100 men, roughly 7 will be rated effeminate, but only 2 of those 7 (29 percent) will actually be gay men. So when you "guess" that an effeminate man is gay, you are likely to be wrong 71 percent of the time (Matteson, 1977a,b).

A factor that contributes to the impression that gay men are effeminate is that sexual orientation is invisible. With racial or ethnic minorities we can see, or hear in their speech, differences that identify them. However, we rarely know someone is gay, lesbian, or bisexual until they tell us—though when we see people who fit the stereotype, we may make the *assumption* that they are gay. Since we tend to notice only the so-called gays who stand out and fit our assumption, almost all those we label "gay" are effeminate. Unless large numbers of gays and lesbians become "open" and visible to us, we have no way of correcting our assumptions.

Ways the Gay Experience is Different from That of Other Minorities

Another way in which LGBT persons differ from many other minorities is that they are born into "straight" families. African Americans, for example, are almost always raised by parents who are also African American, thus they can prepare their children for the discrimination they are likely to experience. In contrast, parents of LGBT youth may not only be straight, but may be prejudiced against homosexuals and thus may reject their own children.

Rates of suicide and of runaway adolescents are much higher for gay and lesbian youth than for youth in general. Many of the LGBT runaways report they did so because of rejection by parents, family, or friends. A high percentage of runaways, regardless of sexual orientation, turn to street prostitution to survive (Dodgson, 2003).

Why Are Some People Homosexual?

Genetic Factors

Genetics plays an important role in the development of homosexuality in men and women. Identical twins are much more likely to have the same sexual orientation than are fraternal twins. In one study of male twins (raised in the same home) when one male identical twin was gay, 52 percent of the time his twin was also gay. In contrast, in fraternal twins, when one was gay the twin brother was also gay only 22 percent of the time (Bailey & Pillard, 1991). A similar but slightly smaller study of male twins found 65 percent concordance for identical male twins, but only 35 percent for fraternal twins (Whitman, Diamond, & Martin, 1993). A study of lesbians with twin sisters also found that a much higher percent of the sisters, 48 percent in identical twins, were also lesbian, compared to only 16 percent among fraternal twins (Bailey, Pillard, Neale, & Agyei, 1993; see also reviews in Bellis & Hufford, 2002, and in Dodgson, 2003).

Genetics accounts for only about half of the variance, however. Yet even in cases in which both twins grew up in very similar circumstances (same family, same age group, same schools, etc.) we often have one gay and one heterosexual twin. We simply do not know what the factors are, in addition to genes, that determine sexual orientation. We do know that family dynamics do *not* seem to be an important factor, despite some mistaken psychiatric theories.

Other Factors

Some evidence suggests that the hormones of a mother during specific phases of pregnancy can effect the later sexual orientation of the baby. Research concerning the role of hormones has yielded confusing results, and should not be interpreted as meaning that prenatal endocrine conditions preordain sexual orientation (Gooren, Fliers, & Courtney, 1990).[1] Dodgson's (2003) review states "there is evidence of increased homosexual orientation among both male and female offspring of mothers who were treated with female hormones (diethylstilbestrol) to maintain their pregnancies" (Dodgson, 2003, p. 4).

Though we are only beginning to unravel the factors involved in sexual arousal and sexual orientation, it is clear that homosexuality exists in every human culture that has been studied, and in every species of mammals that have been observed in their natural habitat (Ford & Beach, 1951). The overwhelming evidence of developmental psychology is that sexual orientation is nearly impossible to change after the person enters puberty. Youth and adults do not "choose" their sexual orientation. Their early development determines what sexual arousal comes naturally to them.

Is Homosexual Behavior Pathological? Is it Immoral?

As counselors, our professional ethics require us to adopt a multicultural perspective in our work. My hope is that this discussion of the issues regarding the gay experience will encourage the reader to take a look at his or her own prejudices in the light of inclusive and body-affirming spirituality. This implies making an attempt to understand the perspective of the gay individual. The limited information we have about how homosexuality develops suggests that for some individuals (both human and other mammals) the "natural" sexual responses are directed toward persons of the same sex. Heterosexuals who have only their own natural responses to judge by are likely to feel that homosexuality is "unnatural." It would be honest to say that *for them* homosexual acts are unnatural. But to the person who, since puberty, has felt the urge to be sexually involved with someone of the same sex—who, for example, has had fantasies and/or wet dreams about homosexual activities—the first experience of actually consummating gay sex often feels ecstatically natural; it is like a "coming home" to who one really is.

It is hard to empathize with an emotional experience someone else has had that is entirely different from our own responses—but that is exactly what we as counselors are called to do. Consequently, we must develop an ethic that takes into account those who are different from us, and respects their very different experience.

Try to think of a situation in which a friend or person you know well has a very different response than you do to some particular event or idea. Have you eventually learned to respect the difference, to think of this person's response as "normal for him or her"? What has helped you learn to be understanding or empathic in this case?

Perhaps the most basic rule of ethics is "do no harm"; at least this is the basic professional foundation for medical ethics, and is part of the Hippocratic oath that medical doctors swear to. So we need to ask, does sex between two consenting adults do any harm when it is between persons of the same gender? Clearly such behavior is "victimless." This does not deny that some sex between adults can be psychologically damaging, but the damage typically has to do with a lack of respect and an insensitivity to boundaries, not with whether it is gay sex or straight sex. And of course sexual contact can transmit diseases, most consequently HIV. However, most of the HIV epidemic in the world has spread through heterosexual sex; the AIDS pandemic cannot be blamed particularly on gay sex.

Mental Health Issues for LGBT Clients

In a landmark study in 1957, Evelyn Hooker sought to determine whether gay men tended to be more neurotic than straight men. (Most previous studies involved sampling errors; the homosexual subjects used were mental patients, though the heterosexual subjects were not. Studies with such a sampling error were almost preordained to discover that gays had mental disorders.) Hooker administered a battery of tests to a matched sample of 30 homosexually identified and 30 heterosexually identified men who were neither psychiatric patients nor prisoners. Psychological profiles and life histories were developed, removing any information that would identify the subjects' sexual orientations. Then expert psychologists were asked to rate the degree of pathology in each of the subjects (Hooker, 1957). "The results showed that the raters could not distinguish between the two groups [the gay and the heterosexual men]" (Masters, Johnson, & Kolodny, 1982, pp. 322, 324).

Building on Hooker's study, Saghir and Robins (1973) studied both lesbians and gay men, comparing them to unmarried heterosexuals (since the rate of certain psychiatric illnesses is higher in single people). Again they discovered that the majority of homosexuals were well-adjusted, productive people with no signs of psychiatric illness (Masters et al., 1982). The Saghir and Robins study did find a higher rate of alcoholism in the lesbian group; other studies of that period provide impressionistic evidence of a higher rate of alcoholism in gay men as well, though sampling problems confound verifying that conclusion. For decades gay bars have provided one of the few safe meeting places for gays and lesbians, so frequenting bars may be motivated more by the need for social relationships with other LBGT individuals than by a thirst for alcohol. But the social situation may encourage overuse of alcohol. Thus it is not surprising that alcoholism rates may be higher among gays. Fortunately, in larger cities many other venues for gay/lesbian socialization now exist.

Previous to these studies, the *Diagnostic and Statistical Manual of Mental Disorders* listed homosexuality as a disorder. On the basis of these two studies and numerous others that followed, both the American Psychological Association and the American Psychiatric Association declassified homosexuality in 1973. By the early 1980s, sufficient research had been done to conclude that "homosexuality by itself is not a form of mental illness, nor is it typically associated with other signs of mental illness" (Masters et al., 1982, p. 324, citing Green, 1972; Hoffman, 1977; and Marmor, 1980).

RELIGIOUS OPPOSITION TO HOMOSEXUALITY

Note: Some of the material in this section is specifically about Christianity, and may not seem relevant to the personal and spiritual growth of those readers whose religious backgrounds are not Christian. In spite of this, it may be worthwhile for non-Christian readers to scan this section, as Christian perspectives continue to have a major impact on our society at large. Those not interested in this material, please skip to the section in this chapter titled "What Threatens Marriage?"

Overcoming Stereotyped Views of Gays and Gay Culture

The most vocal opposition to accepting homosexual behavior has come from fundamentalist Protestantism and from the leadership in the Roman Catholic Church. The opposition claims to be based on the Bible and the tradition of the historic church regarding marriage. Let us examine each of these.

What Does the Bible Say About Homosexuality?

Some will argue that the Bible calls homosexual acts an "abomination," citing Leviticus 18:22 and 20:13: "If a man lies with a male as with a woman, both of them have committed an abomination; they shall be put to death." Though these two verses are frequently quoted, many who quote them fail to note that they were part of a holiness or purity code from 3,000 years ago, attempting to separate the Hebrew people from other tribes in the Middle East (Nissinen, 1998). Here are some other sexual rules from that code (paraphrased by White, n.d.):

- If a bride is found not to be a virgin, she should be stoned to death immediately (Deuteronomy 22:13-21, RSV).
- If a married couple have sex during the woman's period, both should be executed (Leviticus 18:19, RSV).
- If a husband dies and the couple have no children, the widow must have intercourse with each of her husband's brothers in turn until she bears her deceased a male heir (Deuteronomy 25:11ff, RSV). (See more in White, n.d., p. 7.)

And the rules weren't limited to sex.

> They forbid round haircuts, tattoos, wearing clothes with more than one type of fabric, eating pork or shellfish, and others. (White, n.d., p. 11)

Many acts of mixing were seen as violating the created order of male and female and are viewed by the code as "an idolatrous affront to the integrity of the deity" (Lance, 1989, p. 145, citing Shafer, 1978). If the holiness code is applicable today, aren't we obligated to follow all of it, rather than select the rules that fit our own prejudices?

Only eight short passages in the Bible are interpreted by some as condemning gay sex, four in the Old Testament and four in the New Testament. I will speak very briefly about each, but encourage those interested in biblical scholarship to consult Helminiak (2000), Lance (1989), Nissinen (1998), Scroggs (1983), and Wink (1999).

Two of the Old Testament passages describe the destruction of Sodom and Gomorrah and a similar incident in Gibeah (Genesis 19, and Judges 19). Both stories concern visitors to the cities who are protected by their host when other local men threaten to rape them. It is not homosexuality itself that is condemned in these passages; rather it is the lawless, violent behavior in which gangs of men seek to humiliate strangers by forcing them to assume the ("inferior") role of women. (Notice that neither passage criticizes the ethics of the host for being willing to offer his virgin daughters to the local gang of men rather than allow his male guest to be raped. The inferiority of women is taken for granted.) The wickedness of Sodom and Gomorrah is understood by Isaiah (1:10-17) to concern injustice, idolatry, oppression, and the failure to defend the vulnerable—not homosexuality (see Lance, 1989 and Lance, 1992, for details). In fact, the Old Testament prophets *never* include same-sex behavior in their lists of Israel's moral and ethical problems (Lance, 1989).

The passages from Leviticus have already been discussed in terms of the holiness or purity codes. A passage in Deuteronomy 23:17-18, mistranslated in the King James version, "there shall be no *sodomite* of the sons of Israel," contains a confusing Hebrew word *qadesh,* sometimes translated in the Greek Septuagint as "male prostitute," sometimes as "initiating priest," and sometimes transliterated indicating that the Greek translators did not understand what the word meant. Recent research indicates *qadesh* referred to a pagan cultic figure, but whether or not the *qadesh* had a sexual role remains unclear. Read in context, the concern of the Hebrew text was with idolatry and pagan religion, not with homosexuality (Lance, 1989, p. 145). In short, the only Old Testament passages that deal directly with male/male homosexual behavior are those from the purity code, the two passages from Leviticus.

Three of the four so-called homosexual passages in the New Testament come from letters attributed to Paul. 1 Corinthians 6:9-11 and 1 Timothy 1:10 include key words in Greek that we simply do not know how to translate. There is convincing evidence from early Christian writings (especially St. John Chrysotom, fourth century) that neither of the Greek words that were translated "homosexual" (in the King James translation) and "soft or effeminate [men]" or "sexual perverts" or "male prostitutes" (in the Revised Standard Version) are accurately translated (see Lance, 1989; and White, n.d.).

The lesson Paul emphasizes to the Corinthians is that Christians are under a new law, "the law of Jesus, the law of love, that requires *more* of us . . . than strict adherence to a list"—it requires pure heart and good conscience "God does not want us squabbling over who is 'in' and who is 'out.' God wants us to love each other" . . . and leave judgment to God (White, n.d., p. 16).

Romans 1:26-27 is the only passage in the Bible that mentions female homosexuality (Lance, 1989). Paul speaks of women and men giving up "natural" sexual relationships for "unnatural," and burning with passion for members of their own sex. Again, homosexual behavior is secondary to his main argument, but it is clear Paul considers homosexual passion to be unnatural. In context, he is rejecting a life that is focused on lust alone (as he views the activities of Greek fertility temples). He apparently thinks these people are actually heterosexual, but "have given up their heterosexual passions for homosexual lusts" (Romans 1:27, cited in White, n.d, p. 14). Of course in Paul's time no concept existed of homosexuality as a sexual orientation—the word *homosexual* does not even exist in Greek or Hebrew as it was not a concept then. Paul is simply aware of male/male and female/female sexual behaviors, which he assumed occurred in people who were born heterosexual and changed.

He goes on in Romans 12 to clarify his main point, that we are to present our "bodies as a living sacrifice, holy and acceptable to God, which is your spiritual worship." In this section he never raises the issue of homosexuality, though he spells out the matters of practice he views as important (Lance, 1989, p. 148). The important practices include making use of our unique individual gifts, loving in a genuine way, including brotherly affection, giving what is needed such as food and drink even to your enemies, and leaving judgment up to God (Romans 12:3-21).

The last Biblical passage sometimes interpreted as pertaining to homosexuality is Jude 1:6-7, which is simply a reference to Sodom and Gomorrah, and refers to "unnatural lust" (RSV). But the unnatural lust it refers to is sex between men and angels ("sons of gods" or divine beings) (Jude 1:6), not homosexuality, and the Greek words translated "unnatural lust" could more accurately be translated lust for "strange or different flesh." This appears to be a reference to Genesis 6:1-4 (RSV), where "the sons of God saw that the daughters of men were fair" and married and bore children with them, and echoes the sense of the purity or holiness codes that unmatched partners, mixed textiles, or animals that are neither fish nor foul (shellfish) break the divine order of things.

When we exclude passages concerning rape, and concerning sex with angels, we are left with only the two passages in Leviticus (18:22 and 20:13) and one in Romans (1:26-27) that refer to consensual homosexual acts. The first two repeat a law in a purity code most Christians consider outdated. The third involves Paul's belief that homosexual responses come from extreme lust that leads to abandoning one's "natural" interest in the "opposite" gender.

What the Bible *does* say about homosexual behavior is well summarized by Lance (1989):

> The number of biblical texts which refer unambiguously to same-sex relationships is quite small. In several of that small number, the central concern is something else, to which the same sex behavior is incidental or serves as illustration. The prophets never include same-sex behavior in their list of Israel's moral and ethical problems. The issue is never raised in the Gospels. The current interest in the issue of homosexuality and the Bible is *our* interest; it does not reflect the biblical priorities. (p. 140)

What Did Jesus Say?

It is important to notice what is *not* in the Bible. The surviving gospels (Matthew, Mark, Luke, John, Thomas, and possibly the more recently discovered Gospel of Judas) are our only sources for what Jesus said. Nowhere in any of these gospels did Jesus condemn homosexuals or homosexual behavior. However, he did criticize the heterosexual practice of divorce. Jesus said, "You have heard that it was said, 'An eye for an eye and a tooth for a tooth.' But I say to you, do not resist one who is evil. But if anyone strikes you on the right cheek, turn to him the other also" (Matthew 5: 38-39, RSV). Jesus was quoting the Leviticus laws, and implying that they were no longer appropriate in his time. Jesus (and Hillel before him) stated that the second great commandment was to "love thy neighbor as thy self." Jesus did not say "love your heterosexual neighbor"; he placed no restrictions on this love. His parable (the Good Samaritan) implies that anyone in need is our neighbor.

WHAT IS THE HISTORY OF CHRISTIAN MARRIAGE?

The definition of marriage has changed a great deal since biblical times. Even during the centuries in which the various writings contained in the Bible were written, at least three views of the purpose and ethics of marriage existed and are presented within the Bible:

Views of Marriage in the Bible

Male-Centered Polygamous Marriage

The Old Testament marriage was male-centered, and men who could afford it were allowed more than one wife (polygamy) plus concubines. Men's rights to this "property" were protected, though divorce was restricted partly to protect women from poverty. Polygamy was never directly rejected in the New Testament, and was accepted in some Christian groups (e.g., the Church of Latter Day Saints) until outlawed by the U.S. government. As far as I know, the option of women having more than one husband was not discussed, since male dominance was assumed.

Commitment Expected When it was Assured the Couple Could Have Children

In Jesus' time, once a couple were betrothed (engaged), sex was allowed or even expected. The man had the right to revoke the betrothal if the woman was unable to get pregnant. No biblical opposition to this custom exists that I can find. No sex was allowed outside the marriage once a couple were married.

Marriage As Second-Best to Celibacy

Marriage was seen, at least by Paul, as a way to handle men's sexual drives, but inferior to celibacy if the man was capable of remaining celibate. "It is well. . . to remain single as I do. But if they cannot exercise self-control, they should marry. For it is better to marry than to be aflame with passion" (I Corinthians 7:8-9) This view is new to that period of history and was not the focus of earlier Jewish attitudes. (Later in church history, around the fifth through tenth centuries, the superiority of celibacy became the predominant view in the Roman Catholic Church.)

Heterosexual Weddings Outside the Church, Same-Sex Commitments Inside

The development of marriage after the biblical record is not totally clear. Though heterosexual weddings occurred in the first century CE, these were secular events. They were not held in the Jewish temples or the Christian churches. The earliest manuscripts of Christian marriage ceremonies (versus secular ones) are in the sixth century. Over time, the ceremonies moved to the steps outside of the church. It wasn't until 1215 CE that marriage was regarded as a sacred rite of the church.

However, more than 60 manuscripts exist from the eighth century describing life-commitment ceremonies between two males, performed in the church. These manuscripts refer to such ceremonies as far back as the fourth century. A professor and chair of the Department of History at Yale University, John Boswell, received permission to study manuscripts in the Vatican library, and discovered these manuscripts. His books (1980, 1994) interpreted the ceremonies as a form of marriage, which opened a prolonged and still unsettled controversy. Roman Catholic scholars denounced Boswell's interpretation. Questions arose as to why the manuscripts had remained hidden so many centuries.

At least 150 scholarly reviews and discussions of Boswell's books have been published (Halsall, 1998). The ceremonies had been listed in the manuscript index as marriages, and were placed in the section of liturgy with marriages, but some scholars believe they were simply a form of adult peer adoptions; one historian argues that the ceremonies confirmed relationships similar to the Mafia "blood brotherhood" ties (Shaw, 1994). It was hard for participants in the debate to remain objective on so controversial an issue as that of homosexuality being approved within the Roman Church (see Rapp, 1997; Halsall, 1998).

These ceremonies were still going on in France in the sixteenth century; French essayist Montaigne refers to his attending a ceremony at the church of Saint John of the Latin Gate in Rome in which "two males married each other at Mass, with the same ceremonies we use for our marriages, taking communion together, using the same nuptial scripture, after which they slept and ate together" (Boswell, 1994, pp. 264-265). Commitment ceremonies for male couples continued in Rome until the early eighteenth century, and in the Eastern Catholic churches into the nineteenth century, when they were declared no longer a sacrament. They continue in parts of rural Italy today. It appears that these ceremonies were done inside the Christian church before heterosexual marriages had moved inside the church, and the same-sex ceremonies were accepted by much of the church from at least the fourth century to the eighteenth. They were performed for women at least from the twelfth century on (Boswell, 1980). Whether the ceremonies carried implications similar to heterosexual marriages as Boswell believed is uncertain. There seems little doubt that sexual relationships were involved in many of these commitments (Hallsal, 1998), though direct discussion of sexuality was rare in either same-sex or heterosexual documents in that time.

Certainly the discovery of these liturgies brought into question the "historic" grounds for opposition to same-sexed marriage in the church. Whatever the true history may be, given the many changes in marriage over the centuries it is only realistic to expect further changes in marriage as pluralistic and democratic societies evolve.

CAN "THE BODY OF CHRIST" INCLUDE GAYS AND LESBIANS?

It's Not About "Liberal" or "Conservative"

As in any debate, the divisiveness within Christian denominations about inclusion of gays and lesbians comes in part from the emotional investments and attachments of the various parties rather than from the differences in viewpoints themselves. People tend to see their adversary as embodying everything they oppose. So a person taking a liberal stance theologically, and feeling strongly that LGBT persons should be included in all levels of religious decision making and allowed the sacrament of marriage is likely to assume that his or her inclusiveness is part of his or her liberal outlook, and that conservatives will necessarily oppose gay marriages. However, one of the strongest denominations working for inclusion of sexual minorities in Christian institutions is the Metropolitan Community Church (MCC). This church was founded by ministers who were defrocked or refused ordination in other denominations because they were openly gay. A substantial portion of the membership of MCC, probably the majority, are gay or lesbian. Yet theologically, most of the parish churches are fairly conservative.

To cite another example, one thoughtful *conservative* Christian writer has devoted a whole book to the an argument that the traditional doctrines of incarnation and of the Trinity lead to an affirmation of gay *inclusiveness*. Eugene Rogers in *Sexuality and the Christian Body: Their Way into the Triune God* (1999) describes the ways in which liberals and conservatives fail to accurately hear the other. His basic argument is that Christianity is a religion that stresses the incarnation of God—that is, that God took on human flesh in the person of Jesus the Christ. This clearly implies that human flesh is *not* the root of sin or human alienation from God. Rogers further emphasizes that salvation is not essentially an issue of couples, or of gender—if it were, "Jesus as an unmarried man would not be an adequate savior" (Rogers, 1999, p. 185). If Jesus is "the new Adam" who undoes the "Fall" of Adam and Eve (as the writings of the apostle Paul maintain), then Jesus' incarnation and salvation must replace the status of *both* Adam and Eve (Rogers, 1999).

According to classic Christian theology, the new relationship God establishes with non-Jewish Christians is to graft them onto the tree of Israel; that is, to adopt them into the covenant that was first established between God and Israel (the Old Testament, or Old Covenant). The New "Testament" is offered by grace to the (Christian) Church. Non-Jews are *not* naturally part of the redeemed community (Rogers, 1999), but are adopted into it by grace. For Rogers, the "natural" defect of gender, or of ethnicity, or of slavery, is overcome through God's inclusive grace.

> God, in the incarnation, proves able to use even flesh, and even sexuality, for God's own purposes. . . (Rogers, 1999, p. 188)

Rogers argues that the conservative Christian can authentically support gay marriage; Rogers's insights may provide a bridge across the polarized positions. He criticizes his fellow conservative heterosexuals for having been "poor stewards" of the rich theology of marriage. He states that it may actually be those who have been denied marriage, such as gay and lesbian people, who can be "sufficiently uncynical . . . even romantic, about marriage [and] defend the . . . claims about it that the Christian tradition has made" (Rogers, 1999, p. 65).

But Rogers (1999) also takes liberals to task for slipping into accusing those opposed to gay marriage of "homophobia"—using this psychological term to blame, and not hearing the root of the traditionalists' negative emotional reaction to gay relationships as based on a fear for the holiness of the "People of God" (p. 67). While liberals talk of love, they respond to conservatives' fear with blame and judgment. I suspect that Rogers is on target in suggesting that a key motivation for those spiritually sensitive people who are opposed to gay marriage is a *fear* that our culture will lose a sense of holiness or sacredness in regard to the institution of marriage. This fear is heightened by the stereotypic view of gay sex as anal penetration, and the fear of anal sex as dirty, and as involving a man being violated by being in the "female position." (See Lance [1992] for a discussion of this dynamic.) Perhaps the debate would shift if those arguing for inclusion responded to fear with love. "Perfect love casts out fear" (1 John 4:18, RSV).[2]

If you are having difficulty understanding the fear of conservative Christians and/or the politicizing of Christian churches in recent national elections, I strongly recommend reading Ault's (2004) participant-observer study of a congregation in Massachusetts, sensitively described in Spirit and Flesh: Life in a Fundamentalist Baptist Church.

Theological Argument for Gay Marriage

Liberals and civil rights activists are quick to see the parallels between the Christian church's rejection of gays and lesbians and the earlier scapegoating of the black race, or the acceptance of an inferior status for women (I Corinthians 14:33-35), or the tolerance of slavery (Titus 1:9; I Timothy 6:1-2), each of which has been defended on biblical grounds.

If a religious community is to invite LGBT persons as full members of their community it cannot offer them second-class status. If we recognize that the concept of sexual orientation was not understood in biblical times, and that homosexual acts were misinterpreted as against the individual's nature, we cannot base church policy on these mistaken views. A religious community that is inclusive must be willing to ordain and to marry same-sexed couples. That commitment between same-sexed couples was treated sacramentally within the Christian Church even before heterosexual marriages were conducted inside the church, despite the ambiguity about whether the couples were in a sexual relationship, makes it hard to argue that they are of inferior status.

Social Argument for Gay Marriage

Social science suggests that heterosexual marriage benefits modern societies by helping males become less competitive and individualistic and less self-centered. A public commitment to another person in the presence of family and friends helps to tame male's selfish and competitive focus. It is likely that gay marriage would help gay men become even more socially and ethically mature. To deny gay men this commitment does not serve either them or mainstream society well.

Restraint in Sexual Relationships

What liberals often fail to articulate is the important role of discipline, and of moving beyond attachment to one's own wishes and needs to an attitude of respectful restraint, which is necessary to a committed relationship (Rogers, 1999). This is the element Rogers refers to when he speaks of the "sanctification in the asceticism of a common life" (Rogers, 1999, p. 188). Acknowledging the role of

God's unmerited grace in the marriage covenant and the legitimate place for sexual restraint as part of the positive affirmation of one's body *and* one's commitment and sensitivity to the other might permit a deeper dialogue between inclusive and conservative Christians.

WHAT THREATENS MARRIAGE?

The political right-wing in America has it half right when they recognized that a serious threat to marriage exists today (Ventura, 2004). They are also right in recognizing that, unlike in previous stages of culture, we can no longer take for granted that marriage is an institution *only* for heterosexuals. The mistake in the right-wing analysis is that it assumes that the threat to marriage is caused by the possibility of gays and lesbians being married. In fact, the institution of marriage has suffered severe degradation long before the likelihood of gay marriage developed. The threat to marriage actually comes from the extreme form of capitalism that:

- Treats people as "things" to be discarded when thy don't gratify our immediate needs (Ventura, 2004)
- Suggests (through advertisements) that all of our longings and desires can be satiated through consumption of things and seduction of other people
- Fails to value the role of discipline and restraint in the development of a mature human individual living in community

The threat to deep spiritual marriage is not the threat of both partners being of the same gender. Note that two of the traditional and biblical images of marriage use metaphors involving same-sex relationships: the Triune God as the grounds for interpersonal love uses Father and Son, and the metaphor of Jesus as bridegroom to his chosen and adopted people (Israel and the gentile Christians) focuses on a community among males. Rogers (1999) argues that conservative Christianity must embrace both marriage and celibacy as acts of affirming the sexual body and making of them a thankful celebration before God. Furthermore, he argues that a truly triune or biblical theology that recognizes Christian marriage is based on grace and celebration would be inclusive of all three forms of marriage: celibacy (as marriage to a particular ministry), heterosexual marriage (as marriage, sexual constraint, and commitment to a particular person), and same-sex marriage (also, as marriage, sexual constraint, and commitment to a particular person). Marriage does not signify satisfaction, except incidentally. Rather, it signifies sanctification—a covenanted life with God.

> It is no accident, therefore, that God makes a covenant with Israel, and that Ruth makes a covenant with Naomi, Jonathan with David, Hosea with Gomer, and covenant becomes the primary conceptuality for marriage. . . . But as [these] biblical examples indicate, heterosexual marriage does not exhaust [the biblical view of] covenant. [Covenant is] a fluid concept able to assume even same-sex marriages into its trinitarian pattern. (Rogers, 1999, p. 22)

BEING OPEN TO DIVINE SURPRISES

One way to view Christian history is to think of God as continually challenging "his people" to open themselves up to notice and to proclaim that healing (salvation) comes to those who have thought of themselves as "outsiders." At first the early Christians thought of themselves as a small sect of Judaism. Gradually (primarily through the work of Paul) they realized that the "good news" was being accepted by more and more "outsiders." As discussed in Chapter 4, when Jesus met the woman in the region of Tyre and Sidon he at first did not believe she was worthy of God's spiritual food (Mark 7:24-30). He changed his mind. He was open to surprises. At this point I want to present what many readers may feel is a preposterous idea. In the Christian tradition, we are asked to be open to the possibility that the "King of the Jews" was born in the most unexpected of places, in a manger, because there was "no room in the inn" (Luke 2:7). In another gospel it is said that other kings (or wise men) were willing to follow a star to find him (Matthew 2:1-12). The incarnation occurred, not on the throne of David, but in a lower-class stable.

If we are longing for a "model" of a community in which the wholesome and healing power of the spirit is present, where would we look? What subcultures in the West are healthy and reaching out in creative ways? I ask you, now, to consider that the model for redemptive culture in our time may be in a place that many traditional

Christians consider anything but holy—in gay male culture! This proposition is not my original idea, but has been expounded in the writing of David Nimmons (2002), in his book *Soul Beneath the Skin.* He examines the possibility that, in Western culture, the elements that nurture a deeper "soulfulness" are emerging in the gay male community. For many spiritual seekers, looking to the gay community is about as absurd as looking in a manger.

UNDERSTANDING THE GAY SUBCULTURE

One of the opportunities of living in United States is that we have the chance to get to know persons from an amazing variety of subcultures and ethnicities. Unfortunately, often we know them only at a superficial level. If we are open to it, scientific information can help us overcome our biases. Careful studies of gay individuals and of the gay subculture are available and will be surveyed in the following sections. Of course, no amount of information can substitute for direct interaction with people; perhaps the information provided here will lead readers to open up opportunities for dialogue between the gay communities and "mainstream" organizations. To explore having speakers or panelists, search on Google "gay organizations" and the name of your city, or contact the gay information phone line in a city near you.[3]

CRITERION FOR A MODEL SPIRITUAL COMMUNITY

In my own thinking, a model spiritual community in contemporary Western culture would have at least the following attributes:

- The community would foster a positive view of the body, without idealizing a particular body type.
- Pleasure would be affirmed, while simultaneously encouraging nurturing and caring for others, rather than the sole pursuit of selfish or self-centered satisfaction.
- Citizens would be encouraged to develop awareness through both the cognitive and the intuitive learning processes: for example, cognizance of contemporary scientific knowledge, and apprehending a fuller humanness through the fine arts.

- We would be open to the transcendent, without berating our real bodies and our material world.

This list of attributes, developed in the context of these two chapters on the body and sensuality, is certainly not comprehensive. I will use this list later to evaluate Nimmons's (2002) description of the gay male culture. However, you as reader may want to stop reading for a few minutes and jot down the characteristics you would look for in choosing a model.

With this sketch of the ideal spiritual community as background, let us look at Nimmons's (2002) description of the gay male community. His book opens in a particular gay store, which typifies the "faux-outrageous jumble of carnality" that is so common in specifically gay venues. "The soft-core posters in each dressing room . . . the underwear boxes . . . all . . . suggest that what lies beneath the skin is . . . just more skin."

But, Nimmons' (2002) argues, this and scores of places like it are:

> . . . entry portal[s] to the world's newest culture, a tribal homeland where the defaults and protocols of social life shift subtly, and where new rituals and norms hold power. It is a place of different rules and language, where *customs and values are not what they seem* (emphasis mine). (pp. 2-3)

One often hears people who think of themselves as "liberal" stating that "gay people are the same as straight people except for what they do in bed." Though this statement makes some sense in comparing persons merely on their sexual orientations, it also shows a fear of really looking at differences—and especially a fear of acknowledging the gay *culture* that emerged once gay men and women began to affirm themselves and ceased using the straight culture as their model for identity. As one of the earliest American gay rights leaders stated, "I say what we do in bed is the *only* place where we're the same!" (Harry Hay, founder of Mattachine Society, in Nimmons, 2002, p. 4). Nimmons (2002) is well aware that people outside of gay male culture, and many gay men in it, think of that subculture as a very sensuous and sexualized culture, "a body-obsessed, shallow, sexually profligate, consumerist culture" (p. 4). Without denying that there is truth in this caricature, Nimmons invites us to look for the "soul beneath the skin." He points out that for 50 years gay communities have been undertaking a range of profound, spontaneous social experiments. "Under the shadow of a plague [AIDS] many of these changes bubbled unseen" (p. 4). Yet these changes have left their imprint on American life, and have changed fundamental assumptions and givens about how men function—changes that reverberate in the larger American society, and bring the potential to redraw the map of American maledom (Nimmons, 2002). As stressed in Chapter 2 on spiritual development, crises may open the heart to deeper spirituality. To quote from that chapter, research showed some specific changes occurring in men whose partners were dying of AIDS:

Using interviews with self-identified gay men, 20 who were HIV positive and 20 who were HIV negative, Backlund (1990) found that the Fowler protocol for analyzing the faith-development interviews was not particularly sensitive to assessing transition. Backlund developed a more intensive assessment of the interview content, and this measure did show significantly more transitions in faith development for the HIV-positive sample. Having experienced the death of a friend during the previous year was also highly correlated with undergoing transitions in faith-development, for both the HIV-positive and HIV-negative samples.

Some of the ways in which gay male culture differs from the traditional view of masculinity have become evident only since gay men began to converge on specific sections of our major cities, areas that have become "gay ghettos," places where gay men and women settle in sufficient density that measurements of cultural difference are possible.

Low Levels of Violence

First, gays have built a public sphere that is markedly free of interpersonal violence. On the streets, and in public places, this particular male culture has an extremely low rate of violence against others, in contrast to the mainstream culture in which male violence is endemic. A carefully matched study of 10 gay and 10 straight bars in Boystown area of Chicago over a one-year period showed 25 incidents of violence in the gay bars, compared to 49, almost twice as many, in the straight bars. Very similar results come from a study in Denver. "In city after city, the same pattern emerges," the violence rate of gay men in public settings is about half that of straight men. (Nimmons, 2002, p. 16-17). Similarly, comparisons of large public events—parades and festivals—held over the same time period in Washington, DC, showed nine arrests for violence at the Caribbean Festival, the Latino cultural event, and the Fourth of July parade events (combined attendance 575,000 people), but for two gay events (combined attendance 750,000 people), *no* arrests for violence were made (Nimmons, 2002).

Nurturance As a Male Norm

Second, Nimmons (2002) challenges the stereotype of gay lives as a culture of narcissism, hedonism, and self-absorption. If that had once been true, it was markedly changed by the AIDS epidemic. Folkman and colleagues (1994), in a summary of their research on the response to the San Francisco AIDS epidemic, states, "the levels and richness of male caregiving we have documented in this community are simply unprecedented" (Folkman, Chesney, & Christopher-Richards, 1994). Similarly, researchers from the Center for AIDS Prevention Studies (University of California) reported that 54 percent of the men sampled in central city gay neighborhoods had cared for other men ill with AIDS (Turner, Catania, & Gagnon, 1994). Nimmons (2002) states "there is no [previous] known example where more than one in two men took time to care for others unrelated to them by blood, family, or clan ties. Let alone kept doing it for more than a decade" (p. 42).

The caregiving of gay men continues, and is not limited to the AIDS epidemic or to helping partners. Gay men are far more likely than straight men to volunteer in caregiving roles. Another group exhibits high levels of caregiving, robust volunteerism, and enjoys sleeping with men—"We call them women," Nimmons jokes (Nimmons, 2002, p. 43). Straight men also participate in volunteerism, but mostly as little league coaches and scoutmasters and other sport or camping type events, and in fire departments and fraternal organizations. In areas where nurturing is most elicited, for example with spouses and children, "husbands are less likely than wives to help their sick spouses with household tasks . . . and wives . . . [provide] approximately twice as many hours of care as husbands"(Nimmons, 2002, p. 41, citing Folkman et al., 1994).

These differences between gay and straight men have prompted a series of studies of gay altruism, including Badgett's (1998) study of 2,300 people in Milwaukee, Philadelphia, and San Francisco. In this study the gay sample volunteered 61 percent more time to nonprofit organizations (29 hours a month more) than did the heterosexual group; this is markedly above the 18 hours a month average for volunteers in this country. Gay men do not simply volunteer to gay organizations and "take care of our own." They "divide their charitable contributions—in both time and money—almost equally between gay and non-gay causes" (Nimmons, 2002, p. 45). This despite that some of the largest charities in United States have refused to allow blood donation, services, and sometimes even money from gays (most notably Red Cross, Salvation Army, and Boy Scouts) (Nimmons, 2002).

Predicting that gay men might be more altruistic than heterosexual men, Salais & Fischer (1995) used a reliable measurement of empathy to demonstrate that the gay men demonstrated significantly higher empathy than their straight cohorts. Using a very different methodology, the Myers Briggs personality inventory, Nieto (1996) found gays more frequently had "intuition-feeling" personality types. (Recall from Chapter 4 the importance of intuition in good counseling.) The total areas of the Myers Briggs in which these men differed from the usual male population suggested a much greater awareness and sensitivity to relationships. Beginning studies suggest that gay men, compared to straight, are more helpful and more expressive of tender feelings (Taylor, 1983), more responsive to children's needs, and offer children more reasons for appropriate behavior. Gay fathers are stricter (Bigner & Jacobson, 1989), more capable of more humanistic intimate contact (Barba, 1998), and less likely to lie in intimate relationships (Burdon, 1966). Finally, men who live in a male same-sexed household (U.S. census) have a rather different occupational pattern than other men. They are much more likely to manage service organizations; provide some sort of caretaking as a therapist; teach education, theology, kindergarten or special education; do private home care, personal care (cosmetics, hair), or cook; or be a designer, a nurse, a librarian, or a writer (Blandford, 2002).

Alternative Hypotheses About Gay Men's Low Violence and Nurturing

Nimmons (2002) suggests that the nurturing quality of gay culture matured during the AIDS crisis. Although evidence to suggest that the greater nurturing shown by gay males is somehow biologically based is insufficient, it is important to note that many of the personality studies cited were done *before* the AIDS epidemic. This suggests that another "cause" may exist. Surely the experience of being called to care for others (in the AIDS epidemic) teaches much. But the experience of *feeling different* early in life may also be a factor in gay sensitivity.

One might also speculate that overcoming the purity code and the sex-negative moral standards of heterosexual culture played a key role in the emergence of more nurturance and less aggression in gay males. Some anthropological studies suggest a relationship between sexual repression and levels of aggression among diverse cultures. A comparison of sexual freedom in 49 cultures led Prescott (1977) to the conclusion that sensual deprivation is a major contributing factor in physical violence.[4] Whatever the reasons, the lines of Holly Near's (1979) song "Singing for our Lives" appear to be accurate: "We are a *gentle* angry people" (emphasis mine).

A Sex-Positive Subculture

Gays seem to have developed a culture of service—though it appears to be seldom noted. However, since this is a chapter on spirituality and our bodies, let's turn directly to the issue of sex in the gay culture. The usual image is that gay men in the midst of the AIDS epidemic continued to engage in unsafe sex. But after reviewing more than 30 studies, the consistent finding is that between 60 and 70 percent of men who have sex with more than one man reported consistent condom use over the prior six months. This contrasts to only 17 percent of heterosexual men with multiple partners (Binson et al., 1995; Fisher & Fisher, 1992). Furthermore, gay men who are HIV positive tend to reduce risk behavior even more than HIV negative gay men, in order to protect their partners (Nimmons, 2002). Safer sex, Nimmons (2002) notes, should be seen as a complicated form of caretaking. It may be that gay male couples' honesty about multiple relationships makes these relationships safer than heterosexual males' typical practice of keeping their outside relationships secretive.

During the early 1990s I had two opportunities to deal directly with the issues of HIV prevention: I was invited to lead the HIV prevention program on the university campus where I was teaching, and I was funded by the Centers for Disease Control and Prevention (CDC) to lead a research project on safety and risk among Asian-American men who had sex with both men and women. In those years not much research had been done on "bisexuality," and the CDC believed that bisexuals would be the group that would carry the virus from the gay to the straight community. (That prediction was wrong; it was intravenous drug users who became the most important bridge to the heterosexual community, leading to a shift in the numbers of new cases. In the first decade of the epidemic, new cases occurred mainly among gay men; later the majority of new cases occurred in women, as continues to be the case.)

Two findings in our studies deserve mention because they were surprises. First, it became clear that younger men were more at risk if they had sex with other young men; if their first sexual partners were somewhat older men who were more enmeshed in the gay community, these partners were more likely to teach the young men about safer sex, and possibly to share memories about friends and former partners who had died of AIDS. Since the older partners had experienced directly the tragedies of this plague, they took prevention seriously. In addition to age of partner, another variable that proved predictive was degree of involvement in the gay community. Gay youth who were *more* involved in the social structures of gay culture, rather then staying primarily involved in the straight community and only entering gay culture for sex, were more likely to practice safer sex.

An even more surprising finding was that the men in our study who came from conservative protestant Christian backgrounds (these were mostly Korean Americans) were the *most* likely to engage in risky sexual behavior, compared to Chinese Americans, mostly of Buddhist or Taoist cultures, and to Filipino Americans, mostly Catholic (Matteson, 1997). Obviously the kind of culture or community in which a person lives greatly affects how a person lives out his or her sexual life. We can only speculate about why involvement in the gay community or in the Chinese-American or Filipino-American communities provides greater protection from risky sex, while coming from conservative Christianity in the Korean community provides the least protection of these four subcultures. My suggestion is that because conservative Christianity teaches the most *sex-negative* view of the body, it is the *least* protective. As the men discover that their sexual inclinations are strong (probably during adolescence), and that they are turned on by other men (probably during their twenties), most of these Christian Asian-American men have felt in conflict with their ethnic roots. The Catholic boys have the support of other Catholic boys in deciding that their Church, their Pope, and their celibate priest really aren't knowledgeable or experienced in this area; thus they may disregard the teachings of their religious leaders, knowing that many other American Catholics have made the same decision. However, conservative protestant boys from puritan traditions (and most of the mission churches emphasized a puritan view of sex) may have to throw out their religious tradition in order to integrate their sexual urges. They are faced with rejecting one identity (being "religious") in order to explore and discover another (their gay or bisexual identity). Their choice is between continuing to accept what their church is saying, or listening to what their body is saying. Unfortunately, in rejecting their religion, they may also have rejected the norms of cautious and safe behavior. They may have had the kind of "all or nothing response" that is sometimes associated with guilt. That is, once they have broken the sexual taboo, they reason, "I have already sinned; I might as well go all the way" (Matteson, 1997, p. 102). Thus the sex-negative religious background may lead to rejection of social norms that are protective.

In contrast, those Asian Americans whose religious and philosophic traditions are Eastern typically did not grow up in a sex-negative culture. This is not to say that Eastern traditions endorse gay sex. Rather, almost all sexuality is seen as a discrete and private affair. It was not necessary for them to reject their backgrounds to carry out discrete sex with men.

Sexual Mores in the Gay Subculture

But what about the sexual values of gay culture? Don't they undermine spiritual values? During the 1950s and 1960s, an era of huge social and sexual change occurred, partly launched by the women's movement, the pill, the student movement, and the recognition of many youth, women, gays, and lesbians, that the sexual mores passed on from the puritans no longer made sense to them.

> As the walls of the old sexual order came tumbling down, forces within the larger culture moved to defend the ramparts. They tried to discredit, sabotage, and dismantle the collective erotic exploration American was beginning. They tried. . .to roll the clock back and stamp out erotic innovation. They fought abortion, birth control, family planning, pornography, and Internet chat rooms, railed at free love and drug use and condoms and premarital sex. (Nimmons, 2002, p. 78)

As usual, the clock did not roll back. As is typical in American culture, the debate became foolishly polarized between extreme conservative/puritan sexual views, and libertarian/individualistic/hedonistic defenses of the changes. Meanwhile, more and more heterosexual couples (as well as same-sex couples) began to live together without the cultural sanction of marriage, use of birth control and dangerous-when-illegal abortions continued to rise, pornography became more and more common not only in "adult bookstores" but in neighborhood drugstores and on television, and a lack of realistic family planning (backed by United States foreign policy of "gag rules") has resulted in the world population more than doubling in 40 years (Sharif, 2001), endangering the environmental survival of mother earth.

Clearly a sexual ethic suitable for this millennium is necessary. Biblical Christians tend to think they represent the ethic of Jesus' times, with no awareness of the history of sex and marriage. Jewish men in Jesus' time were expected to have a period of "betrothal" to a woman to see if she could become pregnant. (Recall that Joseph was "betrothed" to Mary at the time Jesus was conceived.) If the woman did not conceive, the man was not expected to marry her (Anthony Wei, 2000, personal communication). Having the man's genealogical line continue was considered a higher priority than the woman's needs or feelings. As has been true throughout history, sexual ethics need to be reformulated to fit current circumstances and beliefs.

The gay community realized that the goal of teaching America to "just say no" was not going to work (and HIV prevention research among heterosexual youth has borne that out). "[T]he communal sexual explorations of the 1960s, so aggressively extinguished in the larger culture, continued [in the gay community], deepened, matured,

[and] took new forms" (Nimmons, 2002, pp. 78-79). This experiment was possible partly because of the "sexual privilege of men" (Nimmons, 2002, p. 79). The concept of complementarity in heterosexual relationships is important to understand. To oversimplify: If males play a dominant role, females are scripted for a submissive or dependent role. Inasmuch as males have held more economic and physical power throughout most cultures since the rise of agriculture, they have had more sexual freedom. Heterosexual men for the most part, especially before AIDS, have not practiced monogamy or premarital chastity except as necessary to appease their female partners. Furthermore, research suggests heterosexual men are more likely than gay men to be dishonest with their partners (Nimmons, 2002). As and Simon and Gagnon (1969) pointed out decades ago, in negotiations between dating males and females, the general perception is that it is the men who push down the accelerator toward sex and the women who put on the brakes. Obviously, then, when two men get together, it is likely that neither partner has been socialized to put on the brakes.

The positive side of gay men's freedom to experiment is that gay men,

> informed by our status as erotic outlaws . . . have conspired in a lusty, unapologetic embrace of sex and its myriad pleasures. . . . We were the ones who wrapped up our communal ethics of care in latex technology, called it safer sex, and implemented it more thoroughly, with more bawdy bravura, than any other population on earth. (Nimmons, 2002, p. 79)

Despite this embracing of sexuality, the gay culture is open to its own differences. In fact, more than twice the percentage of gay men—24 percent—are celibate as among straight men. Among male couples, commitment to their emotional relationship has a higher priority than commitment to sexual exclusiveness; that is, in the early years of a committed relationship, male couples practice monogamy, but when they have developed a level of emotional trust, they often accept sexual involvements outside the couple as long as these do not endanger the primacy of the emotional commitment (see, e.g., Forssell, 2006). Levels of sexual sensation seeking among gays and straights are essentially the same (Zuckerman, 1983). But eroticism is both easier in gay culture, and is "more a part of gay men's view of human nature" (Herdt, 1992). However, perhaps the most "shocking" aspect of gay culture is not its sexuality, but that men and men actually become close and caring friends. Michael Foucault, who defined friendship as the core philosophical issue at play in queer men's lives, wrote, "To imagine a sexual act. . . is not what disturbs people. But that individuals (men) are beginning to love one another—there's the problem" (Foucault, 1996).

Let me use Nimmons' (2002) own summary:

> Self-identified gay men are engaged in a striking range of cultural innovations in social practices. Our levels of public violence are vastly lower. We volunteer more often, demonstrating levels of altruism and service quite distinct from other men. Our patterns of intimacy and interpersonal connectedness take new forms. We are redefining gender relations in powerful and novel ways. We have distinct patterns of care taking in sexual and communal realms. We are enacting new definitions of public and private, family and friends, as we are vastly transforming relations of pleasure, community, and authority. We are pioneering a wide range of untried intimate relationships, with new forms, rituals, and languages. (p. 5)

IS GAY CULTURE A GOOD MODEL?

How does this description of the contributions of the gay male community stack up against the criteria listed earlier? In what follows I will evaluate it against the criteria I suggested for a "model" twenty-first century embodied spiritual community. It seems to me that Nimmons has effectively presented data that the gay community has a positive view of pleasure while simultaneously encouraging nurturing and caring for others (rather than the sole pursuit of self-centered satisfaction)—my second criterion. Beyond this, he has elaborated the importance of male-to-male friendship within the community, and the special status of friendships between gay males and heterosexual women. (Nimmons devotes a chapter to each, which I have slighted here.) And there is no question that the gay male culture has "a positive view of the body," the first part of my first criterion. Whether the second part has been fulfilled is questionable: Does the gay male culture value the body without idealizing a particular body type? Nimmons (2002) doesn't deal directly with this. Certainly its icons and imagery idealize the trim and muscle-bound youthful male with a handsome face in much the way that classical Greek aesthetics idealized it.

It is commonly believed that men, compared to women, are overly focused on looks when it comes to choosing their mates. If that were the case, it would make sense that gay male culture would develop an exaggerated focus on being "the beautiful people." As noted earlier, in heterosexual couples a complementarity emerges in regard to certain traits and behaviors. For example, we have described male/female interactions regarding sex as the men "pushing down the accelerator" and the women "putting on the brakes." In same-sex couples, gender scripting continues from earlier experiences—that is, gay males are raised as "males" and continue the male "accelerate sex" role even in a same-sexed relationship; since no female is present in the couple the complementary role is not there to balance. Thus male/male couples are likely to show exaggerated male traits, such as high levels of independence in the couple; female couples may show intense interdependence (Ackbar, 2005).

The speculation that this "amplification" process occurs in the man's focus on his partner's appearance is based on the assumption that only men give physical attraction priority in choosing a partner. However, social experiments as early as the late 1960s demonstrated the importance of physical attractiveness for *both* genders. To cite one example, an ingenious study involved college freshmen who participated in a "computer matched" blind-date dance during orientation week (Walster, Aaronson, Abrahams, & Rottman, 1966). During the dance intermissions, the freshmen were briefly interviewed on some personality and intelligence variables and asked questions regarding their desire to date their partners again. Months later a follow-up was done to determine how frequently the couples had reconnected after the dance. Findings showed that the subject's own attractiveness played no role in how he or she viewed his or her dance partner. The primary determinant of how much the partner was liked, was desired as a future date, and was actually asked out on another date was the partner's physical attractiveness. The attractiveness of one's partner was far more significant, for both men and women, than were personality variables; intellectual variables were of no significance whatsoever.

Studies such as this one forced me to question my belief that men were more "visual" and more focused on physical attractiveness in their partners. More recently it has become common for women's media, and women themselves, to comment more on looks. Perhaps our whole culture has become more visual. But it is also likely that women are freer today to express such feelings, though women may have had such feelings in previous decades as well.

Though Nimmons (2002) makes the case that, in terms of sexual and sensual exploration, gay culture affirms difference and variety, it seems questionable to me that it really affirms a variety of body types. The issue is important from the point of view of individual development; the individual needs to develop a realistic, rather than idealistic, view of her or his own body. The focus on image, on a stereotypic view of external attractiveness—whether it occurs in gay culture or mainstream culture—may distract persons from developing an internally felt sense of their own body.

Returning to the criteria for a model embodied spiritual community, my third criterion states, "It would encourage being well educated, including cognizance of contemporary scientific knowledge, but also valuing intuitive 'knowing' through the fine arts." Considerable evidence suggests that gay men tend to be better educated than their male peers. And the personality data regarding gay males' greater focus on intuition and empathy has already been noted.

The final criterion concerns whether, in gay culture, room exists "for the transcendent, without denying our real bodies and our material world." I think the answer is yes, as witnessed by the altruistic values enacted in nurturing and in volunteerism. But in the gay community the "transcendent" is less commonly expressed through the use of traditional religious symbols. I think this is partly because gay men have been so wounded in their experiences with the institutions of religion. An emphasis on spirituality, rather than religion, is common in persons who have been hurt by clergy (Zinnbauer et al., 1997), and is increasingly common in our culture as a whole ("Where We Stand on Faith," 2005). Twenty-four percent of Americans now describe themselves as "spiritual but not religious."

This stance may be even more common among gays. It is exemplified in one of the greatest pieces of performance art in decades, the pair of plays *Angels in America* (Kushner, 1992). This dramatic work, which focuses on the gay community during the AIDS epidemic, clearly deals with the transcendent.

I have already stated the hope that this look at gay issues will encourage the reader to reassess his or her own prejudices in the light of inclusive and body-affirming spirituality. Besides trying to understand the perspective of the gay individual, we have taken a positive look at gay subculture. Though it is doubtful that a purely cognitive understanding can overcome our years of bias, it is incumbent on us to check whether our view of the subculture is, in fact, based on the *mis*understandings and stereotypes of the mainstream culture. Let us turn now to the implications of inclusive and body-affirming spirituality on our work with clients.

WHAT TREATMENT APPROACHES WORK?

As counselors, we can take essentially three positions working with LGBT clients. One is to try to help the clients give up being gay. Reparative therapy (as it is called by those who believe that something is "broken" in homosexuals and bisexuals), more accurately called sexual orientation conversion therapy, attempts to change LGBT individuals into practicing heterosexuals. It is still practiced by some therapists (Bieber, 1988), mostly those who claim to be Christian counselors. However, the American Psychological Association has taken the position that psychologists who practice reparative therapy are acting unprofessionally, because the weight of the research evidence shows that attempts to change sexual orientation are unsuccessful (Haldeman, 1999). Clinical evidence suggests that the attempts are actually damaging to some clients, as they feed into the clients' guilt and self-deprecation, blaming themselves for their own sexual orientation (Shidlo, Schroeder, & Drescher, 2001).

Another position is to recognize that one is not comfortable working with gays, lesbians, or bisexuals, and referring such clients to counselors who specialize in such work or at least are comfortable and informed in this area. A third position is to accept the client's sexual orientation and work with the specific issues the client raises as his or her problem areas, without assuming that the sexual orientation is the key issue for the counseling.

These latter two seem to me to be legitimate and ethical positions. There is nothing wrong with counselors recognizing their own limitations, as long as they do so in a way that does not blame the client or place a burden on the client. Since clients are already vulnerable, they may misunderstand a therapist's refusal to work with them as an indication that their situation is hopeless. The therapist needs take the responsibility for the decision by saying something such as "I am choosing not to work with you because I think a therapist who has experience with gay and lesbian issues can be more helpful to you," or, "because I have some personal issues that are triggered by the gay and lesbian issue, and it would be a disservice to you." As in other referrals, the counselor should make a specific recommendation about the next step the client can take to find an appropriate counselor; for example, "There is an LGBT information line in [nearest city], and they have a counseling program; they also may be able to name a counselor nearby who is qualified to work with you. I suggest you call [phone number]."

Usually you can find out the number for the nearest gay switchboard, hotline, or information line by looking up "gay" in the city phonebook. A directory to gay information lines can be found by calling The Gay and Lesbian National Hotline at 1-888-THE-GLNH, or by going to the resources page of their Web site: http://www.glnh.org/find/index.html.

The third position (accepting the client's sexual orientation, and working with the specific issues that the client raises as his or her problem areas) is the one I take. Counselors who become comfortable working with gay and lesbian clients have a responsibility also to become knowledgeable about the subculture. If counseling LGBT clients is new for you, one way to become knowledgeable is to admit up front with a new client that you don't have much experience working with gay clients, but that you would welcome the client teaching you about the subculture and special issues. I routinely do this when working with a client from an ethnic group that I know little about. Typically I ask such a client if they know of any particular reading they think would be useful for me. I also sometimes make "field trips" to increase my understanding. For example, a counselor taking on her first lesbian client might find in helpful to attend some meetings of Parents, Families and Friends of Lesbians and Gays. These can be a comfortable setting for meeting with other heterosexuals who are dealing with a son or daughter who has recently come out, or is in other ways exploring what the gay community is like. Some local chapters have parents who have become activists who might offer to go out for coffee and talk one on one with you. Experiences such as these provide more context for working effectively and without bias (see Exhibit 6.2).

EXHIBIT 6.2.
Ways to Avoid Hurting LGBT Clients

1. Remember concerning yourself, we are all prejudiced. Remember concerning the client's family that different levels of movement toward affirmation exist. Tolerance is a step in the right direction; accept it in the family, but know that it's a long way from affirmation. For example, my Aunt's response, on first meeting our adopted biracial daughter Heather, was, "She is so cute. How could anyone hold it against her? She can't help it that she's black." The statement is racist in the sense that it assumes being white is better, and that Heather would want to change if she could. Many attitudes toward gays involve toleration, but are still heterosexist; the implied assumption is that straight is better.
2. Do your homework. Check the facts instead of making generalizations or accepting stereotypes. Read up-to-date material. Do not trust research based on clinical samples (from mental health clinics, clinics, hospitals).
3. Don't assume "different" or "abnormal" means "bad."
4. Even when you can make statistical generalizations, it doesn't help you in making decisions for a particular individual. For example, even though most women are shorter than most men, and less muscular, a woman who can lift one hundred pounds should be eligible for a job that involves lifting. It is not "a man's job"; it's a job for a strong person. Train yourself to think beyond categories of race, sex, age, sexual orientation.
5. Develop relationships with people in a category you tend to stereotype. Choose someone you have a chance of liking. If the only blacks, women, or gays you know are in roles subordinate to yours (clients, employees), you run the risk of viewing them as in some sense inferior. Make conscious efforts to develop *peer* relationships with minority persons.
6. When working with clients from other ethnic, religious, racial backgrounds, or with alternative lifestyles, get formal or informal *supervision* from someone who is from that same group.

DEALING WITH WHAT CLIENTS PERCEIVE AS THREATENING

A case study from my own practice illustrates the use of inclusive spirituality on the part of the counselor. The clients are a father who is highly reactive, and his 15-year-old son. The father, a widowed man in his late fifties, requested a session to discuss his fear that his son might be gay. In the phone interview I asked if the father expected I'd be seeing the son as well. He replied affirmatively, suggesting that he hoped I could change the son. Since I work from a systems perspective, I stated that it would be better to see them together for the first interview. If I saw the father alone first, it would likely be harder to develop rapport with the son, who might feel I've already been given a negative impression of him by his father.

In the initial conjoint session it was easy to sense that the father was intensely involved with the son, his only family now that his wife had died. The son, almost 16, was seeking more independence. The father was an Italian immigrant and regularly attended a church in a Catholic parish in which most of the parishioners were of Italian descent. It was clear that the father had hoped I would affirm what he saw as "Christian" values about homosexuality. The father had recently learned that the son had attended a gay youth group, and he was overtly angry and rejecting of his son. Underneath the anger I sensed a mixture of intense connection with the son and fear concerning the son's future if he were gay. I used that session to develop empathy with both men, without taking sides.

I set up the second session with the son alone. The son almost immediately poured out that he was gay, but that he hadn't told his father yet because he was terribly afraid his father would throw him out of the house. It was clear that the boy's wish to stay in the home was based largely on his need for family and his attachment to his father, not simply on economics. Legally, of course, the father could not abandon the boy, but the possibility of the father emotionally abandoning him certainly existed.

As a developmental psychologist, I was convinced that a "cutoff" from the father could seriously scar the boy. Furthermore, it seems to me more important, more deeply spiritual, to love a child in spite of differences than to be "right" concerning a particular interpretation of the Christian view of homosexuality. So my task as a counselor was to be sensitive to the father's spirituality but to try to connect his love and responsibility as a father to his religious beliefs. Two moral or spiritual issues were motivating the father—his view that homosexual behavior is sinful, or at least a dangerous direction for his son, and his love and responsibility as a father. My task in a session alone with the father was to elicit both of these, and clarify more fully the father-son issue, since he had not yet articulated fatherhood as *also* a moral issue and a spiritual responsibility. When we had enough rapport, I asked something such as, "What is a Christian father's responsibility to a son?" and, after more listening, reminded the father that, though Jesus tells his disciples that following him may "lead son away from father," nowhere in the gospels does Jesus give permission for a father to abandon a son. My intent was to block the father from acting out in anger and rejecting the son; I did so by appealing to his being a Christian father.

I did not see it as my responsibility to engage the father in a discussion about my own theology or ethics, but I did see it as important to his spiritual growth to challenge him within his own system. When fear, or lack of information, have resulted in the client's spirituality being destructive, or at least being too constraining, I believe the counselor must challenge or reframe that spirituality so it can become a resource.

Despite the father's fear and anger, he was part of a deep tradition that emphasized the Father God's love for his Son, and the good father's rejoicing at the return of the wayward son. Furthermore, the bonding between this particular father and son was strong. Further work needed to be done to alleviate the fear on the son's part of being cut off, and to uncover some of the father's misperceptions concerning the dangers of gay culture. The main work was accomplished when the father recognized that he resonated deeply with his religious duty to be a good father and did not want the "homosexual issue" to sever the bonds between himself and his son. My work was facilitated by the son realizing that I had fairly concrete knowledge of the gay community, and that I was not rejecting of it or him.

This example could give the false impression that the process model advocated in this book demands that a counselor embrace everyone. The process model encourages the counselor to explore his or her own reactions enough *not* to enter counseling with persons from a group he or she hasn't yet learned to embrace. When I taught graduate students in counseling, I urged them to get to know at least one member of a particular minority group *as a peer* before trying to work with a client from that minority group. The risk of seeing a minority client is that the professional counseling relationship replicates the one-up, one-down relationship that has been oppressive to that minority. It is very hard to work successfully with someone if you have not had a chance to overcome that one-up role in at least one friendship with someone from that group.

To conclude these two chapters on the body and sexuality, it may be helpful to think of the holistic goals of counseling. Our goal is to move toward loving the whole person: mind, body, emotions, spirit. Loving the body implies moving beyond the mind/body split, and beyond puritanism and its rejection of body and pleasure. It involves moving beyond stoicism to being open to the emotions. It means integrating ways of knowing, to include not just cognitive and rational methods of apprehending but also the more body-sensed intuitive and empathic ways of understanding.

Chapter 7

Overcoming Barriers, Dealing with Differences

POSSIBLE BARRIERS

> Spirituality emerges in the midst of differences through respecting the journey of the other person.
>
> Timothy Pedigo (personal communication)

One of the disciplines that is helpful to my being a spiritually sensitive counselor is spending a few moments before entering a session simply being aware of what I'm experiencing, paying special attention to the barriers that may keep me from being fully present with that particular client. These barriers usually have to do with preconceptions of who the client is. Sometimes the preconceptions emerge from my assessment of the client, especially if I have viewed the client through a category such as those in the American Psychiatric Association's *Diagnostic and Statistical Manual of Mental Disorders* (DSM). Other barriers exist about which we may be less aware—expectations we have of a client because she is a woman, or he is a man, because the client is elderly, or "only" an adolescent, or because of the sketchy information we have concerning racial or ethic background. This ritual helps me get beyond categorical thinking.

As counselors most of us want to view ourselves as tolerant; often we have put real energy into trying to be "color blind" or in other ways eliminate the prejudices and biases with which we grew up. But habitual ways of perceiving and thinking do not go away easily; often a prayer or short meditation is not enough to overcome the barriers of gender, race, ethnicity, religion, or class. We need a context of experiences and learning with the particular category of people whom we are experiencing as "other." When we are seeking to understand a particular ethnic group, for example, it is better, if possible, that we first meet people from that group who are our peers. If our first encounter is with a client in the hierarchical setting of the counselor-client relationship, it confounds the situation, in that we are already in the higher status role. Meeting these people requires a life discipline of seeking to include a variety of persons of different races, ethnicities, and backgrounds in our social and intimate friendship groups.

We have been trained that developing a relationship with the client is crucial, especially in the beginning of counseling. In order to be clear about our own barriers to relationship, we need to unpack the baggage from our personal histories and cultures and examine it. Not that we will throw out all the clothes that we've been carrying around, but we can choose what really fits us, and what belongs to the climate we will inhabit with our clients, and throw out what insulates us unnecessarily.

As counselors who are seeking to integrate spirituality into our work, we value the spiritual sensitivity that we have—or long for—in our own lives. We sense that this spiritual atonement is relevant to our relationships with our clients, but we are conscious of many differences between us and our clients, and this leaves us confused about how to go about integrating the spiritual into counseling sessions. With each client, I ask myself, "Can I really be present with this person?" Sometimes doubt emerges, and I ask myself, "Am I the one who should be his or her therapist?" A central issue concerns how to handle the differences between us and our client so that the differences don't separate us.

Observing Differences

As you read the following anecdote from my experience when our children were young, notice the natural way in which Eric, as a child, is conscious of differences:

> My wife Sandy and I were seated at the kitchen table eating lunch with our two four-year-olds. Sandy and I are both Americans of northern European ancestry. Our two kids, both adopted, are biracial, with both Caucasian and African-American lineage. Eric looked around the table and verbalized his observa-

tions. "I have a flat nose, and Heather has a flat nose. Mommy has a pointed nose, and Daddy has a pointed nose. When I grow up, I will have a pointed nose."

At this age, Eric does not have a lot of cultural baggage around race or age—he is simply and innocently observing. In fact, he is observing with an open mind, or as the Buddhist's say, with a "beginner's mind." He is a good model for a counselor insofar as he feels free to observe what is visible, and to share his thoughts about it without any claim to expertise. However, his conclusion is dead wrong. Speaking as Eric's proud father, I believe Eric was an exceptionally bright and verbal child. He had gathered empirical observations from two groups—-the two adults at the table and the two children at the table—-and he had made a generalization that perfectly fit his data. All the adults at the table had pointed noses, and all the children had flat noses, so he had inferred that when he became an adult, he too would have a pointed nose. Eric may have been a budding scientist, but he didn't yet understand random sampling, and he was unknowingly plagued by the problem of confounding variables. Specifically, both of the adults at the table were Caucasian, and both of the children were biracial, so age and race were confounded in his sample. He had attributed the differences in noses to the wrong variable.

Observing and commenting on differences is not what gets us into trouble. However, classifying things and attributing them to particular causes can lead both children and adults into mistaken beliefs. In American culture, these mistaken beliefs often have to do with the categories of age and race (as illustrated by Eric's classifications) and with gender, physical ability, sexual orientation, ethnicity, and religion. Class is also a key trigger of prejudice but it is often overlooked.

Why is Prejudice Important to the Spiritually Sensitive Counselor?

It is important at this point to clarify the purpose of this chapter, since the content develops in what may be an unexpected direction for the reader. Most current writing in this field focuses on the differences among the major religions. At the same time, most authors comment that spirituality should not be equated with formal religion, and that it is possible to be profoundly spiritual without being involved in traditional or institutional religion. (It is also possible to be involved in religion and be spiritual, of course.) Becvar (1997) states it well:

> From my perspective, spirituality transcends specific religious traditions and accommodates the full range of belief systems. Counseling/therapy with a spiritual orientation focuses on the whole of the client/system and is aimed at the cocreation of a new context within which healing at a soul level is achieved. And it includes a conscious awareness both of the *connectedness of the client and counselor/therapist* and of the *sacred trust* that is bestowed upon counselors and therapists by their clients. (p. 24, emphasis mine)

Since spirituality is so essentially related to *connectedness,* it seems to me that it is crucial to examine whatever divides us, whatever barriers we allow to separate us as humans. The barriers of religion are only one of a group of prejudices and biases and assumptions that have the potential for compromising this connectedness. The *sacred trust* that clients place in us obligates us to discipline ourselves to work to overcome our own prejudices in all of these areas. This requires more self-examination that is common for counselors; a recent analogue study showed that psychotherapists' beliefs about their ability to avoid bias concerning sexual orientation, particularly concerning bisexuality, did not accurately reflect the therapists' actual risk for developing biased perceptions of their clients whose sexual history has included both male and female partners (Mohr & Weiner, 2006).

Of course, a thorough analysis of age, race, gender, physical ability, sexual orientation, ethnicity, religion, and class is not possible in one chapter or even one book. Fortunately, some dynamics of prejudice and bias can be discerned in examining any one of these issues, and these common patterns accelerate the learning curve once a helping person begins the examination.

For this chapter I have chosen gender as the best place to focus for several reasons:

- We all relate to the gender issue as a conscious one in our lives. (Typically those in the majority do not relate to race issues, or ethnicity issues, or issues of being physically challenged as one of their own issues, though in fact the issue of racial conflict *is* a white issue as well as a black, Hispanic, or Asian one.)

- Most of us are already aware that attitudes toward the genders, toward masculinity and femininity, began in the home.
- A solid body of empirical research pertains to the gender issue, and to perceptions of gender. This is less the case for the other issues.
- Almost all of us have opportunities in our daily lives to deal with the other gender, and thus to directly put into practice whatever we learn about ourselves and others regarding gender prejudice. Except for those readers who live in gender segregated communities (monasteries, convents, schools, or colleges that are not coed), we do not have to form new social groupings in order to experience our reactions to gender and experiment with changes.

My basic premise is that the beliefs we have about gender (or race, ethnicity, etc.) clarify the way we perceive and handle human differences. We may enjoy differences or we may perceive them as a threat. We may use differences to inflate our own sense of self-importance, turning a difference into an issue of superiority and inferiority. Most crucially, we may allow differences to distance us. As Lott (2002) elaborates in terms of relationships with the poor, distancing takes on the form of exclusion, separation, devaluing, and discounting, resulting finally in discrimination.

Gender: An Example of How We Handle Differences

Gender and the Deities

Gender and age are arguably the primary categories in human relationships. In small, preliterate societies, age and gender were often the only basis for differentiation in roles (Campbell, 1996); so far as anthropologists have discovered, no human societies exist or existed that have not assigned different roles in terms of gender and age.

When we hear that a couple have just had a baby, the first question we are likely to ask is, "Is it a boy or a girl?" Before we begin relating to the new person, we want to know its gender. Gender is so central to our view of being a person that we find it almost impossible to think about God as a "person" without attributing a gender. The earliest deities that were worshiped appear to have been feminine. Preliterate humans were very directly dependent on nature to provide the animal and plant food they needed, and to bless them with fertility so they would have children to assure the future of their tribe; their worship reflected their awe and dependency on the continued fertility of plants, animals, and the women in the tribe. Images of pregnant animals (in cave drawings) and heavy-breasted and full-bellied females (in miniature sculptures) seem to have been the first expressions of worship. The awesome and revered was pictured as female.

Later, with the emergence of property ownership and agriculture, the gods were viewed as male, defending territory as warriors. Where pantheons of many deities emerged, usually they included both male and female deities. Some deities were viewed has half male and half female, especially in Hinduism and Buddhism, but rarely has the divine been portrayed as without gender, except in academic theology.

The Masculine/Feminine Split

The importance of male/female differences in nature and in social learning is reflected in every society of humans that has been studied having defined gender roles. What is surprising is how varied these roles are in human societies, and how complex the differences are in nature. We tend to assume that all of life is divided into male and female, that only heterosexual behavior is natural, that males and females must get together for the females to produce offspring, that males are usually bigger than females, and that females are usually more beautiful. All of these assumptions are based on overgeneralizations and on cultural biases; they do not accurately describe the varieties of nature.

We forget that most forms of life on our planet, such as bacteria, viruses, and the less complex multicelled organisms, reproduce by various forms of division without the dichotomy of male and female. Some very complex forms of individual life, such as snails, are *both* male and female. In other forms, such as sea horses, it is the males who hold the fertilized eggs and hatch the babies. In some species the males and females look almost identical, for example, bears, raccoons, robins, crows, toads, and houseflies. In some the females are larger than the males, for example, spiders and great horned owls. In many species the males are more splendid, colorful, or ornate in appearance than the females, such as peacocks, roosters, cardinals, moose, lions, gorillas, and guppies.

Observers of mammals have known for half a century that homosexual activity "is inherit in most if not all [species of] mammals including the human species" (Ford and Beach, 1951, p. 143). Scientists and naturalists have documented homosexual behavior in most mammals, and in a huge range of bird species (Bagemihl, 2000). Whether in domestic animals such as cows, or in the wild, as has been recently documented in field research with orangutans ("Swinging Both Ways," 2001), homosexuality is not "unnatural." In fact, what we view as "natural" has been very much biased by our culture's values and assumptions. Bagemihl (2000) also cites documented observations of homosexual behavior in reptiles, amphibians, fishes, insects and other invertebrates, and domesticated animals.

To focus specifically on humans, we must question which differences between male and female are truly "natural" and pervasive, and which are simply overgeneralizations or even misperceptions. Books such as *Men are from Mars, Women are from Venus* (Gray, 1992) encourage us to think stereotypically and to assume that personality traits, styles of communication, and a broad group of behaviors are "naturally" masculine or feminine.

As social scientists and practitioners, we need to answer three questions:

1. Do clear differences exist between men and women in personality traits and behaviors?
2. If so, what factors produce these differences? That is, are the differences socially learned and subject to change, or are they built into the genetic and biological structure of each gender?
3. What impact do gender differences have on our relationships with our clients?

RELATED RESEARCH FROM QUANTITATIVE PSYCHOLOGY

What Gender Differences Really Exist?

In this section, I am hoping the reader will notice the ways her or his assumptions about gender differences may or may not fit the facts.

Make a list of what you personally believe are the ways males and females are different. As you read this section, mark each of these listed items as either being validated by the factual evidence, or not.

A classic review of the empirical research on differences between men and women, *The Psychology of Sex Differences,* was published in 1974 by Maccoby and Jacklin. After reviewing more than 2,000 studies, the authors concluded that many common beliefs about gender differences have no basis in the facts. Girls are not more social than boys, nor are they more suggestible or lower in self-esteem. Girls are not better than boys at rote learning and simple tasks; nor are boys better at higher cognitive processing. Boys do not show higher achievement motivation than girls.

However, based on their analysis of the research, they believed that four areas of gender differences were "well established":

- Men are generally more aggressive than women.
- Men are superior in visual-spacial abilities.
- Men score higher than women for mathematical abilities.
- Women are superior to men in verbal abilities.

These findings need to be reavaluated using the data from the many studies that have been published since then, and the method of meta-analysis, which has since been developed, needs to be used. This is an important new statistical method for quantitatively pooling the results of many different studies of the same issue. Consequently, we can be much more sure about some consistent and sizable differences that occur. On the other hand, a hot debate is ongoing about how large a difference must exist in order to consider it important or significant (see Eagly, 1995, versus Hyde & Plant, 1995, for an example of the debate).

With increased data and better analyses, some areas of gender differences among American respondents seem even more clearly established today:

Aggression

Maccoby and Jacklin's (1974) earlier generalization that men show higher levels of aggressive behavior is validated in more recent reviews of the data using meta-analysis. The difference is moderate in size (Eagly & Steffen, 1986; Hyde, 1984, 1986).

Visual-Spatial Abilities

Newer research allows us to be more specific. Men's superiority in two types of visual-spatial processes, mental rotation and spatial perception, seems to be present in the newer data, although the only large gender difference is in mental rotation—that is, males may not have to turn a map around to know whether a particular turn is a left or a right—they can rotate the picture of the mapped intersection in their heads (Linn & Peterson, 1985; Masters & Sanders, 1993). However, spatial visualization does not show a clear gender difference (Linn & Peterson, 1985), and it has been recently discovered that in the subcategory of visual-spatial abilities women outperform men in regard to memory of spatial location (Silverman & Eals, 1992). So the broad generalization of the earlier studies, that men are superior in visual-spatial processes, does not seem warranted.

Verbal Ability and Mathematical Ability

In two areas of gender differences that Macobby and Jacklin (1974) described as well established, the differences seem to have become smaller and smaller in the ensuing decades: female superiority in verbal ability (Hyde and Linn, 1988) and male superiority in mathematical ability. The failure of men to outperform women in math is especially clear (in later studies) if the meta-analyses are limited to more representative samples. In those studies females actually slightly outperform males (Hyde, Fennema, & Lamon, 1990). It seems clear that the differences in cognitive performances attributed to particular genders in the past were either artifacts of poorer research techniques or have disappeared now that boys and girls are being given more equal opportunities. Meta-analyses comparing different time periods show the differences in scores have grown smaller with each passing decade.

Sex

Although the newer psychological research based on meta-analysis has challenged most of the previously assumed differences, it has uncovered some new differences. In a meta-analysis of 239 different samples, the largest male/female differences concern behaviors and attitudes directly connected to sex. The largest concerns the incidence of masturbation. Females report a much lower incidence of masturbation than males; almost all males have masturbated. The gender difference is enormous [effect size d = .96] compared to cognitive differences (such as verbal or mathematical ability), or differences in the social-personality realm (such as aggression). The other enormous difference is in males' acceptance of casual sex, in contrast to females focus on sex in the context of love (alothough women as well as men become somewhat more accepting of casual sex as they move into adulthood; teens are less accepting).

These two differences are greater than differences in any of the other variables that have been studied comparing males and females. These remarkable differences should not lead us to overgeneralize that most sexual attitudes and behaviors are very different between males and females. Differences in anxiety or guilt about sex, and in attitudes about intercourse in a committed relationship, are only moderate in size. Attitudes about civil liberties for homosexuals and, surprisingly, about masturbation (in contrast to behaviors), as well as attitudes of sexual satisfaction, show no gender differences at all (Oliver & Hyde, 1993). It also should be noted that one of the two large differences (incidence of masturbation) has decreased in size over the period from the 1960s through the 1980s, although it is still much higher for men.

To briefly summarize the results for other personality and social areas in which meta-analyses have been performed (besides aggression):

> The theory that women fear success, and that men are more achievement oriented, has no support from any of the four meta-analyses that have been performed. (Hyde & Frost, 1993, pp. 80-81)

The supposed greater conformity and influenceability of females seems to be demonstrated primarily in studies with male investigators; the difference does not show up when the authors of the studies are female (Hyde & Frost, 1993).

The idea that women more often perform helping behaviors depends on how *helping* is defined. Men do more acts of rescuing, primarily in short-term relationships, but women perform more helping behaviors than men when the type of helping is caretaking in long-term relationships. (Note these studies did not differentiate gay from straight men; see the previous chapter for information on the extraordinary rates of gay males' care in long-term relationships.) Finally, women receive more help from men than from women; men receive about the same from each (Hyde & Frost, 1993).

In small groups, it is not true that men are more active than women. Again, it depends on the type of activity. Both men and women perform more task-oriented behaviors than socioemotive ones, but when positive socioemotive behaviors are performed, it is usually by women (Hyde & Frost, 1993). Men are consistently more active and interrupt more often than women in task-oriented groups (Eagly & Karau, 1991; Wood & Rhodes, 1992).

In specific types of leadership behaviors, no gender differences are clear. But in overall style of leadership, women tend to engage in participative leadership, while men favor more directive leadership (Hyde & Frost, 1993).

The only reported gender difference that is of higher magnitude than the directly sexual differences (masturbation, etc.) concerns females superiority in noticing nonverbal cues, especially visual cues of facial expressions. Females are also more empathic. As infants they do more "reflexive" crying (responding to other infants' cries). As children they show more empathy in responding to pictures and stories than boys. As adults they show more empathy on paper-and-pencil inventories (Hyde & Frost, 1993).

In these last three areas (small group activity, leadership behaviors, and attunement to nonverbal cues) women seemed to be more focused on interpersonal or expressive concerns, and men focused on task or agentic orientation.

Clearly, men as a group are different from women as a group in some ways—though in many ways they have been perceived to be different and are not, and in other ways they once were different but are less different today.

What Factors Produce these Gender Differences?

That some male-female differences have faded away over the decades suggests that those differences may have been due to social roles and learning experiences. This does not mean that those differences that have remained stable are clearly biological—it may be that social conditions surrounding those traits have continued to reinforce them. For example, research on gender stereotypes shows consistently that aggressiveness is a key part of the male role in the United States (Eagly, 1987). Competitive athletics and expectations in military settings heighten levels of aggressiveness in males (Arkin & Dobrofsky, 1978; Stein & Hoffman, 1978). Females are socialized against being aggressive and feel more guilt and anxiety than males when they do show aggression (Eagly & Steffen, 1986).

Both laboratory studies and anthropological observations strongly suggest that aggression is a learned role. In a social laboratory study, Lightdale and Prentice (1994) used a technique designed to make individuals temporarily lose a sense of responsibility and feel anonymous and not constrained by social norms such as gender roles. Under these conditions, differences between males and females disappeared.

The female superiority in empathy and related behaviors may also be a result of male learning of gender scripts. Masculinity, as generally defined in U.S. culture, rewards hiding feelings, seeming rational or tough—and thus works against the development of empathy. "When a boy's own emotional life is closed off, when he can't accurately and openly feel his own feelings, it is unlikely that he has much of a basis for feeling empathic toward others" (Garbarino, 1999, cited in Kenrick et al.,1999, p. 46).

It is also important to remember that almost all of the studies reviewed in the meta-analyses used American subjects, so they tell us about gender differences only in American culture. Margaret Mead's (1935) field studies of New Guinea tribes pointed out that many "personality traits" (such as aggressiveness or nurturance) which are seen as masculine or feminine were not consistently gender-typed across cultures.

> In a mountain-dwelling tribe . . . men and women were more alike than in our culture. Their similarity lay in their passivity, gentleness, mildness, and domesticity. . . . Men and women shared the care of the children and other home duties with less division of labor than that with which we are familiar. (Hilgard & Atkinson, 1967, p. 106, citing Mead, 1935)

Other cultures train both men and women to be masculine by our standards. Among a river-dwelling culture in New Guinea, "both sexes tended to be ruthless, aggressive, and violent" (Hilgard & Atkinson, 1967, p. 106). Some societies believe, as we do, that certain traits and activities are natural for men and others for women, but the specific traits are nearly the opposite of our own. In the lake-dwelling tribe Mead studied, the woman was the aggressive partner, the manager of business affairs. The man was emotionally responsive to the feelings of this children, and he was subordinate to and dependent on his mate. The psychological reversal was so real that the Tchambuli (tribe) interpreted it as biologically natural—even to the extent that the man went into confinement and suffered while his wife had the baby (Hilgard & Atkinson, 1967).

Even in the realm of behaviors leading to mating, what is "natural" is not what our cultural biases lead us to expect.

> There is a widespread belief that male animals of most species always assume complete command of the mating situation and inevitably play the more active role in pre-coital courtship. Nothing could be further from the truth. . . . The relative sexual readiness of the male and female frequently determines which individual will solicit and which will respond. . . . So far as we have been able to ascertain, there is no mammalian species in which sexual initiative rests solely with either the male or the female. (Ford & Beach, 1951, pp. 102-103)

From the cross-cultural evidence it seems clear that unless specific pressures are brought to bear against such behavior (as in our society), women initiate sexual advances as often as men do (Ford & Beach, 1951).

Evolutionary biologists argue that many of the significant and lasting differences between the genders evolved from the different roles that men and women played in early human history, and the issues of mate selection surrounding these (for a succinct introduction, see Buss, 1995). Men's greater interest in casual sex fits their need (in evolutionary history) to seek a variety of partners for carrying on their genetic line. They are more likely to be jealous about sexual infidelity in a woman partner than about emotional involvements. Females, because of their role in carrying the baby and nurturing it, are more concerned with finding a mate who will stay with them and provide for the child. Females are more upset by emotional infidelity in men than by sexual infidelity (Buss, Larsen, Westen & Semmelroth, 1992). Women's greater skills in interpreting facial cues might be associated with their need to assess their mate's emotional fidelity. Men's greater ability to follow spatial rotations is interpreted as necessary to hunting skills, essential to providing for his mate and their children (Buss, 1995).

Using evolutionary biology as a framework for theorizing which gender differences are genetically based is both tempting and risky, given that the field is in its infancy and very few of the supportive studies are cross-cultural. The studies concerning jealousy cited previously have had similar results in three different countries, but all three were northern European or American. The most broadly based finding, tested for 37 cultures on six continents, is that women are more exacting than men in their standards for a short-term mate—they expect him to be able to be a good provider (Buss, 1989). Though it is striking that the only cognitive gender difference that has stood the test of three decades of research—men's superior visual rotation—seems related to hunting skills, Buss fails to note that another physical skill important to hunting—accuracy of throwing—shows no gender difference (Thomas & French, 1985). One of the areas in which male and female differences is shrinking is in athletic performance, which suggests that these differences are highly responsive to environmental forces such as training (Linn & Hyde, 1989). (Note that female Olympic athletes have continued to close the gender gap on the 100 meter dash and the 100 meter freestyle events.) Studies also show that girls grow up in environments that provide less spatial training than is provided for boys (Baenninger & Newcombe, 1989). No evidence supports that the gender difference in mental rotation is diminishing (Masters & Sanders, 1993). Nevertheless, it remains an open question whether this gender difference is due to a biological and evolutionary difference in male brains or to the likelihood that males get more experience in spatial mapping and representation.

The Social Malleability of Gender Differences

Given that social scientists have been studying gender differences for more than three decades, what is most striking is the degree to which gender differences are open to change. Only two of the differences noted in the early review (Maccoby & Jacklin, 1974) turned out to be important in recent studies: men's higher degrees of aggression and their superior skills in visual rotation. Aggression does not seem to be a biologically-based difference, considering cross-cultural differences and the fact that in laboratory studies where other variables are manipulated the gender difference disappears. The only large gender difference that might be considered stable across periods of time and therefore possibly genetic is men's superiority in visual rotation. It is too early to know if certain athletic skills are tied to male genes—we know that in some areas women are closing the gap in athletics.

The important differences found in more recent research are all issues of interpersonal interactions or sexual behaviors. For men, these are interrupting and taking charge in task-oriented groups, a greater acceptance of casual sex, and a higher incidence of masturbation. For women, these are seeking mates who are good providers and attunement to nonverbal cues. The group behavior and leadership styles of men and women are different, possibly due to status and power differences rather than gender. The focus on men as providers may change as women are now more involved in the paid workforce throughout their adult years. The incidence of masturbation is beginning to change as women take more control of their own bodies.

In the social realm, this leaves only men's acceptance of casual sex as a solid difference over time that is not clearly changing in this culture. As noted, the related psychological data concerning jealousy differences is limited to three highly industrialized and male-status-centered societies. The most relevant anthropological or comparative studies come from subhuman primates. Evidence suggests that among those animal species in which regular mates are formed, sexual jealousies are aroused if the dominant male observes another individual attempting to copulate with any of the females in his group. The most prevalent pattern of mating across all primates, including man, is a multiple one in which two or more females are attached to a single male. (Recall from Chapter 6 that this is the pattern for Old Testament marriages.) However, in human societies the majority of males have only one mate at a given period of time, although a man may support more than one sex partner if he can afford it (Ford & Beach, 1951). The continuity of the attitudes toward casual sex over time, and the similarity of the data on jealousy between the three human cultures and the primate comparisons, strengthen the case for evolutionary biological theory.

On the other hand, if men's differences from women in regard to casual sex is biological, it is hard to explain the anthropological data. (We could wish for some methodology similar to meta-analysis that would update our reviews of the data from anthropology.) Of the 185 societies reviewed in Ford and Beach (1951), only 29 formally restrict mating to one partner, and only 9 of these wholly disapprove of both premarital and extramarital sex liaisons. In short, less than 5 percent of human societies the anthropologists had studied believed in lifetime monogamy. Though it is certainly more common for men to have multiple partners than for women, some societies approve of women having two or more men as simultaneous and long-term partners, most notably the Kaingang of Brazil, the Toda of India, and the Marquesans of Polynesia (Ford and Beach, 1951). Especially interesting is that Toda women often marry several brothers, and expressed jealousy among the brothers is practically unknown. In addition, in almost 40 percent of the societies studied, women may have sexual liaisons with other men, although they may not marry them.

Given this breadth of views of what is acceptable for women when looking across cultures, it is clear that if the gender difference regarding casual sex were to hold up at all in studies outside of Euro-American cultures, it certainly would *not* indicate that women are interested in only one man, from the perspective of biology and evolution. Women's concern for the nurturing of offspring may lead them away from casual sex, but it does not necessarily inspire monogamy.

SUMMARY OF GENDER DIFFERENCE FINDINGS

Is Gender Important?

Let's return to the three questions we raised earlier:

1. Do clear differences exist between men and women in personality traits and behaviors?
2. If so, what factors produce these differences? That is, are the differences socially learned and subject to change, or are they built into the genetic and biological structure of each gender?
3. What impact do gender differences have on our relationships with our clients?

To the question "Do clear differences exist between men and women in personality traits and behaviors?" the research suggests that most of the stereotypes have no basis in fact. The data in 1974 suggested that males are more aggressive than females, but studies since then show that the difference is only moderate in size and is decreasing.

The generalization that males are superior (to females) in spatial ability has been shown to hold only for mental rotation of visual images. In another visual-spatial area women have been shown to outperform men; they are better at memory of spatial location.

The cognitive gender differences found in earlier reviews of research have almost entirely disappeared. Male superiority in mathematical ability and female superiority in verbal ability are declining. The belief that women have greater fear of success, or that men are more achievement oriented, has no support in the data from meta-analyses. The generalization that women perform more helping behaviors holds only if we limit "helping" to caretaking in long-term relationships; men do more short-term or rescuing behaviors. The generalization that men dominate and interrupt more in small group settings applies only if the groups are task-orientated. Leadership behaviors are not more frequent in men, but the genders do favor different styles of leadership behavior, with women engaging in participative leadership and men favoring more directive leadership. Women seem to be more focused on interpersonal or expressive concerns, and are more empathic. The only reported gender difference that is of higher magnitude than the directly sexual differences occurs in the area of interpersonal concerns: females' superiority in noticing nonverbal cues, especially visual cues of facial expressions.

It is clear that most of these differences are socially learned and subject to change. Few, if any, of these differences appear to be built into the genetic and biological structure of each gender. Males' greater aggression, for example, does not exist in certain cultures, and when social strictures are removed, gender differences in aggression disappear. Finally, we must recognize that the very search for gender differences has been done in a way that may have confounded two important variables, as the next section will clarify.

Confounding Gender with Hierarchy and Dominance

Before we move to the question of the possible impact gender differences have on our relationships with our clients, we need to note a problem with the isolation of gender as a variable. When we view a group of persons in terms of their gender and notice a difference, the difference may be due to another variable that coexists with gender. Remember the confusion my son made in attributing pointed noses to age rather than race? The confusion was understandable because the Caucasians in his sample were also the adults. A similar confounding occurs in any culture in which males have more power in economic and political decision-making: the women in the sample are also the people with less power. So we don't know if differences such as being more attentive to nonverbals or communicating more indirectly or softly are due to being female, or to being less empowered (Crawford & Gentry, 1995). One interesting approach to finding out is to compare communication strategies in heterosexual couples to those in gay male and in lesbian couples. Falbo and Peplau (1980) found that the individuals who saw themselves as the more powerful partner in the relationship used more direct, interactive strategies (the prototypical heterosexual male strategy), and lower-power partners used indirect, "feminine" strategies, regardless of their gender (cited in Crawford & Gentry, 1995). That is, where gender and power are not confounded (e.g., in lesbian or gay male couples), a pattern of more direct communication from the dominant person occurs, and more attention to nonverbals and indirect expression occurs in the lower-power partner.

Women of color have led the way in recognizing that systems of oppression are linked, and that all of them are based on hierarchy and dominance and are supported by similar social structures (Crawford & Gentry, 1995). The social psychological literature on groups who are in the minority and do not have as much political and economic power, or as high a status, shows that such people tend to be much more aware of the behaviors and habits of the higher status group than vice versa. To take an extreme case, a slave must learn the ways of his or her master in order to survive. The oppressed have more motivation to understand the oppressors than the other way around. Thus, African Americans, immigrants, gays and lesbians, or other minorities are likely to be fairly sophisticated and nuanced in their understanding of the majority culture, whereas members of the higher status group have much more stereotypical and superficial knowledge of the minority cultures. This literature also clarifies how social injustice can persist in targeted groups who seem unaware of the injustice, showing no evidence of unhappiness or rebellion but instead seeming quiescent (Fine & Gordon, 1989, p. 165, cited in Crawford & Gentry, 1995, p. 178).

When we describe male-female differences, looking at this one variable apart from others—gender but not power and status—we may fail to notice that many of the differences attributed to "sex" are really due to power. Furthermore, instead of seeing behaviors or styles of interaction as situation specific, we attribute them to static personality traits.

Once we recognize this dynamic, we realize that some common themes exist in the experience of all of the minorities, whether the category is ethnicity, race, gender, sexual orientation, age, or physical ability. If we tried to summarize research on the differences between African and Anglo-Americans, we would find parallels to the gender differences we have reviewed here. Some differences that were highly significant would turn out to be factually correct, but more closely related to economics and class than to race. The same kind of thought distortions and emotional defenses are involved regardless of which of the oppressions, which of the minorities, we are dealing with. Since we cannot conduct a review of the literature on each of the issues that may separate us from our clients, the "Resources" section of the Appendix offers more specific readings on overcoming racism, ageism, and other specific prejudices. Much of what follows about gender could be restated about racism, ethnic prejudice, anti-Semitism, and the others.

Not only are group differences (such as gender difference, racial difference) often due to issues of power and status, so are some common behaviors in almost all people in certain situations. Consider, for example, the deference a high-ranking military man shows when he is interacting with an officer of even higher rank and status than himself. He does not have a deferent personality style; he is deferent only to those few military men who rank higher than he. In fact, most styles of interaction are situation specific rather than consistent traits of a person. It is important to realize that when our clients defer to us, it does not mean that they are acting out a racial or gender stereotype, or that they have a deferent personality. They may, in fact, be responding to the power and status issues of the counseling situation.

What if gender is not so much about real differences, but is important largely because we habitually pay attention to it?

How Does Gender Impact Our Relationship with Our Clients and their Spirituality?

If we conclude from the review of social science research that gender differences beyond those directly related to sex are not all that great, and are mostly due to social rather than biological variables, or to confounds with power differences, we might ask, "Why should counselors be concerned with gender in their work with clients?" The answer has more to do with expectation and perceptions than with gender itself.

Gender expectations impact our clients' views of themselves, of significant others, and of the divine:

1. Many clients fail to reach their full potential because they accept uncritically the stereotypic limitations for their own gender.
2. In couples, one partner may place unnecessary restrictions on the other due to his or her gender stereotypes. Often the other member has similar stereotypes, but they are less obvious.
3. The three major Western religions (Judaism, Christianity, and Islam) all developed during and after the emergence of agricultural economy, and traditionally identify "God" as masculine. Historically, these traditions were enmeshed in patriarchal culture, though all three have elements within their scriptures and tradition that encourage liberation from traditional women's roles. Nonetheless, the institutions and forms of these traditions have posed a problem for many women. What does it mean to be "made in the image of God" but to consistently visualize God as "Him" or "Father"? Does it fit women's experience to think of God's creative change in the world as coming solely through God's "only Son," and never being mediated through women? Some psychological interpretations of history have argued that the emphasis on Mary the mother of Jesus has increased

> throughout the history of Catholic Christianity as a counter to the overly male-dominated institutions and scriptures of that church. In Judaism, which in its classical forms has been traditionally patriarchal, is also a mystical tradition that focuses on the Sheckhina, the feminine aspect of God, and refers to the divine indwelling on earth (Fishbane, 1999).[1]

On the other hand, religious institutions in the West have been somewhat "feminized." Far more women than men regularly attend Christian worship services in the United States and Europe, whether protestant or Catholic. The traditional paintings, sculptures, and stained glass windows depicting Jesus show him in clothing that, by today's styles, looks feminine (although in fact the common dress for working men in Jesus' time looked similar to our Bermuda shorts). The American ideal of the tough, self-made individualist does not square with the popular image of Jesus as a gentle, nurturing person. Rather, the notion of Jesus as a gentle, nurturing person seems more congruent with the "feminized" depiction of paintings, sculptures, and stained glass. Given these images, it is not surprising that many of our male clients are uncomfortable thinking of themselves as "spiritual."

Often the path of spiritual growth comes from both directions—an expansion of the person's images of God, Jesus, or other symbols of the divine to include both the so-called feminine traits of nurturance, gentleness, and love, and the masculine-identified traits of courage and fortitude, *and* an expansion of one's view of oneself to embrace both traditionally feminine and traditionally masculine traits.

Gender plays an important role in our lives (for both counselors and clients), not so much because it determines our capabilities, but because it determines the scripts society has given us. It is not gender itself, but our distorted perceptions, our inappropriate generalizations, and our false expectations that can hamper our relationships with clients. These three types of distortions can handicap our work with clients, whether the differences concern gender, age, race, class, or other categories.

Distorted Perceptions

Our perceptions of our clients may be distorted because of our own misunderstandings or stereotypes. Some interesting research on perceptions of infants' emotions has been done using videotapes after a toy has been taken from an infant. The infant screamed and cried, with first a sad and then an angry facial expression. When this tape was shown to expectant parents, those men who strongly endorsed the gender stereotypes of emotion more frequently rated the babies that were (arbitrarily) identified as boys as showing anger, and those identified as girls as showing sadness (Plant, Hyde, Keltner & Devine, 2000). The misperception occurred only in the parents who were themselves stereotypic.

Distorted interpretations of expression of emotions are not restricted to infants. Interpretations of adults' emotional expressions are even more likely to be distorted because of gender than those of the infants. In a study by the same authors, college undergraduates were shown slides of men and women expressing sadness or anger, or a mixture. "The slides of men were interpreted as more angry and less sad than the women's equivalent expressions" (Plant et al., 2000, p. 88). These distortions occurred in almost all of the students, not just in those who endorsed gender stereotypes.

If we as counselors continue to have gender stereotypes, we may inadvertently shape our clients' expression of emotions. These and other studies show that we can interpret expressions to fit our preconceptions of what is appropriate for each gender. If fathers teach their sons to label their distress as anger, but teach daughters to label it sadness, the parental stereotypes could train the children to accept their own emotions only when they fit the gender stereotype. Unaware counselors might do the same.

Inappropriate Generalizations

Our clients may not fit the "norm" for their gender, and we may make generalizations that do not apply to this individual because we have focused on their gender and have not noticed their individual values or activities that don't fit the gender stereotype. I recall an incident of this kind of role stereotyping that occurred when our children were in elementary school. I received a phone call from a teacher who asked to talk to my wife. The teacher was concerned about an interaction that had occurred between our daughter and another child, and assumed that my wife should be the one to deal with it. Since I was committed to taking equal responsibility for the child rearing, I resented this gender-biased assumption, though it may simply have reflected an overgeneralization about fathers.

False Expectations

Our expectations for our clients may also be limited because of our views of what each gender can do. An undergraduate woman in a liberal arts college was gifted artistically. She was counseled into teaching art as a career, partly because the faculty did not recognize that she also was very capable at visualizing three dimensional spaces and had an interest in building and construction. It took her years to realize that what she really wanted was to become an architect.

I have already noted that persons of lower status tend to internalize the oppression that they have experienced; this makes them especially vulnerable to the lowered expectations of persons in power, such as their counselor. Thus a woman some decades ago might have believed that women couldn't be architects.

Unfortunately, we have had years of experience during which certain expectations went unchallenged. It was assumed that men should be the ones to dig ditches because "men are stronger." Of course, some men are stronger in the muscle groups needed for digging, but some women also have those strengths. If you are seeking person to do a particular job, you want a person with those strengths—the gender is irrelevant. A husky woman can do it more easily than a frail man. The point is to look for an individual with the appropriate strengths, not to base your search on overgeneralizations. Once we get used to thinking in gender categories, we tend to turn generalizations into rules.

Just as we may unfairly expect too little, we may also expect too much. We may have expectations for changes in our clients that are unrealistic, based on our attempts to make the client more like ourselves. Suppose, for example, that you are working with a young male client who is exploring gay relationships. You might wish he would have more heterosexual experiences and make sure he is gay before he gets himself into situations that will lead to his being labeled and treated as a minority. Though your intentions may be good, and flow from a wish to protect him, it is important to be remind yourself that, if you were seeing a male client who was wanting to have more experience with women, it is unlikely that you would urge him to have more homosexual experiences first in order to be sure that he is straight. It is likely that you have some hidden assumptions in your wish for the gay client to have heterosexual experiences; you might assume that he can change his sexual orientation, or that being gay is inferior to being straight. We send a message to the client that, if he can do something to overcome a homosexual orientation, he should do so.

Just as the counselor's unrealistic expectations can be harmful to the client, so can the client's self-expectations. Recently a married couple in their thirties came to me for counseling. They were feeling overwhelmed by the complications of each having a career yet trying to raise children. They were fighting over who did the most housework. They felt guilty that they weren't "doing it right" in terms of balancing these roles and responsibilities. When I stated that I thought they were behaving quite normally for parents in this period of history, they were surprised and curious. They assumed their problem was one of personal failure, and were expecting themselves to have a clear sense of what they should be doing to balance their work roles and their parental responsibilities. Similar to many in their age group, they were so busy with their work and home lives that they had little time for deep enough relationships with their peers to notice that *most* of their peers with dual careers were feeling the same lack of clarity. Historically, we are in a period radical revision of gender roles. Shared parenting and dual careers is a relatively new experiment. The belief that they should know how to do it right was expecting too much.

Other Differences that Become Barriers

I have used gender differences as an illustration of the ways in which society and culture can exaggerate the importance of a variable and turn it into a barrier. The same questions that structured this discussion of gender differences could be used to analyze most other differences which society has reified into groups or categories (see Exhibit 7.1).

Exhibit 7.1.

Take a moment to review in your mind the basic process which has been illustrated using "gender" as a prejudice:

- Does the data show real differences?
- Do such differences last over history and /or across cultures?
- Is there any reason to believe the differences are actually biologically based?
- If the differences are based largely in perceptions, how might they impact on our counseling.
- Do the distortions manifest themselves in: *distorted perceptions, inappropriate generalizations,* and *false expectations?*

This analysis will not be repeated for race, class, and so on. Theoretically, we could review the social science research and ask, concerning race, for example:

1. Do clear differences exist between Caucasian Americans and African Americans in personality traits and behaviors?
2. If so, what factors produce these differences? That is, are the differences socially learned and subject to change, or are they built into the genetic and biological structure of each race?
3. What impact do racial differences have on our relationships with our clients?

Some brief comments, and some personal anecdotes may be helpful in bringing the discussion back to concrete personal relationships. The important process evaluation concerns whether the person has learned to open himself or herself to new experience, and to bring that experience to bear in his or her daily connections with others. An anecdote concerning my Aunt Lucille provides an example.

> This incident occurred soon after we adopted our second child. Both of our children are biracial (African American and Caucasian). Heather's complexion is considerably darker than Eric's, and it is much more obvious that she has African-American lineage. Some months after she joined our home, I took Heather with me on a visit to my Aunt Lucille, a single woman

in her early sixties, still living in the tiny village in Pennsylvania near the farm on which she and my dad had grown up. Everyone within many miles of that village was Caucasian, and this was about 1971, so if Aunt Lu (as we called her) had ever seen a black person, it was Bill Cosby, and only on television.

Heather was quite a sociable toddler, and after Aunt Lu and I had been conversing a while, and Aunt Lu had offered Heather a couple cookies, Heather walked over to where Aunt Lu was sitting and reached up her arms asking to by lifted onto Aunt Lu's lap. Even though Aunt Lu was not often with children, Heather was too charming to resist, and by the time we were ready to leave, she and Heather had become friends. When we were ready to leave, and I had gotten Heather strapped into the child car seat on the passenger side, and I was seated behind the steering wheel with the window down, Aunt Lu stood by my car window and thanked me for coming. "And thanks for bringing Heather to see me. She is such a sweet little girl," she said. "And she can't help it that she's black."

Many of you, reading this, will recognize that "she can't help it that she's black" is a racist statement. It assumes that being white is superior—that if Heather could help it she would prefer to be white. But if you were Aunt Lu's counselor, and you were to express blame or disgust at Aunt Lu's assumptions, it would show your own failure to recognize that this rural woman is attempting to integrate what is for her a completely new experience—interacting with an African American. Her prejudice is not based on negative feelings toward Heather, but stems from trying to fit this new experience into her past categories and beliefs. In spite of this narrow experience, she has taken in the person of Heather, and allowed it to change her. She has opened herself to experience Heather, not just as black, but as "a sweet little girl." And to that extent, a positive spiritual process is occurring.

Like my aunt, I was raised in a rural area, and prior to college my firsthand experience with African Americans was limited to one girl in my class (from kindergarten on through high school). Unlike my aunt, I grew up with parents who strongly valued appreciating differences, so I went out of my way, once in college, to get to know persons of different backgrounds: black, Jewish, Icelandic, German, Nigerian, to name the backgrounds of a few classmates I got close to in my early years in college. Though I was privileged to have a more cosmopolitan post–high school experience than my aunt, the process of overcoming stereotypes for each of us was similar. Just as Aunt Lu looked at what was desirable through the eyes of a Daughter of the American Revolution, I looked at Judaism and reading the Torah from the perspective of the protestant Christianity. It takes a great amount of effort to begin to see the world from the perspective of a different history than one's own. Each of us overcomes our prejudice in little steps, one at a time.

Race As a Western Denial of Power

I have presented evidence that very few of the differences between genders can be attributed to evolutionary and biological roots. Since gender roles are much more basic to the history of human development and appear much earlier than the occurrence of the subdivision of named races, it is hard to imagine that substantial psychological differences between races would appear if we attempted to measure racial differences with the quantity and quality of research tools available for research on gender differences.

I described earlier the confounding of gender differences with differences in power and status. This problem is all the more acute in the discussions of differences between races. I noted that a person who is being subjected to discrimination may not even be aware of it due to internalized oppression. The reverse is also true. It is very difficult for those in positions of privilege to recognize it.

"I have come to see white privilege as an invisible package of unearned assets which I can count on cashing in each day, but about which I was [meant] to remain oblivious" (McIntosh, 2007, personal correspondence). McIntosh listed a whole series of conditions that she found she could count on most of the time because of her skin color. The list that follows contains less than a quarter of the original list of 46 conditions she discovered, but as you read them, you can see if you generally take any of these for granted:

- I can if I wish arrange to be in the company of people of my own race most of the time.
- If I should need to move, I can be pretty sure of renting or purchasing housing in an area which I can afford and in which I would want to live.
- I can be pretty sure that my neighbors in such a location will be neutral or pleasant to me.
- I can go shopping alone most of the time, pretty well assured that I will not be followed or harassed.
- I can turn on the television or open to the front page of the paper and see people of my race widely represented.
- When I am told about our national heritage or about "civilization," I am shown that people of my color made it what it is.
- Whether I use checks, credit cards, or cash, I can count on my skin color not to work against the appearance of financial reliability.
- I can arrange to protect my children most of the time from people who might not like them.
- I can swear, or dress in secondhand clothes, or not answer letters, without having people attribute these choices to the bad morals, the poverty, or the illiteracy of my race.
- I can do well in a challenging situation without being called a credit to my race.
- I can take a job with an affirmative action employer without having co-workers on the job suspect that I got it because of my race. (McIntosh, 1988, pp. 5-9)

This list consists of small but important conditions that McIntosh realized she could take for granted every day. She did not claim to speak for all white people everywhere, relative to all people of color. She found her list relevant for her, and also very difficult to generate.

"I repeatedly forgot each of the realizations on this list until I wrote it down. . . . for in facing it, I must give up the myth of meritocracy" (McIntosh, 1988, p. 9). It is said that the great biologist Charles Darwin took notes only on the things he observed that didn't fit his theory. "The other things," he said, "are easy to remember." It might be worthwhile for the reader to take some notes if you realize that you are experiencing privilege that others don't have. It may help to sensitize you.

Socioeconomic Class

To touch briefly on the issue of economic class: One of the central myths of American culture is that people get what they deserve—that esteem and prosperity come to those who really work for them. This is one factor that contributes to the depth of racism in United States. Racial differences provide a convenient cover that allows us to hide the extreme and unjust differences in social classes in our culture; we blame the disparities on race. Note that a common stereotype of the "welfare mother" is of a black woman; this despite that the majority of welfare mothers are actually white. Fiske and colleagues (1999) studied the perceptions and emotional reactions people had to 17 different groups that are often stereotyped in the United States. "Welfare recipients were the only group that was both disliked and disrespected, and whose members were perceived to lack both warmth and competence" (cited in Lott, 2002, p. 106). The words *racial minority* and *inner city* are often used as codes for *low income,* and it has been argued that rural poor whites are also "racialized" as "a breed apart, a dysgenic race unto themselves" (Lott, 2002, quoting Wray & Newitz, 1997, p. 2).

The tendency in the United States is to see poverty as an individual problem and to be preoccupied "with poor people's behavior, rather than the social and economic arrangements that perpetuate poverty, inequality, and social exclusion" (Halpern, 1992, cited in Lott, 2002).

Lott (2002) concludes that the dominant response to the poor by the non-poor is that of distancing in the form of exclusion, separation, devaluing, and discounting, resulting in class discrimination. Part of this distancing is to conflate the class issue with the race issue, as the image of the black welfare mother illustrates.

Helping the Client Notice that Some Problems are External

Often individual clients enter counseling filled with self-criticism and self-blame. They may believe that what handicaps them is due to their own errors or pathology. For such clients, it can be freeing and empowering to recognize that some of the "mistakes" they are making, the struggles they are experiencing, are common throughout the culture at this point in history. Using an example already noted, it is liberating for a woman to realize that her struggle with balancing motherhood and working life is not just an individual struggle, but a common problem for women. Similarly, a man's confusion about his role as a father, and his wife's criticisms about his inadequate involvement with children, are part of a historical shift in gender roles for which his parents could not have prepared him. Her struggle and his confusion are not signs of pathology in them as individuals or as a couple.

During the 1990s and early 2000s, most working parents believed we were in a period of economic boom. But 80 percent were no better off in buying power than their own parents were two or three decades previous. Formerly, the working class believed they could achieve the "dream" of owning a house and car and sending their children to college. They believed that their abilities and hard work assured their chances of having a good life. It is not just that the clients have false expectations; now that less working class people achieve this dream, they tend to blame themselves instead of understanding the way our economy has been stacked against them.

THE COUNSELOR'S AWARENESS OF THE CULTURE'S BLIND SPOTS

As a client or counselor begins to see individual struggle in the broader context of the cultural and historic milieu and becomes aware of the influence of culture on her or his perceptions, he or she can begin to question some of what has been, up to this point, taken for granted. Like the proverbial fish who is unaware of the water it swims in until it is removed from the water, once a person gets perspective on his or her own culture, the cultural assumptions are no longer taken for granted. They no longer seem "true," but are seen as one point of view. Not all clients are interested in this area of growth, but it is extremely helpful for us as counselors to become aware of the assumptions and blind spots of our own culture. Alan Rolland (1996), an American who has worked extensively as a psychotherapist in India and Japan, gives two clear examples of Western assumptions which prove invalid when applied to these Asian cultures:

> If an Indian teenage girl comes to an American analyst with out-of-body experiences, would the analyst even begin to consider that these might be due to too much meditating, as turned out to be the case, rather than some dissociated state? (pp. 489-490)
>
> [Or if] patients come to us stating that they have slept next to their mothers for several years, or sometimes into their teens, we would certainly wonder about the mother-child relationship and how it might impact on the patient's current problems and the transference-countertransference relationship. And yet that is traditionally the norm in Asian cultures. (p. 489)

While working on a college campus in India, I had a similar experience. A colleague there, a psychology professor, was concerned that a woman student might drop out of college because of homesickness and family worries. The student had told friends and at least two professors that she missed sleeping with her mother and sister (this is common in India); they responded by telling the student that her worries were trivial.

Although in the United States it would be extremely uncommon for a woman of college age to sleep with her mother and sisters, this was not what concerned her Indian peers and professors—they simply didn't understand why it mattered so much to her. But, once she sensed my desire to understand, the student had no trouble explaining it. Her elder sister died when the student was four years old, and at age ten her father died suddenly of a heart attack. He had two brothers, who traditionally would have taken a fatherly role in their niece's life after her father was gone, but within two years they had also died. This left only the mother, who was not too healthy and in her mid-fifties, and the two daughters. With all of these losses, the longing for the deep connectedness she had felt at home is not surprising or pathological. Despite the losses, her mother had left it completely up to her daughter whether she moved away to college; the daughter made the decision to go. Now she was far from home, and her mother had caught some illness and had become very dehydrated. Fearing the loss of her only parent, she began to fantasize the warmth and closeness of being with her mother and sister again. Had I not known of the cultural acceptance of youth sleeping with their same-sexed parent, I might not have stayed empathic enough to have elicited the sequence of deaths that overdetermined her wish for a return to that connectedness.

Using One's Own Experience

Learning to empathize, to see things through another's personal history and frame of reference, is not simply a cognitive process. Usually the counselor begins to empathize on the basis of some shared feelings—for example, although I've not had to live through the black person's experiences of being treated as inferior because of race, I do know the experience of being treated as inferior by peers. In my junior high and high school years my peers in gym classes in a small mining town viewed me as a klutz. I was usually one of the last to be chosen when they selected team members for a baseball game. That experience of not being acceptable to the majority helps me identify, however imperfectly, with the rejection of person of minority status.

Can you remember experiences in your past that help you identify with certain minorities even though you are not actually from that group?

Steps to Overcoming Prejudice

We do not successfully overcome prejudice by cognitive work alone. Transcending our biases involves developing a deep love of differences.

Next time you are out in nature, when you walk along, take delight in the varieties of nature that surround you. Whether you are noticing the kinds of trees, the multitude of flower species, the different shapes of seashells, or the varieties of bird calls, be conscious that Mother Nature seems to love differences. Can you open your heart to rejoice in differences?

Second, be conscious that prejudice is taught, and therefore it can be untaught. The musical South Pacific says it well:

> You have to be taught
> Before it's too late.

Before you are six or seven or eight
to hate all the people your relatives hate.
You have to be carefully taught.

(Rodgers & Hammerstein, 1949)

We do not simply learn an attitude or feeling such as hate and direct it to the same person our relatives did. We learn a way of thinking and categorizing. We learn from our limited experience and sometimes draw false conclusions from it.

An Experience More Potent than Gender

In the first portion of this chapter I reviewed the material from the meta-analyses of studies of gender differences. In this closing portion, I want to mention a surprising finding from meta-analyses of research seeking to resolve another debate. For decades, social scientists questioned whether psychotherapy was effective at all. In the past decade or so, outcome research has fairly successfully demonstrated the effectiveness of several types of psychotherapy, at least when an appropriate match exists between skilled counselors, the type of therapy, and the problem. When we compare the results from these two different areas of meta-analyses, a very interesting, though somewhat serendipitous, discovery is made. The range of outcome differences between clients receiving therapy and those in control groups is *larger* than the differences between males and females in most of the studies of gender differences (Hyde & Plant, 1995). To state this in simpler terms, people who have undergone psychotherapy show greater differences, compared to people who have not, than men show compared to women. So, as a counselor, when you have doubts about the effectiveness of your work and the field of psychotherapy, remind yourself that psychotherapy has a greater impact on behavior and personality that does gender! If you have not been on the receiving side of psychotherapy, consider allowing yourself to have that experience.

This research result does not mean, of course, that gender has no impact on people. Gender, race, social class—all of these barriers have an impact socially in much the same way an electric fence with no current running through it will still control farm animals. Once the animals have become conditioned to the fence and avoid it, the farmer can turn off the electricity and the animals won't go near it. They never learn that the electricity is no longer on. This seems to me a good metaphor for many of the social barriers that exist in our society. Once children have become fearful of people who are different, they continue to avoid these people, even though, in reality, the differences don't matter. They perceive the differences, and "believe" they matter. They act as if the differences were important, and the differences then function as real barriers, when in fact, they are only *perceived* barriers.

Chapter 8

Why So Much Suffering?

The tragedy of unjust suffering has bewildered and overwhelmed humans for millennia. It has been the subject of works of drama, novels, and treatises of theologians and philosophers. The book of Job (in the Hebrew scriptures) is an example of this, and is considered by some to be one of the most profound pieces of literature ever written. In this chapter we will review the story and message of Job.

But we will also look at a modern rendition of that work. It can be argued that suffering confronts the spirituality of modern man in a new way. Reasons for this include:

- *The loss of an imperialistic religious worldview.* Religious pluralism and the rejection of religious imperialism leave us without a rationalization for such suffering. When you believe your religion is the one true faith, you can rationalize the suffering of those who are not in that faith as part of "God's punishment," or at least of God's chastising of those people to lead them to the true faith. But once you encounter persons from faith traditions different from your own, you begin to realize that they hold their positions with the same integrity and honest conviction that you hold yours. We may suspect they are misinformed about some things, but we can't justify that God would punish them.
- The *effects of modern communication* technologies that disseminate news of tragic suffering across the world. The awareness of events from all over the world provides us with an onslaught of information about the suffering of others, which can be overwhelming. This phenomenon has been dubbed "compassion fatigue" (or empathy fatigue). This includes, for example, an awareness of the genocide of other human cultures. In some cases, most notably Nazi Germany, such genocide was carried

out in the name of Christianity and with the acquiescence of much of the Christian church, which has played a role in undermining the belief in the moral superiority of Christian cultures.

JOB: CONTRIBUTIONS TO AN UNDERSTANDING OF SUFFERING

It has always been easy for people of privilege who live a moral and responsible life to assume that they experience a bountiful life because they are favored by God. The author of Job seems intent on pushing the reader or listener to an understanding of the problem of suffering that is deeper and more realistic than this.

The story line is simple. Job is an upright man, a firm and faithful follower of God. He has everything: a wife, seven sons and three daughters, "a very great household" including a huge livestock farm, many servants, and so much wealth that "this man was the greatest of all the men in the East." (Job 1:1-3, RSV)[1] His sons were so wealthy they "feasted in their houses" each day.

"There was a day when the sons of God came to present themselves before the Lord" (1:6), and the Tester was among them. (The original Job poem predates concepts of a devil or Satan figure; the Tester is understood more as a questioner or a court advocate.) He had been visiting earth and checking things out. God asked him if he had noticed "my servant Job . . . a blameless and upright man?" (1:8). The Tester argues with God, stating, of course Job is devoted to you—you've given him everything. But check out what will happen if you take away "all that he has"—will Job then still bless you? God takes up the challenge, and gives the Tester the power to take anything he likes from Job, but not to actually touch him physically (1:9-12).

Soon after, Job is at home when a servant rushes in and reports that he and other servants were out in the fields plowing with oxen, when foreigners attacked them and killed the oxen, the other livestock that were with them, and all the servants but this messenger (1:15). In rushes another farmhand from the pastures, reporting that another tribal group has killed the servants that were guarding the camels, and have stolen all the camels (1:14-17). While that farmhand is still speaking, yet another messenger rushes in and tells Job that his daughters and sons had all been eating together at the eldest son's home, when a tornado destroyed the house and everyone but this messenger was killed. Devastated, Job tears his clothes, shaves his head, and falls to the ground worshipping God:

> Naked I came from my mother's womb, and naked shall I return; the Lord gave, and the Lord has taken away: blessed be the name of the Lord. (1:21)

When the Tester and God next converse, the Tester has to admit that Job has been faithful, even after losing all his possessions and servants and children. But, he argues, if God actually "touches him" physically, Job will "curse thee to thy face." (2:5). God relents and gives the Tester permission to physically touch Job. The Tester afflicts Job's whole body with painful boils. Even Job's wife becomes convinced that Job was being too good to be true, given all that he's suffered; she advises Job to "curse God and die." But instead he remains faithful.

Three friends hear of all that has gone wrong for Job, and come to mourn with him and comfort him. When they see his condition they are so moved that they also tear their clothes and sit down with him, and are present with him in silence for a whole week, "for they saw that his grief was very great" (2:13b).

In their presence, Job finally breaks down. He wishes he'd never been born (3:11), or had been stillborn (3:13)—at least he then would have had peace. He screams out to his friends, longing for death (3:24, 21).

Finally the first friend, Eliphaz, asks permission to speak. He begins by crediting all of the support Job has given to others when they've been down (4:4). Now it's Job's turn to have troubles, he says—and since the innocent and upright are never punished, Job's suffering means in some way he has sinned (4:8). After all, no human is without sin (4:17). This friend beautifully communicates a plea to Job to confess his sin, to understand the afflictions are God's way of correcting him and purifying him (5:17). In this way Job can be redeemed.

Job responds that he is being judged unfairly (Chapter 5 through 10), that he has no right or power to judge God, but if he dared speak the bitterness of his soul he would ask God to show him what he has done wrong (10:1-2). Then Job gains strength, and says directly to God, "You know that I am not wicked!" (10:7). It seems to be a no-win situation—If I sin, I get punished, and if I am righteous, I am not supposed to lift up my head. "I am totally confused" (10:15b King James Version). If I'm no good no matter what, why did you make me? (10:18, 19). Please, leave me alone; just let me die (10:20).

At this point the second friend, Zophar, rebukes Job (Chapter 11). "A man full of talk" will not be justified (11:2). We can't possibly fathom God's ways, and it is arrogant to think we can. You deserve even worse than God has given you (11:6b).

Job argues back: I am not stupid (12:3), I know that God is more powerful, that he makes and sustains all that is. I know this as well as you (13:2). You are not one who can heal me—you are telling me lies! (13:4). You would be wise to keep silent (13:5) and not pretend to speak for God (13:7). Leave me alone; let me speak directly with God—I'll take the consequences. "Though he slay me, yet will I trust in him: But I will maintain mine own ways before him." (13:16). I refuse to be hypocritical and confess sins I haven't done. Tell me, what sins have I done to deserve this? (13:16, 23-24).

The first friend soon takes up the argument again (Chapter 15), echoing the ideas of his colleague, that Job is uttering "speeches which can do no good" (15:3) and turning his spirit against God (15:13). And Job responds "miserable comforters are you all!" (16:2). The third friend, Bildad, chimes in, agreeing with the others that Job "knoweth not God." (18:21). Job cries out to them "Have pity on me, have pity on me, O ye my friends: for the hand of God has touched me. Why do you persecute me, just as God does? (19:21-22, KJV).

The argument continues, with all three friends assuming Job's guilt, and Job protesting that they "wrongfully imagine" his sinfulness (21:27). He again pictures himself arguing his case before God (23:4-6) and being found innocent (23:10)—but he can no longer find God.

> Oh, that I knew where I might find him. . . Behold I go forward and he is not there; and backward, but I cannot perceive him. (Job 23: 3, 8).

Job refuses to give up his integrity (27:5). He lists the laws and ethical expectations he believes God has set forth and argues that he has followed them (Chapter 31); he longs for written reports from his adversary of where he has failed (31:35). At this point the three "friends" give up trying to argue, but a younger man not previously mentioned, having been deferent to their age, now feels free to speak: None of the three of you has been able to convince Job. Surely God will not do something wicked (34:12); Job has not only sinned, he has compounded it with rebellion against God (34:37). The young man follows his condemnation of Job with a direct challenge to Job: "Listen to this. Be still, and consider the wondrous works of God" (37:14). The young man refers to "fair weather" coming from the north, and to God's "terrible majesty."

Having been introduced, God himself now speaks to Job out of a whirlwind.

> Where were you when I made the foundations of the earth? Answer me that, "if you have any understanding?" (38:4)

In a series of rhetorical questions asserting God's power and Job's lack of understanding, the author brings the drama to a poetically powerful climax. Finally God asks Job: "Shall the man who argues with God teach him? You that reprove God—let him answer that!"

With this show of power and majesty, Job is beaten down. In the ending to the book, the epilogue, Job now sees himself as vile, and says he has spoken enough, he will proceed no further (40:5). Again God describes His incredible power and glory, and states, "Look on every one who is proud, and bring him low" (40:12). God compares Job's arguing with Him to a small fisherman trying to use normal hooks to catch a sea monster (Chapters 40 and 41).

Again Job answers with total submission: "I uttered things I knew nothing about" (42:3). "I abhor myself, and repent in dust and ashes." (42:6). Now that Job's pride is totally broken, God dismisses the three friends for failing to be as submissive as Job. They are commanded to make a sacrificial offering, and "my servant Job will pray for you" (42:8). At the very end, God restores all of Job's family to him, and makes him twice as rich as he was before (42:10).

In this ending to the story, though not in the original dramatic poem, Job succumbs to the magnificent and powerful God like a slave to an oriental potentate. He abandons his questions concerning why he should have to endure such great suffering, since, though he is not perfect, he is a remarkably good person. He surrenders to the position of his friends and inquisitors—that he has no right to question God.

Textual Studies

The central narrative with the poetic dialogues between Job and the friends, and between Job and God, were recognized as an important piece of Hebrew literature. Textual studies of the Job manuscript suggest that the opening and the ending of the story are later additions (Anderson, 1971). Some scholars believe that the additions were a compromise to make the dialogue less of a challenge to the theistic tradition of Judaism. Ending the story with Job's final submissiveness may have been intended to placate the traditional views that we have no right to challenge God's actions or impugn his justice. Certainly traditional theism has not been comfortable with questioning either the omnipotence or the goodness of God. Unfortunately, sufficient textual evidence is unavailable to determine whether or not this more acceptable ending was part of the original text.

Implications of the Book of Job for our Beliefs about God and Evil

Every character in the book of Job, and most current readers, would like to believe the following three statements:

1. God is all-powerful and causes everything that happens in the world. Nothing happens without His willing it.
2. God is just and fair, and stands for people getting what they deserve, so that the good prosper and the wicked are punished.
3. Job is a good person. (Kushner, 1983, p. 37)

The story of Job seems intended to highlight this theological problem. The friends of Job believe statements 1 and 2, and conclude that 3 must be false. Throughout the poem, Job insists on his own goodness, and argues that he does not deserve the bad things that have happened to him.

But the ending takes a turn. God speaks directly to Job—*not* about His being just or fair or even loving, but of His own power and majesty. Job succumbs, giving up his claim to goodness, stating that he has said too much, and leaving unsettled the issue of God's fairness.

Whether or not the ending is authentic, one can argue that, psychologically, the ending is not convincing. We have already reviewed social science data, and argued that being willing to challenge accepted conventional religious views is healthy (see Chapters 2, 3, and 4). The Job dialogues appear to be a direct challenge to the orthodox view that suffering is a consequence of one's personal sins. In many respects the theological discussion between traditional Judaism of the time and the Job poems is similar to that between Voltaire's dramatic criticism in *Candide* and eighteenth century optimism (expressed by the character Pangloss) (Voltaire, 1946). Though written more than 20 centuries later than Job, both masterpieces recognize that the prevailing religious or philosophical view of their times—that the righteous are rewarded, and only the sinful suffer—is discordant with careful observation. Both have the courage to challenge the conventional wisdom.

Blaming Oneself for External Events

A series of social psychology experiments attempted to investigate a phenomenon closely related to the themes of the story of Job. The expectation—that if one is faithful and repentant, everything will end well—is not only contrary to the facts, but we now know from these experiments that such Pollyanna expectations can lead to psychologically destructive processes. Such beliefs frequently feed into outsiders viewing someone's bad fortune as evidence of the person's guilt. The seminal work in this field is Lerner's (1980) classic, *The Belief in a Just World: A Fundamental Delusion.* It reports a variety of experiments testing the patterns of thought and behavior related to belief in a just world, and, as the title suggests, the research leads to Lerner's conclusion that the belief fosters delusional thinking. In order to maintain the comforting belief of our own deservingness, we need to believe that others also get what they deserve. So when we become aware of outcomes that appear to be unjust, we convince ourselves that the victim somehow deserved his or her suffering. This leads to the pernicious tendency to blame the victim.

The 1988 film *The Accused,* based on a true story, illustrates this tendency: A 21-year-old divorced mother had been drinking and socializing in a bar in Massachusetts. Urged on by their peers, several male patrons seized her, tore her clothes off, and gang-raped her on the barroom floor and then on the pool table, as others cheered and watched. Many people who saw the film attributed blame to this victim, implying that she deserved this fate. "She had no business being in the bar," stated one observer (Myers, 1990, p. 361). If it is a just world, then people can be blamed for their fate. The wealthy and healthy can see their fate as being deserved and the fate of the less fortunate as equally deserved, thereby linking good fortune and virtue. In a survey in the United Kingdom, 33 percent of respondents agreed that women who had been raped are usually to blame for it (Wagstaff, 1982). Along similar lines, in 1968, right after the assassination of Martin Luther King Jr., when a representative sample of Americans was asked what their strongest reaction was, one-third of the sample chose the answer, "He brought it on himself" (Rokeach, 1970).

We don't always blame the victim, however; we do so when such a tactic helps us maintain the sense of our own deservingness and justice (Deaux & Wrightsman, 1987). We seek ways to distance ourselves from the victim, to be certain that we are different and therefore safe (Lerner, 1970).

Further research in social psychology raised a mitigating note to the blameful tendency of belief in a just world. Observers saw videos of "learners" being punished with electric shocks (as in the Milgrim experiments described in Chapter 4). Some of the observers were asked, while watching, to "imagine how you would feel if you were subjected to the same experience. . . . Concentrate on the way you would feel while receiving the treatment . . . think about what your reactions would be to the sensations you would receive" (Alderman, Brehm, & Katz, 1974, p. 344). Other observers were instructed to simply and objectively watch the learners movements. Those in the first group, asked to imagine their own feelings, were less likely to blame the victim than observers who were instructed to observe carefully the specific reactions of the victim without sympathy. Vicariously experiencing the victim's suffering appears to eliminate the tendency to derogate the victim; simply observing suffering does not (Alderman, Brehm, & Katz, 1974).

If we somehow believe that the plagues of Job might fall upon *us,* we are less likely to see Job as a deserving sinner. Thus, alongside the tendency to blame the victim lies an equally pernicious tendency for people to blame themselves for catastrophes that befall them—an inward-directed form of the belief in the just world.

The belief in a just world does not have exclusively negative consequences, however. In fact, the evidence suggests people are strongly motivated to eliminate the suffering of innocent victims—but often are afraid that if they act in caring ways, they will loose their own "just place" in the world. In caring, we feel vulnerable to doing more than our just share and thus becoming a victim ourselves. However, in situations in which people feel assured they won't loose their own status, they can be generous and self-sacrificing in their efforts to relieve unjust suffering (Lerner, 1980). The data clearly "disconfirm the myth that we are all out to get all we can for ourselves, regardless of what it might cost others." (Lerner, 1980, p. 189). Rather, we care about receiving what we ourselves deserve first, but if that is somewhat assured, we long for others to be treated justly as well (Lerner, 1980). This tendency to want what is good for others, not just for self, is even more evident in situations in which good communication occurs among a fairly small group, and altruistic norms and rules to regulate self-serving behavior are established (Myers, 1990).

In situations in which people can take responsibility for their behaviors, it is appropriate and effective for them to be self-critical when their actual behaviors are incongruent with behaviors they have publicly affirmed. For example, if people agree that in order to prevent AIDS they should practice only safe sex, and they make a public statement to that effect, they are more likely to actually practice safe sex if they are reminded that sometimes, in the past, they have failed to do so. In short, consciously promoting self-criticism is effective in encouraging responsible behavior that is within our control (Dickerson et al., 1992; Stone et al., 1994). However, people who blame themselves for events that are outside their own control are at greater risk for depression; as stated, this kind of self-blame is especially likely among people who are invested in believing the world is just. These individuals assume personal responsibility for a wide array of negative life events that are outside their own control. For example, results of longitudinal studies of people who become depressed after bouts of rheumatoid arthritis suggest that many of them, even prior to the episode of pain and suffering, were predisposed to blame themselves for other (unrelated) negative external events (Chaney, Mullins, Wagner, Hommel, Page, Doppler, 2004).

One might think that pain itself, or at least chronic pain, might be a cause of depression. It is true that pain is related to depression, but not necessarily in the way one would expect. People who are or were depressed are more tuned in to pain; they notice it more than the average person. Patients who had a recent depression paid greater attention to their pain and engaged in more pain catastrophizing than did their never-depressed counterparts.

The effects of depression seem to continue long after the depressive episode. Even patients who had a depressive episode more than four years ago continued to believe that they had relatively less personal control over their pain than did patients without a history of depression. Tested on days when they reported having had a good night's sleep, patients with a history of depression, either recent or remote, were less able to inhibit catastrophizing about pain than were never-depressed patients. A history of depression also left recently depressed patients more apt to refrain from social, vocational, and personal activities when they were in greater pain. Recently depressed patients were more likely, when their pain increased, to experience negative and positive mood changes, threats to their perception of personal control, and doubts that their pain coping strategies were effective in reducing their pain. When their fatigue increased, they were less confident that they had exerted personal control over their pain that day (Tennen, Affleck, Armeli, & Carney, 2000). In short, it is not physical pain that leads to depression, but the interpretation of that pain compounded by a tendency to view oneself as the cause of negative events.

This research leaves us with the question, "What helps a person step outside this pattern of self-justification or self-blame?" How do we stop being "tuned into pain," and shift to being responsive to pleasure or to small experiences of joy? The Alderman, Brehn, and Katz (1974) research suggests that one key lies in shifting from an attitude of blaming to one of empathy. Perhaps it is a sense of connectedness, more than of pleasure, that allows us to absorb pain without responding with blame. These conjectures go beyond what the "just world" research was designed to explore.

A CONTEMPORARY JOB STORY

A rewrite of the story of Job in modern form was accomplished to considerable literary acclaim by Archibald MacLeish, who called his dramatic poem *J. B.* He summarized the viewpoint of Job's friends and their case against Job in these lines:

It's rank irreverence—
Job there on the earth . . .
On his dung heap
Challenging God!
Crying to God.
Demanding justice of God!

(MacLeish, 1958, p. 9)

In doing so, he highlighted the theological issue. The friends argue that God is so powerful and just, we humans have no right to challenge Him. But the question raised by unjust suffering is precisely that—is God just, is God righteous? After Job has been pounded down, and has lost everything, God responds to Job's questioning by displaying His power and glory. As Nickles, a character in *J. B.*, says:

"What's the Power to a broken man
Trampled beneath it like a toad already?
What's the Glory to a skin that stinks!"

(MacLeish, 1958, p. 136)

In other words, what kind of answer to suffering is it to show that God is more powerful and man has no right to question him? Like the friends of Job, we who were raised religious are likely to want to dodge the question of unjust suffering. It is easier to believe that somehow we have not observed correctly, that "nobody ever gets anything that isn't coming to them" (as Kushner [1981] phrases Job's friends' position). We want to keep believing in God's goodness and power, and in a just world. Yet even God (in the whirlwind speech) has trouble keeping the Leviathan (sea monster) in check. Kushner interprets this speech, "If you think it is so easy keeping the world straight and true, to keep unfair things from happening to people, you try it!" (Kushner, 1981, p. 43). The position of Job's friends and of traditional religion—saying that everything works out for good in the end—may comfort us, but it leads us to blame the bereaved and the unfortunate, as evidenced in the powerful tendency for belief in a just world. And friends telling someone in Job's position to "cheer up" is anything but empathic (Kushner, 1983, p. 38).

MacLeish (1958) sharpens the dilemma:

If God is God, He is not good,
If God is good, He is not God;
Take the even, take the odd,
I would not sleep here if I could
Except for the little green leaves in the wood
And the wind on the water. (p. 11)

I take the latter three lines to mean, given the suffering, "I would not stay here on earth if I could help it," but it is nature that makes it tolerable—that part of nature which is so beautiful and puts me at peace.

To push the issue further, if we directly face the contrast between the God we have been taught to believe in—a just and all-powerful God—and the experience we observe—that of unjust suffering—we are likely to conclude that God cannot really be all good, unless we assume that God is *not* all powerful and that some suffering and evil are beyond His control. This is the conclusion Rabbi Kushner (1983) reaches in his book *When Bad Things Happen to Good People*.

Kushner's attempt to face the issue head on reminds me of a similar attempt, by a pastor, that I observed forty years ago but still remember clearly. I related this incident in an earlier chapter, but will retell it here. I was still a youth when I heard a sermon by a famous preacher, George Buttrick. I had spent the summer working in the state of Minnesota, and had gone out of my way to travel to Minneapolis to hear him. The huge church on Hennepin Avenue where he ministered seemed especially somber during the first portion of the service, but I thought perhaps that impression was just my reaction because I normally had attended small churches where everyone knew me. Not far into the service, Reverend Buttrick mentioned what apparently many of the congregation already knew: the previous evening, a car full of youth from this church had been in a terrible accident, and five of the youth were now dead. Buttrick had totally revised the service and his sermon in order to address his grieving congregation and this catastrophe. He began by giving voice to the feelings and questions he knew those in his congregation were asking: Why did such a terrible thing happen to these relatively innocent young people? Why are we, as parents, suffering this tragic loss, when we have done our best to raise these youth within the church? Where is God in this mess?

Then Buttrick stated his own questions and doubts. He acknowledged that such catastrophic tragedies challenge traditional religious thought. He stated humbly yet clearly that he did not have answers. He suggested that, in all honesty, we need to be open to *not* having answers. But—and this was his only clear message of faith—the one thing he knew was that God was suffering *with* them in this tragedy. God was present, not as an omnipotent figure, but as a sensitive and loving parent, who himself had suffered while his son died, and was suffering now, with these parents and parishioners.

The central Judeo-Christian message, according to Buttrick, MacLeish, and Kushner, is *not* about the power or omnipotence of God, but that the God of justice and love suffers with us in our experiences of injustice and suffering. (This is not apparent in the original Job story—the message seems to be "accept the will of God submissively.") MacLeish (1958) goes so far as to rewrite the ending of the Job story—or, more accurately, of the Job poem as recorded in the Hebrew scriptures. In *J. B.,* Job's wife abandons him in his suffering. But in the last act, instead of reaffirming the power of God, MacLeish (1958) ends the play with Job's wife returning to him carrying a branch of forsythia. Job angrily tells her to go back to wherever she'd been. She replies that the city is nothing but ashes now.

> She looks at the twig in her hands.
> Sarah: Among the ashes!
> I found it growing among the ashes,
> Gold as though it did not know. . ..
> J. B.: Curse God and die, you said to me.
> Sarah: Yes
> She looks up at him for the first time, then down again.
> You wanted justice, didn't you?
> There isn't any. There's just the world. . . .
> J. B.: Why did you leave me alone?
> Sarah: I loved you.
> I couldn't help you any more.
> You wanted justice and there was none—
> only love.
>
> (MacLeish, 1958, pp. 149-152)

Kushner summarizes:

> MacLeish's Job, *J. B.*, answers the problem of human suffering, not with theology or psychology, but by choosing to go on living and creating new life. He forgives God for not making a more just universe, and decides to take it as it is. He stops looking for justice, for fairness in the world, and looks for love instead. (Kushner, 1983, p. 145)

Whereas the Hebrew scripture of Job ends with the glory of God, it is not a satisfactory ending for modern man. *J. B.,* by contrast, concludes with Job's wife saying:

> "The candles in churches are out.
> The lights have gone out in the sky.
> Blow on the coal of the heart
> And we'll see by and by . . .
> Blow on the coal of the heart and we'll know . . .
> We'll know . . ."
>
> (MacLeish, 1958, p. 153)

Albert Camus, the great French novelist, developed a similar view in response to the sufferings of disease and war. In his masterpiece *The Plague* (1948), a visitor (Tarrou), trapped in the quarantined city, and a doctor (Rieux) have spent months trying to understand the situation and minister to the sick and dying in the plague-infested Mediterranean city. The rules of the quarantine make it hard to carry on a normal social life. The two men struggle to cope with the needs of the people and yet to enforce measures that will restrict the transmission of the virus within the city. Exhausted, while they are walking and talking by the shore one night, they stroll out onto a pier. Tarrou raises the issue of how to become a saint when one doesn't believe in traditional religion. Dr. Rieux offers,

> "I feel more fellowship with the defeated than with saints. Heroism and sanctity don't really appeal to me. . . What interests me is becoming a man."
>
> "Yes, we're both after the same thing," [Tarrou responds] "but I'm less ambitious."

> Rieux supposed Tarrou was jesting, and turned to him with a smile. But, faintly lit by the dim radiance falling from the sky, the face he saw was sad and earnest. There was another gust of wind and Rieux felt it warm on his skin. Tarrou gave himself a little shake.
>
> "Do you know," he said, "what we should do now, for friendships sake?"
>
> "Anything you like, Tarrou."
>
> "[Let's] go for a swim." (Camus, 1948, p. 255)

They impulsively break the rules and dive into the ocean for a swim. In those precious moments together, moments in which neither regulations nor viruses overwhelm their consciousness, they sense the deep bond of their friendship.

> . . . and a strange happiness possessed [Rieux]. Turning to Tarrou, he caught a glimpse on his friend's face of the same happiness, a happiness that forgot nothing, not even murder. (Camus, 1948, p. 256)

Camus asserts that it is such transcendent moments of deep relationship that make human life meaningful, despite the meaninglessness and injustice of the plague. In both MacLeish's and Camus's literature, justice (a just world) cannot be assured—but glimpses of love allow us to go on.

Camus was a secular existentialist, MacLeish (1958) was raised a protestant Christian, and Kushner was a Jewish rabbi, yet each was deeply spiritual and each came to a similar answer to the question of suffering. All Reverend Buttrick was sure of was that "God is with us in our suffering." Whatever theological resolution you or your clients reach to this problem, it is clear that our ministry as counselors is to be with our clients in their suffering.

THE COUNSELOR

To truly be with our clients, we must come to grips with our own suffering. This means at least the following:

- Developing some perspective on where one's own level of suffering stands in comparison with that experienced by others. The comparing game doesn't resolve any personal issues. But it does force a person to recognize whether or not he or she has led a comparatively privileged life, and therefore may have been more protected from some areas of suffering than those who are less privileged.
- Paying attention to the ways we run from our own suffering, and the ways we face it and cope with it. Noticing our own coping mechanisms may help us to avoid the assumption that the methods of coping we use are appropriate for everyone.
- Looking for the spiritual meaning, or lack of meaning, of the suffering. Where does our own suffering fit with our sense of the purpose and meaning of our life? What revisions in our expectations and beliefs does it demand?

Pain: Coping and Accepting

For both ourselves as counselors and for our work with our clients, it is helpful to distinguish between coping skills and the "serenity to accept the things that can't be changed,"[2] which I will refer to as "letting go." When we, or our clients, are suffering with chronic pain, it is helpful first of all to learn both general coping skills and specific skills that are effective in the management of chronic pain. A variety of skills have been shown to reduce pain, including "acknowledging and expressing feelings appropriately, assertiveness training, developing self-acceptance and self-esteem, exercising . . . meditation . . . relaxation" (Cole, 1998) and, when appropriate, procedures for encouraging "letting go."

Guided imagery and relaxation have both healing and preventive effects. Not only do they result in increased strength in patients who have suffered injury, but they reduce anxiety and decrease the likelihood of further injuries, a controlled study with knee surgery patients determined. Thus they make it more likely the patient will reengage in life (Cupal & Brewer, 2001).

In addition to learning the skills that help the person handle stress, chronic pain sufferers need to accept realistic goals rather than looking for a "cure" or for complete freedom from pain (Cole, 1998). The acceptance of realistic goals may be viewed as a first step in movement toward the next phase of dealing with pain. Folkman and Lazarus's (1988) distinction between coping efforts aimed at the perceived source of stress (i.e., problem-focused coping) and efforts to regulate one's emotions as a way of adapting to a stressful encounter (i.e., emotion-focused coping) has guided coping theory and research for decades.

Emotion-focused strategies are less likely to be used unless problem-focused strategies have also been attempted. Typically, a phase of problem solving, figuring out when coping skills are successful in reducing pain, precedes a more realistic reassessment of what pain relief is possible and what changes in lifestyle are necessary. Eventually, a "letting go" of expectations for cure may occur. A study using a method of within-individual measurements showed that when efforts to directly influence pain were not successful (and resulted in a higher level of pain the next day), the respondents on that second day switched from trying to influence pain to trying harder to adjust to the pain (Tennen et al., 2000).

My own experience with chronic back pain fits with the research just surveyed. In context, although in my earlier life I had endured a number of physical hardships, each of these had only been a temporary interruption of my overall sense of well-being and health. In 2003, when my back problems began, chronic pain was new to me. When chronic back pain began to limit my favorite retirement activity, overseas travel, I had to realize that this time the illness might not be temporary, but something I would have to endure the rest of my life. My first priority was to figure out which kind of treatments helped me. I was seen and evaluated (with every diagnostic approach currently used for spine and muscle assessment) by five different types of medical professionals; each of the different professions had somewhat conflicting theories, and each had their own favorite treatment plans. Conducting my own experiments with different pain killers, exercises, stretches, use of heat or cold, supportive cushions, etc., and keeping careful and methodical records of the levels of pain I experienced with each, helped me sort out, one approach at a time, what worked best for me.

Once I had done all that seemed possible to reduce the pain, I shifted to the inner work of learning to accept pain, rather than fight it. This process was helped particularly by frequent reading of Buddhist writings on suffering. (I especially recommend that those dealing with frequent pain read Brach, 2003; Chodron, 2000; and Cohen, 2002). Paradoxically, after accepting at a fairly deep level that this pain might be a part of my daily experience for the rest of my life, I began to feel considerably better, and was able to stop completely the use of codeine, and later to give up pain medicine altogether except on days I was making long flights or driving for many hours.

Relinquishing unrealistic goals and letting go of control is a continuous process. Though the letting go actually seems to have helped to produce an improvement, I can't unambiguously state that it was the cause. There are no guarantees about the future. I must acknowledge the possibility that the pain may come back. However, with the letting go and the decrease in pain, I have developed an increased confidence in my ability to cope with and relax into pain—this has resulted in a reduction in my fear about facing a return of the pain.

Embracing Our Own Suffering

Perhaps the greatest gift of suffering is that it can lead us to acknowledge what we don't know or understand, and thus help us achieve "a beginner's mind," the ability to "face into the large openness." This embracing of the unknown, moving forward without a clear belief or map, seems to be a crucial ingredient of the spiritual search today.

An image from the great Italian novelist Ignazio Silone (1963) comes to mind: "The ancient and serene Mediterranean sky, populated with shining constellations, is now clouded over" (Silone, 1968, p. 127). Faith in past centuries may have provided a fairly clear path and a particular direction. In today's times, such clear guidelines are rare. Instead, we may have no clear sense of where our path leads. "But the little light which survives, glowing around us, gives off at least enough light as we walk on so that we can see where to put our feet" (Silone,1968, p. 127).

And that is enough.

To some this may seem a lack of faith. Silone (1968) states that "this is not enough to constitute a profession of faith, but it will do as a declaration of confidence" (p. 126). For me, when I am actually in the experience, it feels more like a lack of hubris, a humble acknowledgment that it is not for me to know, but for me to trust that the light will be provided as needed.

A BRANCH OF FORSYTHIA

I have already spoken of a modern version of the book of Job, and with it, a recognizing of the limits of God, or the limits of the holy. Though I am very much a lover of nature, and often find that being in the serenity of nature is extremely important in helping me to let go and to accept pain without becoming depressed, to actually *be* in nature itself (in contrast to viewing Disney World images of nature) provides me with constant reminders that pain and suffering are built into existence; deconstruction and decay are continuously present, making room for the new. The animal world is a world that includes "tooth and claw" (as philosophers fighting the rationalism of the eighteenth century were fond of pointing out). Nature grounds us, but also forces us to face that reality is not all lovely and beautiful. In the Buddhists sense, nature puts us in touch, but it takes away the false grounding, and leaves us in open, empty space.

Suffering and the Lack of Solid Ground

The book of Job instructs us that in many instances suffering appears to be meaningless—there is no moral "reason" for it. The person suffering is no more "sinful" than others around who do not suffer. When no learning occurs, the suffering, instead of providing new information, may tip the person's mental balance toward disturbance or instability. Sometimes this instability is creative—it cracks open a space for new light to shine through. But sometimes it is destructive, more than the person can bear.

The twentieth century version of Job, *J. B.*, powerfully presents the sense of meaningless suffering, in some contrast to the orthodox Christian story, which claims that Jesus' suffering will somehow make the world better. On the level of individual salvation, this Christian claim cannot be proved or disproved. However, on the level of social salvation, it seems clear that Christ's sacrifice has *not* saved the world from continued famines, plagues, and wars. It is hard to argue from either nature or history that the *world* has been redeemed, even if some *individuals* may have been. Though plenty of evidence suggests that psychological factors affect physical health, little evidence confirms that dogmatically correct religious beliefs correlate with longer life (Sagan, 1997). At the individual level, the spiritual learning from suffering is largely not a learning of new information or belief, but of new humility and openness.

What Can I Learn from Suffering?

An empathic learning is gained from chronic pain—a greater awareness that others also suffer, and that your own experience may open you more deeply to others.

If you haven't yet practiced the meditations on extending empathy to others' suffering, I suggest you do so now. See particularly Chapter 12, Jack Kornfield's (1993) Exercise 5: Meditation: Transforming Sorrow into Compassion

---

Constructive approaches to suffering include the following:

- Coping, figuring out what I can change
- Letting go of that which I can't change
- Changing my expectations of myself

Examples include reassessing how much I can get done, overcoming my reluctance to ask for help from others, paying others to do jobs I used to do myself, clarifying my limits, and refusing to do the things that hurt my back such as moving furniture, pulling heavy things.

Kushner (1983) argues that some pain (such as that caused by kidney stones) is meaningless and no one wants to repeat it. Other pain, such as giving birth, is meaningful and women are willing to endure it again (Kushner, 1983).

> [P]ain makes some people bitter . . . others sensitive and compassionate. It is the result, not the cause, of pain that makes some experiences of pain meaningful and others empty and destructive. (Kushner, 1983, p. 64)

We still are left with the question of why the meaningless pain, such as kidney stones, exists. Kushner (1983) recognizes this bigger question, and states clearly that he doesn't know why "God created a world in which there is sickness and disease," but is comforted that at least pain, sickness, accidents "follow the laws of nature, which make sense" (p. 65). "Centuries ago," he states, people found reassuring proof of God in stories of miracles." Today, if anything "we find proof of God precisely in the fact that laws of nature do not change."

Job, or our own neighbor with a degenerative disease, will not be comforted by lessons in biology, natural sciences, or theology, "he needs to be told that what is happening to him is dreadfully unfair . . . that the God I believe in did not send the disease and does not have a miraculous cure that he is withholding" (Kushner, 1983, p. 68) "All we can say to someone [suffering] is that 'vulnerability to death is one of the given conditions of life'" (Kushner, 1983, p. 71). We can't explain suffering; all we can do is rise above the question of why this is happening, and begin to ask the question "what do I do now this has happened?" (Kushner, 1983, p. 71).

For many, the issue of suffering raises not just the question of injustice, but the sense that God is hiding, that if no pattern allows us to count on God's justice, how can we trust his presence (Anderson, 1971)? The Job portrayed in the dialogue poem of the Hebrew scripture speaks for all "who feel themselves the victims of a meaningless and evil universe, when faith is swallowed up in the abyss of doubt and God seems to have vanished. What kind of God is this who hides himself from me?" (Anderson, 1971, p. 240).

The answer Job is given is not an all-embracing rationale, but "an experience, a direct confrontation with the sovereign God. . . The God who is God" (Anderson, 1971, p. 241). This is the God who, in a time of anxiety and doubt, is found at the center of the storm (Anderson, 1971).

One interpretation of the Job story, implied in Anderson's commentary, is that the suffering is made meaningful because it leads to a direct experience and interaction with God. A similar explanation of suffering is given in the gospel of John. Most scholars do not take the words attributed to Jesus by John to be those of the historical Jesus. John has Jesus argue that the blind man suffers not because of his sins but "that the works of God may be shown forth in him" (John 9: 1-3, discussed in MacKenzie, 1968). The parallel argument would be that Job, and we, suffer, so that we are forced to face the power and presence of God.

When we experience suffering, our immediate response is to feel that something is wrong. The corollary which usually follows is to try to figure out who to blame for what went wrong. Is it because some human has sinned? Or is it something God has willed, perhaps for some greater good?

An alternative orientation is the first noble truth of Buddhism: "when we feel suffering, it does NOT mean that something is wrong. . . . Suffering is part of life, and we don't have to feel it's happening because we personally made a wrong move" (Chodron, 2000, p. 40).

RESEARCH ON WHAT HELPS THOSE IN PAIN

Benefits of Disclosure of Physical Pain

It is generally assumed by counselors that it is helpful for clients to express their emotional pain. Counselors are less likely to be aware of the benefits of expressing physical pain. (Most of the research studies of pain involve subjects who are suffering physically. The obvious reason is that it is too intrusive to study mental and emotional suffering in the person directly affected.) Studies of patients' disclosure of physical pain have shown that patients who share their pain show a variety of indications of better functioning than patients who hold it to themselves. These differ with the circumstances, but include decreased absenteeism from work, faster reemployment, better grade point average, better mood, fewer health problems or symptoms, fewer health center visits, improved liver function, and better immune function. (Esterling, Antoni, Fletcher, Margulies, & Schniederman, 1994; Francis & Pennebaker, 1992; Greenberg & Stone, 1992; Greenberg, Wortman, & Stone, 1996; Pennebaker & Beall, 1986; Pennebaker, Colder, & Sharp, 1990; Pennebaker, Kiecolt-Glaser, & Glaser, 1988; Pennebaker, Barger, & Tiebout, 1989; Petrie, Booth, Pennebaker, Davison, & Thomas, 1995; Spera, Buhrfeind, & Pennebaker, 1994).

All of these studies listed were conducted using healthy subjects, typically college students. Kelley, Lumley, and Leisen (1997) wanted to determine whether the positive results of studies with healthy subjects would apply to those who have physical illnesses. They conducted a controlled study of rheumatoid arthritis patients. The experimental group was encouraged to talk into a tape recorder about an important stressful life event for 15 minutes a day over four consecutive days. Not unexpectedly, "the most frequent topic was difficulties with rheumatoid arthritis" (mentioned at least once by 61 percent of patients). At first the disclosure resulted in more negative moods in the patients, but at the three months follow-up, those patients who had expressed their pain had less disturbance in mood and better physical functioning in their daily activities. A subgroup of the experimental group—patients who experienced larger increases in negative mood after talking—actually improved physically. They demonstrated improvements in the condition of their joints at the three months test. These improvements were not correlated with subjective measures of pain. The authors concluded that the effects of a stressful experience appear to be mediated by one's emotional processing of the event. As one patient summed it up: "Talking about my problems was hard at first and upset me for a while, but over time, I think it helped me." It is impressive that simply talking to a passive tape recorder has such positive effects; how much more powerful would the benefits of expressing oneself to a human who really listens be?

It is worth mentioning that far more research studies are available on the effects of secondhand suffering than on the direct experience of suffering; we will look at that material in a later section on caregivers.

Staying With the Client Suffering from Emotional or Mental Pain

Almost all forms of counseling correctly assume that clients who disclose their mental and emotional pain feel better. Though counseling theories differ about how to intervene, they have in common a recognition of the importance of careful listening, following the leads of the client (e.g., Egan, 1994).

One of the most common areas of suffering that counselors hear from their clients concerns conflicts with their families of origin. Sometimes such struggles go on for decades. "Donna" is an example.

Well into adulthood, she wanted to learn a new way to be with her mother (Felder, 2004). The client's mother, in phone call after phone call, would get furious at Donna for minor things that Donna's daughter had done that did not meet the grandmother's expectations. These tirades invariably elicited angry, guilty, and hurt responses from Donna, and resulted in a distancing between Donna and her mother. In the sessions with Felder, her therapist, Donna gradually shared a shift she was experiencing in her feelings about her mother—a shift that Felder himself was wishing for in his relationship with his father.

One week after Donna's mother's had waged a tirade about her granddaughter's failure to sound enthusiastic when she thanked her for an unattractive blouse Grandma had sent her for her birthday, Donna shared that she had found herself able, during this latest phone conversation, to remain calm and to listen empathically to her mother. It suddenly became clear to her that her mother just needed a little validation that she was a decent grandmother, and a worthy human being. So Donna took a breath and said, "Mom, I completely understand what you're saying. If I were in your shoes I'd be wanting my granddaughter to give me a real affectionate thank-you as well. I'm going to talk to her and hopefully we'll make some progress on this in time for the holiday presents."

In response, Donna's mother calmed down a bit. She was silent for several seconds, whereas before she'd been yelling and carrying on.

> In that silence I felt love for my delicate and complicated mother. For a moment we were just a mother and a daughter hanging out calmly together on the phone. We chatted for a few minutes more and it felt great—just two women connecting after years of trying to change each other. (Felder, 2004)

The therapist comments that he could see the heaviness lift. Donna's mother hadn't changed much, but Donna had significantly changed her internal response to her mother. Following this session, the therapist, being humble and open enough to learn from his client's growth, called his own father. As usual, the father responded to Felder's sharing by interrupting and shifting from his son's disclosure to a story about himself:

> I realized I could either go back to the old ways of feeling put upon, or try the new way of finding meaning in each interaction. I couldn't change my dad, but I could choose to feel compassion, decency, and relaxation.
>
> So, like Donna, I took a deep breath and began to participate fully in conversation about what was going well and what was difficult for my father and stepmother that week. Then, for a few moments, they listened to what was going on in my life. For the

> first time in years, we were simply hanging out on the phone, and connecting like old friends. It felt wonderful. (Felder, 2004, p. 87)

Both of the relationships just described were between adult children and one of their parents. Even counselors who are experienced at listening carefully to their clients can have difficulty listening to their own relatives. Felder openly shared this difficulty, but he learned from his own client that it was possible to change such a relationship. In a commentary on this case, Molly Layton (2004) describes how she had a practice of taking a morning swim in the pool, but habitually would dread the plunge into the cold water, grit her teeth, make the dive, and swim "like mad . . . until at last that water and my body were one." She uses this as a metaphor:

> I was reminded of this dive into the pool while reading about the plunges that Donna and therapist Leonard Felder took. It also reminded me how we're presented every day with some noxious experience that stops us up, shuts us down, and gives us the opportunity to ask ourselves, *why not experiment with opening up?* (Layton, 2004, p. 87; emphasis mine)

This way of responding to noxious events, to suffering, has many names. Layton (2004) goes on to note two secular labels:

> Wilfred Bion called it "patience." The poet Jon Keets called it "'negative capability,' the capacity to stand without knowing, without 'irritably reaching after facts.'"(p. 85).

Layton (2004) provides a third label taken from Buddhism:

> The therapist's expertise abides in his tolerance of his own state of "not-knowing," which the Buddhists call "bodhichitta," an opening of the heart, an enlargement, a facing into a large space. (p. 87)

The typical Western view of Buddhist practice as attempting to face absolute "emptiness" is corrected by Layton's translation of bodhichitta as "facing into a large space." This phrase makes more understandable the Buddha's teachings of facing life with a "beginner's mind."

It is intriguing that modern secular psychology tends to cite Buddhist teachings more frequently than those of Christianity. This may be partly because Buddhism developed a more explicit "psychology" of states of awareness than did classical Christianity. However, the teachings of Jesus on being "born again" are also about awareness, and imply facing life with a beginner's mind. The view that, to be "saved" we must repent—which literally means "to turn around"—is clearly a metaphor for both shifting psychological perspective and for changing behavior. While the Buddhist emphasis is on awareness, the Christian admonition suggests more—a change in direction or action. Together, they sum up the changes both Donna and Felder experienced: an internal "shift" and a new way of responding.

It is helpful to ground ourselves in the events themselves, and not get too lost in the words about events. The redemptive events Donna and Felding experienced involved a letting go of guilt as well as of anger and hurt. One of the dangers in the Christian tradition has been the temptation to hang on to guilt, as if the glory of God's salvation is dependent on and directly correlated with the profundity of one's experience of guilt. Some Christian theologies seem premised on hanging on to feelings of guilt, as if letting go of our guilt means we would no longer experience gratitude for the shift, the sense of wholeness.

Group Suffering

To this point most of the methods I have suggested for dealing with suffering have focused on the individual's physical or psychological suffering, and have been individual interventions. It is also important to point out the group and cultural aspects of suffering.

Judging by the feedback that I have received following workshops I've conducted, one of the most powerful interventions I've made has come at the end of the workshop, when in a simple acknowledgment I thank each member for taking the risk to really be vulnerable. I then ask that we remember that we each come from our own histories, and the suffering we experience comes not just from our personal twisted past, but also from each of us carrying the burden of the twisted paths of our family, racial, and ethnic histories.

I try to convey both the feeling of being grateful for the sharing and of the sensitivity of being in tune with a deep suffering that is far greater than each of our individual personal histories and the specific incidents that we have experienced.

RESEARCH ON THE RISKS OF EMPATHY: THE COSTS OF CARING

This section reviews three pieces of research concerning "vicarious suffering" and its effects on helping professionals (such as burnout, etc.). The costs of caring for helpers who are emotionally involved has been termed *compassion fatigue* by Figley (1995). Emergency workers are exposed to events involving human pain and suffering on a daily basis. Using the theoretical frameworks of emotional and cognitive empathy, Regehr, Goldberg, and Hughes (2002) studied a group of paramedics (EMTs) to understand factors that lead to higher levels of distress for these service persons. Though many EMTs routinely cope effectively with emergency situations, an occasional case may precipitate symptoms of depression or PTSD (posttraumatic stress disorder) in a worker. In the work that emergency workers do with victims of violence, "empathy may be expressed as a cognitive awareness of the distress of victims while maintaining an emotional distance or, alternately, it may involve an emotional connection with the victim. It is conceivable that having an emotional connection would increase vulnerability to symptoms of traumatic stress" (Regehr et al., 2002, p. 508). Events involving much blood and gore, or direct threats to the worker's life, were *not* likely to be viewed by EMTs as the most traumatic, although they were frequently reported. "One of the techniques [EMTs] often use is to deal with the events cognitively and technically while maintaining an emotional distance" (p. 509). Certain events, however, trigger more emotional empathy:

> The most commonly reported events defined by respondents as traumatic for themselves were suicides and violence against children. . . . Respondents indicated that the impact of these events was due to the fact that they were unable to understand why something like this might have occurred. Some commented

> that they were trying to make sense of something that was inherently nonsensical. Others felt the disparity between what they wanted to believe and what they were witnessing. . . . Still others worried about families who lost a member at Christmastime. . . . The sacred holiday only accentuated the incongruity they felt. (Regehr et al., 2002, p. 510)

According to the authors, the most debilitating stress in emergency workers was precipitated by the death or injury of someone whom the worker viewed as cut off from relationship to others; that is,

> an individual who died alone, without the support of others; a child who did not benefit from a loving, caring environment; a family devastated by loss; or an individual so alienated that he took his own life. In this process of contextualizing the individual, the paramedic develops an emotional connection to the individual or the bereaved family members. (Regehr et al., 2002, p. 511)

Thus, the EMTs move beyond a cognitive understanding of the loss or suffering to experiencing emotional empathy in these situations and identifying with the vulnerability of their clients.

Certainly empathy had positive effects: "there is considerable evidence that empathic doctors and nurses provide higher quality care and have patients who express higher satisfaction with service" (Regehr et al., 2002, citing Jarski, Gjerde, Bratton, Brown, & Matthes, 1985; Squier, 1990; Wheeler & Barrett, 1994). But empathy may also have its costs to some service givers.

In another study of helpers, this time crisis-line volunteers, Kinzel and Nanson (2000) observed that these volunteers are often exposed to horrific accounts of human pain and suffering. They frequently feel good about the work they are doing, reporting "having made a positive contribution toward changes in the lives of others" (Black, 1992, p. 6), but they can also get overloaded. Among the signs of overload or burnout are recurring nightmares, intrusive thoughts, and negative emotions such as impatience with hotline callers (Cyr & Dowrick, 1991). The most commonly used defense mechanisms of the hotline workers fit three categories:

1. Avoidance: avoiding different situations and people, consuming alcohol or drugs as an escape, and magical thinking—wishing that the situation would get better miraculously.
2. Detachment or mental disengagement: This mechanism may reduce stress initially, but may reduce empathic listening, and may eventually lead to the volunteer quitting.
3. Feeling personally responsible for the client's suffering: This reaction is aggravated in crisis-line work by callers being anonymous and the volunteer rarely knowing the outcome of his or her attempt to help (Cyr & Dowrick, 1991).

As a consequence of exposure to:

> graphic accounts of sexual abuse experiences and to the realities of people's intentional cruelty to one another . . . the hotline counselor, through his or her empathic openness, is vulnerable to the emotional and spiritual effects of vicarious traumatization. (Figley, 1995, p. 151)

The serious risk of enduring repeated vicarious traumatization is that the service worker's inner experience or schema about the self (Figley, 1995) and the world (Schauben & Frazier, 1995) may become transformed. The sentiment "the world is an ugly place" (Cyr & Dowrick 1991, p. 349) expressed by a crisis-line volunteer suggests a transformation of this individual's schema of the world. (Kinzel & Nanson, 2000).

One way to help prevent burnout is to provide the caregivers with information about burnout. Cyr and Dowrick (1991) found that only 54 percent of their sample of 30 volunteers answered yes when asked, "Have you ever felt burned out from working on the crisis line?" (p. 350). Yet, when the volunteers were asked indirectly about burnout (by checklists indicating behaviors and feelings), 97 percent implied they had or were experiencing symptoms of burnout. Information may assist the volunteer in recognizing signs that they are getting overwhelmed, and that this experience is a result of the situation rather than due to their own deficiencies (Kinzel & Nanson, 2000).

In both crisis work and counseling, being aware of the signs and monitoring one's own stress can lead to appropriate actions such as seeking more support from other volunteers, asking for closer supervision, and limiting the amount of time one is subjected to vicarious trauma. For counselors, the last may require making sure one has a mix of clients, including some whose issues involve less trauma, and whose goals in counseling are focused more on personal or spiritual growth. Inexperienced counselors should be especially careful to limit the number of clients they work with who are reacting to trauma that elicits strong emotional responses in the counselor. Counselors who have a number of such clients may need a supervisory arrangement that allows for immediate debriefing after difficult sessions. Kinzel and Nanson's (2000) recommendations to hotline agencies concerning immediate debriefing are available by accessing their article online.

FORGIVING THE UNIVERSE: SOME PERSONAL REFLECTIONS

> Returning to the modern rewrite of Job, the author (MacLeish, 1958) has J. B. respond to the problem of human suffering, not with theology or psychology, but by choosing to go on living and creating new life. J. B. *forgives God for not making a more just universe,* and decides to take life as it is. He stops looking for justice, for fairness in the world, and looks for love and beauty instead. (Kushner, 1983 p. 145, emphasis mine)

Personally, metaphysics and systematic ethics no longer interest me. Though these disciplines attempt to reach to the skies with intellectual scaffolding, it seems to me the base of the scaffolding cannot support the weight of the structure, so it all collapses. Therefore I make no claims to know what the ultimate integration of love and power and justice may be.

I cannot know the consciousness of God. However, I do trust that conscious decisions have value. We need to choose the God or gods we worship with care. It matters what or who we worship. And it matters to whom we pray. In short, the disciplines of the spirit matter. Not that our decisions are simply rational; they are not. But the process of reaching conscious decisions involves integrating our information and our values. When we make a commitment, when we get engaged and make a pledge or a vow, we are joining our values and passions to our plans and actions.

Inasmuch as we claim to believe in a God of love, and choose to value and worship love, it would seem that we must keep learning how to treat the universe as a lover. In a long and committed love relationship—e.g., in the forty-six-year-long relationship I've had with my wife—I have learned to love her not only for all the wonderful qualities she has, but also *in spite of* the personality quirks and idiosyncracies that I don't exactly like. She has done the same with me. Similarly, I take it as my spiritual task to learn to love the universe in spite its flaws. Incredible suffering appears to be an intrinsic part of the universe. It is not explainable, it is not always meaningful, and it does not make sense in terms of the beliefs I was taught about a good and all-powerful God. I can adjust to the imperfections of the universe, such as the annoying way everything gets "dirty" and has to be cleaned up. I have reconciled myself to the sad fact that all life is finite and eventually dies, realizing that these losses are part of constant change and make possible both progress and new possibilities. They are Shiva, the third member of the Hindu Trinity—who destroys to make way for the new.

What is hardest for me to square with the concept of a loving God is the tragic suffering—the injustice of it, the way it "falls on the unjust" but also on the just, and most of all the way it overwhelms some people and just closes them off so that they cannot possibly grow from it. For me, the pervasive suffering is the most serious "flaw" in the universe. But, like it or not, the suffering is there. I believe it is my task, even though I can't figure out the reason for this suffering, to love the universe in spite of the suffering. In short, I believe the path of spiritual growth involves softening to the pain, bearing it, and "forgiving" the universe for being what it is.

In no way does bearing the suffering diminish the process of giving thanks for all that is wonderful in the universe. In most days and weeks, the spiritual path is a joy, not some difficult drudgery. As Jalál Al-Din ar Rumi has said, "if loving does not include celebration I'll have none of it!" Yet, just as the suffering doesn't negate the joy, the celebration does not erase the struggle with pain, and eventually—for rare moments at a time—the surrender of forgiving the universe.

For me at least, the struggle is not about believing or not believing, or even about accepting grace. The struggle is about the worthiness of what we value most deeply—love—and the practice of becoming at one with the love. The process of accepting what is and letting go of resentment is transformative. The act of letting go is neither passive nor inert. It is an act. There is a place for acts that try to change the social structures that perpetuate injustice or suffering, but there is also a place for letting go and letting oneself be changed by accepting what is. After we've tried to do what we can do, and it still is not enough, each of us needs to get beyond the "call" of our particular "mission" and honor that which we can't change or control.

We can do all we can to alleviate suffering in the world. Nonetheless, suffering we can't change will remain, suffering we can't justify, suffering as an inevitable part of human life. So far as I can see—which is only one step ahead—our calling is to let go of the claim to understand, and to forgive the universe.

PART III: HELPING AND HEALING

Chapter 9

Staying with Process

WHERE TO FOCUS

Redefining Growth, Identity, and Mental Health

The goal-directed or developmental models of growth are likely to be culturally biased, as was noted in earlier chapters. However, it is possible to conceptualize growth differently, focusing not on a particular goal or direction, but on the process. What I am suggesting is that we not focus primarily on either a progression of stages (Erikson or Piaget or Kohlberg) or a goal (Maslow or Rogers), but on a process of openness to experience and evidence. Before I describe this more fully, let me return to some material on adolescence (noted in Chapters 2 and 4), because it is central to my thinking about process.

In the study of adolescent identity, it was initially expected that the healthy consequence of the identity process was the formation of a firm identity. Erik Erikson's (1968) insights on identity development were operationalized by James Marcia and colleagues' (1993) structured interviews, through which youth were classified as belonging to one of four statuses: *foreclosure* youth, *diffusion* youth, *moratorium* youth, and *identity achievement* youth.

During several decades of research, these categories continued to be used as convenient research tools, but it became increasingly clear that the initial formulation was biased toward men, and failed to note the complex interaction between the formation of identity and the development of interpersonal intimacy (see Matteson, 1993a). It also became clear that the functional identity status for adults in a fast-changing, pluralistic, multiethnic society, is not the "achievement" of a fixed identity. Rather, it is the commitment to a process, which includes taking a stance, but also involves re-opening the search among alternatives whenever the person is confronted with new and relevant information. (I have taken the liberty of repeating three sentences that appeared in an earlier chapter, to remind you of this shift from identity as *status* to identity as commitment to a *process.*) The *meta-commitment* is to making life decisions through *continued exploration.* In short, rather than the static result that the phrase "achieved identity" implies, what is needed is a more fluid and open identity. In many ways the mature, healthy identity is closer to a continued moratorium (Lifton, 1961), though the sense of crisis or confusion subsides as the person becomes comfortable with the process of uncertainty and openness in some areas, while decisions and commitments may remain settled in other areas (see Matteson, 1975).

What does it mean to value openness, and at the same time acknowledge the need for limits, boundaries, and closure? Are these best conceived as pulsations, alternations between opening and closing? And if so, is openness really the criterion, or does some value above openness incorporate both sides of this alternation?

Thus a shift has occurred in the theory of adolescent development from viewing identity process as ending in a particular status to a sense of that the mature result is an openness to an ongoing process. As Sam Keen puts it, "I have no identity that will not be lost and found and lost again" (1994, p. 149). It is not, however, a fluidity that is totally molded by the social environment without the power to participate and shape that environment. The achieved identity does involve an integration of the various parts of self, and, consequently, an integrity in relation to the outside "realities" and the outside social context. A center of values exists, but those values include a recognition of indefiniteness, ambiguity, and uncertainty, as well as a willingness to continued exploration.

It is likely, in previous centuries—when traditional cultures changed very slowly, new knowledge was acquired slowly, and the inhabitants of almost any specific nation or area were relatively homogeneous—that a foreclosed identity was fairly functional. Not so in today's world. It seems crucial to develop an identity that is at least somewhat independent of tradition, if not critical of it. And it seems necessary to take a stance that is accepting and open to change—even change of ones very self.[1]

Focusing on Process

The emphasis on process I am proposing (as opposed to many of the developmental models) does not assume a specific direction or goal. The stance I take is that the mentally healthy persons do more than "function" in the social environment; they can also critique that environment. They do more than understand and assimilate their particular cultural traditions; they can criticize them, and transcend them. In short, they are persons who develop an openness to changing identity, and possibly changing society.

Optimal Functioning and Values

It appears that, no matter what model we choose in order to assess mental health, we are involved in value judgments. I believe a criterion based on optimal mental health may be more useful for defining spiritual health than is a deficit approach. The previous discussion of mental health uses statements of optimal functioning. In contrast to models that emphasize the absence of symptoms, or adaptation, or goal-directed development, the focus on process that I am proposing attempts to clearly articulate what is valued. It is true that the use of optimal definitions as criteria leaves the majority of the population falling short of the standard (Sue, Sue, & Sue, 2000), but this does not make it inappropriate for assessing healthy experiences, events, or approaches to spirituality. It is better to meet the value issue head on rather than to allow value criteria to enter surreptitiously in intuitive or unexpressed judgments.

Previous models of mental health often failed to acknowledge that the criterion of mental health necessarily involves value judgments. Consequently, the judgments were made sub rosa, and tended to be ethnocentric. Cognitive and analytic methods increase the risk of the counselor imposing his or her own belief structure on the client. In contrast, experiential counseling methods do not encourage the counselor to focus on beliefs or opinions. By centering the sessions on the client's process using experiential methods, such as focusing, or Gestalt, or other intuitive and sensory approaches, the counselor rarely enters a direct discussion of dogmas or beliefs. Even opinions are typically recognized as a mixed expression of feelings and externalizing; in Gestalt work, clients are often encouraged to change an opinion statement into a statement about themselves.

Spiritual Growth and Process

Since spiritual counseling supports the commitment to process as a central component of identity, the actual sessions with a client need to focus on the process going on in the client, and the process between the client and counselor. The interview focuses on the individual's movement and growth, and interventions are chosen not only to fit the stage the individual is in, but to assess whether or not the individual is open to further movement. The process approach shifts the focus to whether the client is continually expanding his or her awareness of new information and new experience, and expanding his or her circle of acceptance—both of self and of others.

Summary of the Emphasis on Process

In practice, the emphasis on process directs the counselor to stay intuitively aware of the relationship, sensitive to the subtle openings and closings of the client and of the counselor himself or herself, and openness to the unfolding of life itself. This is not a vague and amorphous process, but a process of contact—with one another, with reality. The emphasis on process, as a derivative of the growth model, values growth, but growth is not predefined as movement toward autonomy or toward principled morality, or attaining the next stage. It is viewed as the process of expanding, making contact, and integrating.

Counseling Theories in which Process is Central

Historically, the client-centered approach of Carl Rogers was one of the first major theories to attempt to allow the client's emotional process and the client's own worldview to be the focus of the therapeutic interactions (although certainly classical psychoanalysis was attentive to the client's process). Rogers had first labeled his approach "nondirective," but consciously renamed the approach "client-centered" when he realized it was not actually "nondirective" since the reflections of the client's responses subtly encouraged the client to move more and more into feelings. Rogers, in describing the fully functioning person, emphasized such persons' openness to *experiencing*. Rogers' personality theory stated:

> When the individual perceives and accepts into one consistent and integrated system all his sensory and visceral experiences, then he is necessarily more understanding of others and is more accepting of others as separate individuals. (Rogers, 1965, p. 520; see also Rogers, 1961)

Eugene Gendlin's (1978) focusing approach grew out of client-centered therapy. Gendlin related experiencing to the creating of meaning, and developed a body-based method for accessing this subjective experience (Gendlin, 1962, 1970). Focusing provides examples of process interventions in spiritually sensitive counseling.[2] Focusing is not the only experiential approach that could be used in a way that is congruent with the emphasis on process. Numerous experiential approaches and techniques can be accommodated to this purpose, and can be fruitfully integrated into a counselor's work if they are tailored carefully to particular clients. (Some of these are used in Part IV of this book.) It should also be noted that some similarity exists between the focusing approach with its "felt sense" and the type of "mindfulness meditation" advocated by many Buddhist practitioners. Mindfulness can be described as even-hovering attention to experience (Timothy Pedigo, 2001, personal communication), and, similar to focusing, it is a method of staying in the stream of thoughts and feelings but not being pulled under by them. However, it is useful to describe the focusing approach more fully since it is one of the few process approaches that his been fairly concretely explicated.

A seminal work in the focusing approach, and so far as I know the only work to clearly articulate a step-by-step approach for using experience to guide spiritual growth in counseling, is Elfie Hinterkopf's (1998) *Integrating Spirituality in Counseling*. As Hinterkopf applies the focusing approach to spiritual issues, the client becomes the judge of his or her own process; the method for making this assessment is the use of a "felt sense" in experiencing a problem, and later a series of "felt shifts" in one's relationship to the problem. I will briefly describe these two processes. See Hinterkopf (1998) and Gendlin (1962, 1970) for a more detailed description.

"A felt sense is made of many interwoven strands, like a carpet. But it is felt . . . as one." (Gendlin, 1978, p. 82). An example is when you have been listening to a discussion, and are about to say something relevant and important, but others are still talking. You don't have the exact words prepared, but you do have a felt sense of what you want to say (Gendlin, 1978). It is not just an idea; it is experienced in the body.

Focusing is an approach for guiding the client in attending to his or her body as the client approaches a problem, clarifying the crux of the problem, finding the words that feel just right for it, and moving underneath the original feeling to more of "the whole of it." This sort of cycle is repeated, and at points a "felt shift" occurs; the client has a sense that something has changed. Again, this is not simply a mental change, but a body shift. The issue is worked on gently, with these little shifts. It may not be resolved in one session—but the little shifts allow a perrson to reach a point where it is okay to go out in the world and see what happens, being aware of the little changes that have occurred, and then return to continue the process (Gendlin, 1978).

It is much easier to understand this process when one experiences it with someone who has used it and can teach it. Words are inadequate in describing a process that is only partly cognitive. (See Appendix for resources.) Two examples of Hinterkopf's work with clients appear at the end of this chapter.

Hinterkopf's (1998) model for spiritually sensitive counseling is noteworthy, not only because it so clearly explicates how to follow process, and the advantages of doing so in the spiritual area, but because the issue of evaluation is directly addressed in the distinction between a "felt shift" and an "inner critic." Because the inner critic can block growth, it is important that the counselor be alert to when that process is occurring. The critic is usually experienced as coming "at me," while the felt shift is experienced as "from me" (Hinterkopf, 1998, p. 41). Both a felt shift and an inner critic are experiences of the client, and it is the client's own evaluating that is central. However, the counselor plays an important role in helping the client to differentiate between these two experiences (see Hinterkopf, 1998, Chapter 6).

Hinterkopf makes no claims that this model is value-free. In the context of this discussion of healthy spirituality, it needs to be noted that the model assumes that one's own "felt sense" is a valid test of the direction of growth—that is, that the individual (at least in the context of a client-counselor relationship) is the authority for spiritual growth. Thus the individual client is her or his own authority regarding what changes are needed to facilitate her or his own growth.

Beyond the Individual

Though both focusing and mindfulness meditation have been explicated primarily in terms of the individual practitioner, both can be successfully practiced in group settings. The *sanga* (regularly meeting meditation group) not only provides support for continuing the practice, but often enhances the meditation experience itself.

However, spiritual work may also be done in groups. As I have noted, my own use of the emphasis on process has emerged partly in the context of a seminar in spirituality and counseling, which met for a series of workshops. I have been impressed that, once the students understand the need for safety and design interventions to limit any attempts of group members to proselytize others in the group, the group norms become very supportive of individual process, and feedback helps to prevent flights into airy fantasy. These experiences convinced me that it is possible to develop group norms that help the members focus on the emotional and body-experienced process, and that keep the group from getting distracted by talk about beliefs or evaluations of the content of the spiritual experiences.

I am reminded of Sam Keen's (1994) metaphor that the spiritual journey is like mountain climbing:

> The idea that the heroic journey must be taken by a solitary individual fits neatly into the modern ideology of individualism. But it is a very dangerous half-truth that applies only to the first phase of the spiritual journey in which we explore the illusions of the psyche and our autobiographical truth. Those who try to go it alone end up isolated, alienated, and prey to all forms of madness. . .
>
> From here on, the only way we can avoid the dangers and illusions to which solo climbers are susceptible is to rope up, stay in communication with each other, search for consensus, and reflect on our common experience. (p. 95)

It would be premature for me to predict exactly where my suggested combination of focusing and group work will lead. I do see it as a challenging direction for future counselors interested in the process of spiritual growth to use the group setting for feedback. This might help to get us beyond the individualistic emphasis of Western psychology, and allow the process to include both the individual's felt sense and the group's collaborative evaluation. It should be noted that Hinterkopf herself has taught focusing in Japan and Korea, and notes the issue of individualism versus connectedness (Hinterkopf, 1998), although as far as I'm aware she has not written about the advantages of group process.

Little information is available on the benefits and risks of engaging in leading groups for spiritual development, yet it is a challenging direction for future counselors interested in the process of spiritual growth to explore, especially because of the opportunity for peer feedback, as well as for support and encouragement on the journey.

WHAT QUALITIES ARE REQUIRED OF THE SPIRITUALY SENSITIVE COUNSELOR?

Perhaps the most important quality necessary for working with clients in a spiritually sensitive way is attending to and responding to the client's process. This has been stressed throughout the first section of this chapter. Doing this involves both empathy and intuitiveness, which have also been discussed earlier. A central premise of this book is that the spiritual counselor must undergo an examination of his or her own spiritual development. All of this requires commitment to continual growth in one's capacity to be open and caring.[3]

Three other qualities of counselor behavior in spiritually sensitive counseling are worth discussion:

1. *Self-disclosure* may be particularly helpful in spiritually sensitive counseling, partly because the client is discussing material that is not necessarily valued in our "bottom line" culture (see Lerner, 2005, Chapter 1). Self-disclosure can reassure the client that the counselor values the spiritual quest in his or her own life. As in all therapist self-disclosures, one needs to take care not to shift the focus of the interaction to the counselor for extended periods. The focus of the session is appropriately on the client, and immediately after counselor self-disclosure, it is important to listen for how the client has interpreted the disclosure, and what it meant to the client.

In situations where a value difference exists between the client and the therapist, a particular type of self-disclosure is needed in which the therapist shares his or her own value stance in a way that does not imply that the therapist's own way is "the right way" for everyone. This means standing beside the client as another human who sees the need to be clear about a moral issue. However, the counselor does not stand *above* the client, but realizes that the client will have to make his or her own decision on what is moral. As Doherty (1995) stresses, it does mean treating the issue *as a moral issue,* not just an issue of self-interest.

In Chapter 3, I began discussion of a composite case from my own practice whom I called "Dan." Dan was one of eight or ten bisexual married men I was seeing in a therapeutic men's group. My own values are that important information that impacts a significant relationship should be shared with the other person—in this case, Dan's wife. So when Dan disclosed that he was having a relationship with another man in order to explore the "gay" side of his bisexuality, I had no trouble empathizing with his need to explore this important area of his own identity. But I was very uneasy that he wasn't telling the truth to his wife, whom he claimed was his closest friend. In this particular case, the issue was confounded by Dan's disclosure risking personal rejection both for his homosexual behavior and for his infidelity with his wife. It is particularly important that I, as therapist, not encourage shame in the client regarding issues that are genuinely identity issues. In another setting, the counselor's attitude toward gays and bisexuals might easily have been suspect, but the men in this group knew the group I was leading was sponsored by a gay organization, so it was unlikely that Dan would have misinterpreted my addressing the infidelity issue as a criticism of his bisexuality.

One might argue that Dan put a higher value on maintaining their love than on truth, but his leaving his wife out of the decision-making process suggested her equality was compromised. It is important to remember that earlier, when Dan had tried to include her, she had opted out. As in so many human ethical decisions, two ideals may be in conflict. To Dan, "truth" seemed less important than "love." (See Exhibit 9.1.)

The issue I have tried to illustrate in the Exhibit 9.1 description of my relationship with Dan is a value clash. As a process therapist, I cannot know the ultimate moral truth for Dan, but I need to work openly with a moral issue when it's what's involved. The way to do so, I believe, is through self-disclosure. But I can have no expectation that self-disclosure will function as persuasion. To the contrary, it is self-disclosure as a peer, a fellow traveler in the identity search and the search for a moral path.

EXHIBIT 9.1.
An Example of Therapist Self-Disclosure

I shared with Dan, in front of the group, that it is my own experience that whenever I am dishonest on an important issue that affects both me and my significant partner, the dishonesty builds a barrier between us. Even if nothing is said, I believe that my partner experiences the barrier. We both sense that there is something between us, something unspoken, and it weakens the trust. So I have come to a decision not to keep such secrets, even if working through the issues is painful and frightening.

My words deeply affected Dan. I can't remember his exact words, but he stated that he longed to be more open with his wife, and that he had tried to share some of his feelings toward men with her, but it had scared her and pushed her away. She had told him not to say any more. Dan stated that he envied me and that my partner and I could be open on very difficult issues, but it seemed his wife could not tolerate this. It seemed a wall stood between them whichever way he handled it, honestly or dishonestly. So he chose not to risk losing her altogether. From his perspective, he loved her too much to insist on absolute integrity for himself.

Future sessions included some reassessment on Dan's part concerning whether he was underestimating his wife's ability to deal with the issue. But the moral issue itself, the issue of his own honesty versus his holding on to the relationship, was not reconsidered. I felt that Dan had heard my input as it was intended—as a concern for his own moral integrity as well as for his wife's well-being. But nothing in his own perception of the dilemma had changed. What had changed, in me, was that I developed a new respect for our differences. I became more humble about my "rules" for intimate relationships; perhaps they don't apply to every couple. At the very least, I'm not in a position to judge Dan's marriage.

2. *Returning to characterological issues:* Though portions of a client's work with a therapist may focus on the spiritual path the client is trying to discern, this work is part of a process of the client discovering and possibly redeciding her or his life. Whatever events or experiences are discussed, they need to be treated in the larger context of the growth process the client has undertaken with you as counselor. This may go without saying: whenever the client shares an experience, be it a profoundly spiritual one or a mundane and practical one, it becomes part of understanding the next steps on the client's path. No matter how revelatory the experience, it must be reconnected to the

day-to-day life of the client. It may open up new options, or shine light on elements of the client's life and mission that he or she has not previously recognized. But, almost immediately after the "new" is recognized, some of the client's typical ways of handling life will likely pop up. An anxious and self-deprecating client of mine, in the midst of a fairly lengthy series of interviews, shared with some excitement that in the previous week he had attended a meeting of a group of men who were dealing with a life-crisis similar to his own. Quickly he squelched the excitement and stated, "Well, that's really nothing. Lots of men get together with other men just to talk men's talk."

I responded, "It sounds like you're minimizing how big a step that was for you." He was, in fact, doing something he'd fantasized doing for more than a decade but had never been able to take the risk. Now that he'd taken the risk, he returned to his self-effacing style. Later in the session he went back to my comment. "You were right," he said. "I guess I *could* take credit for that. I don't know if I'll try it again, but at least I did it."

3. *Recognizing one's own limits, or underestimating one's strengths:* Counselor self-disclosure may also be appropriate because of differences between the counselor and client. With any long-term client, a therapist at times will realize ways in which the client's struggle is different from his or her own, and the path that is right for the client is not obvious to the counselor. At these points the relationship may become more of a peer relationship; the counselor may simply need to say to the client, "This is not something I have gone through," or "I can tell that experience is important to you. I must state honestly, I have never had an experience quite like that. I'm really interested; tell me more."

One danger is that we will set up rules or expectations for psychotherapists that feed into the tendency of some counselors to underestimate their own relationships with their clients. A fear of doing it wrong may inhibit some counselors from doing it at all. For example, a secular counselor who is very humble about his own progress on a spiritual path, who honestly acknowledges how difficult it is for him to meditate, and who is regretful about a number of relationships in his history that he feels he "bungled," may be quite capable—in spite of these flaws—of staying with a client who is longing for a deeper spirituality. Assuming that this counselor takes the spiritual search seriously, it would be a loss for the client if this counselor were to refer his clients to a "specialist" once they indicate the need for spiritual counseling.

Among the counseling competences expected to be included in masters programs in counseling, the Association for Spiritual, Ethical and Value Issues in Counseling (ASERVIC, a division of the American Counseling Association) has recommended two that are of special relevance to spiritually sensitive counseling:

1. Demonstrate empathy for understanding spiritual and transpersonal communication
2. Use the client's religious, spiritual, or transpersonal beliefs in the pursuit of the client's therapeutic goals as befits the client's expressed preferences, or admit inability to do so in such a way that honors the client (Fukyama, 2000).

The last point, concerning admitting inability, implies not only honoring our client's therapeutic goals, but entering into the spiritual dialogue as a "student" who can learn from the client's tradition and experience, not as a "guru." In Chapter 3 I discussed a Catholic client of mine: A Lithuanian woman client of mine, "Mary," was struggling with her Catholic heritage. . . . What Catholicism meant to her . . . turned out to be quite different than the official doctrines of the church. Her view of Catholicism also proved to be much different from how I, coming from a different culture and different religious heritage, had understood (or misunderstood) Catholicism. An approach that is frequently helpful is to make the client the expert. "I know a bit about Catholicism, of course, but tell me what your belief is and how it impacts your decisions on this issue."

We can place ourselves "below" our clients, to learn from them about their traditions and life experiences that are different from our own. And, when there are irresolvable value differences, we can place ourselves on the same level with our clients, as in the last case concerning Dan, the bisexual husband.

There does seem to be one way in which it is appropriate for the therapist or counselor to place himself or herself "above" the client, and that is in terms of knowledge and leadership regarding the process of counseling itself. We are not "experts" in how to live our clients lives outside the therapy room; we are experts in the process of therapy.

I have mentioned the fear that practitioners will use the increasing interest in spirituality among counselors as an excuse to propagate their own religious opinions or beliefs, and in Chapters 3 and 4 I discussed safeguards against this misuse. An additional safeguard against propagating beliefs is implicit in the focus on process.

Unlike previous models (medical, psychosocial, and growth models), the emphasis on process does not lead to a content-orientated method of doing spiritually sensitive counseling. Cognitive and analytic methods increase the risk of the counselor imposing his or her own belief structure on the client. Experiential methods decrease that risk.

The emphasis on process implies using an interactive and process-orientated method. The counselor-client relationship is a collaborative one, and grows out of the common humanity of the client and the counselor, not out of some special spiritual authority of the counselor. The growth in acceptance includes genuine acceptance of each other's real differences. This distinction is crucial to protect the client from the imposition of the counselor's values on the client.

By centering the sessions on the client's process using experiential methods, such as focusing, or Gestalt, or other intuitive and sensory approaches, the counselor rarely enters a direct discussion of dogmas or beliefs. Even opinions are typically recognized as a mixed expression of feelings and externalizing; clients are usually encouraged to change an opinion statement into a statement about themselves.

One of the elements that almost all experiential approaches have in common deserves mention here: the counselor frequently needs to teach the client to "slow down." "Speed is the enemy of the spirit" (Keen, 1994, p. 152). The rush to formulate concepts, beliefs, and answers often gets in the way of the actual process of experiencing, of being aware, both within and without. Simple relaxation techniques—to move the client's attention to the body tensions themselves and to let them go—may be stepping stones to then learning focusing and other approaches. These approaches are used in Part IV of this book.

Consider turning to Chapter 11 and trying Experiment 5, "Relaxing." If you haven't done some of the experiments before that, you might go back to them after completing Experiment 5. If you are not familiar with the focusing approach, you can find an example in Experiment 4 "Clearing a Space," in Chapter 13.

The changes that such means of "slowing down" make in the brain process appear to be directly related to changes involved in transcendent experiences. In short, when we teach such methods, we may be setting clients on the path to greater receptivity to spiritual experiences.[4]

Examples of Process Work with Beliefs

Two additional cases, both from focusing work, may be helpful to specifically illustrate work with areas of beliefs, in contrast to work with value issues.

Hinterkopf (1998) notes the importance of being sensitive to the terms that are used by the client. She gives an example of using nontheistic terms with "Mr. K.," who had said that he was spiritual but had difficulty relating to the term *God.*

> After discussing the issue involved, I asked him, "What is your experience of being related to something greater than yourself?" The client said, "It feels like getting in touch with a larger background where you're aware of feeling connected to everyone and everything else." Then I asked him, "How does getting in touch with a larger background feel in your body right now?" He said, "It feels more relaxed. My body feels bigger and there is a quiet energy. My head feels clearer." When the client said "I think I just had a spiritual experience," I agreed. Had I insisted on using the term *God,* instead of affirming the client's words, I would have run the risk of hindering or negating the client's spiritual process. (p. 79)

Notice in this example that the counselor focuses on the client's felt experience, using his terms, but also checking out whether another phrase, "greater than yourself," fits the client's experience. No attempt is made to persuade the client, only to find the language that fits the experience for the client.

Another example from focusing work further illustrates this focus on the client's process, without getting hung up on differences in beliefs. Hinterkopf (1998) advises:

> In supervising counselors I have sometimes heard counselors tell clients they cannot relate to the client's experience because it is unfamiliar to them. This unfortunate and unnecessary response usually stops the client's psycho-spiritual process and leaves the client feeling isolated. (p. 79)

Hinterkopf goes on to illustrate the handling of unfamiliar or unexpected spiritual content, without getting lost or distracted by differences in belief:

> A Chinese woman from a Buddhist background talked about feeling "very tired much of the time." At first she thought it was a physical tiredness from her busy schedule and not enough sleep. But then she realized that her tiredness was due to "too many reincarnations without enough enlightenment."
>
> After the counselor reflected her new realization, the client continued: "Life is getting old for me." She explained that she knew that she wasn't here to just live this life but that she was here to get enlightened. Again I responded empathically and reflected her felt sense words. I then suggested the question, "Perhaps you could ask yourself 'What does this whole thing need?'" After spending some time with her attention directed inside, she received the answer, "Light and love in the heart area." She realized that she was so tired because she wanted to achieve enlightenment by herself. She said, "Instead I now realize that I need to *receive* enlightenment—that enlightenment is a gift, a moment of grace when I remember to receive light and love from the universe. This is the only way to receive enlightenment." With this answer her tiredness disappeared. I suggested that she stay with her new feeling of easing." (Hinterkopf, 1998, pp. 79-80)

The change or "felt shift" that occurs for the client does not come from the counselor engaging in conversation about the beliefs, but from facilitating the experiential process. In this case, the new "insight" that is achieved is the client's own rewording of her experience.

In both of these cases, the client is encouraged to experience more deeply. In the first, the counselor's question about his "experience of being related to something greater than yourself" opens him to access an experience that he wasn't in touch with. In the second, the question about what the whole thing "needs" leads to the client's accessing her needs for love from others and the Other. In neither case do the questions or leads involve the counselor imposing his or her beliefs on the client. The questions are based on the process.

IN CLOSING

One of the frustrating things about process, for many novice counselors is that it is so open-ended. But that is the truth about life, and it is appropriate that this chapter end in an open-ended way. Two themes have recurred throughout this chapter but remain unresolved. The first is the question of cultural bias. Is the focus on process itself culturally biased? Is it a historically limited phenomenon? I think the answer is yes to both of these questions. The concept of an emphasis on process emerges in the current context of psychology and counseling, which values multiculturalism and openness as opposed to dogmatism and tribal or exclusive orientations. And it emerges at a time in history when, if values that are limited to one race, one tribe, or one religious group are affirmed, it can lead only to divisiveness and war. The only kind of identity that can work in a pluralistic and fast-changing world is an open identity—an identity committed to the process of change and expansion itself. We cannot claim that this is a value orientation that would have worked in previous times, or is universal. We can only argue that it is the most functional approach for our time.

The second unresolved theme is the issue of "fruits" and the dictum "by their fruits you shall know them." What would be the early fruits of counseling with a emphasis on process? I believe they may not be ethical acts so much as attitudes. The client may show an increased openness, a sense of being accepted and accepting others, rather than a well-developed empathy or skill of connecting. Only later might behavioral changes occur, measurable fruits. But these later fruits would be expected to flow from a personal center of seeing and being, from wisdom, rather than from opinion or belief. Remember that the earliest descriptions of the healing acts of Jesus and Buddha were so described—as flowing from a personal center of being and wisdom. Perhaps fruits are not the first results. Perhaps the real test of healthy spirituality is whether this kind of process is occurring.

Chapter 10

Continuing the Spiritual Journey: Reaching for a Spirit-Filled Life

> There are two major groups of people in the world—those who want certitude and those who want understanding.
>
> Karl Rahner, German Jesuit theologian

Our spiritual journey may lead us in any of several directions including: involvement in issues of advocacy or justice, concern for the ecology of the planet, exploration of other forms of spirituality than one's own tradition, and experimentation with practices such as art, movement, meditation, or listening to poetry read aloud, any of which may be new to us. This chapter on charting one's own journey does not advocate a particular direction, but focuses on ways to keep the process going. So many adults in our culture look back at their youth and their passionate concern for what they thought mattered, and ask themselves, "Where has my spirituality gone?" Without a clear process for setting priorities, it is easy to drift into keeping up materially, or climbing up in status, or simply trying to be "happy" in the midst of a task-filled agenda of things to do. Maintaining a spirit-filled life involves clarifying what helps the reader stay in touch. Options to be explored include obvious self-care concerns such as getting enough sleep, eating healthful foods, and exercising, but also "care of the soul" through movement, self-designed rituals, taking breaks and vacations, and listening to music with the mind free of words.

There are, of course, a number of assumptions in the way I have written about the spiritual paths. As the title to this chapter suggests, I do not conceive of the spirit-filled life as being a simple matter of beliefs or concepts. Though it is important to clarify what one believes and discern which beliefs are helpful and congruent with one's understanding of this world (Chapter 4 discusses this process), a spirit-filled life has more to do with making choices for meaningful involvements than with dogmas or belief systems. Even the terms *meaning* and *understanding* may imply a more cognitive process than I intend; what I am envisioning is a passionate and embodied process. (See discussion of "engaged passion" in Chapter 5.)

A colleague of mine, Jon Carlson, along with two other counselor educators, Jeffrey Kottler and Brad Keeney, spent a week in a Bushman village in southwest Africa. They witnessed a Kalahari healing ceremony. Keeney, who had been coming to this village several times a year, explained to Carlson and Kottler that Bushman shamans do pretty much the opposite of what we do as therapists: rather than conducting their work in secrecy when someone is afflicted with a mental or physical problem, they bring together the whole community to hold a healing dance and ceremony.

> The Bushman believe that when someone is in trouble, whether through a curse, a physical malady, or some emotional difficulty, the community should come together to hold a dance. Once the drums start beating, the villagers start chanting and the shamans start moving rhythmically. Then spontaneous movements begin to take place—movements that resemble something between seizures and uncontrolled wiggling. They believe that it's this shaking that transfers healing energy from the healer (and the ancestors) to the afflicted. (Kottler, Carlson, & Keeney, 2004, p. 24)

In a conversation before the ceremony, the Bushman shaman, Cgunta, carried on a discussion with Kottler, trying to understand our Western form of healing, psychotherapy.

> "What is it that you do with your people?" Cgunta asked politely through our translator . . .
>
> "Well, people come to see me in my office, I mean the place where I work. We sit down together and we talk about what's bothering them . . ." Kottler responded.
>
> "There's a fire where you work?" Cgunta asked.
>
> "No, actually no fire . . ."

> "The whole village is there?"
>
> "Ah," [Kottler hesitated] "You see, in my culture, in my village, someone comes to me alone, or sometimes with his or her family. That's when we talk about things and try to figure out what's going on and what we might do to make things better."
>
> "You *talk about* problems with these people?" Cgunta said, very puzzled . . . "And tell me," he said with a grin, "have you ever helped anyone doing this?"
>
> When I got to the part about clients scheduling specific appointments for private conversations, alone, without anyone else around, Cgunta became more and more tickled by the absurdity of how this sounded to him. I then described how clients sit still in a chair . . . and we tell then to calm down in the most soothing way we can . . . and sometimes even recommend certain drugs to help people relax. Cgunta found this too funny, since the whole idea of calming an upset person down was the most ridiculous idea he'd every heard. Kottler tried to explain that they needed to be calm to "think clearly enough to comprehend what their anxious symptoms might mean."
>
> "What, then happens to the mystery?" he wondered, shaking his head. (Kottler et al., 2004, p. 55)[1]

When I speak of a spirit-filled life, I do not necessarily mean a calm one. I certainly do not mean one without mystery and awe. The meaningful life I'm referring to may come from listening to the still, small voice within. But it may also come from, or lead to, active involvement in service. Music, dance, and other arts may be important to one's spiritual path in modern times, as well as in prehistoric times. They court a spirit of connectedness, not of privacy and isolation. In many respects, the spirit-filled life is closer to the traditions of native people—indigenous tribes in Africa, or in Peru, but also in the "sweat lodges" of the plains Indians of the Americas—than to the orthodoxy of psychotherapy. The inadequacies of traditional psychotherapy are partly due to its structuring of an intense, two-person relationship that is inherently unequal and authoritarian, yet does not have the safety of community involvement. This contrasts to the community-based and experience-based rituals and dances through which the shamans work. This weakness of authority-based therapy has been thoroughly critiqued for decades (see, for example, Kramer & Alstad, 1993;

Laing & Esterson, 1999; Masson, 1988; Szasz, 1961). Therefore it will not detain us here.

But an experience-based spirituality alone is not enough. In traditional societies, based almost completely on face-to-face relationships and personal mentors, intense spiritual experiences can be contained and shaped into socially constructive behaviors. But in modern societies, with so much of the teaching being done by impersonal authorities rather than mentors, deep experiences, if they occur at all, are likely to go unshared and become privatized. Or they may lead to a tribalism that is totally malfunctioning in a multicultural setting. This has been stated with biting sarcasm: "It takes a village to raise a child to hate all of the people in the next village" ("Cynical Sayings," 2003).

It is not easy to sustain a sense of life as meaningful on a day to day basis. If we are not intensely involved in a cause, or a life project, we may find ourselves bored or consumed by the minutia of life, feeling at the end of the day that we've not done anything meaningful. On the other hand, if we *are* heavily involved, it is easy to get overwhelmed, to feel pushed by the needs of others, or to become obsessed about the outcomes of our endeavors.

PRACTICE

Bo Lozoff and his wife Sita lead a community for ex-offenders that provides a humane and supportive setting while the former convicts make the move back into the mainstream culture. In his inspiring book, *It's a Meaningful Life, It Just Takes Practice* (Lozoff, 2001), he makes the basic point that thinking about a meaningful life or a spirit-filled life won't get you there; you have to get involved. You have to practice acts of love to learn the art of loving (Fromm, 1956).

Central to a spiritual life is choosing the experiences that help you connect with the sacred. Whether you decide to pursue your path of spirituality by maintaining a connection with one of the organized religious groups, or whether you follow a less traditional path, the way is not easy. Any path requires practice. Even if you have given up traditional forms of worship, or of prayer, you must look deeply at yourself, seek out your own form of community, and find your own style of expression. The inner and the outer practice are both crucial, and Lozoff addresses both. But, as I suggest in Chapter 11 (Experiment 3:

Ambivalence and Shuttling), the inner and outer practices are deeply connected. It's not a question of "which comes first?" They support each other and grow from each other.

COMMUNITY

Lozoff (2001) devotes more than half his book to the outer practice, the path toward community. For most of us, beginning to practice involves forming some mutually supportive relationships. This is true whether we think of the spiritual path as centered in meditation, or in the art of loving.

This discipline of practice does not grow out of duty (although for some, this is a start). Spiritual replenishment comes from the giving and receiving of blessings (Casey, 2005). We give and are given blessings both in our relationships with other people and in our relationship with "the creation"—with nature and the cosmos. One measure of the spiritual life is the extent to which we take every experience in life as a blessing. Another measure is our willingness to respond by giving blessings to life—to others and to the universe (the environment). Sometimes it is very hard to take what comes and receive it as a blessing; this struggle is expressed in the African-American spiritual "I didn't know I'd have to pray so hard" (Casey, 2005). Sometimes when we are hit by reality, we respond by hardening, or with anger, when what is needed in is even deeper receptivity.

This development of the inner spirituality involves clarifying what helps the reader stay in touch. Though the previous chapters reflect some of the main areas in which we must struggle to find an authentic spirituality, I think the key area—which I have not addressed directly to this point—concerns community. It seems paradoxical, but the spiritual path involves two orientations toward community. First, it is your journey and no one can tell you which direction to go. But second, you do not need to walk your path alone—you need feedback and support. Sam Keen (1994) uses the metaphor of the necessity of roping in with other climbers on the steeper ascents of mountain climbing. A person needs community, especially if he or she moves away from the institutions of religion. I strongly encourage my counseling students, once they leave the academic cloisters, to initiate a clinical support group.

During the years my wife and I were completing our graduate education in Boston, we became involved in a church that had a very active pastoral ministry, as well as an active prophetic ministry. The primary preaching minister was also involved in a number of social action projects, and encouraged the parishioners' involvement—yet there was an openness to different political and cultural opinions. When we moved to a much smaller college community, we couldn't find a church that had a ministry that fit our needs. Each Sunday we would visit a new church, attending not only the worship service but the adult Sunday school or Bible study class. And we would ask, "are any of you in a church group that supports your own ministries to others and your causes?" No such group seemed to exist in this area, but frequently after the service or class a person or two would come up to us and say, "If you find such a group, please call us; we would like to be in one too." So we shifted our goal, and continued to visit other churches, but primarily to collect the names of others who wanted that kind of spiritual community. A few months later we put out a letter to all whose names we had collected, announcing the first meeting of a spiritual support group, to be held in our home. More than 20 people arrived for the first meeting. They included two former nuns; a priest; several ministers; people in counseling, social work, and related fields; several faculty from the small university where I was teaching; and others. Though there was some attrition when we settled into regular meetings and closed the group, the group continued to meet for well over a year. It became a powerful support, and a major force in our own spiritual growth.

It was a lesson for us both: if you can't find what you need, initiate it. Since it was a peer-run group, with no assigned leadership, initiating the group did not require us to have special skills in group leadership, or special gifts of ministry. It simply required that we state our needs, be open to possibilities, and do a little communication to get things going.

A Community of Acceptance Opens the Way to Deeper Experiences of the Sacred

My current support system includes meetings twice a month of a clinical support group. And every year or two I attend a conference that centers around poetry, music, art, mythology, and storytelling.

Just before I left for this conference in a recent summer, I visited a woman from my church who was in hospice. Alice is nearly the same age as I am, and had a virulent cancer spreading to her brain. When I got back home from the conference, I learned that Alice had died. Someone who knew her even more deeply than I did, speaking at the memorial service on Sunday, stated that when you became Alice's friend, "she would never spare you either her excellent cooking—or her criticisms!" That seems to me a good definition of true friendship and real support. It is a relationship that is honest, speaking the truth in love. The community attending the conference I had just returned from is of that quality. We continue the communication between conferences by means of a collection of letters or essays sent to each of us every month, to which each of us contributes regularly. These communities do not hide me from the hard truth, yet they are nourishing.

It has been said that "a good friendship—and a good group—is one that provides both support and confrontation." Is this an adequate starting point in defining friendship?

Expanding Our Communities

Most important, we can take stock of our own patterns of socializing. If we have fallen into the path of least resistance and find almost all our socializing is with people of our own age group, our own race, our own type of work, and our own socioeconomic status, we can consciously begin developing a more diverse reference group, one that has members from many cultures or subcultures. We can use these people to check out our own assumptions and perceptions.

Dad's Cloud

I am especially open to the spiritual when I am in a community of people I have learned to trust, and am close to nature. Some years ago the conference mentioned previously took place on a campground near an ocean bay. The event I am remembering occurred on a beautiful summer day. Our afternoon workshop was held in an old timber lodge. About 40 or 50 of us, who had chosen to learn a new breathing meditation, sat in a big circle in the quiet darkness before a huge fieldstone fireplace. For several successive afternoons our meditation leaders were an Ojibwe couple; this husband and wife were teaching us a form of meditational breathing that involved excitation. Rather than the calming practice of most Eastern meditation, the breathing involved some mild hyperventilating. During the breathing exercise, when the instruction was given to return to normal breathing but to follow one's visual fantasies, I felt a call to leave the lodge and walk down the grassy hill to the bay. On the dock were several empty kayaks. I put on a safety vest, slid a kayak into the water, pulled it even to the dock, laid a paddle across it, and climbed in. The water was calm so it was easy to glide quietly out into the bay and around the shore to where I had no view of the camp or of those attending the conference. There I felt at one with nature, alone yet connected. Some time passed as I continued to paddle, facing out into a large body of calm water, seeing only the water, the horizon, and low lying clouds near the horizon. Then, gently and beautifully, one of those clouds began to grow upward, upward, billowing and white but tall as an enormous thundercloud. It was amazing—surreal and quite beautiful. My attention was fixed on it, and yet I was aware of the calmness around me, and felt very connected to all that was. Connected, with a sense that the cloud was a warm and loving "other." Then I heard a voice. Not an actual sound, not something that could be recorded, but a distinct and clear voice—that of my father. My father had been dead for 20 years; I had grieved him, and for several years he had spoken to me in dreams, yet this was no dream. I knew I was on the bay, that a supportive community was back on shore meditating.

A rich belly laugh roared from the cloud—the laugh of my father's loving voice. In my dreams I had heard his wishes, and the assurance of his love for me, with a touch of sadness. But I had forgotten his wonderful laugh. It was as if he were saying, "Don't worry yourself for me, and don't remember me with longing or sadness. Remember my laugh."

It was one of the most moving mystical experiences I have had. I've hesitated to tell it to people, as it could be taken as magical or miraculous or labeled a hallucination, and I don't believe it was any of those. I'm sure if someone had been in another kayak nearby, they would not have heard my father. In one sense, this all happened "in my head." But I am also sure it wasn't a hallucination—if a porpoise or a sudden wave had upset my kayak I would have snapped back to reality just as a daydreaming driver on the turnpike jerks back into the practical world when his or her mind is needed there.

I see no need to explain it. I'm simply glad that, at that point in time, I was open to the experience; it was a powerfully *integrating* experience. It brought joy to my heart—not just my father's joy, but the joy of all creation.

Often our theories of perception and of the nature of reality prevent us from experiencing a fuller and deeper reality. We let words and reason interrupt our direct experience. Thus we cut ourselves off from new messages and revelations and states of being that can help us heal and grow into a more complete person. Notice that such experiences are not about beliefs. For me, they do not change my view of the physics or metaphysics of nature. They don't break any natural laws. But they break into our stuck places.

Involvement in Relationships

One can become involved without having to make dogmatic commitments. One only needs to vow to take the next step, out of curiosity, wonder, and love, even though we can't see clearly where it will lead (Casey, 2005). Just as we can decide to go on the next date with a person who intrigues us or elicits our sense of beauty, so we can "date" the parts of the world and the paths of the spirit. We can look at the realities around us head on, face the pain, ugliness, the hell, directly, a step at a time. When we are repulsed or face ugliness, we can go deeper. Remember Jeffers' poem about a forest fire:

> Beauty is not always lovely; the fire was beautiful, the terror
> Of the deer was beautiful; and when I returned
> Down the back slopes after the fire had gone by, an eagle
> Was perched on the jag of a burnt pine. . . .
> The destruction . . . brings an eagle from heaven. . . .
>
> (Jeffers, 2000)

Good or bad, beautiful or fearful, we can face it and explore it. We don't need to feel rushed into commitment until we've developed a relationship with a particular path, until we've explored it sufficiently to know it is, for us, a portal to the sacred. And even then, it need not be our only path.

TWELVE GATEWAYS THAT CAN LEAD TO THE SACRED

Along with accepting ourselves, and affirming differences, comes the recognition that different people come to the sacred along different paths. It is hard to find the right language, because almost every word or phrase that seeks to point to the sacred also contains assumptions or symbols that derive from a particular path. The sacred is beyond language. In some Jewish theology, the holy is not named, but called "the Ineffable." This is implied in Moses's interaction with the burning bush. When he asks for the name of the holy one that is revealed in the burning bush, the response is "I am who I am." Even the word *sacred* has it's problems, as it is often used in contrast to the *secular* and can be misunderstood to imply that the sacred is "other worldly"—a metaphysical statement that is itself too restrictive. Some people will be called to paths that they themselves describe as "other worldly," but others are called to live in this world, but not of it (John 17: 16-18; Romans 12:2). There is no way around these word problems, short of silence or music and art. And there *is* a sense, when standing on holy ground, that music, art, or silence are more appropriate than words.

You cannot assume that the sacred will come at your bidding. But you can build on your past experience, and your present expectations.

What are the activities or places in which you have experienced the sacred in the past? From what you know about yourself today, where do you expect you will meet the sacred at this point in your life? And what do you need to do to keep open the gateways, so that the holy can enter your life?

As a starting point, take a look at each of the following twelve descriptions of what others have experienced as portals to the sacred, and get a sense of which ones could be gateways for you. (*Note:* I am grateful to David N. Elkins (1998) for his description of eight "nontraditional paths to spirituality" described in the second half of his book *Beyond Religion.* He devotes a chapter apiece to the paths of relationship, the feminine, the arts, the body, nature, psychology and psychotherapy, mythology, and dark nights of the soul. If my brief and personal descriptions of any of these pathways do not make sense to you, I urge you to read the corresponding chapter on that path in Elkin's book.)

Since I do not see the traditional religions as necessarily negative or immature paths, I have listed them as the first two "gateways" to the sacred. However, if the first two paths no longer work for you or for your client, or if—as is unfortunately common—you or your client have been wounded, even traumatized, by people in the institutional church, you may be more reachable via one or more alternative paths.

Besides the first two paths involving traditional religion, I have added two nontraditional paths to the eight Elkins uses: excitation and exercise, and social causes. This results is a total of twelve gateways to the sacred.

You may be aware of still others. My purpose here is not to develop an exhaustive or logical category system, but to evoke enough concrete options to elicit your interest and help you design the next steps on your path.

Gateway One: The Religion of One's Ancestors

For many, the way "home" is through returning to the religion that was part of their childhood, or at least of their family tradition. Many, many persons who have felt that their lives have become meaningless or superficial feel a sense of "being home again" when they reencounter the sacred, so it is not surprising that one way to be open to that experience is to open oneself to what one deeply "remembers." Martin Prectel, a Mayan shaman and the finest storyteller I have heard, tells the wonderful Mayan story of a man who, in his life travels, becomes broken and scattered. He is given the task of revisiting the places of his journey and re-membering—literally reassembling—his body (Prectel, 1998).

One of the dangers of contrasting "spirituality" to "religion" is that it disregards the spiritual gifts handed down from generation to generation by way of the institutions of religion. "Through our religions, we humans have preserved history's greatest wisdom teachings" (Maugans, 2002). Certainly the Roman Catholic and Eastern Orthodox churches played an important role in preserving scriptures, including the Job story (see Chapter 8), the prophetic literature, the letters attributed to Paul, and four of the gospel narratives. The role of monks as scribes was crucial in preserving these documents through the Middle Ages. (On the other hand, more than 200 other gospels were deliberately destroyed by the institutional church, and one, Thomas, was suppressed and only recently discovered [Ellerbe, 1995].)

Convincing evidence suggests that the black/white civil rights movement of the 1960s would not have occurred were it not for the role of the black protestant churches, and later, of some of the mainstream churches. In the 1980s the development of "liberation theology" led Catholic orders in Latin American into the movements to counter corrupt dictators and their subsidizers in North America (Bellah, 1996).

In short, it generally takes institutional effort to preserve important socially transforming teachings and writings, and the church has done this, even at times preserving writings that challenged the orthodoxy of their time, such as the central drama of Job (see Chapter 8). On the other hand, institutions may preserve traditions that, in current society, are out of date or even harmful—traditions that are circumscribed in one era of time, yet are revered as if they were *the* "true tradition." Such traditions may be used to justify treating certain targeted "others" as inferior or dangerous. An example of this, covered in detail in Chapter 6, is the destructive treatment of homosexuals and women perpetuated by church regulations derived from patriarchal times.

Institutionalized religion is still important to the majority of Americans—64 percent consider themselves religious, even more (79 percent) now consider themselves "spiritual" ("Where We Stand on Faith, 2005), yet the fastest growing category on surveys that ask people to state their religious affiliation, is "none" (Killen, 2005). Some are concerned that the shift in Western culture from supporting organized religion to supporting spirituality without organized form will result in a personal and private form of practice that does not involve commitment to improving the social order. At the very least, we must acknowledge that the paths of history and social change are complex and ambiguous, and it is unfair to paint organized religion as always in the wrong. For some it is the early training ground for their spirituality, although they move on. For others it is the way "home."

Gateway Two: Exploring Another Tradition

One of the great advantages of growing up in a multicultural society is that it is relatively easy to explore traditions other than the "faith of our fathers." Although I grew up in a town of fewer than 2,000 people, three protestant churches and one Roman Catholic church stood within the village and within walking distance of my home. So when I was in early high school, I began attending occasional services in churches that represented traditions somewhat different from the one in which I was raised (though all of these were Christian). This interest in the differences became a lifelong passion. When I went to college, I explored Judaism. Later I became interested in India and read Hindu scriptures and literature about Hinduism; still later I was profoundly influenced by Buddhism. Although for some periods I was not directly involved in a religious institution, it's hard to recall a time when I wasn't reading the literature and absorbing the scriptures of the traditional religions.

It is easy to get a misimpression of a religion if one only reads about it and does not get involved with a regularly meeting group, or travel to a country in which that religion is widely practiced. A common misimpression is an idealization of the "foreign" religion. It is similar to the classic admission of Linus, one of Charles Schulz's *Peanuts* characters: "I love humanity, it's the people I can't stand!" When you travel in a country that is majority Hindu, or majority Buddhist, you begin to see the same ambiguities, the same mixture of inspiration and prejudice, of love and narrow-mindedness, that you know in the religion of your family of origin. But beyond that disillusionment, if you gets involved in an ongoing group—for example a meditation sanga—you begin to see the depth of people, and feel the connectedness that you can't observe simply by attending the services of another place of worship. Similarly, many "helping groups" have their own rituals and strategies, for example, the twelve-step plans of AA and related "Anonymous" groups; they seem to represent an integration of the spiritual and secular in our society.

It is important for each of us to try to empathically enter the worldview of those with very different beliefs from our own. An example of this is a remarkably empathic and perceptive study, published as a book, *Spirit and Flesh: Life in a Fundamentalist Baptist Church,* and presented in a film, *Born Again.* James M. Ault (2004), a sociologist, describes 10 years of his life getting to know the congregation of a fundamentalist church in an attempt to understand the alliance between such churches and the politically radical right. I have seldom read a nonfiction book that helped me connect and empathize so much with a group that holds rather different beliefs and values than my own.

In short, if the religious tradition you or your client grew up in no longer seems to nurture and challenge you, it may be a valuable experience to explore a different one. At the very least, it will provide you with a broader basis from which to evaluate organized religions.

Gateway Three: Relationships

For the past two days I have been feeling uncommonly joyful. However, three or four days back I woke up feeling a bit depressed, and randomly opened a book on my bedstand, seeking guidance the way some people open a Bible hoping God will show them the relevant verse. Out popped a poem by Rumi (the great Persian Sufi poet of the thirteenth century):

> Today . . . we wake up empty
> and frightened. Don't reach for the key to the study
> and begin reading. Take down the dulcimer.
>
> Let the beauty we love be what we do.
> There are hundreds of ways to kneel and kiss the ground.
>
> Jalál Al-Din ar Rumi (Moyne & Barks, 1984).

I mentioned to my wife how beautifully that poem had captured my feelings so many mornings when I lay with unopened eyes, sensing the echoes of yesterday's news of war, the suffering of friends I visit in hospice and at a rehabilitation center—sad or tragic events that sometimes crowd out the sunlight. It isn't till I get out of bed, see the sunshine, view the beautiful woods nearby, smell the lilacs (this week), or (a week ago) observe the wildflowers, that the beauty awakens the joy in me.

But yesterday morning and today were different. I woke up feeling joyful. *What is different?* I asked myself. It is not that I have avoided listening to the news, or that I haven't been in touch with those in pain. Both tragedy and pain were present. But two days ago I had sung some hymns in a community I treasure. I had spent some time playing with two of my grandchildren. I had met with a friend of 30-some years. And I had taken part in a leisurely discussion with my wife about some things that mattered.

The difference, in a nutshell, was that I was holding the joys and sorrows in a constant sense of relatedness. The highs and lows were set in the context of community. In addition, throughout the day were periods of silence, times when I could "catch my breath" and deepen my roots. So I felt connected, but also grounded.

To treat relationships as one's top priority is not easy in our urban Western culture, although perhaps the majority of other cultures do so. As an immigrant from Argentina expressed it when asked about the differences between his country and United States: "In Argentina we work to live, but in America you live to work." He pointed out that from Monday to Friday we go to lunch with work associates, and talk mainly about work. "In Argentina we would never talk about work at lunch. We would talk about our families, our friends, or what we are doing in our lives" (Elkins, 1998, p. 224). Elkins' chapter on relationships (especially pp. 225-230), as well as such books as *The Lexus and the Olive Tree* (Friedman, 1999) describe America's transition away from a society of face-to-face relationships.

Accepting Self

The flow between in-breath (taking in others) and out-breath (knowing and expressing self) grounds us, and seems central to spirituality. I've written in previous chapters about meditation and breathing, and about breath itself. Most basic human activities, from breathing to daily routine chores can be enriched with spiritual meaning by keeping consciousness alive to the present reality. Mindfulness meditation provides a discipline for achieving this (Hanh, 1976).

In the chapters on crisis and development I've stressed finding one's own stance with authenticity. Particularly in the chapter on suffering I've emphasized becoming aware of your own responses and the importance of nurturing a tender respect for yourself. This central ethic of loving oneself and loving the other is as basic to relationships among sentient beings as is the law of gravity (the mysterious mutual attraction of material objects) to physics. Since many good books are totally devoted to the whats and hows of relationships, it's not necessary to survey the whole territory here—but I do wish to make two points about laws and generalities.

Respecting Others

As far as I know, all sentient life requires relationships with other sentient living creatures. *Love* may be too big a word for the first phases of human relationships; loving implies a deeper presence than most of us are capable of at first. Relationships usually begin with respect, and work and play their way up to love. No relationship can grow without respect. Even our casual interactions, when they are constructive and growing, are dependent on a respect for one another, and for oneself. Our relationship with ourselves can grow more and more positive if we begin with simply respecting ourselves as we are right now. I'm not implying that really respecting ourselves is easy, but it is a more realistic beginning point than trying to "love." So I argue, instead of trying for too much, simply start with respect. Receiving life as a blessing involves enough awareness to recognize the barriers we set up within ourselves, and finding ways to nurture who we are rather than trying to make ourselves look better. Spirituality is not about smiling all the time. It is about breathing in deeply, and getting in tune with the deepest reality. It is rooted in authenticity.

This inward-looking practice is itself relational:

> This above all: To thine own self be true
> And it must follow as the night the day,
> Thou canst not then be false to any man.
>
> Polonius, in Shakespeare's *Hamlet*

Affirming Differences

A second point concerns differences. Every rule, law, or generalization we make risks ignoring the differences. Though I find it useful to invoke the metaphor of breathing to describe relationships—the flow between in-breath (taking in others) and out-breath (knowing and expressing self)—we deny respect if we are not open to the differences in the patterns of even this basic flow between self and other. One of my closest friends, I'll call him Ed, thinks of himself as an introvert and perceives me as an extrovert. And I'm sure he's right that we are very different in the patterns of our self/other process. I wake up happy on the morning after a day of much connection, punctuated with moments of alone time. My guess is Ed most appreciates a day of solitude, punctuated by one or two phases of deep connecting. So it is for our clients: to achieve balance, some need more time for self, some need to invest more in others. Giving to others can be a direction of growth for clients experiencing depression, boredom, and lack of meaning, but a person cannot give himself or herself to others if he or she has no "self" to give. A client who is compulsively giving, or giving because it's "women's role," may need a different challenge—to find himself or herself spiritually the client may need to move inward.

Of course this description of our differences is somewhat caricatured. For example, when I described myself as waking up happy after days of feeling connected to others, I left out that, following that particularly good day, I fully enjoyed spending the next morning and afternoon completely alone, and totally without media entertainment or news. So the differences (and the categories) may not be as simple as they appear at first. It isn't necessary to take any of these descriptions of patterns literally. The key point is, if you are to let others in you need to be observant of and respectful toward the particular individual you are relating to, knowing that she or he is not simply the mirror of yourself.

Gateway Four: The Feminine

Just as it is valuable to explore other religious traditions, it can be a rich experience for men to explore in themselves the aspects of personality that are traditionally thought of as feminine. (I can't speak personally about the reverse, women exploring the masculine. It appears that ever since women entered the workforce outside the home they have had to deal with a basically masculine culture; I suspect far more women have integrated aspects of masculinity into their personal lives than men have integrated femininity into theirs.)

Crossing over Gender Roles

A large body of research exists in social psychology that seeks to determine whether masculinity, or femininity, or a mixture labeled "androgyny," is most functional. Sandra Bem's research and rethinking of the scales of masculinity and femininity made credible the concept of androgyny, in which an individual has high levels of *both* masculine and feminine personality traits and behaviors (1974). At first androgyny was presented as uniformly positive, stressing the advantages of flexibility, being capable of both agentic and communal behaviors. Later a careful piece of research using multiple measures of mental health led Jones, Chernovetz, and Hansson (1978) to challenge Bem's view; Jones and colleagues concluded that for both men and women (in American culture), functionality has to do primarily with high masculinity. Still later it was recognized that the items about emotional vulnerability were inflating the correlates of the femininity scale with dysfunction (Lifshitz, 1978). Positive communal items such as interpersonal awareness, however, correlate highly with one important mental health measure: self-esteem.

In addition to problems of sex bias in certain instruments,[2] much of the debate was aggravated by a failure by researchers to place data from specific studies into the broader context of the developmental processes of identity and intimacy. I have already noted that Erikson's assumption that identity must precede intimacy holds for men but not women. This difference results in a different path to healthy personality for women than for men. Women do not need to be androgynous to achieve intimacy, but higher scores on masculine traits *do* seem to be necessary for women move on to identity achievement. Conversely, men do not need to be androgynous to develop an achieved identity, but intimacy seems to develop only in those men who have higher levels of some feminine personality traits. In reality, masculine and feminine characteristics are not opposites, and high levels of one do not necessitate low levels of the other, but because the culture continues to view these traits as polarities, an individual needs to demonstrate achievement in the "sex appropriate" area first (that is, men must prove their masculinity; women their femininity) or they will loose social support (Matteson, 1993b).

When gender roles are studied in developmental context, it seems clear that both males and females require a flexible integration of masculine and feminine behaviors to obtain positive mental health. But this isn't sufficient. Mental health also requires the ability to explore alternatives and then to invest in concrete commitments (Matteson, 1993b).

For American men, an active and externalized style is socially encouraged. Quietly waiting, looking inward, and then expressing tender and vulnerable emotions at first seems "weird" for men. Despite all of the discussion of gender role changes since the second wave of the women's movement (beginning in the 1950s), women continue to be socially punished if they show masculine traits without having first demonstrated competence in the roles that are traditionally feminine. For men, the social ostracism that can come from seeming "feminine" is even more severe—unless they have already proved their "manhood."

Unfortunately, we all lose from social arrangements that encourage agentic or masculine traits and ignore feminine traits—or vice versa. This is sometimes recognized by men once they become fathers and realize their inadequacies in trying to nurture and care for the infant. While the mother has been given many years of training in caring for baby dolls, the father—unless his parents went out of their way to teach him—usually must take instructions from his wife to get through more than an hour of infant care. This puts him in another bind, since men are supposed to be leaders and give instructions (or orders) to their wives. All of society's subtle indoctrination that he should dominate may make the new father negative toward accepting leadership from his wife, and his new fathering responsibilities may evoke feelings of incompetence and inferiority. At its worst, this results in his "proving his manhood" by abusing his wife or child, or in his flight from the home to be "with the boys," or eventually, in separation and divorce.[3] Developmental psychologists largely agree that men's masculine identity is more fragile than women's feminine identity because men are much more likely *not* to have had a lot of time and connection with their fathers (compared to women with their mothers). Since this issue was thoroughly discussed in my earlier writings (Marcia et al., 1993; Matteson, 1975), and has been updated by more recent experts in male development such as Ronald Levant and William Pollack (1995), further elaboration is not necessary here.

When men begin to explore a broader model of masculinity—because of the crisis of divorce, or a sense of disappointment in the traditional male role, or other reasons—they often find it deeply enriching. It comes as a relief to realize "I don't have to be *on top* of everything all the time." If men stop being so active, and just let go, they may begin to feel a subtle but new sense of joy in life. Similarly, they may find it is a release to cry, rather than hold everything in. It is comforting just to be close, without feeling one has to perform sexually at every opportunity. It feels refreshingly authentic to simply state "I don't know," rather than compete to have the answers, or to defend an opinion on every subject.

For some men the experiences of being in an ongoing men's group, where they can finally be vulnerable along with other men, and where they learn to accept nurturing from *men* rather than continually expecting it from women, are rich sources for rethinking and re-experiencing what it means to be a man. It is valuable for men's groups and conferences to include different generations of men, as both younger and older men benefit when a mentor relationship is formed. The lack of models for intimate male-to-male relationships is well known in gay culture. But it harms straight men as well—as poet and leader in the mytho-poetic wing of the men's movement Robert Bly has pointed out for several decades (Bly, 1990).

I frequently walk in a forest preserve near my home. Though I generally go at times when I think few people will be there as I like being in nature alone, it's not uncommon that I will meet someone walking toward me on the paved path. Often they are wearing sports clothes, including a T-shirt with a slogan or some message on it. Recently I met an African-American woman, probably in her fifties, wearing a T-shirt that said in large letters WORSHIP ME. Since many African-Americans wear shirts testifying to their faith, I was expecting the smaller print to say something about Jesus, perhaps with a biblical citation. Instead, as I got closer, above the WORSHIP ME were the words "I am a Senior!" I know the feeling expressed on the woman's T-shirt. When I was teaching youth in psychology and counseling, I sometimes had the opportunity to become a role model or mentor for men who were struggling to integrate the feminine. Now that I am retired, it is much rarer that I get a sense of being treated as a mentor or an elder. In our youth-oriented media, most of the heroes and heroines are decades younger than I. Young men having personal relationships with older men as mentors, so basic to development in traditional societies, is extremely rare today. So I am particularly happy when I'm with my grandson, or my son-in-law, and feel moments of being a mentor again.

However, it is not sufficient that young men have older men as models. They need males who honor the females around them, and the feminine within themselves. Traditional religions have been ambivalent about this. On the one hand, conservative religion in particular can be a "haven of patriarchal attitudes and masculine biases" (Elkins, 1998, p. 109; Ault, 2004). On the other hand, "my conservative church was one of the few places I could hear adults talk openly about love, kindness, and forgiveness" (Elkins, 1998 p. 109). Even crusty old farmers sometimes found the courage to express their gentler emotions at church. The worship services, with their music, prayers, and sermons, were often nourishing to the soul. So in this sense feminine values were honored, and both men and women were encouraged to nurture and develop their souls (Elkins, 1998).

It is rare that men dare to be affectionate and intimate with other men, or risk being vulnerable and asking for nurturance from other men. After my first trip to India I recall showing a series of slides to some American undergraduate students. Viewing some street scenes, a male student noted several pairs of adult Indian men walking hand in hand. The student asked, "Is homosexuality more common there?" "No," I replied, "but sustaining deep male-to-male friendships is common." How much of American men's fear of closeness with other men comes from identifying it with homosexuality?

The process men undergo when they let in the feminine, letting go of the barriers and the expectations, is not just a psychological release. The process of opening the gateway—of opening up to a broader view of manhood than the limited roles portrayed by supermasculine icons—from the superhero cartoons to the John Wayne movies—may lead to a new receptivity to the stories of men such as Jesus, Buddha, Gandhi, and King. New receptivity in a man permits him to sense others' needs, and to be nurturing. This can be a slow process, but intuitive people around such a man begin to notice his changes. Gradually the man becomes less armored, easier to touch, so he himself receives more nurturing. All of this opens the way for the spirit (which in much of Christian tradition is viewed as feminine) to enter and be embraced by him. Even men who are not particularly invested in traditional masculinity find it helpful to expand their images and metaphors for the sacred to include feminine symbols.

A receptivity to sense the holy in the fertility of women can occur in childhood. One of my own earliest memories of being overwhelmed by awe occurred when I was only seven. I was walking down the sidewalk in our neighborhood, and saw my dad driving toward home. Dad saw me, pulled over, and urged me to jump in and see what he was bringing home. Dad was glowing, and Mom, in the front seat with him, just returning from the hospital, was holding the tiniest, most beautiful little baby I had ever seen. This was my new sister Carol. It seemed to me so amazing that my mother had been able to create something so wonderful in her belly.

I remember for years thinking it must be wonderful to be a woman and be able to be so creative. In church, I worshiped a Father God, but at home I was in awe of the Mother Goddess. And since I loved nature, when I witnessed such miracles as the budding of trees in the woods near us, I thought of it as Mother Nature's blessings. If someone had asked me about my concepts of God, I would have verbalized mainly male-dominated symbols, but if I had been asked about experiences of awe and wonder, female symbols would emerge. Of course I later realized men can be creative too, but not in such a direct and embodied way. I was not unique in thinking of God as male, but having rich feminine associations with the divine. In the "Personal God Project" (see Griffith, 1999), some of the respondents who initially described God as a kind father, when asked, "What relationship in your own life most reminds you of the one you have described with God?" described relationships with women, including mothers, grandmothers, and "our housekeeper, who taught me about love that lasted through hard situations."

Our clients' experiences are richer than their conceptualizations, or the words they use to describe God. We can help them draw on their experiences rather than reinforcing their constricted representations.

> Heidegger came to the conclusion that true art is always a revelation of truth . . . *aleitheia,* [the Greek word for] the kind of truth one sees when something reveals its essence or true nature. (Elkins, 1998, p. 123, citing Heidegger, 1975)

Throughout the medieval period, the church was both the guardian and the keeper of the arts. Specifically religious art, music, and storytelling can often penetrate the soul when the left-brained and academic dogmas cannot. However, possibly because art and artists are bearers of the spirit, they were the first to break away from the church during the Renaissance. Artists often speak of their inspiration coming from beyond them—as a "muse"—or simply share an awareness that a creative idea or work seemed to unfold itself, possessing a life of its own. Though I am not a skilled poet, I love poetry and occasionally write poetry, primarily for my own enjoyment. At one time in my life I fell in love with a person, and some days later, after a deep meditation period, "awakened" with a complete poem in my mind. The only poetry I'd written in years was in free verse, but this time I wrote without stopping, and eight verses of four lines each, in rhyme and iambic pentameter, poured out. Only minor editing was needed. It is a mystery to me how such things happen—it did feel like a muse must have whispered it to me. Art, like infatuation, seems to transcend the boundaries and control of the ego.

Similarly, music has the power to transport us beyond our linear or thought-bound ways of perceiving. Each of us has our own tastes, and there's no merit in arguing that one style of music is more able to act as a portal for the sacred than another. Often music that expresses a deep longing is experienced as sacred, whether it be a classic (such as the "going home" theme in Dvorak's *New World* symphony) or a country song. Other music can express the dark nights of the soul, such as Bob Dylan's "Hard Rain's A-Gonna Fall." Early in my preparation for my ministry to others I found myself turned off by some of the music of the classical period (some Mozart and Haydn) because it did not seem to me to reverberate with the pain and tragedy I saw around me. In contrast, I was moved by Beethoven's symphony No. 9, which spends three movements working through the pain and grief, and the bittersweet sense of nature, and only then breaks out in a "Hymn to Joy" that transcends the tragedy. Even then, the tragic echoes in the background. I found myself playing Toscanini's recording of symphony No. 9 again and again.

Similarly, I loved the way Rembrandt's painting of the resurrected Christ at Eméus showed a radiating face in the midst of a very dark canvas.

> The same sensitivity that opens artists . . . makes them vulnerable to the dark . . . It is no accident that many creative people—including Danté, Pascal, Goethe, Nietzsche, Kierkegaard, Beethoven, Rilke, Blake, and Van Gogh—struggled with depression, anxiety and despair. (Elkins, 1998, p. 124)

Later in life, when the tragic did not seem so overwhelming, I discovered the incredible luminosity of the paintings of Van Gogh. At the literal level, the old shoes, or the wrinkled and twisted sunflowers may seem limited and mundane, but the shimmering lighting and the texture of the thickly applied paint says things words cannot convey. (See Edwards, 2004, for a biography that focuses on Van Gogh's spirituality rather than his pathology.) In the most intense experiences of creativity, you feel no sense of an "I" that is in control, an "I" that is responsible for the variegated images that flash spontaneously through the mind (Elkins, 1998, p.131). From this perspective one can more easily understand the medieval artists who designed and crafted the gothic cathedrals and were content to remain anonymous. Their work was simply "for the glory of God."

Gateway Six: The Body

Many people with Catholic or conservative Christian backgrounds find it hard to recognize the body as a gateway to the sacred. Yet the importance of dance in ancient religious ceremonies, the role of thoughtful choices about diet and exercise in promoting a sense of wellness, and the connections between ecstatic spiritual experiences and sexuality, all point to the body as important in spiritual life. Since I have already devoted a chapter to the subject (Chapter 5), I will simply remind the reader at this point that it is crucial to explore and seek out your own individual path. An example of this as it concerns the physical postures of meditation follows.

After about two years of trying to learn sitting meditation, I switched to a kind of moving meditation that flowed from my feeling. Some might call it a type of modern dance, though as I did it, it was certainly not a performance art! After a couple of years of using my own style of meditating, I went to a conference in which American Buddhist leader Jack Kornfield taught loving kindness meditation, and psychotherapist Stanislav Grof used a type of highly expressive self-guided therapy (see Kornfield, 1993 and Grof, 1988). Also on the program was a man who led classical sitting meditation twice a day. During a question-and-answer period, a woman in the audience explained that, because of a back problem, sitting meditation was hard for her physically, and she wanted to develop her use of lying meditation. The trainer countered that the classical sitting pose has thousands of years of use, and is the correct pose to use. The woman seemed terribly disappointed. Given my usual distaste for dogma, I wanted to do what the strategic family therapists call "spit in the soup"; that is, do something to upset a dysfunctional and rigid system. I wanted to spit in this trainer's soup.

It happened that I had in my suitcase some materials I had brought from my recent trip to India, but had not had time to read yet. One of these was a pamphlet on Buddhist meditation, showing several long-used and valuable postures. One of these postures was the classical lying posture. So I carried it with me to the various sessions the next day, and sure enough, I spotted the woman who had asked the questions. I handed her the pamphlet, stating I didn't need it. Then with a smile I told her, "I just want to be sure you understand what the classic postures are," and I pointed to the lying down posture. She smiled, and when she passed me the next day, she thanked me heartily.

Teachers or mentors always run the risk of turning their individual experience into a dogma. Spiritual seekers mustn't let such rigidity keep them from exploring and testing out their own way. Notice that Chapters 10 through 12 of this book include alternative forms of relaxation exercises and meditation. All bodies are not the same and no one posture fits all. As indicated in the description of the African ceremony earlier in this chapter, energetic and active forms of dancing have long been part of many spiritual traditions. So I will continue to dance as I meditate.

Gateway Seven: Excitation and Exercise

In a workshop on spirituality that I recently led as part of a men's conference, several men noted that a path to the spiritual for them was a form of regular exercise, such as running; the aspect of exercise they were pointing to went far beyond exercise as a way to keep the body fit. They described with enthusiasm the special experience that they have when they maintain a steady excitation—they enter an altered state. This, of course, parallels the experience of tribal dancing described earlier in this chapter, and it has been noted in Glasser's work *Positive Addictions* (1976). In Chapter 4, I wrote in some detail about activities that are done with such full engagement that other thoughts and cares and concerns disappear and a oneness of mind emerges; Csikszentmihalyhi (1990) has studied this experience and labels it *flow.* Obviously both running and dancing are physical activities; it makes sense to describe them after presenting the path of the body. Grof and Grof (1990) write:

> One may also discover the transcendental realms unexpectedly during physical exercise, such as dance or sport. This is perhaps due to focused concentration on the activity, bodily exertion, or increased breathing rate; the same elements are involved in techniques developed by many meditative practices, which allow one to go beyond the ordinary, logical world. (p. 65)

The basketball player Patsy Neal describes such an experience:

> There are moments of glory that go beyond the human expectation, beyond the physical and emotional ability of the individual. Something unexplainable takes over and breathes life into the known life. . . . Call it a state of grace, or an act of faith . . . or an act of God. It is there, and the impossible becomes possible. . . . The athlete goes beyond herself: she transcends the natural. She touches a piece of heaven and becomes the recipient of power from an unknown source. (in Grof & Grof, 1990, p. 65)

In contrast to tribal dancing that is done in groups, the present-day athletes who experience running or other exercising as mind altering most frequently mention sports that they practice alone. This may be a consequence of our cultural expectation that spiritual and mind-altering experiences are individual. It is important for me to include this particular path, because it is not one that I have experienced myself. I can comprehend it, in part because it parallels my own experiences with mountain hiking. As in running, the mind-altering experience while hiking is most common when one is alone and physically exerting oneself. In the mountain setting, the experience is amplified by, and partly dependent on, the beauty of the scenic setting.

Though I myself have not had the experience of positive addiction to exercise, I want to honor those who have, especially the men in my workshop who suggested it as an additional path. It points to you as a reader being able to discover gateways this author has not yet opened. Remember this when, at the end of the chapter, you are invited to use a worksheet and make your own list of spiritual paths.

Gateway Eight: Nature

Aborigine people in almost every inhabited area of the world have recognized the sacredness of mountains, lakes, streams, oceans—places where the beauty, grandeur, and awe of nature is present. Early American transcendentalists such as Emerson and Thoreau believed that spirituality was more effectively achieved through a personal experience with nature than in a church building. I grew up guided by parents who loved to go to state parks, and in their later years traveled to some of the wonderful national parks in the United States. My father's parents lived on a farm set in a very beautiful valley, and when they retired, they installed a "picture window" (new in those times) so they could continue viewing the beauty of their natural setting. Thus it came as a surprise to me that many Americans living right in the midst of nature don't appreciate it. The first house my wife and I bought, in our late twenties, was near the top of a small hill with a panoramic view of the rolling hills and valleys to the northwest of us. Soon after we moved in, the farmer across the road, ready for retirement, added a cozy extra room to his small house. His best view, like mine, was to the northwest—but he didn't even place a window in that wall. From his perspective, he had spent his work life conquering and subduing nature to feed his livestock and his family. Nature was something to work against, not to enjoy. Yet, in the original meaning of the word, we are all "pagans," that is country dwellers and "people of the earth" (Elkins, 1998, p. 210).

The competitive spirit of Americans, and the belief for centuries that nature was boundless and could be exploited to the fullest, has made us the worst polluters, per capita, in the world. We worry about the huge populations of countries such as India and China, but in fact Americans represent less than 6 percent of the world's population, but consume 25 percent of the world's energy.

In contrast, most Native Americans felt in tune with nature, and honored it. This is not to deny that they killed animals and plants—they were, of course, dependent on these for food—but as a whole they did not kill unnecessarily. For example, if a group of Native American men needed to fell a tree in order to build a canoe, they would first offer a prayer, apologizing for having to kill the tree, and thanking the tree for being willing to provide the material they needed. Many of the practices for planting and for hunting were environmentally respectful, although we have some aspects of preserving or restoring the environment today through more advanced science that were not understood by native tribes.

The renewed interest among spiritually sensitive people in nature-based ceremonies such as celebrations of solstice, and of the cycles of the moon and the seasons, are a modern attempt to honor our reciprocity with nature. We depend on nature for our very existence. Yet, unless humans learn to live in cooperation with nature, and provide the planning and protection that is necessary for this beautiful network to be sustained, we will destroy the very foundation we depend on. Unfortunately, our culture's worship of "free enterprise" often ignores that every corporation is a fully owned subsidiary of planet earth (Nader, 2000).

Of all of the gateways to the sacred, nature touches us with its gifts, but also reminds us of our dependency and our need to give in return. Experiences exist in nature can be primarily receptive—standing silently in awe of the unfathomable depths of the starry night, witnessing the vast carving and painting of the Grand Canyon, or walking around the mysterious sculptures of the rocks of Yosemite. These are truly encounters with the sacred. But to really appreciate nature and live in tune with it, more of an interaction is required. The aesthetic beauty of a snowcapped mountain can be experienced standing miles away, but when one hikes on the glaciers of Mt. Rainier—wearing crampons for secure traction, carrying a sharp walking stick for the balance that is maintained naturally by our four-footed friends—the majesty and sovereignty of that enormous volcanic mountain is mind-blowing. Trekking in the Katmandu valley, aware of peak after peak of mountains older than all of humankind, thousands of miles of uplifted bedrock larger than anything else on earth, one feels a humbling sense of smallness, mixed with the joy of being alive and being strong enough to be there, grateful to stand on so solid and holy a ground.

David Elkins (1998), in his chapter on nature as a path to the sacred, describes his experience in standing among the giant redwood trees in California. "I was overwhelmed not by their size, for I had expected that, but by their sense of solid eternal presence and, for lack of a better word, their *indifference* to the affairs of humankind" (p. 223). Here is the poem Elkins later wrote to them:

Now I know why my foremothers
worshipped trees
and danced their moonlight rituals
in darkened groves.
Here amid your pachyderm trunks
there is power and some huge warmth
inviting midnight's fires and rituals wild
to hold aback centuries of darkness
that hover close by.
And you alone survived to tell
of those pagan days
and the patience it takes
to make a life.

(Elkins, 1998 p. 51)

Yet there are smaller, more delicate encounters with the sacred in nature that can be just as life-enhancing, or healing, even if less dramatic. Bird watching, one of the most popular and fastest growing hobbies in the United States, is something that many people, including those with disabilities who are homebound, use to bring nature to their windows. Experts tell us that feeding wild birds does not upset the balance of nature and is a way for many people to find more meaning in their lives through an appreciation of the diversity and complexities of avian life (Banziger & Roush, 1983; Banziger, 2006, personal communication).

I have described earlier a mystical experience I had of remembering and hearing my dad's laugh in the midst of a billowing cloud, and I have stated that simply being open to encounters, without trying to rationalize or explain them, can result in a sense of nature delivering messages to you. Several times in my life animals or birds have allowed me to get surprisingly close to them, almost as if they can sense that I am in an open and vulnerable state, and therefore not frightening or dangerous to them. From this mutual respect sometimes springs a "message"—not (in my experience) actually in words, but in awareness. As with the cloud, in each of these experiences I am aware that if other people were present they would not hear the message. The encounter is a personal encounter, and the reassurance I get from the message comes as an I-Thou experience, a sense that the encounter transcends me and my own ego, and unifies me with something/someone much greater than I.

Gateway Nine: Self-Exploration through Psychology and Psychotherapy

In the century that has passed since Freud first published his theories, the fields of study dealing with mental illness and mental health (especially psychology, psychiatry, psychotherapy, counseling, and social work) have become remarkably influential. Almost any bookstore in the nation has a section of self-help books and other materials to assist one in achieving a better life through exploring and changing one's thoughts, feelings, and behavior. Though we can complain that too much of this material is purely self-serving, and may actually encourage conforming to society rather than transforming it, we must also realize that many people would not have begun a search for a deeper life were it not for these influences. One of the blocks to spiritual exploration may be the tendency of those in academic circles to denigrate authors and presentations that are not as sophisticated or academically solid as their own. I remember in the mid-1960s, while I was attending a fairly prestigious seminary, one of the great European protestant theologians of the time came to America and spoke on several campuses. In a question-and-answer period, he was asked about a particular theological position that was developing in secular theology, and in his response he spoke disparagingly of one of my favorite professors, calling him "a paperback theologian." In class the next day, that professor responded with a smile, noting that protestantism had begun because of the writings of a "paperback theologian" (referring to the pamphlets and treatises that Martin Luther distributed thanks to the newly invented printing press). He continued, saying he could only wish his own writings would have as positive an impact. Certainly many self-help writings have weaknesses and shortcomings—but don't let snobbery deter you from exploring recommendations that you feel may lead to growth.

Although I believe the scientific method has tremendous value, as does replicable research (and I have tried to review such research throughout this book), I agree with Elkins that psychotherapy has far more in common with artistic processes than it does with medical and mechanistic models. I believe the best way to understand therapy is to approach it as an artistic endeavor and to use the creative process as its central metaphor (Elkins, 1998). Approaching therapy as a creative act need not inhibit our studying the process scientifically, just as other aspects of the creative process have been usefully studied. We can use the scientific method to check our work, so that dogma and superstition don't prevail, and at the same time recognize that we are dealing with a process that is human and mysterious and can't be reduced to medical or mechanical schemas.

Another response to psychological reading material is to overidentify with it. When I taught undergraduate students, especially in the abnormal psychology courses, I used to caution them about "psych student syndrome," a parallel to "med student syndrome" in which medical students begin to believe that they are infected with every disease they study. But in reality, I am glad when students "overidentify" if it leads them to examine their own lives. The central issues of mental illness are human issues, not something experienced only by patients. It is hard to think of life vocations that contribute so much to one's own personal growth as do psychology and counseling or psychotherapy. Therapists would be in denial to sit in sessions with client after client and not find they use some of the defenses the clients are using, or enact dysfunctional patterns the clients are enacting. Letting in these insights is not easy, and having a support group and regularly making use of supervision that involves self-examination greatly enhances the likelihood that these revelations will be sacred events rather than stressful bumps contributing to depression.

The ability to gain perspective on oneself rather than staying lost in one's egocentric viewpoint has long been valued, but the tools for doing so have been profoundly sharpened by the modern social sciences.

Gateway Ten: Mythology

Though words can never capture the transcendent, storytelling can be very helpful in communicating a sense that something far bigger than our personal egos is involved. Stories take us to the eternal dimension. They often begin with a statement similar to inducing a trance: "Once upon a time" or "In the time before all time" or "In another time, like this time, but unlike this time." The listener knows that what is being told is not historical—it's "just a story." Yet she or he also knows that some kind of Truth will be involved, although it is not literal truth. The characters in the story are bigger than life. They may be called "heroes," or "goddesses," or given names such as "Adam" (which simply means "Man") or "Eve" (which simply means "Mother"). Thus the stories are about us. Yet they are more than us.

What is mythology? On the broadest level, we can say that a people sharing a system of religious belief has a common myth. In this sense a myth expresses metaphysical truths and gives answers to the basic questions of life (Edinger, 1994). Myth is not used here in it's vernacular meaning; there is no implication that the story is "false," but a recognition that the truth is not at the literal level. Probably no one did more than Joseph Campbell (1968, 1996) to help Americans realize that mythologies function at a nonliteral level, revealing a truth that transcends facts. "Their force lies not in what meets the eye, but in what dilates the heart" (Campbell, 1979, p. 48). In a tribal society, in which only one belief system is present and empathic knowledge of competing beliefs from other tribes or nations is uncommon, the believers make no distinction between literal and mythic truth. But in a multicultural setting is an awareness that the story is a way of framing the facts to make sense of them, and that other competing ways are possible.

Jungian psychologist Edinger (1994) states that

> the Greek myths are sacred scripture, no less than the Hebrew Bible and the New Testament. Certainly the Greek myths and what was built on them—the science and philosophy and literature—form some of the basic roots of the Western unconscious. (p. 3)

The specific technique Edinger (1994) suggests is listening to a myth or story and asking, "How have I had an experience like this one?" (p. 3). Certainly most Westerners, if they don't let the prejudices of religious training stand in the way, find that they reverberate with Greek myths in much the way that they resonate with the teachings of Jesus, or the prophets, or the Hebrew stories of creation.

Elkins (1998) suggests that one reason mythology touches us at such profound levels, and why we are so fascinated by these ancient stories, is because they are replete with personifications. That is, a particular human characteristic is displayed in a character, such as a hero, who personifies it. Personification is one of the dialects of the soul; it is congruent with the imaginal and poetic nature of the deeper levels of the psyche (Elkins, 1998, p. 199).

One risk, if we draw on too limited and biased a sample of myths, is that we will assume that patterns occuring in many cultures are built into the human psyche. An example is male dominance/female inferiority. Modern social sciences, through the study of other cultures and ethnicities, provide evidence that male dominance has *not* defined all human societies. In fact, in some societies women have "veto power" over men's destructive wishes. For example, in Navajo culture, the women's council can veto the men's decision to go to war. In fundamentalist Christian churches, the men have official decision-making power, but the male leadership is dependent on the good reputations of the individual men, and the women, through prayer circles, have the power to sabotage a man's reputation (Ault, 2004). In many nomadic gathering societies, men and women are of essentially equal economic power and social importance. The experience of male dominance is a socially determined experience—not a transcendent archetypal pattern.

One can consciously search for and collect myths and stories that challenge this norm. (For example, try "Googling" for three words together: "myths female superiority.") Becoming acquainted with the plurality of mythology, and the similarities *and differences* in myths across cultures, helps to guard us against taking our own myths too literally or condemning another group's myths and sacred stories as inferior or evil.

One of the great advantages of mythology over dogmatic or creedal religion is that, in many ways, myths are themselves pluralistic. For example, even if one's knowledge of mythology is limited to the gods and goddesses in the Greek pantheon, they provide such a variety of personality types that one can use them systematically to look at issues from a variety of perspectives and evoke forgotten elements of one's own personality, rather than staying in a rut. At least two Jungian authors have used the Greek pantheon in this way: Jean Shinoda Bolen in her pair of books, *Goddesses in Everywoman* (1984) and *Gods in Everyman* (1989), and Edward Edinger (1994) in *The Eternal Drama: The Inner Meaning of Greek Mythology.* Their use of many gods or goddesses to enrich the reader's personality suggests a personality theory based on the metaphor "multiple personalities" in contrast to the more typical personality theories that view the self as a unified entity. Sandra Watanabe-Hammond (1987, 1990) calls her approach "cast of characters," and likens the individual to a drama with many characters. She does not treat the client as just the central character in the play, but as a system of interactions between all the characters in the play. Richard C. Schwartz (1995, 2002) refers to the person as "the family within" and calls his approach "inner family therapy," or IFT. (See also Goulding & Schwartz, 1995.) Videos of Richard Schwartz directly working with clients are particularly helpful (Schwartz, 2002). Mythology comes alive in the counseling session when these approaches are integrated in a spiritually sensitive counselor.

Gateway Eleven: Dark Night of the Soul

The dark night is a period of aridity, a dry period in which the life of the senses seems dormant or dead—a period in which the human soul seems separated from the source of spiritual life. This gateway is different from most of the others. No one would consciously choose this way. Nonetheless, it can be a portal to the sacred.

The phrase "dark night of the soul" is a derived from a great spiritual classic by the Christian monk St. John of the Cross (1542-1591).[4] Written soon after St. John's escape from prison, his two-part work form a full treatise on mystic theology. He has been called "the most sublime of all the Spanish mystics . . . he soars aloft on the wings of Divine love to heights known (only to a few of even the saints)" (Peers, 1958, p.) The depth of the "dark night" can only be understood in the context of the profound experience of light and love.

Since mysticism emphasizes direct experience in relating to the divine, it should not be surprising that much of mystic literature (regardless of culture of origin) uses the analogy of romantic love to describe the interaction between the individual and God. The fifteenth century Indian poet Kabir writes:

> If you don't break your ropes while you're alive,
> do you think
> ghosts will do it after?

> The idea that the soul will join with the ecstatic
> just because the body is rotten—
> that is all fantasy.
> What is found now is found then.
> If you find nothing now,
> you will simply end up with an empty apartment in the City of Death.
> If you make love with the divine now, in the next life
> you will have the face of satisfied desire. (in Bly, 1977)

In spiritual life, as in romantic life, the path of love need not begin with commitment. More frequently, the positive experiences begin with a meeting and an opening. The meeting is often a happenstance. It is an act of grace. The universe comes to meet you. Just as one may fall in love, one may fall into a spiritual experience or awareness (Fromm, 1956). As anyone who has learned to dive knows, although you can put yourself into a position in which falling is possible, you then have to let go. As has been noted in previous chapters, this means being open, having a "beginner's mind."

And just as we may "fall in love," we may experience a terrible falling out of love. As noted in the section on Gateway Five: The Arts, "the same sensitivity that opens artists . . . makes them vulnerable to the dark" (Elkins, 1998, p. 125). The mystic, similar to St. John of the Cross, may "soar aloft on wings of Divine love," but he may also descend to the depths. This descent, the experience of painful separation from the Loved One, is felt as a living hell.

The experience of the dark night of the soul is not limited to mystics or those with artistic sensitivity, however. For many, tragic experiences or existential crises may open up the self to the life of the soul. The routines and the values they have been conforming to suddenly seem superficial, and the experience of a death of someone close to them, or of unexpected failures, or a gradual sense of meaninglessness, crack the self open and let in a transcendent light. "Priorities rearrange themselves with lightning obviousness, and the house that ego built collapses . . ." (Elkins, 1998, p. 249). By experiencing adversity, the soul breaks loose and grows wiser (Elkins, 1998).

Though the dark night is a period of aridity, it differs from clinical depression in that the person views it as a period of spiritual trial. The person becomes detached or disinvested in the senses for their own sake (Washburn, 1994). Two special risks exist in this state. One is that, though the state is not clinical depression, it may bring on ideas about—and possibly attempts at—suicide. A less dramatic risk is that the journeyer will confuse the need for inner detachment with an outer isolation, "acting out externally, letting go of family and social roles" (Grof & Grof, 1990, p. 61) The suffering, and even the aridity, are seen by St. John of the Cross as signs that the pilgrim is on the right path. He cites the Psalm of David, "In a desert land, without water, dry, and without a way, I appear before You to be able to see Your power and Your glory." This period of dispossession includes the loss of the more immature views of God (Washburn, 1994, p. 233).

In classical Christian thought, even the Christ, after his death, must descend into hell. On the cross, Jesus cries out about the loss of God: "My God, my God, why have you forsaken me!" The Apostles' Creed proclaims the classical Christian view: "He descended into hell. The third day He arose again from the dead." St. John of the Cross argues that when the priest or monk becomes disinterested in the repeated rituals and the prescribed prayers, it is again a good sign that he is reaching into a deeper place in his soul.

In mythology across many cultures is a recognition that spiritual development often involves moving deeply downward (facing death, hell) before one can move upward into joy and communion (Deardorff, 2004). This theme appears in the mythology of such diverse cultures as Iraqi, classical Greek, medieval European, Chinese, Japanese, and the Hopi and their Native American predecessors, the Anasazi. The earliest of all known epic stories, the myth of Inanna, portrays the numinosity of procreation and giving birth; this leads to the worship of the fertile female goddess. But this goddess must go to the depths of the underworld (Wolkstein, 1988).

Another version of this theme of descent is the Phoenix myth. The phoenix bird arises from the ashes of ruin. It's best known form is the Arabian myth, but the Phoenix is first referred to by Hesiod in the eighth century BCE, and later by the famous Greek historian Herodotus, fifth century BCE. The myth has Chinese, Japanese, Russian, Egyptian, and Native American counterparts, with the Phoenix also referred to as the Firebird, and other names, all associated with the sun (Lady Gryphon, 2005). Medieval Christian culture, especially Dante's *Inferno,* which portrays Beatrice leading the protagonist through hell and back. The Anasazi and Hopi Native Americans tell the story of the flute-playing hunchback, Kokopelli, who is asked to lead the journey through the deep tunnel to enter the new world (Deardorff, 2005; Sharp, 2005). Often, as in the Kokopelli story, it is a wandering minstrel, a messenger from the unknown, who leads the people away from culture-bound structures: Taliesin in Celtic mythology, and most notably Orpheus in Greek mythology (Deardorff, 2005). Orpheus's "songs could charm wild beasts and coax even rocks and trees into movement. . . . He was one of the Argonauts, and when the Argo had to pass the island of the Sirens, it was Orpheus' music which prevented the crew from being lured to destruction" (Hunter, 1997). His love for his wife, Eurydice, was so great that, when she was killed by the bite of a poisonous snake, he went down to the underworld to lead her back to earth. His passion led him to break the rule that he must not look back at Eurydice. "Just before the pair reached the upper world, Orpheus looked back, and Eurydice slipped back into the nether world once again" (Hunter, 1997). In his inconsolable sorrow, he spurned the love of other women, who then attacked and beheaded him—but even in death, "Orpheus' head floated down the river, still singing, and came to rest on the isle of Lesbos" (Hunter, 1997). The lesson seems to be that failure to follow the rules is sometimes life-giving (bringing rocks and trees to life), but can also be fatal. But even in death, true beauty cannot be silenced.

Miller argues that the motif of descent into hell is archetypal in nature, fundamental to the human soul, universal in scope, yet dead in the wake of ecclesiastical literalism and theological rationalism (Miller, 1989, cited in Deardorff, 2004).

According to Dante, the inscription at the entrance of hell reads "Abandon all hope, you who enter here." During the descent, we may "lose all hope."

What Can We Do When We Are in the Midst of a Dark Night of the Soul?

It is important for both the struggling person, and for the counselor, not to confuse the dark night with psychopathology.[5] The dark night is a period of devastating self-insight, a facing of what Jung called "the shadow." The poet D. H. Lawrence understood that this phase is the beginning of transformation, and reflects the devastation in his poem *Phoenix,*

Are you willing to be sponged out, erased, canceled,
made nothing?
Are you willing to be made nothing?
dipped into oblivion?
If not, you will never really change.

Lawrence (1964)

Out of these depths comes a more realistic, more profound unity with the sacred. The loss of ego turns out to be a blessing in disguise. Only a small percent of people experience a profound dark night of the soul, but many of those who do, at some point experience a shift—for some a sharp turnaround, for others a gradual ascent—in which the loss of self is now felt as a positive mystical experience.

More than once when I
Sat all alone, revolving in myself
The word that is the symbol of myself,
The mortal limit of the Self was loosed,
And passed into the nameless, as a cloud
Melts into heaven.

Tennyson (1885)

The loss of hope during the dark night does not foreclose staying open to possibilities that may emerge, such as gateways (Ventura, 2005). In the midst of the desert, one suddenly experiences a subtle movement of wind, as if a door has opened. When one intuits an open door, it is not important to rationally comprehend what is happening. In one of his poems, Ventura (2005) cites his father's advice:

It is not necessary to understand
the opening of the door
to feel the wind.

Ventura (2005)

This union of the self with the whole may remain gentle, "a dissolution of ego structures that is necessary in order to reach a larger definition of self," or it may lead to dramatic episodes of blinding light or visionary states. These may be overwhelming and frightening if the individual is not ready to let in so much energy (Grof & Grof, 1990). They may lead a person to think of himself or herself as very special, superior, as St. John of the Cross clearly warned. These states may feel so rich that one hates to leave them and come down from the mountaintop. On the other hand, the vision from the mountaintop can make someone, similar to Dr. Martin Luther Jr., fearless about death, and happy to move forward toward the promised land of justice and love (King, 1968).

Based on a vision near the end of her life, another great Spanish Christian mystic, Teresa of Avila (1515-1582), describes the journey inward as moving through seven palaces inside of palaces, to where, in the innermost chamber, one achieves union with God. Her seven stages in some ways parallel the psychological stage theories reviewed in Chapters 2 and 3, and provide a navigational tool, used in conscious cultivation of silence, stillness, and surrender, which may help a person move more gently from the dark night. Here is a "translation" of her vision into steps of inner movement (based on her Treatise on the Spiritual Path, 1577):

1. Cultivate self-knowledge, humility, and discipline.
2. Seek wise counsel, guidance, and instruction.
3. Beware of self-righteousness, entitlement, and autonomy.
4. Think less, love more; cultivate a contemplative practice.
5. Balance wild abandon with clear discernment.
6. Suffer the agony of separation, trials and self-doubt.
7. Experience union with the Source and express love of the Source by loving and service to one another. (Starr, 2005, p. 36)

It is also important for the person undergoing the dark night and spiritual transformation to realize that these linear or stage concepts are metaphors; this is mythology and should not be taken as a simple progression. Washburn develops a much more complex progression, but cautions that once a person has experienced a descent and then an ascent, the process is not over. Spiritual development continues to have ups and downs (Washburn, 1994).

Is the Dark Night Also a Cultural-Historical Event?

Just as the dark night of the soul may occur in the spiritual journey of an individual, the phrase is also apt for describing some historical and cultural changes that have been going on since just before the beginning of the twentieth century. Some might say that Western culture is currently in a dark night of the soul. A number of theologians and religious writers and teachers in the twentieth century have expressed the sense that the presence of the sacred has been diminishing in human experience. The phrase "the death of God" first appeared in a short parable in Neitzche's book *The Gay Science,* which centers on a character who walks the streets announcing the death of God (Neitzche, 1887). Decades later the great Jewish theologian Martin Buber used the image of an "eclipse" to describe the sense that God was not present, although the metaphor suggests God ("the sun") is still there but temporarily can't be seen or known. Influenced by Neitzche, the consummate masterpiece of the great German composer Wagner was a mythological drama in four complete operas, referred to as the *Ring Cycle.* The cycle ends with *"Götterdämmerung"* ("The Twilight of the Gods"), although Wagner himself seems to have been ambivalent about whether modernism needed to reject the Christian belief in God (see discussions of "Parsifal"). Certainly Neitzche's rejection of the classical Christian doctrine influenced a number of protestant theologians, sometimes referred to as existentialist Christians. One of the greatest of these theologians, Paul Tillich, emigrated from Germany to the United States during World War II; he preached and lectured about "The Shaking of the Foundations," and published a series of sermons under this title (Tillich, 1955). Almost 60 years after Neitzche, the more radical expression of this experience, the theology that "God is dead," and the experience of mourning the loss of God's presence, became widely discussed on seminary campuses and in university religious programs.

Thus, an experience that the sixteenth century saint understood as part of his individual spiritual voyage, by the twentieth century seemed to describe, at least for some, a cultural crisis and a shift in worldviews. The anxiety that comes with shifts in worldviews and uncertainty about the future is exacerbated by the political manipulation of fear. As "Granny D" Haddock (2005) noted, "Great leadership comes from love, and great societies come from confident, mass empowerment." But since 9/11, many of our political leaders have led from fear and anger and "are forever dividing and punishing the people instead of uniting, encouraging and empowering them." Both foreign policy and economic policy have been designed to encourage fear, and to take away the sense that one's work can lead to security. The destruction of the working class and the focus on the uncertainty of government safety nets such as social security "gives people great fear for their own futures" (Haddock, 2005).

A crisis in trust, then, may not indicate a sign of weakness in one's personal spirituality, but rather may reflect a sensitivity to the conditions of our time in history. In spite of the seriousness of this experience of the descent, and the question of what it means when a whole culture is in descent, a sense is still felt that by going deeply into the experience, one can come out of it even closer to the sacred. As Tillich (1955) rightly saw, a parallel exists between the current period of descent and the experience of sin at the time of the Reformation. At that time, faith needed to incorporate the experience of redemption in spite of sin. In our time, trust needs to incorporate the experience of redemption in spite of doubt. The descent into the depths may be qualitatively different for modern humanity than it was in earlier centuries, because the individual spirit is burdened with doubt and discouragement, moreso than with guilt. The faithful response to redemption may have as much to do with social or interpersonal action as with individual morality. Trust may lead to working for interpersonal changes that will affect important relationships, or to social changes that can redeem the structures of human society as well as the individual.

Wagner's "Twilight of the Gods" implies a redemptive social change as part of the effects of the diminishing power of the gods: the door is opened for a fuller humanity, now that the gods no longer dominate. Can a cultural mythology develop that will inspire the type of personal narrative that encourages constructive change? A psychological investigation of the personal narratives that affect adults provides a suggestion of the kind of modern myth that is needed. In a study seeking some of the sources of truly generative adult lives, the authors analyzed the internalized life stories of 40 highly generative and 30 less generative adults with similar demographic profiles. They discovered that the highly generative adults were more likely to reconstruct the past and anticipate the future as variations on a prototypical commitment story. This story has the following elements:

- The protagonist or hero enjoys an early family blessing or advantage, but is sensitized to others' suffering at an early age.

- He or she is guided by a clear and compelling personal ideology, a value system that serves as a compass or rudder, providing stability over time.
- This internalized myth involves transformation; bad experiences are redeemed, resulting in good outcomes, and goals are to benefit society in the future.

Such internalized commitment stories sustain and reinforce the modern adult's efforts to contribute in positive ways to the next generation (McAdams, Diamond, de St. Aubin, & Mansfield, 1997).

For the mystic, and for many others who are confronted with hell-like experiences, "our task is not to endure the pain and difficulties of life, but to give ourselves over to the soul and to that which is greater than ourselves" (Elkins, 1998, p. 259). We move through the dark night of the soul to a richer experience of the spirit.

Gateway Twelve: A Social Cause—Activism

When Luther first articulated his view of the "ministry of all believers"—the concept that all Christians, not just the priest or the pope, are called to their vocations—it seemed grandiose to some. For a ditchdigger or garbage collector to claim his or her work as a ministry to others might make some people laugh, but I think the opposite is grandiose—to believe that only the ordained ministers, or kings, or presidents, are doing the total work of the sacred in the day-to-day life of men and women is to put too much of history on the shoulders of the leaders. It is to take a "Great Leaders" view of what matters in history, when increasingly historians are recognizing that the trends and themes of history are due not just to leadership but to social movements of the masses. The entire web of humanity is interconnected. Each individual, each common man and woman, has a role to play. This is not a "claim to power" (although it is empowering), but a humble statement of one's connectedness in the total web of being.

Luther developed his concept of the "priesthood of all believers" as a view of vocation, or "calling." When I transitioned from the parish ministry to a combination of teaching and counseling, I continued to feel my work was a ministry, but my vision of ministry was broader than the church or a particular religion. Two aspects of Luther's view of vocation seem too limited for our time. First, Luther articulated the idea of vocations in an almost totally Christian context, whereas we need to understand our callings in a multireligious and multiethnic context. Second, Luther's doctrine basically justified the status quo of his society, *except* in relationship to the Roman Church priesthood and hierarchy. The Reformation led to a radical challenge of the hierarchy of the church, the dominant international institution of his time. But the role of one's work may also challenge the nation state, or the business enterprises and global economy of our day. Given today's context, with the conflicts between nation states, and the pervasiveness of international capitalism or "globalization," it seems important that a contemporary doctrine of vocations should include a critique of our official jobs and their complicity with the false gods of nationalism, consumerism, and corporate greed.

I do not assume everyone should be a political activist. But I do see it as part of my own calling *not only* to be a counselor/educator, but to be informed on certain key social issues, to make decisions about when and how to lead, or to join actions that seek to make our society more caring and just. My volunteer work as co-leader of a local social action group has provided me a chance to meet a number of people who do not see their official jobs as "ministries," but who are passionately involved in specific attempts at social change—for example. an unskilled union laborer who is actively opposing urban sprawl, a mother of adult children who is a dedicated peace activist, a retired person who regularly volunteers for Habitat for Humanity, and a former health educator who helped spur the formation of our suburban hospice organization. Often these volunteers believe that their social or community action is their ministry and gives meaning and significance to their life in a way that their job does not.

Many hours of social investment and activism involve pure "grunt work," just as with most employment. Occasions of breakthrough also occur, occasions when the barriers between groups of people are broken down, and humanity seems as one. These are occasions one will remember all of one's life. It is in these events that social activism can become a gateway to the sacred. I will share two of these.

My first venture into social justice issues began with my high school honors paper; I wrote about the Supreme Court decision arguing that racially "separate" schools were inherently unequal, and thus illegal (*Brown v. Board of Education,* 347 U.S. 483 [1954]). This led me into a series of protests and boycotts while I was still in high school and continuing through my 12 years of higher education, culminating in my participating in voter registration in Raleigh, North Carolina, in 1967. By then I knew by heart songs such as "We Shall Overcome," but had sung them mostly with other white northerners in safe settings. In Raleigh we worked in the black ghettos in teams consisting of a black college student (usually from Raleigh or nearby) and a white student (such as myself, from Boston University). Although I worked with different teammates each day, in each case I felt a new sense of how important getting out the "negro" vote was to these students. I also felt a sense of appreciation from them for our white involvement as comrades in the fight. After days of work together, the group of students bonded; some of the participants from Raleigh no longer were "negro students" to me, but were "Tony" and "Elli" and "Samantha." When we joined in a parting ceremony before those of us from Boston boarded a bus to return, we formed a big circle, arms around each others' shoulders, singing "We Shall Overcome" with a passion I'd never before experienced. We were all in tears, partly because we hated to leave, partly because we knew the danger these youth were exposed to, but mostly because we felt united in the cause of justice as brothers and sisters fully believing that where one person is denied justice we all suffer.

The second experience I want to share is a quieter one—in fact, it mostly took place in silence. It occurred in 2003. Again I was part of a group of people coming from many states and backgrounds; again some of us had traveled some distance to join others, this time in Indianapolis. The action was a silent vigil, standing quietly in a line two blocks long on a sidewalk facing a city convention center. The center was hosting the governing convention of a protestant denomination that was distributing to their youth a booklet arguing that sexually active gays, lesbians, and bisexuals are condemned by God. They had chosen to write about us, but they refused to dialogue with us—with LGBT Christians and their allies. We were protesting that there should be "no action about us without us!"—a basic guideline for maintaining respect (Brethren Mennonite Council for Lesbian and Gay Concerns, 2005). The organization holding the vigil was founded by two ordained ministers who had become a gay couple. The group's methods were completely nonviolent, and opposed the denomination's "spiritual violence" against gays' natural orientation. The grandson of Mahatma Gandhi had helped develop the approach, and the organization's name, Soulforce, is a translation of the Hindi term for Gandhi's method. To participate, we had to undergo training in this method and agree to a set of principles that, among others, included these statements about our adversary:

1. My adversary is also a child of the Creator; we are both members of the same human family; we are sisters and brothers in need of reconciliation.
2. My adversary is not my enemy, but a victim of misinformation as I have been.
3. My only task is to bring my adversary truth in love (through relentless but nonviolent action). (SoulForce, 2005)

As delegates to this convention would pass us, coming in or out of the convention center, our group would hand them flyers explaining the reasons for our vigil. However, we were instructed that each time we prepared to pass out a flyer we were to look the particular person, the adversary, in the eyes, and ask ourselves silently, "Do I really believe this person is also a child of the Creator? Do I accept him or her as my brother or sister?" Unless we could feel at that moment that we were passing information to another child of the Creator, we were simply to look down, stand in silence, and instead of acting, focus inwardly on our own need for reconciliation. The intent was that we will speak the truth (as we know it) only in *love*. That is, we will not interact in a way that expresses anger, or treats the adversary as inferior; we are all sisters and brothers in need of reconciliation.

During the several days of the vigil, before each period of standing on the sidewalk across from the convention center we would meet for meditation, led by the minister who trained Martin Luther King Jr. in Gandhi's method of nonviolence. This meditation period was very much an act of community. So when we were on the line and standing face to face with an adversary we did not stand alone, but stood as part of this community.

Though I have participated in numerous rallies, vigils, and demonstrations, never have I felt so keenly that each encounter was not just an effort for justice, but a prayer for my own humanity. In this way of being, there really was "soul force," a spiritual stance that transcended our own egos or opinions.

WHERE DO WE GO FROM HERE?

Certainly these are times in which spirituality takes discipline and practice. Yet "spirituality is accessible to all those who are nurturing their souls and cultivating their spiritual lives" (Elkins, 1998, p. 26). We know from research in positive psychology that assessments that help people choose specific actions that fit their unique personalities can lead to increased happiness (Seligman, Steen, Park, & Peterson, 2005). The three most effective actions (of those used in this study) were:

- Write and deliver in person a letter of gratitude to someone who has been especially kind to you but has never been properly thanked.
- Each evening for a week, write down three things that went well for you that day. In addition, write down what you believe caused that thing to go right.
- Assess your top strengths, and use one of them in a new and different way. Do this every day for a week. (The assessment they used can be found on their Web site: http://www.authentichappiness.sas.upenn.edu/, but you may try your own way of assessing your top strengths.)

Now is the time to do another assessment: Which gateways to the sacred described in this chapter do *you* need to structure more frequently into the daily bustle of your life? Notice that I say "gateway*s*," for many of us will want to combine several of the approaches. Worksheets 10.1 and 10.2 are intended to help you in that assessment.

Many of the paths or gateways involve ambiguity. Both inspiration and discouragement can ensue from organized religion, from relationships, from the body, nature, mythology, and social involvement. The dark night of the soul directly expresses the "negative" side of this ambiguity. In short, *no* assurance can be given that opening one of the gateways will always lead to inspiration. But the more aware you become of the personal effects of each gateway for yourself, the more wisely you can choose your path. You can, for example, choose music that moves you through and beyond despair, or go to places that inspire you. You do have some control, especially if you develop what in monastic life were called "the disciplines of grace," and you take time to practice (Lozoff, 2001). We do this "nurturing our souls, cultivating . . ." (Elkins, 1998) by consciously recognizing which life experiences

- help us to open,
- help us to experience the sacred, and
- help us to love.

This is not to say that it's all up to us, and that culture and circumstances don't matter. They especially matter when immature leaders use them to emphasize fear and anger, encouraging disempowerment. No matter how disciplined we are, we'll have circumstances and times in which hope doesn't come.

> Sometimes all you can do in life, in the harder moments, is to put one foot in front of the other. . . . But do not act from anger; the defense of freedom and fairness comes best from a loving and tolerant heart. . . . You will always come to some new victory, despite your darkest worries and despair. (Haddock, 2005)

To paraphrase Bo Lozoff (2001), spiritual life is possible, but it takes practice. It is not easier than being traditionally religious—it requires consciously making room for the sacred, making time and place for the transcendent, the holy, in everyday life. It requires the discipline to seek those particular experiences of the sacred that are most powerful for you—to open the gateways, and to allow them in.

Worksheets 10.1 and 10.2 are intended to aid you in planning your own practice, to follow up on the reading you've just done. The first is for your own use. The second is to help you do an assessment with one or more of your clients.

Work Sheet 10.1. Your Own Spiritual "Plan"

List your current practices; note the number of times each week you do each one:

PLANNING A MORE SPIRIT-FILLED LIFE

1. Choose from the list below the practices or experiences that you already have done, but intend to to *increase* in your life. (Mark these on the list with an "I.")

Traditional Religion

Attending worship
Meditation

Alternatives:

Visual arts (P2)*
- Music
- Dance
- Poetry

Body (P3) movement
- Message
- Relaxation
- Sexual connection

Relationships (P7)
Feminine (P1): Receptivity
- Emotion

Psych: Counseling (P4)
- Journaling

Narratives:
- Reading, drama, movies, story

Mythology (P5)
Nature: (P6)
- Scenery
- Animals
- Beauty

Dark nights of the soul (P8)
- One's own suffering
- Being with others' pain
- Being with the dying

---

*"P" refers to Pathways, by number, elaborated earlier in this chapter.

2. Choose from the list above the *new* experiences you want to explore. (Mark these on the list with an "E.")

3. Now set some priorites. Choose two current practices to increase (you marked them on the list with an ""I") and two new ones to explore ("E"). List those in the spaces below:

   Increase:
   a.
   b.

   Explore:
   a.
   b.

   Set a realistic schedule for each of the four items, such as "every day," or "every Tuesday and Saturday," and write it after the choice.

4. Support your commitment by telling a "buddy" whom you will ask to support you in this commitment. List two or three buddys:

   ____

   ____

   ____

5. Journal your responses to the changes you experiment with (step 3). If you haven't already, I encourage you to buy a notebook in which to journal, or set up a journal file folder in your computer, so you have a regular place to keep you "spiritual journal."

6. Evaluate and revise the plan. Mark in your datebook a time to review your new explorations, and decide how to continue on the basis of your assessments.

Worksheet 10.2.
An Assessment To Use With Your Clients

PART ONE

(*Counselor:* Read through this list and consider copying it to go over with your client)

Tasks for Maintaining a Spirit-Filled Life

1. Sense what you passionately value. Explore it. Affirm it.
2. Be open to learn what "reality" or life experience calls you to give up, to surrender, or at least to hold more loosely.
3. Go where you sense life's spark.
4. When exploring, let loose of expectations.
5. Notice when you have the courage to be authentic.
6. Choose some deep friends who will support your growth unconditionally.
7. Choose to be with some people who are not like you, or who directly challenge you.
8. Decide whether you need a spiritual "community." Consider initiating a spiritual support group.
9. Find a way to express your values and commitments. For most, this means "walking your talk," finding specific action that puts flesh on your ideas. For some, it means to literally "express" them in art, music, or drama. Give out what is experienced internally so others can witness it.
10. Developing a practice, in time, in space. Experimenting with what forms of prayer, meditation, or sacred movement are right for you and participating in this practice daily, or at least regularly. Finding places in nature, or spaces in buildings, or putting together an "altar," "centering point," or devotional center in your home that provides a visual reminder for you to get centered or connected to your spiritual self. (See Work Sheet 10.1 for more ideas.)
11. Clarify what media or arts help you grow spiritually. Visit and revisit such art, music, readings, etc. (Note that if others generally don't recognize some music, or a certain book, as spiritual, that doesn't mean it's not spiritual for you.)
12. Incorporate pilgrimages into your vacations; go to places that have historic or traditional connections to your spiritual heroes or guides, or places in nature that seem especially spiritual to you.
13. Find a counseling supervisor or spiritual coach who will work with you on expanding the spiritual dimension in your work with clients.

PART TWO

(*Counselor:* Write up an assessment of which of the above are your clients' strengths and/or weaknesses. Do some conceptual work to clarify how you see your client on the issues listed.)

What feelings and judgments does this assessment raise for you? Where do you feel judgmental or pushy in relation to that particular client? Which are issues you feel fairly comfortable bringing up with your client?

PART THREE

(*Counselor:* Explore with your client what issues he or she wants to work on. If the client has included some spiritual issues, it may be useful to share with him or her which of these issues you have thought about and feel comfortable working with in relation to the client. Find out which ones the client wants to work on with you.)

PART IV: EXPERIENTIAL APPROACHES

The experiential portion of this book is organized around three domains: the self, oothers, and the spiritual dimension. This division of topics into these three is somewhat arbitrary and does not imply a metaphysical hierarchy or a sequence of spiritual maturation. In using Part IV of this book, it is not generally necessary to pursue the experiments in sequence. However, it may help you to stay grounded if you start with Chapter 11 on self, and complete at least the first section before jumping to Chapter 12.

Within each of these chapters, peruse the Concepts and Introduction sections first, then try one or more experiments. After that, read the Cautions and then decide whether to pursue more experiments in that section, or to explore another domain. Within each chapter the experiments often follow a progression, but it's perfectly okay when you read one set of instructions and that particular experiment doesn't interest you, to jump ahead to the next. I think it will be clear whether or not you need to go back to the previous one to understand it.

These experiments or exercises have been tried by a number of people; many were used in the classes I taught and workshops I led on spirituality and counseling, but this does not mean they are just right for you. Sometimes you may want to adapt them to fit your needs. On the other hand, if you feel like exploring, it's often worth trying something new just as it is, without modifying it. It usually feels a bit uncomfortable to move into something new, but that's what exploring is about. When you have tried something new, you might make some notes on that page about what you would change for the next time you go back to that experiment.

Think of this experiential section of the book as a personal workbook that you can keep revising to make it more valuable for your future explorations.

Chapter 11

Centering the Self

GROUNDING THE SELF

Concepts of Grounding

Groundedness is simply being where one is, part of reality, as embodied in flesh and blood. At least two of the classic poses of the Buddha show a grounding. In one, the Buddha is standing; in the other he is meditating while seated cross-legged, and he is touching the earth with one hand. The classical Buddhist name for this second posture places it in the context of his vow to meditate until he achieved enlightenment. Thunder, lightning, and other threatening events tried to interfere, but Buddha touched the earth, asking nature to bear witness to his resolve. The firmness of resolve is not a toughness, and the gentle, relaxed face of representations of the Buddha reflect the artists' awareness of this.

Similarly, the Hebrew view of resolve is embodied in flesh and blood. Recall the pledge of Abraham's servant, sealed by putting a hand "under the thigh"[1] of Abraham—an intimate, physical, solid connection (Genesis 24:2,9, RSV). Awareness of our groundedness reaffirms our solid connection with earth. It is not ethereal; it is solid. It is not "alone"; it is dependent.

Cautions

Grounding experiments are very safe. I have used them both in group settings, such as classes and workshops, and in exercises to try alone (with written instructions similar to those that follow), and have never had a student or client report a disorienting or frightening experience. However, the students or clients had come to know me, and the classroom meetings or sessions had become a place of safety and trust. Since you as reader probably do not know me, and since no interpersonal trust has developed with peers in a group context, I encourage you to be aware of your inner reactions when you first read an experiment. If you feel in some way it might be bad for you, before you begin it, make some modifications such as those listed in the "Modifications to Reduce Anxiety" section in the Appendix, or discontinue the attempt to do the exercise altogether.

The experiments that follow seek to remind you of your own connection with the solid ground beneath you. You do not need to change anything or make anything happen; just become aware of what is.

Experiment 1: Dependence and Contact

The intent of this experiment is to physically experience one's dependence, to make solid contact, and to express gratitude.

Step One

Choose a room containing a bed or with carpet that will allow you, later, to lie down comfortably. If it would be comfortable to go outdoors and lie on a blanket on the ground, that is even better.

Begin in a comfortable sitting position. Experience the weight of your body pushing into the mattress or carpet. Think of gravity as pushing you through the material and holding you against Mother Earth. Experience your dependence on the earth to hold you up. Allow yourself the feelings of dependency and give thanks to Earth for it's support.

Step Two

Try saying something to the earth, such as, "I did not arrive on this earth of my own doing. Thank you, Mom, for bringing me into the world. Thank you, Mother Earth, for receiving me. I thank you, mothers, for the gift of my life and my consciousness on this earth."

Pursue this type of conversation. Perhaps, as you express the various ways you are dependent on the earth, it will feel right to lie down, and state, "I am totally dependent on you; without your bounty, I could not exist." Again, write your own script.

Return to standing up. Take a stand as a person. "I am here. I am standing on this ground. This ground supports me. This is a legitimate space. My position here is a gift. And it is not the whole, but it is my place. With your grace, I am here." Remember, you do not have to be someone other than who you are. Think of Martin Luther's words, "Here I stand; I can do no other." The resolve comes from the reality of who he is.

Explore through writing the script how it feels to acknowledge both a dependency and a claim to a space. One possible direction: "I can stand in this space, even though I don't understand everything that makes this possible. I accept the mystery of my existing here. It is important that I be clear where I am. I do not need to claim that I have the whole truth—only that this is where I am at this time. I feel supported by Mother Earth in this place, and give thanks."

Follow-Up

In the next few days, when you are standing, be conscious of the weight against the soles of your feet. When you are seated, experience the weight of your body pushing into the seat. If you meditate, experiment with having one hand relaxing in a position that allows some fingers to touch the ground.

Experiment 2: Quiet Self

Being fully human makes us real. Reality can't be defined, it can only be experienced. Be alert to those brief moments during the day when you experience your fundamental self behind a breath, a feeling, a sensation. Before you jump out of bed tomorrow, see if you can catch the fleeting hint of being, pure and simple, before the mind starts chattering. This still, silent, nameless state is very satisfying. It cannot be touched by thinking, talking, or doing (Chopra, 1995).

Experiment 3: Ambivalence and Shuttling

In the Introduction I shared two of the splits that I felt in my own development. I noted that, at this stage in its development, the field of counseling seems to be poised between focusing on its own identity, and being ready to immerse itself in a larger Self, an identity that transcends its own. That is, focusing on the human self only as a psychological construct, or focusing on the human self with it's ethical and spiritual dimensions. I suspect most of us, at our best, will shuttle back and forth between involvement in concerns greater than ourselves, and reexamination and nurturing of our selves. I am not arguing here for a selfless life, only for a life that is concerned with more than self.

Our tendency, when we experience ambivalence or feel split, is to choose one side of the split and try to bolster it, and to suppress the other polarity. Rarely can this produce integration or healing. Instead, we need to attend to both poles, moving between them—-sometimes a new integration will emerge.

It may not be clear at first that shuttling is important to grounding. Yet one of the main ways we stay ungrounded is that we try to ground ourselves in one side of a polarity, the side that fits our image of ourselves. But the polarity is not overcome, and we continue to shuttle back and forth in our feelings. Therefore I encourage you to avoid getting into an intellectual argument about these experiments, but to dive into the experience of shuttling. It is better to *experience* this than to try to grasp it as an abstract conceptualization. If this experiment doesn't work for you, move on to the other grounding experiments, and later come back to "the shuttle" and try it again.

The Shuttle (Using "the Empty Chair")

Step One: Choose a "split" you feel in yourself. I've briefly noted some splits I have felt in myself: masculine versus feminine, Eastern versus Western, spiritual versus self-centered. If you resonate with one of these, you could choose it. Or you may be aware of some other split in your personal experience. Chose one for now. (You can repeat this experiment at another time using another split.)

Step Two: Find a place where you can be alone, unobserved, and unheard. Situate two chairs facing each other about as far apart as you would usually sit when conversing with a friend. I will refer to each side of the split as "left" and "right," but it will likely be more effective if you give each side a descriptive name (such as "masculine" and "feminine") and simply use "left" or "right" to refer to the chairs you sit in for each side. Sit in one chair and state "I am the [left] side." Try to experience those qualities in yourself that belong to that side. Say them out loud, but as you name them, try to feel them, move as they would, act them out, use the appropriate voice tones and volume. For example, "I am the masculine. I am *strong*."

Step Three: Shift to sitting in the other chair. Repeat this process with the other side. For example, "I am the feminine. I am gentle. I am graceful. But I am weak." Again, continue until you feel into that experience. Sometimes it helps to exaggerate your gestures or voice tones.

Step Four: Begin a dialogue between the two sides. For example, "I am masculine, and I want you, 'feminine,' to understand that I want to be dominant." Continue until you sense a response inside yourself from the other side.

Step Five: Then shift chairs; be the other part. Example, "I *do* understand that you like to dominate. But I'm feeling crushed. I need a chance to express myself."

But don't let me write your script. Begin writing your own. Don't worry if parts of it don't resonate or feel authentic. Keep the script flowing, and some real dialogue will emerge. Sometimes it will surprise you. Stay with the surprises. When you get anxious and want to leave, try to shuttle to the other side and express the response. However, if your anxiety grows, discontinue the experiment, and go to the "Modifications to Reduce Anxiety" section in the Appendix.

It may take some practice for you to get used to this strange way of talking between parts of yourself. Be creative. Modify the technique to fit yourself. Later, you may go back to these instructions and find you've integrated some of this and can try more. Embodying the parts, instead of intellectualizing them so they remain impotent words, helps most people really access and know them. Shuttling keeps you from a phony position and aids deeper integration. Viewing films of Gestalt therapy, especially some of James Simkin (Simkin & Obern, 1980) and Fritz Perls (1973a,b), may be useful. The shuttle may be mechanical at first, but it allows us to engage different parts of ourselves with deeper awareness

Experiment 4: Movement and Balance

Clear an area so you can move freely. Accept the limits of what is available—you can do this experiment with only a six-foot by six-foot space, if necessary. Standing in a relaxed position, with flexed knees, read the following:

Have you ever watched someone meditate though movement, such as tai chi? Or have you observed the flowing, effortless way in which some basketball stars, such as Michael Jordan, can move? Or watched ice skaters in smooth, fluid movements? The purpose of this experiment (as in all of these exercises) is *not* to accomplish a "good" performance, but to explore, become familiar with your reactions and your relationship with your body, and to learn to accept it or expand it, or set limits on it.

In this experiment, try not to "script" things ahead, but to move and experience. Let the movement keep "writing itself," developing its own choreography, seeing what emerges. If the space makes it safe to do so, close your eyes. Try to stop "seeing" your movements; just feel them from inside. The process is not to watch yourself but to *sense* yourself and follow the senses as they shift and change.

If you get stuck, try just walking for a while, or rocking, or simply shake and wiggle parts of you that want to be shook or wiggled. Find what feels pleasing, or what stretches you, or what pushes you. Experience yourself in your body. The grounding this time is in interaction with the foundation, the floor or earth beneath you. Ground yourself in your body senses. Learn to trust the flow.

Many people are surprised to find that a movement that becomes interesting and is repeated or expanded leads to some feelings—sometimes ones you weren't aware you were "carrying around." The word motion is in emotions. Emotions are there to move us, so let them do that. If an emotion has been waiting to be expressed, it may have lodged between you and the ground, possibly keeping you from getting grounded. Flow with it, and through it (for additional movement and balance exercises, see Exhibit 11.1).

NURTURING THE SELF

Cautions: Nurturing experiments almost never increase anxiety, or produce frightening experiences. Neither do they result in persons feeling overwhelmed or disoriented. In group settings it is not uncommon for some participants in relaxation experiments to fall asleep, and then to feel embarrassed. It is helpful if the leader states that some members are likely to fall asleep, that this is perfectly okay, and that we will gently wake them when it is time for the group to move on to the next activity. In individual work, occasionally persons

EXHIBIT 11.1.
Additional Movement and Balance Exercises

Variation 1

Some people find it hard to get moving, but are used to dancing to music, and find music helps them "free up." It's probably best, unless you have a specific feeling in mind, to choose music with a variety of moods and tempos so that you can discover which one "moves you" at this point in time.

Variation 2

If you have a friend whom you trust and who would be willing to do the movement experiment with you, try it in two phases.

Phase One

Step One

Choose which of you will first be the moving person, and who will simply witness. The main task of the witness is simply to watch and sense what the movement of the friend feels like to you. With a witness present, the mover can move more freely with his or her eyes closed, counting on the witness to guide him or her away from any object or obstruction that could hurt the partner. The main focus of the witness, however, is simply experiencing how the friend's movement affects you. Plan on allowing the movement to go on for about ten minutes (unless the mover requests a longer or shorter period).

Step Two

Sit down together. The witness simply describes, clearly from his or her own person, not as an interpretation, what the witness saw and felt. Allow this to go on uninterrupted for five minutes, or until it feels complete to the witness.

Step Three

The mover may now share anything he or she would like to about what the experience was like for him or her. In this step the witness should limit responses to reflecting feelings, listening carefully. Avoid interpretations.

Phase Two

Switch roles. The person who was "witness" now becomes the "mover," and vice versa. Again go through the previous three steps.

are uneasy or feel guilty about their self-indulgence. I simply treat this as valuable information for them—to be aware that they are not really sure they deserve to feel good.

Experiment 5: Relaxing

The first goal of this exercise is for you to lead yourself through a deep muscle relaxation exercise, and reach a relaxed state. Many recordings are available of various mental health professionals and workshop leaders giving relaxation instructions, and you may want to purchase one of these.

However, if you have a cassette recorder, I would encourage you to dictate the instructions onto a tape so you can hear your own voice leading you into relaxation. Hearing your own voice makes it easier to make the transition to internal self-leadership of your own relaxation. Eventually you want to be able to silently lead yourself into a relaxed state.

Step One: Preparations

Find a quiet place were you can be alone and unobserved, and where you can sit comfortably but in an upright position so that your neck easily supports your head. (Lying down or sitting in a recliner may encourage sleep. The purpose here is to calm oneself but remain alert and awake.)

Step Two: Beginning

(Pause between each of these instructions, giving yourself time to experience them):

- Sit with both your feet touching the ground, and without your arms crossed.
- Pay attention to your breathing. Breathe slightly slower and deeper than usual, but breathe naturally. Gradually just let your breathing control itself, and continue to feel your breathing. Feel the air coming in—-and going out. Feel it in your nose, your throat, your lungs, the movement in your belly, and so on. In—and out. In—and out.

- Now begin the muscle relaxation (step three). Move systematically through each muscle group, from head to toe.

Step Three

- Keep breathing easily and relaxing.
- Now relax the muscles in the top of your head, in your forehead, and above the ears. (It may help you to picture a comfortably warm egg broken on the top of your head, and sense the egg oozing down, and the warmth relaxing all those muscles.)
- Breathe gently, and now relax the muscles around your eyes, around your nose.
- Now relax the muscles in your jaw, in your tongue, in your lips—relax all of the muscles of your mouth and throat.
- Scan all the muscles of your head—and if anything feels tense, gently relax it.
- When you're ready to continue, relax the muscles in your neck, and in your shoulders.
- Relax the muscles in your chest, and in your upper back.
- Moving to your arms, relax the muscles of your biceps, of your whole upper arm, in your elbows, your forearms. Picture the tension in your arms seeping like sand down into your hands—and then flowing through your hands and out the ends of your fingers. Relax all of the muscles in your hands and fingers.
- Again, scan the muscles in your shoulders, arms, hands, and fingers. Just let all these relax.
- Now pay attention to your stomach area. Relax all of the muscles in your gut. Let the relaxation flow down into your groin. Relax the muscles in your groin, and in your hips.
- When you're ready, relax the muscles in your thighs and quadriceps, all the upper part of your legs.
- Relax around your knees, your calves.
- Let the tension seep down your legs into your feet, and out through your toes. Let all of the tension go, until your lower body feels very relaxed.
- Finally, once again scan your whole body from head to toe.
- If any part is still tense, increase the tension; really tense up those particular muscles. Now, on the out breath, let all that tension go. Relax those particular muscles (for relaxation exercises, see Exhibit 11.2 and Exhibit 11.3).[2]

EXHIBIT 11.2. Toe-to-Head Relaxation Exercise: Systematic Relaxation Moving Upward from Toe to Head

- Keep breathing easily and relaxing.
- Now relax the muscles in your feet, beginning with your toes; just letting them dangle.
- Now relax your ankles, your lower legs, especially your calves.
- Relax the muscles around your knees, the muscles in your upper legs, the quadriceps, and especially the muscles in your thighs.
- Just let all of the muscles in your lower body relax. Perhaps it will help you to imagine being on a safe beach, and the warm water of the ocean is lapping at your toes, and gradually each wave flows over your toes, your feet, etc., and then flows out, carrying away all the tension.
- When you are ready, let the relaxation flow from your thighs up into your groin. Relax the muscles in your groin, and in your hips. Now pay attention to your stomach area. Relax all of the muscles in your gut.
- As your stomach relaxes, gradually relax the muscles in your lower back. Relax the muscles first in the tailbone, and then move up the spine, relaxing, relaxing, work your way to the upper back.
- Now gradually move your attention around to your chest. With each breath, relax the muscles in your chest.
- Moving to your arms, relax the muscles of your biceps, of your whole upper arm, in your elbows, your forearms. Picture the tension in your arms seeping like sand down into your hands—and then flowing through your hands and out the ends of your fingers. Relax all the muscles in your hands and fingers.
- Now move your attention upward, to scan the muscles in your shoulders. Just let your shoulders relax.
- Now feel the relaxation moving upward to your neck. Relax all the muscles in the back of your neck—and then in the front. Relax the muscles in your jaw, in your tongue, in your lips—relax all of the muscles of your mouth and throat.
- Breathe gently, and now relax the muscles in your nose, around your eyes, and up your forehead. Now relax the muscles in your scalp, so your whole head is relaxed.
- Scan all the muscles of your head—and if anything feels tense, gently relax it.
- Just let your body breathe itself. Just let yourself lie gently, totally relaxed against the ground or chair. Just experience the relaxation. Just be.

EXHIBIT 11.3.
Scanning

Keep breathing easily and relaxing. Simply scan your body. If you sense an area of tension, pay attention to the muscles that are tense. Then contract them; increase the tension; really tense up those particular muscles. Now, on the out breath, let all of that tension go. Relax those particular muscles.

Visualize the contrast between the taut, tense muscles, and the loose, comfortable muscles when you are relaxed. Repeat the contracting of the muscles in the area that was tense.

Then relax again, and scan your body. If you are aware of another area of tension, repeat the process.

Experiment 6: Self-Soothing

This experiment works best if you begin with a complete relaxation exercise from Experiment 5, and when you are relaxed, continue, using the following step. Thus it has been labeled as step four.

Step Four

Now that you are relaxed, keeping your eyes closed, gently move or change positions to be more comfortable.

Step Five

Now touch yourself and hold yourself in any way that helps you feel nurtured. For example, if it feels good to hug yourself, do it. If you feel like gently stoking your left arm with your right hand, do that. As you sense what your body wants, just allow it to emerge.

Step Six

Try saying something such as, "You are my body, my temple, and I love you, so I will give to you whatever good feeling you want. I will lay it on your sacred altar.[3]

Step Seven

If it's comfortable, continue to flow and nurture yourself/be nurtured for at least ten or fifteen minutes. If not, notice if you have any bad feelings and wish to withdraw, do so. Take a break, or go back to reading the cognitive section of the book.

If you feel ambivalent, you might move to the shuttle, and play out some of your ambivalence and see where it leads.

Note on Foundation Experiments

The previous experiments form a foundation for much of the experiential work in the remainder of the book. I refer to these experiments as a foundation because these techniques involve moving from ideas and feelings to an embodied experience. The more embodied and grounded the foundation, the more solidly you can build on it.

If you have trouble with these experiments, you may want to try the experiments that follow, but it may be valuable also for you to regularly return to the previous foundation experiments and see if they become more comfortable. However, if you return to Experiments 1 through 6 and regularly find them difficult, you may find it valuable to seek out a counselor or therapist who is trained in experiential techniques. Ask if they would agree to a few sessions working with you on these or similar experiments.

Chapter 12

Focusing on Others

The focus of this chapter is your relationships with others. More specifically, the first part of the chapter is intended to help you sort out whether you need a spiritual community to support you in your journey and growth. These exercises are intended to be done alone.

The second part concerns the spiritual act of giving to others, and receiving from others. Some of the exercises can be done with a friend, if this seems right for you. The third part again includes exercises to do on your own. They are concerned with inclusiveness as a goal of spiritual practice and the process of moving beyond ones own tribe.

SELF AND SPIRITUAL COMMUNITY BACKGROUND

Many of the exercises in this chapter and the next make use of guided meditation or guided imagery. Although they can be called "meditations," they involve directing or focusing thoughts and feelings. They are somewhat different from meditation, which attempts to quiet the words and verbal voices within us (which we will save for Chapter 13, the relationship with the spiritual).

In this first section, Experiments 1 and 2 both have to do with exploring your self in relation to desiring or choosing a spiritual community. Experiment 1 asks you to look at your own spiritual journey and consider choosing a community in relationship to where you are in your journey. Experiment 2 asks you to look at different "parts" or "roles" of your self, and consider which parts of your self would be affirmed by specific communities.

Experiment 1: Cycles of your Spiritual Life

Introduction

The purpose of this exercise is to help you review some of your past spiritual journey in order to make decisions about the next steps. The exercise, found in Exhibit 12.1 may also help you decide whether you desire a spiritual community at this phase in your life.

EXHIBIT 12.1.
Cycles of Your Spiritual Life

Sit comfortably and naturally, letting yourself feel present and at ease. Let go of any plans and feel the natural rhythm of your breathing. Then, when you have become quiet, reflect back over your whole spiritual life. Remember how you first became awakened to the life of the heart and the spirit. Remember the sense you had at that time of the possibilities, of the mystery, of the divine. Bring to mind the years that followed, the early spiritual teachers and the sacred places that inspired you. Survey the following year, remembering the systematic practices you have followed, the cycles you have gone through, the situations that have taught you the most, the unexpected lessons, the times of solitude, the times of community, your trials, your benefactors, your guides, your recent practice. Be aware of the problems you encountered as well, their difficulties, their teachings.

Enjoy this reflection, seeing it as a story, an adventure, appreciating its cycles and turns with a sense of wonder and gratitude. Then feel yourself resting in this moment today with an openness toward your life ahead. Let yourself sense what may lie ahead of you: the next natural stages of your life, the incomplete areas of your life, the dimensions of spiritual practice you may be called upon to include.

As your own spiritual guide, become aware of what situation might be beneficial for you. If your present life allows, should you seek a period of solitude and aloneness, or choose to become involved in a spiritual community? Does your spiritual practice call you to a period of service for others, or is it the season to devote yourself to your career, creativity, home, and family? Do you need a teacher, or is it best now to rest on your own resources? If your present life doesn't allow you to make those choices, what cycle are you being presented with? How can you best honor both your choices and your life situation and include them in the opening of your heart and the cycles of your practice? Sense how you can be true to yourself and true to the dharma, the Tao that is unfolding in your life.

Source: Adapted from Kornfield (1993)

Experiment 2: Who Am I?

The next exercise is an extension of the work on self presented in Chapter 11. However, its intention is different. The purpose of using this exercise here is to survey some of the "roles" and "aspects" of yourself as you *consider seeking a spiritual community.* If you are clear you do *not* need a community at this time, move on to Experiment 3.

In many spiritual traditions, repeatedly asking yourself the question "Who am I?" or a variation such as "Who is carrying this body?" is the central practice offered for awakening. Teachers such as Ramana Maharshi and great Zen masters from China and Japan have used the repetition of this simple and profound question to guide students to discover their true nature. In the end, it is a question we must all ask ourselves. Without being aware of it, you take many things as your identity: your body, your race, your beliefs, your thoughts. Yet very quickly, with sincere questioning, you will find yourself sensing a deeper level of truth.

The question "Who am I?" can be asked alone in your own meditation practice, and it can also be done with a partner. One of the most effective ways to inquire into this question is to sit together with another person and ask this question over and over, letting the answers deepen as you go on. See Exhibit 12.2.

EXHIBIT 12.2.
Who Am I?

To do this, let yourself sit comfortably facing a partner, prepared to meditate together for 30 minutes. Decide who will ask the question for the first 15 minutes. Look at your partner in a relaxed way and then allow the questioner to begin asking the question, "Who are you?" Let the answers from the person responding arise naturally, saying whatever comes to mind. Once an answer has been given, after a brief pause, the questioner can ask again, "Who are you?" Continue asking this question over and over for a full 15 minutes. Then you can switch roles, giving your partner equal time.

As this question is repeated, all sorts of answers may arise. You may first find yourself saying, "I am a man," or "I am a woman," or "I am a father," "I am a nurse," "I am a teacher," "I am a meditator." Then your

(continued)

(continued)

answers may become more interesting: "I am a mirror," "I am love," "I am a fool," "I am alive." Or whatever.

The answers themselves do not matter, they are part of a deepening process. Just keep gently listening for an answer each time you are asked. If no answer arises, stay with that empty space until one comes. If confusion, fear, laughter, or tears arise, stay with them too. Keep answering anyway. Keep letting go into the process. Let yourself enjoy this meditation.

Even in this short time your whole perspective can change and you can discover more about who you truly are.

Source: Kornfield (1993), pp. 213-214

After completing the meditation in Exhibit 12.2, sort out your responses in relation to the question of joining a community. You may long for an ideal community—one that can listen to, understand, and accept every important aspect of yourself. More realistically, you can benefit from a community that accepts most aspects of yourself, but if an important aspect remains hidden for fear of rejection, or is in fact rejected, you may need to seek another community in which that aspect of yourself can be recognized and acknowledged. It may be helpful to list all of the important aspects of yourself that emerge during this exercise, and systematically survey them as you consider a particular community.

Step One

If you haven't already done so, make a list of all the important aspects of yourself that emerged during this exercise. For convenience, choose one word, or an initial, that will refer you to each "aspect" of yourself on this list, or simply number the list, and refer to it.

Step Two

A. If you have one or more specific communities you are considering joining or becoming involved in as a source of support for your spiritual journey, list those systematically.

B. If you do not have particular communities in mind for possible spiritual support, make a separate list of your most important reference groups at present (e.g., "my work group," "friends from college," "long-time friend").

Step Three

Using each of the possible communities as headings, place under each heading the numbers, or the reference words, that refer to aspects of yourself that you believe you could be open about within that community. Are any aspects of yourself totally left out? An aspects for which you have no community that you believe you can be open about them?

Continuing the Work

Hopefully doing the previous steps has provided some awareness of where you presently stand in relationship to potential communities. There is no simple way to process and use this information; your choice of what community or communities to get more invested in may involve factors not surveyed here, and may emerge intuitively rather than by some calculation of what aspects are accepted, hidden, or left out. But be conscious that those aspects of yourself that are left out by your reference groups may produce shame or hiding. A vital and full spirituality involves bringing your *whole* self before the divine.

It may be especially important to find one person with whom you can share any hidden parts, either a close friend or a counselor. In exploring those parts, you may want to ask a friend for ideas of other interpersonal relationships you might develop that would allow those hidden parts to become more open.

GIVING AND RECEIVING FROM OTHERS

In this section the focus is shifted from community to a dyad, a deep interpersonal friendship or committed relationship. Experiments 3, 4, and 5 are designed to be experienced with a person you trust: a friend, partner, or family member.

Cautions

The only caution that needs noting is that if you choose to involve a friend or partner (which can be very helpful in this section), select someone you know well and trust. If no such person lives near you who can join you in these, you might consider involving someone nearby whom you are beginning to trust—but simply ask that person to help you with one particular experiment. Before you ask, read through Experiments 3 and 4, and decide which one you'd be more comfortable doing with that person. Then ask him or her just for that experiment. If it works out well, you can ask if he or she would like to do more with you another time. The experiments in this section are likely, if you are ready, to intensify the intimacy of the relationship.

Experiment 3: Being Really Present

The following exercises can be done with a person you trust, but they can also be done alone, as a way of expanding your awareness of your relationships with others.

Breathing Experiment for Two

See Exhibit 12.3.

EXHIBIT 12.3.
Being Really Present: Breathing Experiment for Two

In this exercise the person with whom we wish to make contact ("partner") is requested to lie comfortably on a bed or on the floor as is suitable, with his or her clothes and belts loosened, glasses removed, arms laid gently by the sides, legs uncrossed—open-bodied. The partner is instructed to just breathe naturally. There is nothing you need to do but feel what is happening.

(continued)

(continued)

The "follower": To encourage a recognition that the partner's experience, no matter how mundane or remarkable, is totally the person's own, the follower should sit next to but not touch the person lying down. If the meditation takes the partner to the nondualistic space beyond old mind, he or she will not think it was due to some intervention on your part, some magic done on him or her, but will sense its rise within as dependent only on himself or herself.

Sitting approximate to the partner's midsection, let your eyes focus on the rise and fall of his or her abdomen with the inhalation and exhalation of each breath. Encourage the person to breathe naturally, not to control the breath or to hold or shape it, but to allow it to be naturally comfortable. Without further communication, allow yourself to let go of your normal breath rhythm and begin to breathe as the other person breathes. As you notice the other's abdomen rising, inhale. As you notice the abdomen falling, exhale. Completely let go of your breath and take on the partner's respiration rate. Breathe his or her breath in your body.

It is important that once you tune in to another's breath, you do not "lock in," but keep the eyes steadily focused on the rising and falling abdomen of the person lying down, so that you can be attuned to even the subtle changes within the person's respiration, as different states of mind and different feelings come and go. Even if a state of great peace comes over you, do not close your eyes and disconnect from your partner. Let your attention be very closely attuned to even the subtlest changes in the rising and falling of your partner's abdomen so that your breath too can accommodate these changes.

Taking a few breaths, perhaps eight or ten, begin to breathe his or her breath in your own body. As you both exhale, allow yourself to make the sound ahhh with each exhalation, allow this sound to drop deeper and deeper into your body until your belly breathes the ahhh of your partner's exhalation. It is important that the other person is able to hear your ahhh, that it is audible and clear. Don't float off into some inaudible whispered ahhh, which may be pleasant to you but breaks connection with your partner.

Each mutual in-breath is taken silently. As your partner lying before you exhales silently, from your belly, past the heart, out of the mouth comes this great sound of letting go, the deep ahhh of release to be heard by your partner as if it were his or her own. The person lying down need not make any sound.

As with all of these meditations, it is important to make them your own—any type of experimentation is valid. But for the first half dozen

(continued)

(continued)

times you do it with someone, allow your partner to maintain silence and encourage the deepest ahhh, the deepest letting go of that profound sound within.

Maintain this breath connection, breathing your partner's breath in your body, making ahhh on the exhale, for as long as it is comfortable. In the course of this practice, any number of states of mind may arise. Some feel a peace beyond understanding. Others moving toward this peace notice fears of intimacy, sexual energy, doubt, arising and dissolving momentarily in the breath.

Just stay gently with it. But let your partner know that he or she is in control, and anytime your partner wishes to stop the exercise, he or she need only silently raise a hand and you will stop. No force here, just an allowing of the miracle of the heart to present itself as it will and demonstrate how profoundly we share being.

This deceptively simple practice has been found to be of exceptional use to many. In hospitals we are familiar with numerous nurses and physicians who use this practice with those who are in considerable anxiety or tension. For those unable to sleep in a hospital environment, many may discover that halfway through the meditation their partner is snoring comfortably. Let it be. Don't force conclusions. Allow the meditation to be the teacher. Any preconceptions are just to be seen as another thought, another bubble floating through the overlapping vastness of a shared reality. Some speak of not being able to tell whose feeling it was that arose at any point along the process of this practice. Conversation after the exercise about what was happening during different stages often allows the connections to deepen that much further. This is an aspect of its potential to deepen relationships.

Source: Adapted from Levine (1987), pp. 58-60.

Experiment 4: A Forgiveness Meditation

Experiment 4 is especially valuable for persons who are still hurting from a broken relationship, but it can be valuable to anyone who has been in a relationship and has unfinished issues that need forgiving. This is to be read slowly to a friend or silently to yourself. See Exhibit 12.4.

EXHIBIT 12.4.
A Forgiveness Meditation

Begin to reflect for a moment on what the word forgiveness might mean. What is forgiveness? What might it be to bring forgiveness into one's life, into one's mind?

Begin by slowly bringing into your mind, into your heart, the image of someone for whom you have some resentment. Gently allow a picture, a feeling, a sense of that person, to gather here. Gently now invite that person into your heart just for this moment.

Notice whatever fear or anger may arise to limit or deny their entrance and soften gently all about it. No force. Just an experiment in truth that invites this person in.

And silently in your heart say to this person, "I forgive you."

Open to a sense of his or her presence and say, "I forgive you for whatever pain you may have caused me in the past, intentionally or unintentionally, through your words, your thoughts, your actions. However you may have caused me pain in the past, I forgive you."

Feel for even a moment the spaciousness relating to that person with the possibility of forgiveness.

Let go of those walls, those curtains of resentment, so that your heart may be free. So that your life may be lighter.

"I forgive you for whatever you may have done that caused me pain, intentionally or unintentionally, through your actions, through your words, even through your thoughts, through whatever you did. Through whatever you didn't do. However the pain came to me through you, I forgive you. I forgive you."

It is so painful to put someone out of your heart. Let go of that pain. Let them be touched for this moment at least with the warmth of your forgiveness.

"I forgive you. I forgive you."

Allow that person to just be there in the stillness, in the warmth and patience of the heart. Let him or her be forgiven. Let the distance between you dissolve in mercy and compassion.

Let it be so.

And now gently, giving yourself whatever time is necessary, allow the other person to dissolve as you invite another in. Having finished so much business, dissolved in forgiveness, allow that being to go on their way. Not pushing or pulling them from the heart, but simply letting the person be on his or her own way, touched by a blessing and the possibility of your forgiveness . . .

Now gently bring into your mind, into your heart, the sense of someone who has resentment for you. Someone whose heart is closed to you.

(continued)

(continued)

Notice whatever limits his or her entrance and soften all about that hardness. Let it float. Mercifully invite the person into your heart and say to them, "I ask your forgiveness."

"I ask your forgiveness."

"I ask to be let back into your heart. That you forgive me for whatever I may have done in the past that caused you pain, intentionally or unintentionally, through my word, my actions, even through my thoughts."

"However I may have hurt or injured you, whatever confusion, whatever fear of mind caused you pain, I ask your forgiveness."

And allow yourself to be touched by their forgiveness. Allow yourself to be forgiven. Allow yourself back into their heart.

Have mercy on you. Have mercy on them. Allow them to forgive you.

Feel their forgiveness touch you. Receive it. Draw it into your heart

"I ask your forgiveness for however I may have caused you pain in the past. Through my anger, through my lust, through my fear, my ignorance, my blindness, my doubt, my confusion. However I may have caused you pain, I ask that you let me back into your heart. I ask your forgiveness."

Let it be. Allow yourself to be forgiven.

If the mind attempts to block forgiveness with merciless indictments, recriminations, judgments, just see the nature of the unkind mind. See how merciless we are with ourselves. And let this unkind mind be touched by the warmth and patience of forgiveness.

Let your heart touch this other heart so that it may receive forgiveness.

So that it may feel whole again.

Let it be so.

Feel their forgiveness now as it touches you.

If the mind pulls back, thinks it deserves to suffer, see this merciless mind. Let it sink into the heart. Allow yourself to be touched by the possibility of forgiveness.

Receive the forgiveness.

Let it be.

And now gently bid that person adieu and with a blessing let them be on their way, having even for a millisecond shared the one heart beyond the confusion of seemingly separate minds.

And now gently turn to yourself in your own heart and say, " I forgive you," to you.

It is so painful to put ourselves out of our hearts.

Say, " I forgive you," to yourself.

Calling out to yourself in your heart, using your own first name say, "I forgive you" to you.

(continued)

(continued)

If the mind interposes with hard thoughts, such as that it is self-indulgent to forgive oneself, if it judges, if it touches you with anger and unkindness, just feel that hardness and let it soften at the edge. Let it be touched by forgiveness.

Allow yourself back into your heart. Allow you to be forgiven by you.

Let the world back into your heart. Allow yourself to be forgiven.

Let that forgiveness fill your whole body.

Feel the warmth and care that wishes your own well-being. Seeing yourself as if you were your only child, let yourself be bathed by this mercy and kindness.

Let yourself be loved. See your forgiveness forever awaiting your return to your heart

How unkind we are to ourselves. How little mercy. Let it go. Allow you to embrace yourself with forgiveness. Know that in this moment you are wholly and completely forgiven. Now it is up to you just to allow it in. See yourself in the infinitely compassionate eyes of the Buddha, in the sacred heart of Jesus, in the warm embrace of the Goddess.

Let yourself be loved. Let yourself be love.

And now begin to share this miracle of forgiveness, of mercy and awareness. Let it extend out to all the people around you.

Let all be touched by the power of forgiveness. All those beings who also have known such pain. Who have so often put themselves and others out of their hearts. Who have so often felt so isolated, so lost.

Touch them with your forgiveness, with your mercy and loving kindness, that they too may be healed just as you wish to be.

Feel the heart we all share filled with forgiveness so that we all might be whole.

Let the mercy keep radiating outward until it encompasses the whole planet. The whole planet floating in your heart, in mercy, in loving kindness, in care.

May all sentient beings be freed of their suffering, of their anger, of their confusion, of their fear, of their doubt.

May all beings know the joy of their true nature.

May all beings be free from suffering.

The whole world floating in the heart. All beings freed of their suffering. All beings' hearts open, minds clear. All beings as peace.

May all beings at every level of reality, on every plane of existence, may they all be freed of their suffering. May they all be at peace.

May we heal the world, touching it again and again with forgiveness. May we heal our hearts and the hearts of those we love by merging in forgiveness, by merging in peace.

Source: Adapted from Levine (1987), pp. 98-101.

If you have just completed the exercise in Exhibit 12.4 with someone you had not been close to, do the following:

Step One

Suggest to that person that you each spend a few moments writing down your reactions, in your own "journals."

Step Two

After you have done that, suggest that you each mark "okay" any of what you have journaled if it's something you would feel comfortable sharing, something you want to share as a way of continuing the intimacy that you have felt between you.

Step Three

Let your partner know if you have something you would like to share, and ask if he or she feels ready to listen, or would rather end at this point. If your partner is ready, go ahead. After sharing, be sure to ask whether your partner wanted to share anything. After the two of you have finished, it may be useful for you to continue doing some journaling.

Experiment 5: Meditation—Transforming Sorrow into Compassion

Introduction

When we feel distanced or out of touch with others, one of the easiest ways to connect is with compassion for their pain and sorrow. Often (not always) the anger we feel toward others is a result of our defense against our own pain; they have hurt us, and it's easier to project the emotion and blame them, than to be vulnerable and feel our own pain. This meditation teaches us to gradually, gently, extend the compassion to broader and broader circles of humanity. See Exhibit 12.5.

EXHIBIT 12.5.
Meditation—Transforming Sorrow into Compassion

The human heart has the extraordinary capacity to hold and transform the sorrows of life into a great stream of compassion. It is the gift of figures such as Buddha, Jesus, Mother Mary, and Kwan Yin, the Goddess of Mercy, to proclaim the power of this tender and merciful heart in the face of all the suffering of the world. Whenever your own heart is open and uncovered, the awakening of this stream of compassion begins within. Compassion arises when you allow your heart to be touched by the pain and need of another.

To cultivate this quality, you may wish to practice the traditional meditation for the practice of compassion and for the transformation of sorrows in the fire of the heart.

Let yourself sit still in a centered and quiet way. Breathe softly and feel your body, your heartbeat, the life force within you. Feel how you treasure your own life, how you guard yourself in the face of your sorrows. After some time, bring to mind someone close to you whom you dearly love. Picture this person and your caring for him or her. Share in the person's pain, and meet it with compassion.

This is the natural response of the heart. Along with this response, begin to actively wish him or her well, reciting the traditional phrases, "May you be free from pain and sorrow, may you be at peace," while holding him or her in your heart of compassion.

Continue reciting these phrases in this way for some time.

Notice how you can hold the person in your heart. Then let yourself be aware of his or her sorrows, his or her measure of suffering in this life. Feel how your heart opens naturally, moving toward the person to wish him or her well, to extend comfort.

As you learn to feel your deep caring for this person close to you, you can then extend this compassion to others you know, one at a time. Gradually you can open your compassion further, to your neighbors, to all those who live far away, and finally to the brotherhood and sisterhood of all beings. Let yourself feel how the beauty of every being brings you joy and how the suffering of any being makes you weep. Feel your tenderhearted connection with all life and its creatures, how it moves with their sorrows and holds them in compassion.

Now let your heart become a transformer for the sorrows of the world. Feel your breath in the area of your heart, as if you could breathe gently in and out of your heart. Feel the kindness of your heart and envision that

(continued)

(continued)

with each breath you can breathe in pain and breathe out compassion. Start to breathe in the sorrows of all living beings. With each in-breath, let their sorrows touch your heart and turn into compassion. With each out-breath wish all living beings well, extend your caring and merciful heart to them.

As you breathe, begin to envision your heart as a purifying fire that can receive the pains of the world and transform them into the light and warmth of compassion. This is a powerful meditation that will require some practice. Be gentle with yourself. Let the fire of your heart burn gently in your chest. Breathe in the sorrows of those who are hungry. Breathe in the sorrows of those who are caught in war. Breathe in the sorrows of ignorance. With each out-breath, picture living beings everywhere and breathe out the healing balm of compassion. With every gentle in-breath, over and over, let the sorrows of every form of life touch your heart. With every out-breath, over and over, extend the mercy and healing of compassion. Like the mother of the world, bring the world into your heart, inviting all beings to touch you with each breath in, embracing all beings in compassion with each breath out.

After some time, sit quietly and let your breath and heart rest naturally, as a center of compassion in the midst of the world.

Source: Adapted from Kornfield (1993), pp. 226-227.

MAKING A CONTRIBUTION

Experiment 6: Meditation on Service

Introduction

Discovering where you are needed involves opening yourself to hear the needs of the world. In that sense, it involves being receptive to the sounds and sights outside you. It also means listening to yourself, and learning to accept your own strengths and special gifts. This meditation is intended to be done alone, to help you with both looking in and looking out. See Exhibit 12.6.

EXHIBIT 12.6.
Meditation on Service

Step One

Pick a quiet time. Let yourself sit comfortably, being at ease and yet awake. Feel your body sitting and feel the gentle movement of your breath. Let your mind be clear and your heart be soft. Reflect on the bounteous gifts and blessings that support all human life: the rain, the plants of the earth, the warm sunshine. Bring to mind the many human benefactors: the farmers, parents, laborers, healers, postal workers, teachers, the whole society around you. As you feel the world around you, be aware of its problems as well: the needs of its people, its animals, and its environment. Let yourself feel the movement in your heart that wishes to contribute, the joy that could come with offering of your own unique gift to the world.

Step Two

Then, when you are ready, pose the following questions inwardly to yourself. Pause after each one and give your heart time to answer, allowing a response from the deepest level of your compassion and wisdom.

Imagine yourself five years from now as you would most like to be, having done all the things you want to have done, having contributed all the things you want to contribute in the most heartfelt way. What is your greatest source of happiness? What is the thing you've done by which you feel the world is most blessed? What is the contribution you could make to the world that would give you the most satisfaction? To make this contribution to the world, what unworthiness would you have to relinquish? To make this contribution to the world, what strengths and capacities would you have to recognize in yourself and others? What would you have to do in your life today to begin this service, this contribution? Why not begin?

Source: Adapted from Kornfield (1993), pp. 302-303

Experiment 7: Meditation on Equanimity, Accepting What Can't be Changed

Introduction

Even when we have heard and accepted a form of calling to service, we need to learn to accept both what we are, and what we are not able to accomplish. This mediation by Jack Kornfield calls upon the "serenity" prayer, which was discussed in Chapter 3.[1] See Exhibit 12.7

EXHIBIT 12.7.
Meditation on Equanimity,
Accepting What Can't be Changed

Equanimity is a wonderful quality, a spaciousness and balance of heart. Although it grows naturally with our meditation practice, equanimity can also be cultivated in the same systematic way that we have used for loving kindness and compassion. We can feel this possibility of balance in our hearts in the midst of all life when we recognize that life is not in our control. We are a small part of a great dance. Even though we may cultivate a boundless compassion for others and strive to alleviate suffering in the world, we still will be unable to affect many situations. The well-known serenity prayer says, "May I have the serenity to accept the things I cannot change, the courage to change the things I can, and the wisdom to know the difference." Wisdom recognizes that all beings are heir to their own karma, that they each act and receive the fruits of their actions. We can deeply love others and offer them assistance, but in the end they must learn for themselves, they must be the source of their own liberation. Equanimity combines an understanding mind together with a compassionate heart.

To cultivate equanimity, sit in a comfortable posture with your eyes closed. Bring a soft attention to your breath until your body and mind are calm. Then begin by reflecting on the benefit of a mind that has balance and equanimity. Sense what a gift it can be to bring a peaceful heart to the world around you. Let yourself feel an inner sense of balance and ease. Then begin repeating such phrases as "May I be balanced and at peace." Acknowledge that all created things arise and pass away: joys, sorrows, pleasant events, people, buildings, animals, nations, even

(continued)

(continued)

whole civilizations. Let yourself rest in the midst of them. May I learn to see the rising and passing of all nature with equanimity and balance. May I be open and balanced and peaceful. Acknowledge that all beings are heirs to their own karma, that their lives arise and pass away according to conditions and deeds created by them. May I bring compassion and equanimity to the events of the world. May I find balance and equanimity and peace.

Source: Kornfield (1993), p. 331.

Chapter 13

Seeking the Spiritual Dimension

When we attempt to center the self, not everything is in the control of the conscious ego. We have some control, but we need outside perspectives to become aware of parts of ourselves that we have hidden from our conscious self. When we shift our focus to others, as the last exercise in the previous chapter showed us, we are in dialogue, and can be responsible only for our side of the dialogue. We can practice really listening, but when parts of ourselves are triggered that react defensively, we need to return our focus to soothing, or temporarily separating from, those parts in order to maintain the contact with the other person.

But as we move toward encounter with the sacred and growth in the spiritual, we seek to have all of our parts accepted and exposed. The role of the ego is much different. The process is mostly one of surrendering control, rather than maintaining control.

This is true even in deep personal relationships with another human. As we really learn to trust, we stop trying to control. In a very real sense, this is true in self-exploration. Eventually, as we mature, we approach our self with curiosity; "What new and surprising thing are you going to display to me today?"

So growth and control are only remotely co-related, and yet we have a sense in which the "self" is present, and takes a stand. It involves submission: "Here I am Lord, take me." But it is not simply submission as in a lord and master relationship; that is, the self is not obliterated. It can stand before the holy with authenticity. My purpose here is simply to state this issue. Various personality theories have grappled with the issue, and used different words to try to point to the authentic self that is more than the defending self, the Self with a capital "S" that is open to the Whole, etc. Once again, when we enter the space of experience and meditation, words fail us, and the reader is cautioned, when following these exercises, to not let the words hang you up. Stay with the experience.

Over many years I have regularly kept a spiritual journal. In an entry some years back, I was trying to articulate how we work out our values. What I wrote seems to apply here, to the broader question of how we interact with the holy, the spiritual. To quote my journal:

> It's some mixture of experimenting and listening. Both putting out, trying things, and being open and receiving. I seldom hear answers in words. I sometimes get the feelings, including the reassurances, in visions of color, in imagery. I meditate through movement. Static meditation only helps me for a period of relaxing, being receptive. But the real taking in comes with the movement.

But, once again the caution. My way may not be your way. We can learn from one another, and we can get feedback from the spiritual communities that we chose, but, ultimately, we must each find *our* way, the way we are called to walk.

EMPTYING THE SELF

Introduction and Concerns

The value of emptying or surrendering the self is recognized in both Buddhist and Christian thought, as well as in secular use of meditation, and in psychotherapeutic techniques such as "clearing a space" (focusing) (see Gendlin, 1978, or Hinterkopf, 1998) and "asking parts to step back" (Internal Family Systems).

Jesus states, "For whoever would save his life will lose it, and whoever loses his life for my sake will find it" (Matthew 16:25; Mark 8:35; Luke 9:24, RSV). However, this concept is paradoxical, and can easily be misused or misunderstood in ways that reinforce a negative view of self. Emptiness can be confused with impoverishment, a withdrawal from life rather than a liberating freedom (Kornfield, 1993). The American Buddhist teacher Jack Kornfield (1993) begins his excellent chapter titled "No Self or True Self" with a succinct statement of the paradox:

> There are two parallel tasks in spiritual life. One is to discover selflessness, the other is to develop a healthy sense of self, to discover what is meant by *true self.* Both sides of this apparent paradox must be fulfilled for us to awaken (p. 205).
>
> If we have a deficient sense of self, if we perennially negate ourselves, we may easily confuse our inner poverty with selflessness, and believe it is the road to enlightenment (Kornfield, 1993, p. 204).

For some people the concept of emptying the self, of surrendering the self or giving the self away, seems scary. It is very hard to find the right words for the experience—and perhaps there are different experiences for different people. We have moments when we reach a sense of "no ego," no self in the sense of not needing to be defensive or have any walls. Some may experience a further shift to no boundaries—being "one" with the universe. Others may feel a loss of boundaries, but a spectator self exists who is aware of the experience. However, that self is not an "I" or "ego" that is separate from the experience.[1] Perhaps the central element of the experience is the letting go of one's self-concept, being open to the experience itself rather than preconceived views of what the reality of the experience must be.

Some people feel negative connotations in the phrases *emptying* or *surrendering,* but are comfortable with the images of "at one" or "totally open."

Concepts of Emptiness

It is clear that Jesus did not intend that his followers berate or devalue themselves. His summary of the Torah (Law) was, "You shall love the Lord your God with all your heart, and love your neighbor as yourself" (as cited in Matthew 19:19, 22:39; Mark 12:31,33; Luke 10:27, RSV). To love your neighbor as yourself implies that one should love oneself.

Similarly, both Kornfield and Welwood, in presenting the central teachings of Buddhism to Westerners, caution against "trying to make a 'spiritual bypass' around life's problems" (Kornfield, 1993, p. 203; the phrase *spiritual bypassing* was coined by Welwood, 2000). These two books provide valuable discussions of the complex interaction between personal or psychological work and spiritual process. The desire

> to find release from the earthly structures that seem to entrap us . . . has been a central motive in the spiritual search for thousands of years. So there is often a tendency to use spiritual practice to try to rise above our emotional and personal issues—all those messy, unresolved matters that weigh us down. (Welwood, 2000, pp. 11-12)

It is generally agreed by those who seek to integrate spirituality and counseling or psychotherapy that the task of self-development cannot be skirted or leaped over in the process of spiritual development. Stated another way, "You must be somebody before you can be nobody" (Kornfield, 1993, p. 205). Even apart from psychotherapy, research in human development has suggested that transcending self, at least in the sense of the ability to connect with others in a caring and mutually valuable way, is correlated with the maturation of an authentic self (Orlofsky, Marcia, & Lester, 1973).

The Practice of Emptying, Opening

Whatever fears the concept of emptying yourself may evoke, let me assure you that the practice is unlikely to be sudden and revolutionary. All of our habits work against giving up our mental chattering, our distracting ourselves, our settling down to real quietness, openness, peace. The concept may be radical, but the practice is slow and steady and safe.

In this section, following the conceptual material, are five exercises. The first (Experiment 1) is an early experiment in meditation. It is followed by more guided exercises, one (Experiment 2) in monotheistic language (which may be easier for persons of Jewish, Christian, or Islamic backgrounds to relate to), and one (Experiment 3) in language that is neutral about (does not assume) belief in God (Buddhist). Experiments 4 and 5 are in secular language and are based on two psychotherapeutic traditions, focusing (Experiment 4), and Internal Family Systems (Experiment 5). The practice(s) have roots in the different religious traditions, but it is not important to know those roots if religious traditions have negative implications in your personal history. Skip the next paragraph if this is the case.

In the Western religions, the practice is associated with the giving up of willfulness, epitomized in the prayer of Jesus in the garden of Gethsemane, "not my will, but Thine, be done." It is helpful to realize that this prayer, in most of the gospels, follows three years of Jesus' movement between prayer and ministry, beginning after the baptism with a period of dealing with temptations in the wilderness, and moving beyond them. A parallel experience is depicted in the life of Gautama (The Buddha)—again an experience of temptation by Mara, a devil-like character—and years of discipline, teaching, and meditation, culminating in the experience of Awareness or Enlightenment.

In some of the exercises that follow, I use the word *meditation* to indicate a discipline of self study and emptying of self because it seems to have become a more acceptable word across many traditions than is the word prayer. Historically, meditation was a carefully developed discipline in the Hindu and the Buddhist traditions, but the word was also used in some of the Western religions, and the word seems to be acceptable to secular humanists and to spiritual atheists in a way that the word "prayer" is not.

However, I know of several humanists or atheists who regularly pray. Prayer may be a valuable spiritual practice even for those who do not believe in the traditional personal God who will intervene in response to prayers of intercession. Persons with deep spiritual longings, but with secular beliefs, may pray to express their longings (Keen, 1994, *xvi-xvii*). One of the exercises (Experiment 2) in this chapter is a prayer of self-surrender. Another exercise (Experiment 4) uses the therapeutic method based on Gendlin's (1978) focusing, and on R. Schwartz's "putting parts of the self aside" (Goulding & Schwartz, 1995).

It may be easiest to begin with the experiment that is most familiar to your own previous tradition or practice. But I would strongly encourage[2] the reader to try each of the experiments, both to explore expanding one's own practice, and to have some experience in the approaches that may be most familiar to some of your clients or prospective clients. Keep in mind that it may take repeated use of a new method to eventually recognize the contribution it is making in your life.

Note to Those Who Already Practice Meditation

The following section, and Experiment 1, are written so that persons with no experience in meditation will be able to follow. If you already practice meditation, feel free to revise the experiment to fit your level of practice. However, I suggest you read the following section and consider exploring some options that have not fit into your particular form of practice.

Concepts regarding Meditation

"Precise and deep meditation shows us emptiness everywhere" (Kornfield, 1993, p. 201). Beginning meditation cannot hope to do so, and this experiment is intended only as an introduction, or an appetizer that I hope will lead you to read much more on meditation (see Appendix) and consider practicing some form of meditation. Meditation is often misperceived to involve a particular experience of concentration and intensity. Instead, in this beginning practice, I suggest you focus on letting go.

It is helpful to experiment with different ways of doing meditation to determine what works best for you. A number of my closest friends and fellow psychotherapists are far more experienced meditators than I am, and some of them believe that traditional sitting meditation works best for introverts, while extroverts often do better with moving meditation. Several choices need to be made that can be thought of as levels of stimulation. Do you choose to meditate:

- *Standing, with slow movement (tai chi, walking meditation), or seated and still?* If seated, you need to explore whether the traditional lotus position is comfortable for you, usually with a cushion that allows your seat to be slightly higher than your feet. If you prefer to sit in a chair, it's usually best *not* to be relaxing into the back of the chair, but to have to maintain the upright back and head. This requires you to stay alert, and when/if you do become drowsy, the early sense that you are losing your balance will bring you back to alertness.
- *With your eyes open or closed?* The traditional position is to have the eyes partially closed with a soft focus on the ground about six feet in front of you. But if you tend to get drowsy, it may help to close your lids but turn your eyes upward, which for

most people reduces the tendency to fall asleep. Some forms of meditation involve gazing at a meditative object such as a mandala. A variation, if you are outdoors or near a window, is to look at one point in a natural setting. You will have to experiment to see if the visual stimulation enhances your meditation, or distracts you. If I am meditating with the intention of reminding myself of my place in the whole of life, nature often enhances my meditation. If I am emptying myself, I do better without the visual stimulation.

- *With or without words?* The process of meditation at first makes us very aware of the constant chatter of words that goes on in most of our minds. The most common beginning meditation is to pay attention to your breathing. The focus on the breath, in the nose, throat, lungs, and the muscles of the belly, may provide a sensual focus that leads us away from the words. Sometimes a single word or a simple phrase is helpful: a word that has sacred meaning to you, such as "love," or the holy Buddhist word "Ohm." At times a simple phrase will come to me in the meditation, and repeating the phrase is helpful.

I hope that these options help those who are new at meditation to realize that it does not need to be a highly regimented and uniform practice. You can bring your own self, your creativity, to the practice. This is not to deny that discipline is needed—especially the discipline of making time for regular meditation. One of my friends tells of a particular meditation that he believed could be helpful to him, but he had to practice it repeatedly for two or three months. Then suddenly it had a profound effect.

Experiment 1: Beginning Meditation

Step One

Find a place were you can be alone, unobserved and unheard. Before you actually begin the meditation, simply sit and be aware of what comes to your mind. Allow yourself five to ten minutes in which you may jot down some notes of the unfinished business that at first preoccupies the mind. Things you haven't done, things you have forgotten, write them down so it's easier to let them go.

Step Two

Now put aside your paper, and just observe the busy mind that wants to keep doing, accomplishing. Let go of "doing" anything with the thoughts or feelings that emerge. If it helps your observation to label the process, simply label the ideas "planning," or "remembering," or "judging," as you sense yourself reacting in these ways.

Step Three

As you experience each thought or feeling or image, briefly label it, but then let it go. I picture this as watching thoughts, feelings, images swim by like small fish, and noticing them, but not stopping them—simply let them pass out of your vision. Usually we pursue thoughts, allowing them to develop, chattering away in sentences inside our heads. In this meditation, we briefly hear the thoughts, but we don't pursue them, we let them go. The practice here is simply to be aware—not to change or control or pursue anything. Just notice what goes on in your body and mind, and let the noticing itself be the only change. Let go of all attempts to hang on to thoughts or feelings. Simply experience what is, without trying to change or control it.

Step Four

If it feels comfortable, simply allow yourself to sink gently, slowly, into simply *being,* without effort or thought.

Experiment 2: Prayer of Self-Surrender

Some spiritual people who reject traditional concepts of God have difficulty with prayer, because they associate it with beliefs in an external being who will grant special favors to those who say the right things or make requests in a particular way. I would encourage readers with such concerns to read the following as a dramatic form. The advantage of this dramatic form is that it encourages us to express ourselves in much the way we would talk to someone who is physically present. This face-to-face style promotes highly personal expression. Surely the divine is open to the most personal forms of expression.

Step One

Silently read each of the sentences of the following prayer. Cross out any that don't seem right for you, so that what remains is to some degree your own composition. Of course you may add lines, if you like.

Step Two

Find a place where you can be alone and not be heard, and read the prayer aloud. (Read only the sentences you have chosen to retain.) When a sentence strikes a chord in you, read it again—perhaps a bit louder. Allow the resonance to flow (see Exhibit 13.1)

EXHIBIT 13.1.
Prayer of Self-Surrender

Oh God
Oh Heavenly Father
Holy Mother
Divine Spirit
Compassionate Guide
Help me to silence my own desires, and simply be in Your presence.
Take from me the ego that constantly intrudes and fails to rest quietly and humbly in Thy Presence.
Drain from me the tensions, the defensiveness, that wall me off from being absorbed in Thee.
Take from me the restlessness that keeps me from lying peacefully amid all that is Holy.
Help me to breathe easy, not trying to prop myself up, simply trusting in Thy Grace.
Open me to feel Your love and acceptance, so that I have no need to prove myself.
Empty me of all assertions and claims that divide me from You.
Breathe Your breath into me. Hollow me out as a vessel, and fill me with Your Love.
With each outflowing breath, empty me, so that, with each incoming breath, I may take in and be filled by Your Love.
And in the silence that follows, let me rest in Thee.
Amen.

Experiment 3: Healing Through Sensing Life-Giving Emptiness

The Buddhist understanding of emptiness is not that of Western physics; emptiness does not imply a vacuum. Emptiness is nearly synonymous with openness, having porous boundaries, and being connected to all things. An abbreviated quote from Kornfield's (1993) section on "Healing through Emptiness" may clarify:

> In Buddhist teaching, "emptiness" refers to a basic openness and nonseparation that we experience when all small and fixed notions of our self are seen through or dissolved. We experience it when we see that our existence is transitory, that our body, heart, and mind arise out of the changing web of life, where nothing is disconnected or separate. The deepest experiences in meditation lead us to an intimate awareness of life's essential openness and emptiness, of its everchanging and unpossessable nature, of its nature as an unstoppable process. . . .
>
> We ourselves are a process, woven together with life, without separateness. We arise like a wave out of the ocean of life, our tentative forms still one with the ocean. Some traditions call this ocean the Tao, the divine, the fertile void, the unborn. Out of it, our lives appear as reflections of the divine, as a movement or dance of consciousness. The most profound healing comes when we sense this process, this life-giving emptiness.
>
> As our meditation practice deepens, we are able to see the movement of our experience. We note feelings and find that they last for only a few seconds. We pay attention to thoughts and find that they are ephemeral, that they come and go, uninvited, like clouds. We bring our awareness to the body and find that its boundaries are porous. In this practice, our sense of the solidity of a separate body or a separate mind starts to dissolve, and suddenly, unexpectedly, we find out how much at ease we are. As our meditation deepens still further, we experience expansiveness, delight, and the freedom of our interconnectedness with all things, with the great mystery of our life. (Kornfield, 1993, p. 51)

In discovering the healing power of emptiness, we sense that everything is intertwined in a continuous movement, arising in certain forms that we call bodies or thoughts or feelings, and then dissolving or changing into new forms. With this wisdom we can open to one moment after another and live in the everchanging Tao. We discover we can let go and trust, we can let the breath breathe itself and the natural movementof life carry us with ease. (Kornfield, 1993, p. 52).

See Exhibit 13.2 for an exercise in developing a healing attention.

EXHIBIT 13.2.
Developing a Healing Attention

Step One

Sit comfortably and quietly. Let your body rest easily. Breathe gently. Let go of your thoughts, past and future, memories and plans. Just be present. Begin to let your own precious body reveal the places that most need healing. Allow the physical pain, tensions, diseases, or wounds to show themselves.

Step Two

Bring a careful and kind attention to these painful places. Slowly and carefully feel their physical energy. Notice what is deep inside them, the pulsations, throbbing, tension, needles, heat, contraction, aching, that make up what we call pain. Allow these all to be felt fully, to be held in a receptive and kind attention.

Step Three

Then be aware of the surrounding area of your body. If there is contraction and holding, notice this gently. Breathe softly and let it open.

Step Four

Then, in the same way, be aware of any aversion or resistance in your mind. Notice this, too, with a soft attention, without resisting, allowing it to be as it is, allowing it to open in its own time.

Step Five

Now notice the thoughts and fears that accompany the pain you are exploring: "It will never go away," "I can't stand it," "I don't deserve this," "It is too hard, too much trouble, too deep," etc. Let these thoughts rest in your kind attention for a time.

(continued)

(continued)

Step Six

Then gently return to your physical body. Let your awareness be deeper and more allowing now. Again, feel the layers of the place of pain, and allow each layer that opens to move, to intensify or dissolve in its own time. Bring your attention to the pain as if you were gently comforting a child, holding it all in a loving and soothing attention. Breathe softly into it, accepting all that is present with a healing kindness. Continue this meditation until you feel reconnected with whatever part of your body calls you, until you feel at peace.

Later Follow-Up

As your healing attention develops, you can direct it regularly to significant areas of illness of pain in your body. You can then scan your body for additional areas that call for your caring attention. In the same way, you can direct a healing attention to deep emotional wounds you carry. Grief, longing, rage, loneliness, and sorrow can all first be felt in your body. With careful and kind attention, you can feel deep inside them. Stay with them. After some time you can breathe softly and open your attention to each of the layers of contraction, emotions, and thoughts that are carried with them. Finally, you can let these, too, rest as if you were gently comforting a child, accepting all that is present, until you feel at peace. You can work with the heart in this way as often as you wish. Remember, the healing of our body and heart is always here. It simply awaits our compassionate attention.

Source: Adapted from Kornfield (1993), pp. 53-54.

Experiment 4: Clearing a Space

The first step in the counseling process, called "focusing," is to clear a space emotionally. In this structured meditation, I will describe only the first aspect of focusing, which I will divide into substeps. For a readable description of all six steps, see Hinterkopf (1998), Chapter 7. See Exhibit 13.3.

EXHIBIT 13.3.
Clearing a Space

Step One

Take an inventory of the problems or issues that currently provoke troublesome feelings for you. You may want to actually list them on paper.

Step Two

In a gentle, friendly voice, ask yourself, "How am I feeling now?" Name whatever stands in the way of your feeling all okay right now.

Step Three

Check to see how the issue that has emerged as a block feels inside. Sense the whole vague complexity involved in that issue. Notice how the whole issue feels in your body.

Step Four

Now use your imagination and chose a way, visually, to picture setting this problem aside. You might picture setting the problem on the floor, outside yourself. You might put it in a picture frame. Or sealing it up in a box or some other container. However you contain it, you might imagine it gradually moving farther away from you, until it's in a distant corner.

Step Five

When you have contained the problem, and/or moved it aside, ask yourself, "How would it feel if I didn't have that whole issue?" When that feeling has been described, go back to step two and name another issue that seems to stand in the way of your feeling okay.

Repeat the cycle until it feels that all of the problems that matter at the moment have been set aside. (It is not necessary to cover every item on your list, if some issues don't emerge as blocking your feeling okay at this time).

Final Step

When all the issues seem "set aside," stay with the sense that emerges. Some people feel less tense, more relaxed, calm, and centered. You may feel expanded, peaceful, more accepting of yourself or others, and of your life. In this meditation, do not try to go back to one of the problems (which would be the next step of focusing), but just stay in the sense of spaciousness, emptiness.

Source: Adapted from Hinterkopf (1998), pp. 52-53.

Experiment 5: Asking "Parts" to Step Back

A number of therapists have developed counseling approaches that encourage the client to think of himself or herself as having many parts that often function as separate "selves." Almost all of us have had the experience of internally arguing with ourselves, with different "voices" or "parts" in ourselves taking opposing points of view.

Much can be learned by pretending that we are "multiple personalities" and naming and getting to know each of the different "voices" that occur with any frequency in our inner dialogues. It is especially helpful to do this with a close friend, with whom you can share your reactions. It is not suggested that you try to work as a counselor or therapist with the "parts" of your client until you know your own parts well, and until you have supervision in how to safely access and approach clients' parts (see Schwartz, 1995, especially pp. 98-105).

The goal is to help yourself "find the place within from which [you] can reach out and connect with all the parts and listen to their fears and hopes, instead of a place chosen by only the dominant parts" (Goulding & Schwartz, 1995, p. 163). This inner leader comes from a state of "psychophysical centering" involving a somatic and psychological sense of well-being (p. 164).

Caution: Most people who do this experiment find it interesting, helpful, and freeing. A few people may begin to feel a bit anxious or disoriented during steps 3 or 4. If you experience this, feel free to stop the experiment. You may want to go to the section titled "Modifications to Reduce Anxiety" in the Appendix. If it interests you later to try the experiment again, try it with a friend or counselor present. See Exhibit 13.4.

EXHIBIT 13.4.
Asking "Parts" to Step Back

Step One

One procedure for encouraging this state is to picture a room, and to picture your centered self standing outside the room.

(continued)

(continued)

Step Two

When a "part" or feeling seems to make you reactive, or pulls you away from a sense of well-being, focus exclusively on that part, and picture what that part looks like. Once you get an image of that part, put the part in the room by itself, and let your centered self look at the part through a window.

Step Three

Ask yourself how you feel toward the part in the room, and whether you feel anything extreme (anger, envy, extreme sadness, fear hopelessness) toward the part. If you do feel such strong reactive feelings, take this as a sign that another "part" is influencing you.

Step Four

If there are such feelings, address this other part. Go back to step two. Ask that second part to "step away emotionally."

Step Five

Continue in this manner until the self feels alone outside the rooms, experiencing curiosity and compassion or empathy for the parts in the rooms, but does not feel irritation, impatience, anger, or fear.

Step Six

Simply experience this centered self, empty of the reactive and interfering parts.

Source: Constructed from the "room technique," Goulding & Schwartz (1995), p. 151.

In a therapeutic situation, the self in leadership would begin a dialogue of curiosity and empathy to get to know the first part. Gradually the reactive parts would be worked with and "unburdened." R. Schwartz (1995) teaches an emptying of self from "contaminating parts" in order to be open and receptive to others, instead of reactive (see also Goulding & Schwartz, 1995, Chapter 9).

EXPRESSING GRATITUDE

Experiment 6: Giving Thanks for Simple Things (and Contact with What/Who is Around You)

This exercise can be done alone or in a group. If in a group, one person volunteers to slowly read the experiment so all can hear. If alone, read a paragraph, then act it out, then read the next paragraph, then act, and so on.

Step One

Stand and move where room is available to reach in all directions. Close your eyes and place your feet in a solid stance, about as far apart as the end of your shoulders. Leaving your feet stable, let the rest of your body move in any way that loosens it up, helps you feel alive and ready to make some contact with others. Move and make sounds, and just enjoy the movement.

Step Two

Now, slowly let your eyelids open just a slit—so a little light but no clear images come in. Be aware of what this experience is like for you. If it is negative in some ways, allow that. But now, pay attention to what you like about it.

In your mind, silently, give thanks for what you like about the light coming it, the colors you like, any sounds you hear and like.

Now open your eyes, let them wander all around the room. Sense something you are attracted to.

Give thanks for the attraction.

Step Three

Now begin to move toward what attracts you. If others get in the way, or someone you are attracted to moves another direction, feel your feelings, but let them go, and shift to a new attraction.

Stay with your feelings. Don't avoid the negatives or the critical, but concentrate on what interests you, what and who attracts you. And inside yourself, or on your face, silently give thanks.

Continue to move and feel. Move toward what interests or attracts you.

Step Four

Continue to give silent thanks for the very simple things that surround you. Don't limit your thankfulness to big things. Give thanks for the sights, the sounds, that tell you your alive.

And behind these, for the air you breath that keeps you alive.

For the fact that you can see. Hear.

For the fact that you are *not* alone in this world.

Stay in the present, even if these relationships are new and not deep yet—be thankful for them.

Give thanks for the many directions you can reach.

For the potential that is here but not yet fulfilled.

Step Five

Now close your eyes again, and slow down. Feel what is going on in you. What feels unfinished.

Are there any longings that have been stimulated—any potentials that you long to have completed?

Sometimes the deepest sense of the spiritual comes to us in our longings.

Step Six (If in a Group)

Ask yourself is there *anything* in this experience you'd like to share with the group when you open your eyes?

Open yourself to hear the sharing of others.

Then open your eyes and rejoin the group.

Step Six (If Alone):

Get your journal or some writing paper.

First, write down all the reactions that seem significant.

Second, put a mark beside those you wish feel you want to follow up on in some way. Consider ways you can do that.

SEEKING GUIDANCE

Experiment 7: Trading Places with a Spiritual Guide

This experiment has three steps. Begin by reading it all the way through. Try the remember the three parts. See Exhibit 13.5.

EXHIBIT 13.5.
Trading Places with a Spiritual Guide

Step One

Close your eyes and picture yourself in the middle of an instance of one the greatest difficulties of your life. It may be a difficulty at work or it may be in a personal relationship. You can remember it, picture it, imagine it, think about it, feel it—whatever way your own heart and mind best sense it. Let yourself reexperience the scene vividly, the people who are there, the difficulties and how you react to them. Let it reach its worst height. Notice how your body feels in the midst of this and how you act and what state your heart is in.

Step Two

Then imagine you hear a knock on the door that you must answer. Excuse yourself and step outside, where you find waiting for you someone such as the Buddha, Jesus, Mother Mary, or the great Goddess of Universal Compassion. One of these beings has come to visit you. He or she looks at you kindly and asks, "Having a hard day?" "Here," the guide suggests, "Let me trade places with you. Give me your body and let me show you how I might handle this situation. You can remain invisible while I show you what is possible."

So you lend your body to the Goddess, Buddha, Jesus, or whomever, and invisibly follow him or her back into the thick of your difficulties. Let the conversation and problems continue as before, and simply notice what you are being shown. How does Jesus, Buddha, Mary, or whoever

(continued)

(continued)

respond to the situation? With silence? Let the guide show you the way. Stay with the guide while he or she teaches you.

Step Three

Then the guide will excuse himself or herself again for a moment and walk back to the place where you met him or her. The guide lovingly returns your body to you, and before the guide leaves he or she touches you gently in the most healing way and whispers a few words of advice in your ear. Listen to these heartfelt words of wisdom and kindness. Hear them, imagine them, sense them, know them in whatever way you can, and let them be just what you need to live wisely.

Source: Kornfield (1993), pp. 164-165.

Experiment 8: A Messenger

Before beginning this guided imagery, go through whatever procedure helps you to feel physically relaxed. Turn back to the relaxation exercise if this seems appropriate (Chapter 11, Experiment 5).

Magic Carpet

Make yourself comfortable in a seated or lying down position in which you can relax for 20 or 30 minutes.

Experience in some detail the feel of the surface you are sitting or lying on. Be aware of how your body pushes against it. Look around you, and take in what you see, where you are. Be conscious and whisper to yourself, "I am in my house, sitting in this easy chair," or whatever words describe your situation in the here and now.

Now imagine that you are on a magic carpet. In a minute it is going to move you gently to a place in nature that you love. Imagine that very gradually the carpet gently lifts you up, a few inches off the floor, and moves you slowly to the ceiling. The ceiling just fades away and you can see the sky above your house, and gradually the carpet takes you up and up, easing you through a layer of soft white clouds. Your carpet is now just above those clouds, and the clouds are beginning to separate a bit and you can see down below a scene you know, a place you've always liked, either in your travels, or in your imagination. You can see a spread of land that looks lovely, and off a ways, you can see a pleasant woods. The carpet lowers you carefully, slowly, and sets you down in the midst of that spread of land.

Gradually the intuition comes to you that a creature is there for you. This gentle being has something to give you, a special message.

The Special Message

You approach, slowly, not wanting to scare it.

The creature rises, comes toward you—and . . .

. . . places a small object in your hand.

Take time now to feel that object in your hand, to ponder its meaning.

Now the creature says something—only a few words. You can hardly hear them, so you bend down to put your ear nearer. The creature repeats the few words, and by listening very carefully you make out the message. (Pause and listen.)

Then the creature turns, and walks slowly away.

You sit down and take a few minutes, right now, to take this all in.

Now you notice that you've actually sat down on the Magic Carpet.

The Return

Slowly it begins to rise. You look down and bid good-bye to this special place. In your mind, you also bid good-bye to the special creature you met there.

The white clouds return, and obscure where you've been. In only a short time, the clouds thin, and you can recognize from this view that you are returning slowly to your own house, to where you were 20 or so minutes ago. The roof mysteriously softens, and makes a space for the carpet to carry you into the house, into the room where you were relaxing, and feeling the weight of your body against the fabric, you recognize the texture of the rug or furniture that you had felt earlier. And as you gradually reopen your eyes, and look around, you can feel that you are safely back to where this trip began. But, knowing all is well, feeling home again, take a minute to remember: Remember the gentle creature. Remember the message the creature gave to you. Just take this moment to feel what all this has meant to you.

THE EXPERIENCE OF LONGING FOR THE HOLY

Experiment 9: Deep Longing

In our culture, when a person expresses a deep dissatisfaction concerning life, we are likely to jump to the conclusion that it is a symptom of dysthymia or depression, but it may also be the deep longing of the soul. The Psalms, as well as the words of Paul, speak of deep longing as an expression of the soul:

- Lord, all my longing is known to thee. My sighing is not hidden from thee. (Psalm 38: 9, RSV)
- As a hart longs for flowing streams, so longs my soul for thee, O God. (Psalm 42: 1, RSV)
- For the creation waits with eager longing for the revealing of the sons of God . . . and not only the Creation, but we ourselves . . . groan inwardly as we wait for adoption as sons [of God]. (Romans 8: 19, 23, RSV).

The poetry of the mystics is filled with longing. It's in the stories of the Persian poet Rumi, and in the verses of the Indian poet Kabir. The following meditation, by Tara Brach (2003), helps us to focus this.

Meditation: Discovering Your Deepest Longing

Sit comfortably, in a way that allows you to be present and at ease. When you feel settled, ask yourself, "What does my heart long for?" Your initial answer might be that you want to be healthy, to lose weight, to make more money, to find a partner. Ask again and listen deeply, accepting whatever spontaneously arises. Continue in this way for several minutes, asking yourself the question, pausing and paying attention in an accepting and nonreactive way. Perhaps your answer will begin to deepen and simplify. Be patient and relaxed — with time, as you listen to your heart, your deepest longing will emerge. This longing might be expressed as the longing for love, presence, peace, communion, harmony, beauty, truth, or freedom.

When you recognize what you most deeply and truly long for in this moment, surrender to that longing wakefully. Say yes, allowing the energy of your deepest longing to fill your body, to suffuse your heart and awareness. What is your experience like when you fully inhabit your deepest longing? Continue to meditate, experiencing longing with an open and embodied presence.

This beautiful reflection can also be explored between two people. Sit comfortably, facing each other. Decide who will first be in the role of questioner and who will respond.

After a time of becoming quiet and relaxed, one person gently asks, "What does your heart long for?" and the other responds by saying aloud what first comes to mind. Whatever the answer, the questioner simply says, "Thank you," bows or otherwise acknowledges the response, and then asks the question again. This continues for an agreed upon length of time.

Before you switch roles, pause for several moments of silence so that the person who has been answering the question can inhabit his or her experience of deepest longing with a full and embodied awareness. In the same way, after the second person has had a turn responding to the question, take a few moments of silence. When the meditation is complete, you might spend a few minutes sharing your individual experience.

At any moment throughout the day, if you find yourself driven by wanting, the question, "What does my heart really long for?" will help you reconnect to the purity of spiritual yearning. By pausing and asking yourself at any moment, "What really matters? What do I most care about?" you awaken your naturally caring heart (pp. 159-160).

THE DANGER OF HOLINESS

Experiment 10: The Shadow of Your Form of Spiritual Practice

I sincerely hope you will continue to find experiments for your own spiritual growth beyond your work with this book. What follows will be the final experiment that I will guide you through in this book. Thus it seems appropriate to take an overview of our spiritual practices. Chapter 10 of this book, in the section titled "Where Do We Go from Here?"—and especially the section titled "Twelve Gateways that Can Lead to the Sacred"—surveys spiritual practices you may choose to explore. The two worksheets within Chapter 10 (Worksheets 10.1 and 10.2) may help you with that exploration. This meditation on your spiritual shadow is another resource in that process of overview and assessment.

Though it is crucial to develop and practice in some concrete way, almost any concrete form that we give to our spiritual practice casts a "shadow." Karl Jung used the image of the "shadow" to talk about the side of your own public persona that you may not be aware of, but that inevitably results from that particular persona.

The shadow of your particular spiritual practices are bound up in the total shadow of your unique personality. In this meditation we are focusing only on the part of the shadow related to your spiritual practices. The intent is not to do away with this shadow—that would be about as likely as doing away with your actual shadow on a sunny day. The purpose is to bring more of it into awareness, which may in turn lead to revisions in the way you practice. See Exhibit 13.6.

EXHIBIT 13.6.
Meditation: Reflecting on the Shadow of Your Form of Practice

Just as every community has a shadow, every set of teachings will also have areas of shadow, aspects of life that they do not illuminate wisely. Every style of teaching will also produce its near enemy, the way that particular teaching can be most easy misused or misunderstood. It can be useful to take some time to reflect on the strengths and limitations of the practice you have chosen to follow. You can then consider to what extent these are issues in your own spiritual life. The following examples hint at the possible shadows you may encounter.

- Insight meditation and similar Buddhist practices can lead to quietude, to withdrawal from and fear of the world.
- The emptiness taught in Zen and nondualist Vedanta can lead to a related problem, to being disconnected and ungrounded.
- Any form of idealistic, otherworldly teaching that sees life on earth as a dream or focuses on higher realms can lead one to live with complacency, amorality, and indifference.
- Physical practices such as hatha yoga can lead to bodily perfection instead of awakening of the heart.
- Kundalini yoga can lead students to become experience junkies in search of exciting sensations of body and mind rather than liberation.

(continued)

(continued)

- Those such as Krishnamurti and others who teach against any discipline or method of practice can lead people to remain intellectual about spiritual life without providing any deep inner experience. Practices that involve a great deal of study can do the same.
- Moralistic practices with strong rules about what is pure and what is not can reinforce low self-esteem or lead to rigidity and self-righeousness.
- Practices of tantra can become an excuse to act out desires as a pseudo form of spiritual practice.
- Devotional practices can leave clarity and discriminating wisdom undeveloped.
- Powerful gurus can make us think we can't do it ourselves. Practices of joy and celebration such as Sufi dancing may leave students lacking an understanding of the inevitable loss and sorrows of life.
- Practices that emphasize suffering can miss the joy of life.

As you reflect on these shadows, consider your own spiritual path and tradition. Let yourself sense its strengths and weaknesses, its gifts and the ways it can be misused. Notice where you may be caught and what more you might need. Remember that there is nothing wrong with any of these practices per se. They are simply tools for opening and awakening. Each can be used skillfully or unknowingly misused. As you mature in your own spiritual life, you can take responsibility for your own practice and reflect wisely on where you are entangled and what can awaken you to freedom in every realm.

Source: Kornfield (1993), pp. 270-271.

Appendix

Additional Resources

MODIFICATIONS TO REDUCE ANXIETY

Many persons, when they read the experiments in this book, feel perfectly safe to go ahead and try them, and sense no need to make modifications. Others sense some fear or apprehension. If you are among this fearful group, several practices might help you reduce your anxiety so that you can go ahead with an experiment. Consider making as many of the following modifications as you like, and any others that come to your mind, before starting the experiment.

Deep Breathing

Often anxiety is simply a result of facing something new, but not allowing yourself to take in enough oxygen for the new situation. Think of each experiment as climbing a small hill. When you exercise you need more air. As you go higher, the air gets thinner. Climbers learn to take slow, deep breaths. It is important that you not take fast shallow breaths, which could cause you to hyperventilate. Climbers on a steep incline, or in heavy snow, do a hesitation step, something similar to the slow "step, and pause; step, and pause" that you may have done when you marched in a graduation ceremony. Apply this to the reading of the experiment. Read, and breathe. Read, and breathe. Read, and breathe.

Inviting a Friend to Assist You

For certain new experiences or paths, it is best to have a companion. In this case the companion does not need to be your guide, since the instructions will guide you. The companion simply needs to be someone who can be with you, and stay present, attentive, caring. Probably you would simply ask him or her to sit silently nearby. The most you would want the friend to say would be, "I'm here if you need me," if he or she sensed you were getting anxious.

If the friend you would choose cannot physically be present at this time, you might schedule a time that's convenient and delay doing the experiment. Another option is to have him or her listen in on the phone, and you know the phone is right there if you need to stop the experiment and talk.

Incorporating a Comforting Object into the Experiment

Perhaps you remember Linus in the Peanuts cartoons, who never went anywhere without carrying his blanket. Physical objects, especially ones that are cuddly and soft, can be very reassuring to adults, not just to kids. If it's just the feel of it, fine. Or perhaps the object is a stuffed animal or doll, and is also an "imaginary friend." This is also fine. Keep it with you or near you as you do the experiment. If you still are uncomfortable, simply spend time with the "comforter" and forget about doing the experiment at this time.

Setting an Alarm

Some travelers on a journey (such as the spiritual journey this book is encouraging) feel comforted to know that a particular segment of the journey is limited in time. Perhaps you remember long rides to your grandma and grandpa's house, and your parents saying "in fifteen more minutes we'll be halfway there and we'll stop for a stretch."

Perhaps you know that you can tolerate a new experience for at least 15 minutes (or maybe it's half an hour—set your own limit). Set a watch for that time, and promise yourself a break at that point. Then resume the experiment, probably backing up a step or two to get back into it. Do it in segments in the time stretches that seem right for you.

Note: Take some time to consider which of these modifications would be helpful to you. Do what you need to do to put those modifications in place. Then go back to try the experiment. Of course, if it still doesn't go well, skip that experiment. Perhaps you will take a break and come back to it when you feel calmer. Or move on to check out the next experiment.

WORKSHOPS AND TRAINING SESSIONS

Authentic Movement

Authentic Movement Institute
P.O. Box 11410
Oakland, CA, 94611-0410
Phone: (510) 237-7297
http://www.authenticmovement-usa.com/index.htm

Focusing

Dr. Elfie Hinterkopf's (1998) book *Integrating Spirituality in Counseling* is being republished by The Focusing Institute. The Focusing Institute Web site is http://www.focusing.org/. Dr. Hinterkopf, who offers workshops and individual sessions in focusing, may be reached at focusintexas@yahoo.com.

Multiple "Selves" or "Parts" Work

Cast of Characters Approach

Sandra Hammond (formerly Sandra Watanabe-Hammond)
E-mail: sandrahammond100@earthlink.net

Internal Family Systems Approach

The Center for Self Leadership
Dr. Richard Schwartz
Phone: (708) 383-2659.
E-mail: IFSCSL@aol.com
http://www.selfleadership.org

BOOKS

Most of the books listed here are helpful in understanding a perspective or minority group not typically covered in the main body of psychological literature. I have listed only books that are not already noted in the References.

Canda, E.R. & Furman, L.D. (1999). *Spiritual diversity in social work practice: The heart of helping.* New York: The Free Press.

Dass, R. & Goodman, P. (1987). *How can I help?* New York: Alfred A. Knopf.

Davis, M., Eshelman, E.R., & McKay, M. (1995). *The relaxation & stress reduction workbook (4th edition).* Oakland, CA: New Harbinger Publications.

Goodrich, T.J., Rampage, C., Ellmann, B., & Halstead, K. (1988). *Feminist family therapy: A casebook.* New York: W. W. Norton & Co.

Kim, Y.Y. (1988). *Communication and cross-cultural adaptation.* Philadelphia, PA: Multilingual Matters Ltd.

Libby, R.W. & Whitehurst, R.N. (1977). *Marriage and alternatives: Exploring intimate relationships.* Glenview, IL: Scott, Foresman and Co.

McGoldrick, M., Giordan, J., & Garcia-Preto, N. (2005). *Ethnicity & family therapy (3rd edition).* New York: Guilford Press.

Mijares, S.G. & Khelsa, G.S. (Eds). *The psychospiritual clinician's handbook: Alternative methods of understanding and treating mental disorders.* Binghamton, NY: The Haworth Press.

Notes

Introduction

1. It is arguable that this is already happening, at least in global structures such as the World Bank and the International Monetary Fund.

Chapter 1

1. Some attempt has been made to revise the D.A.R.E curriculum in light of these criticisms; new research is needed to determine if the revisions succeeded.

Chapter 2

1. Fowler (1981) cites the linguistic and cross-cultural work on world religions of Wilfred Cantwell Smith (1963).

2. Humor can be risky if the client is insecure or experiences the humor as a put-down. As always, the counselor needs to watch for nonverbal responses and notice if the humor may have been taken as being laughed *at,* not with. If unsure, the counselor may need to check out the client's response by looking directly at the client and asking, "I'm not sure how you took what I just said. (pause) Did you think I was making fun of you?"

Chapter 3

1. The "serenity prayer," used by Alcoholics Anonymous, is a part of a prayer attributed to Reinhold Neibhur, but Neibhur is quoted as attributing the prayer to an eighteenth century theologian, Friedrich Oetinger (Conners, Toscova, & Tonigan, 1999). Neibhur was a contemporary of Bonhoeffer who had emigrated to the United States and had brought Bonhoeffer to Union Seminary in New York City twice during Bonhoeffer's struggles with Nazism. Bonhoeffer aborted the second trip, deciding he needed to be in Germany taking his stand. He was martyred there by the Nazis. So the issue of what could and could not be changed was not an academic one for these two men.

2. Egypt has a one-party democracy that tends to be theocratic. Kuwait is an emeritus of princely power. Sudan is a democracy that honors Islamic independence fighters. All three studies were done in the mid- to late 1980s.

3. In Washburn's (1995) charting of Wilber's (1999) stages, from which I have paraphrased these summaries, the stages are not numbered.

Chapter 4

1. This is not to say that ancient persons had no "crises" of faith. Certainly there were conflicts between the belief systems of particular tribes or groups, and when they met each other they had to deal with their differences. Ethical conflicts also occurred, for example, when the behaviors of their leaders seemed incongruous with the highest values of their traditions.

Chapter 5

1. This statement holds for the four cannonical Gospels, but also for the Gospels attributed to Thomas, Mary Magdalene, James, and the others translated in *The Complete Gospels* (Miller, 1994), as well as for the rediscovered Gospel attributed to Judas, so far as I can tell from the *National Geographic* report (Cockburn, 2006).

2. Places of worship seem to be places where stimulation of the senses is heightened—of the ears by music, of the nose by incense, of the hands by water, of the tongue by bread, and of the eyes by wondrous buildings. Regarding the latter, a group within the American Institute of Architects is studying the relationship between neuroscience and spiritual experience as expressed in architectural styles of places of worship (Ratzinger, 2004).

3. The body of social psychological research on "self-focused attention," noted early in this chapter, is relevant to this issue.

Chapter 6

1. A series of studies by Günter Dörner (1972, 1976, 1977; Dörner et al. 1980) suggested that when adult gay and straight men are given a dose of certain hormones, the gay men have physiological reactions that are more similar to the reactions of woman than do the straight men. Dörner believed that although the gay men's bodies are completely "male," including their hormones, an area of the brain has the "female" response. Possibly this is the same area that determines who one is sexually aroused by. In short, sexual orientation may be determined by the way a particular area of the brain has developed. However, later studies with larger samples failed to find this different response, and the interpretation Dörner gave it has been refuted (Gooren et al., 1990).

2. An example of an attempt to respond to fear and hate with love is described in Chapter 10, my experience in a Soulforce vigil.

3. One can usually find the gay information line by looking up "gay" in the city phone book. A directory to gay information lines can be found by calling The GLBT National Help Center, at 1-888-THE-GLNH, or by going to the "resources" page of their Web site: http://www.glnh.org/find/index.html..

4. Prescott's conclusions are dismissed by Zillmann (1984), but he fails to note that Prescott's view is based not on the data from marital sex alone, but on data from

touch or lack of touch in childhood and from attitudes toward adolescent sexuality, which she believes form the foundation for full acceptance of marital sex. Zillmann ignores the fact that those variables are highly predictive of measures of violence in the 49 societies. (See also McElroy, 1983.)

Chapter 7

1. The mystical tradition within Islam, Sufi, led to the meditative practice of whirling dervishes. Islamic cultures today are likely to enforce rigid gender roles. Formal religious leadership is almost solely in the hands of men, and seating in the mosques is still gender segregated, yet I noticed on a recent trip to Turkey that performances of whirling dervishes there regularly involve both men and women.

Chapter 8

1. Throughout this section I have used quotation marks only when I am directly quoting the Hebrew Scriptures. Text that is paraphrased is not placed in quotations. The scriptural quotations are from the Revised Standard Version. A few verses come from the King James Version; these are marked.

2. As noted previously, the "serenity prayer," used by Alcoholics Anonymous, is a part of a prayer attributed to Reinhold Neibhur, but Neibhur is quoted as attributing the prayer to an eighteenth century theologian, Friedrich Oetinger (Conners et al., 1999).

Chapter 9

1. The emphasis on process in this work may obscure the role of closure. Again, the identity development model is helpful since it articulates that growth experience entails an interaction between "opening" and "closing" (opening to search among alternatives, then closure or decision making). Even though the closure is never final, and reopening issues is healthy, closure does play a role in development and in the spiritual journey

2. For another example of responding to process rather than to belief, see the subsection on race in Chapter 4, in the section titled "Textual Criticism and Scriptural Authority."

3. Development of research methods for measuring intuitiveness is already well underway (Rea, 2001), and measurements of cognitive openness have been available for decades (Rokeach, 1960), although measuring emotional openness and caring is more difficult. I do believe that it is appropriate for professionals who supervise counselors-in-training and have trainees who are interested in spiritually sensitive counseling to provide them with feedback on their intuitiveness and caring and to indicate the importance of these traits for doing spiritual work with their clients.

4. The neuropsychology of "altered states of consciousness" is beyond the scope of this chapter (see Wenkelman, 1997).

Chapter 10

1. "Classical sociologists" (Tonnies, 1957) have made the distinction between "gemeinschaft" societies, which are made up of small, homogeneous village communities and are based on personalized and communitarian principles, such as the Bushman, and "gesellschaft" societies, which are similar to our own, complex societies including large urban areas, where the private is separated from the public, and where relationships are impersonal, instrumental, and narrow. In the former, helping is done through community cleansing rituals such as those Kottler describes, while in the latter, helping is usually done through paid professional relationships. One might argue that the Bushman approach might work as effectively as "talk therapy" in those area of our gesellschaft society that are more physically active (adolescents) and less verbal (low socioeconomic status) (Dr. George Banziger, Social Psychologist, Carlinville, IL, April 2006, personal correspondence).

2. A detailed discussion of the measurement problems in integrating Eriksonian research with gender role research can be found in my earlier work (Matteson, 1993b, especially pp. 91-98).

3. This reactivity is equally true of women if placed in a similar bind. See experimental evidence in Matteson (1991).

4. In translation, the two books are titled the *Ascent of Mount Carmel* and the *Dark Night.*

5. For help with the clinical differentiation, see Grof & Grof (1990), pp. 43-45 regarding psychosis; Washburn (1994), p. 232 regarding borderline and pp. 254-256 regarding psychosis.

Chapter 11

1. "Under the thigh" is a euphemism for touching the genitals. Putting the hand on the genitals may relate to the descendents of the man, who are to enforce loyalty if the oath is broken, emphasizing the life-and-death importance of the oath (Brueggemann, 1962).

2. Repeat these exercises until all of your major muscle areas are relaxed. Once you have practiced several of these formats for relaxation, you may have a sense of what works best for you, at least for the time being. This is a good time to photocopy pages from this book, cut and paste, and develop a script to read to a tape recorder, which you can then listen to until you can self-lead. Notice that imagery is used at points in these instructions. Cross out any imagery that does not work for you—for example, is the warm egg on the head helpful or distracting? Is the ocean lapping at your feet relaxing or fear producing? Which works best for you when there is tension: simply relaxing it, or deliberately intensifying it and then relaxing it? When you have edited to produce the script that works best for you, you may want to make a cassette tape of it to use again and again until you can lead yourself into deep relaxation without needing the tape.

3. If this wording doesn't seem right for you, substitute one of the following:

Option one: Try saying something such as, "My body is made in the image of the Holy. I will treat it as Holy. I will honor it, and nurture it, and please it." This is a first step in honoring others and the spiritual body as a whole.

Option two: Try listening for any sense that a loving divine being is accepting you and affirming your nurturing your body.

Chapter 12

1. See footnote 4 of Chapter 3, and Conners, Toscova, & Tonigan (1999), p. 237.

Chapter 13

1. Both Western and Eastern psychologies have a long history of trying to define the self. It is not the purpose of this book to deal with the highly abstract controversies of essential versus existential views of self. However, the various methods of practicing meditation raise interesting conceptual questions. Is there any "self" except in relationship to an object, an "other"? Is a sense of "no self" simply a derivative of the method of closing the eyes and stopping the internal stimuli, so there is no way to be in contact with (or relationship to) "other," and consequently no experience of self?

2. Counselors interested in exploring this approach, in addition to reading Schwartz (1995) and Goulding & Schwartz (1995), are encouraged to read Sandra Watanabe-Hammond (1987, 1988), and to contact the Center for Self Leadership (see Additional Resources in this book.)

References

Achtemeier, P.J., (Ed.) (1996). *The HarperCollins Bible dictionary.* San Francisco, CA: Harper.

Ackbar, S. (2005). Re-defining fusion in lesbian relationships: Relating attachment, social support and outness to intrusiveness and closeness-caregiving. *Division 44 Newsletter, 21*(3), 9-11.

Alderman, D. Brehm, S., & Katz, L.B. (1974). Empathic observation of an innocent victim: The just world revisited. *Journal of Personality and Social Psychology, 29,* 342-347.

Altizer, T.J. (1966). *The gospel of Christian atheism.* Philadelphia, PA: Westminster Press.

Amend, E.R. (2000, August 7). Misdiagnosis of asperger's disorder in gifted youth: An addendum to "Misdiagnoses and dual diagnosis of gifted children" by James Webb, Ph.D. Paper presented at the American Psychological Association Annual Convention, Washington, DC.

Anderson, H. (1971). The book of Job. In C.M. Laymon (Ed.), *The interpreter's one-volume commentary on the Bible* (pp. 238-252). Nashville, TN: Abingdon Press.

Appleton, W.S. (2000). *Prozac and the new antidepressants* (Rev. ed.). New York: Penguin (Plume Book).

Arkin, W. & Dobrofsky, L.R. (1978). Military socialization and masculinity. *Journal of Social Issues, 34*(1), 151-168.

Aronson, J., Blanton, H., & Cooper, J. (1995). From dissonance to disidentification: Selectivity in the self-affirmation process. *Journal of Personality & Social Psychology, 65,* 178-182.

Aronson, J., Cohen, G., & Nail, P.R. (1999). Self-affirmation theory: An update and appraisal. In E. Harmon-Jones & J. Mills (Eds.), *Cognitive dissonance: Progress on a pivotal theory in social psychology* (pp. 127-147). Washington, DC: American Psychological Association.

Aspinwall, L.G. & Taylor, S.E. (1997). A stitch in time: Self-regulation and proactive coping. *Psychological Bulletin, 121,* 417-436.

Astin, J.A., Anton-Culver, H., Schwartz, C.E., Shapiro, D.H., McQuade, J., Breuer, A.M., Taylor, T.H., Lee, H., & Kurosaki, T. (1999, fall). Sense of control and adjustment to breast cancer: The importance of balancing control coping styles. *Behavior Medicine, 25,* 101-109.

Atkinson, B. (1999, July/August). The emotional imperative: Psychotherapists cannot afford to ignore the primacy of the limbic brain. *Family Therapy Networker, 24*(4), 22-33.

Ault Jr., J.M. (2004). *Spirit and flesh: Life in a fundamentalist Baptist church.* New York: Alfred A. Knopf.

Backlund, M.A. (1990). *Faith and AIDS: Life crisis as a stimulus to faith stage transition.* Unpublished doctoral dissertation. Palo Alto, CA: Pacific Graduate School of Psychology.

Badgett, L. (1998). *Creating communities: Giving and volunteering by gay, lesbian, bisexual and transgender people.* Amherst, MA: Working Group on Funding Lesbian and Gay Issues/Institute for Gay and Lesbian Strategic Studies.

Baenninger, M. & Newcombe, N. (1989, March). The role of experience in spatial test performance: A meta-analysis. *Sex Roles, 20,* 5-6, 327-344.

Bagemihl, B. (2000). *Biological exuberance: Animal homosexuality and natural diversity.* New York: St. Martin's Press.

Bailey, J.M. & Pillard, R.C. (1991). A genetic study of male sexual orientation. *Archives of General Psychiatry, 48,* 1089-1096.

Bailey, J.M., Pillard, R.C., Neale, M.C., & Agyei, Y. (1993). Heritable factors influence sexual orientation in women. *Archives of General Psychiatry, 50,* 219.

Bandura, A. (1997). *Self-efficacy: The exercise of control.* New York: Freeman.

Banfield, E.C. (1958). *The moral basis of a backward society.* New York: Free Press.

Banziger, G. & Roush, S. (1983, October). Nursing homes for the birds: A control-relevant intervention with bird feeders. *Gerontologist, 23*(5), 527-531.?

Barba, J.F. (1998). Sexual orientation and the capacity for intimacy. In *Dissertation Abstracts International, 5* (10B), 5635.

Barrett, M.J. & Butler, K. (2002, March-April). Can we talk? Let's end our conspiracy of silence about our ambiguous boundaries. *Psychotherapy Networker,* 32.

Bassett, P.E. (1985). Faith development and mid-life transition: Fowler's paradigm as it relates to personality profile. Unpublished doctoral dissertation. Waco, TX: Baylor University.

Baum, G. (1977). Rethinking the church's mission after Auschwitz. In Fleischner, E. (Ed.) *Auschwitz: Beginning of a new era? Reflections on the Holocaust* (pp.). New York: KTAV Publishing House, Inc.

Baumeister, R.F. (2003, February). Ego depletion and self-regulation failure: A resource model of self-control. *Alcoholism: Clinical and Experimental Research, 27*(2), 281-284.

Beckman, T. (1998) The case of Wagner. Retrieved from: www4.hmc.edu:8001/Humanities/Beckman/Nietzsche/Case.htm.

Becvar, D.S. (1997). *Soul healing: A spiritual orientation in counseling and therapy.* New York: Basic Books.

Bellah, R.N., with R. Madsen, W.M. Sullivan, A. Swidler, & S.M. Tipton. (1996). *Habits of the heart: Individualism and commitment in American life.* Berkeley, CA: University of California Press.

Bellis, A.O. & Hufford, T.L. (2002). *Science, scripture and homosexuality.* Cleveland, OH: Pilgrim Press.

Bem, S.L. (1974). On the utility of alternative procedures for assessing psychological androgyny. *Journal of Counseling and Clinical Psychology, 45,* 196-205.

Bergin, A.E. (1980). Psychotherapy and religious values. *Journal of Consulting and Clinical Psychology, 48,* 95-105.

Bergin, A.E. (1983). Religiosity and mental health: A critical reevaluation and meta-analysis. *Professional Psychology: Research and Practice, 14,* 170-184.

Bergin, A.E. (1991, April). Values and religious issues in psychotherapy and mental health. *American Psychologist, 46*(4), 394-403.

Bethge, E. (1979) *Prayer and righteous action in the life of Dietrich Bonhoeffer.* Belfast: Christian Journals.

Bettleheim, B. (1970). *Obsolete youth: Towards a psychograph of adolescent rebellion.* San Francisco, CA: San Francisco Press.

Bi, W. (1990). *The classic of the way and virtue: A new translation of the Tao-te ching of Laozi.* R.J. Lynn, trans. New York: Columbia University Press.

Bieber, I. et al. (1988). *Homosexuality: A psychoanalytical study.* Northvale, NJ: Aronson.

Bigner, B. & Jacobson, R.B. (1989). Parenting behaviors of homosexual and heterosexual fathers. *Journal of Homosexuality, 18*(1/2), 173-186.

Binson, D. et al. (1995). Prevalence and social distribution of men who have sex with men: United States and its urban centers. *Journal of Sex Research, 32*(3), 245-254.

Black, B. M. (1992). Volunteers serving survivors of battering and sexual assault. *Response, 14*(4), 2-9.

Black, E. & Neilhardt, J.G. (2000). *Black Elk speaks: Being the life story of a holy man of the Oglala Sioux.* Lincoln, NE: University of Nebraska Press.

Blandford, J. (2002). Gay and lesbian career choices. (unpublished manuscript, cited in Nimmons, 1999).

Blanton, H., Cooper, J., Skurnik, I., & Aronson, J. (1997, July). When bad things happen to good feedback: Exacerbating the need for self-justification with self-affirmations. *Personal and Social Psychology Bulletin, 23*(7), 684-692.

Blum, L.A. (1980). *Friendship, altruism, and morality.* Boston, MA: Routledge & Kegan Paul.

Bly, R. (1977). *The Kabir book.* Boston, MA: Beacon Press.

Bly, R. (1990). *Iron John: A book about men.* Reading, MA: Addison-Wesley.

Bolen, J.S. (1984). *Goddesses in everywoman: A new psychology of women.* San Francisco, CA: Harper & Row.

Bolen, J.S. (1989). *Gods in everyman: A new psychology of men.* San Francisco, CA: Harper & Row.

Bonhoeffer, D. (1953). *Prisoner for God.* New York: Macmillan.

Bonhoeffer, D. (1997). *Letters and papers from prison.* New York: Simon & Schuster.

Bonhoeffer, D. (2000). *The cost of discipleship*. Minneapolis, MN: Augsburg Fortress Press.

Borg, M. (Ed.) (1999). *Jesus and Buddha: The parallel sayings*. Berkeley, CA: Seastone.

Boswell, J. (1980). *Christianity, social tolerance, and homosexuality: Gay people in western Europe from the beginning of the Christian era to the fourteenth century*. Chicago, IL: University of Chicago Press.

Boswell, J. (1994). *Same-sex unions in pre-modern Europe*. New York: Villard.

Bowen, M. (1978). *The Use of Family Therapy in Clinical Practice*. New York: Aronson.

Boyer, P. (2001). *Religion explained: The evolutionary origins of religious thought*. New York: Basic Books.

Brach, T. (2003). *Radical acceptance: Embracing your life with the heart of a Buddha*. New York: Bantam Books.

Brethren Mennonite Council for Lesbian and Gay Concerns (2005, winter-spring). Guidelines for establishing and maintaining respect and "fair play" in the church's dialogue about the inclusion of gay, lesbian, and bisexual people in the church. Retrieved October 1, 2007, from: http://www.bmclgbt.org/fairplay.shtml.

Brown, H.B. (1958). A final testimony. Speech given at Brigham Young University, March 29.

Brueggemann, W. (1962). *The interpreter's dictionary of the Bible*. Nashville, TN: Abingdon Press. sv "Thigh."

Burdon, W.M. (1966). Deception in intimate relationships: A comparison of heterosexuals and homosexual/bisexuals. *Journal of Homosexuality, 32*(1), 77-91.

Burtt, E.A. (Ed.) (1955). *The teachings of the compassionate Buddha: Early discourse, the dhammapada, and later basic writings*. New York: Mentor (New American Library).

Burwen, L.S. & Campbell, D.T. (1957). The generality of attitudes toward authority and non-authority figures. *Journal of Abnormal and Social Psychology, 54*, 24-31.

Buss, D.M. (1989). Sex differences in human mate performances: Evolutionary hypotheses tested in 37 cultures. *Behavioral and Brain Sciences*, 12, 1-49.

Buss, D.M. (1995). Psychological sex differences: Origins through sexual selection. *American Psychologist, 50*(3), 164-168.

Buss, D.M., Larsen, R., Westen, D., & Semmelroth, J. (1992). Sex differences in jealousy: Evolution, physiology, and psychology. *Psychological Science, 3*, 251-255.

Campbell, J. (1968). *The hero with a thousand faces*. Princeton, NJ: Princeton University Press.

Campbell, J. (1970-1980). Interviews by Michael Thoms, New Dimensions Radio, National Public Radio, date approximate.

Campbell, J. (1979). *The flight of the wild gander*. South Bend, IN: Regency/Gateway, Inc.

Campbell, J. (1987/1997). The wisdom of Joseph Campbell. (In conversation with Michael Toms, tape 3 of 4.) New Dimensions. Distributed by Hay House, Carlsbad, CA.

Campbell, J. (Ed.) (1988). *Myths, dreams, and religion.* Dallas, TX: Spring Publications.

Campbell, J. (1996). Joseph Campbell audio collection (Vol. 1: Mythology and the individual). Tape 1: The celebration of life. St. Paul, MN: HighBridge Company.

Campbell, J. with B. Moyers, B.S. Flowers (Ed.) (1990). *The power of myth.* New York: Anchor Books.

Camus, A. (1948). *The Plague.* S. Gilbert, trans. New York: Alfred A. Knopf.

Casey, C. (2005, June 4). ViPPresentation at the 31st annual Great Mother Conference. Lake Nebagamon, Wisconsin.

Cauthen, K. (2006, spring). Grace: More than forgiveness of sins. *The InSpiriter, 10*(3), 1, 8. Retrieved October 1, 2007, from http://www.wabaptists.org/inspiriter/TIS2006-04.pdf.

Chaney, J.M., Mullins, L.L., Wagner, J.L., Hommel, K.A., Page, M.C., & Doppler, M.J. (2004, May). A longitudinal examination of causal attributions and depression symptomatology in rheumatoid arthritis. *Rehabilitation Psychology, 49*(2), 126-133.

Chittister, J. (2002a, July-August). The faith will survive. *Sojourners Magazine, 20-21,* 23-25.

Chittister, J. (2002b) From where I stand. *National Catholic Reporter: The Independent Newsweekly.*

Chodron, P. (2000). *When things fall apart: Heart advice for difficult times.* Boston, MA: Shambhala Publications.

Chopra, D. (1995). *The way of the wizard: Twenty spiritual lessons for creating the life you want.* New York: Random House.

Church, F. (2001, November-December). A theology for the 21st century. *Unitarian-Universalist World,* 18-25.

Cockburn, A. (2006, May). The Judas Gospel. *National Geographic,* 81-95. Retrieved fromAvailable at: http://www7.nationalgeographic.com/ngm/gospel/feature.html.

Cohen, D. (2002). *Turning suffering inside out: A sen approach to living with physical and emotional pain.* Boston, MA: Shambhala Publications.

Cohen, G.L., Aronson, J., & Steele, C.M. (1997). When beliefs yield to evidence: Reducing biased evaluation by affirming the self. Unpublished manuscript.

Cole, J.D. (1998, June). Psychotherapy with the chronic pain patient using coping skills development: Outcome study. *Journal of Occupational Health Psychology, 3*(3), 217-226.

Coles, R. (1986). *The moral life of children.* Boston: Atlantic Monthly Press.

Conners, G.J., Toscova, R.T., & Tonigan, J.S. (1999). Serenity. In W.R. Miller (Ed.), *Integrating spirituality into treatment: Resources for practitioners* (p. 237). Washington, DC: American Psychological Association.

Cooper, G. (2001, September-October). When presence matters more than progress: Racism in the DSM. Clinician's digest. *Psychotherapy Networker*, p. 18.

Cooper, G. (2002, March-April). Studying the power of prayer. Clinician's digest. *Psychotherapy Networker*, p. 18.

Crawford, M. & Gentry, M. (Eds.) (1995). *Talking difference: On gender and language.* Thousand Oaks, CA: Sage Publications.

Csikszentmihalyi, M. (1990) *Flow: The psychology of optimal experience.* New York: Harper & Row.

Cupal D.D. & Brewer B.W. (2001). Effects of relaxation and guided imagery on knee strength, reinjury anxiety, and pain following anterior cruciate ligament reconstruction. *Rehabilitation Psychology, 46*(1), 28-43.

Cynical sayings (2003). *The Washington Post,* December 7, p. D2

Cyr, C. & Dowrick, P.W. (1991). Burnout in crisis line volunteers. *Administration and Policy in Mental Health, 18*(5), 343-354.

Dalai Lama & Goleman, D. (2003a). *Destructive Emotions: How can we overcome them?* New York: Bantam Books.

Dalai Lama & Goleman, D. (2003b). *Healing emotions: Conversations with the Dalai Lama on Mindfulness, Emotions, and Health.* New York: Bantam Dell.

Dawn: The Internet edition. Citing "The State of World Population 2001" report of the United Nations Population Fund (UNFPA).

de Gruchy, J.W. (Ed.) (1999). *The Cambridge companion to Deitrich Bonhoeffer.* Cambridge, UK: Cambridge University Press.

de Santillana, G. (1955). *The crime of Galileo.* Chicago, IL: University of Chicago Press.

de Waal, F. (1982). *Chimpanzee politics: Power and sex among apes.* London, UK: Jonathan Cape.

de Waal, F. (1996). *Good natured: The origins of right and wrong in humans and other animals.* Cambridge, MA: Harvard University Press.

DeAngelis, T. (1990, July). Relentless cheeriness may mask repression. *American Psychological Association Monitor on Psychology,* 14-15.

Deardorff, D. (2004). *The other within: The genius of deformity in myth, culture, & psyche.* Ashland, OR: White Cloud Press.

Deardorff, D. (2005, June 5). Deformity, music and creativity. Presentation at the 31st Great Mother Conference. Lake Nebagamon, Wisconsin.

Deaux, K. & Wrightsman, L.S. (1987). *Social psychology* (5th ed.). Pacific Grove, CA: Brooks/Cole Publishing Co.

DeLaurentis, H. (1985). "Maturity in faith": An interdisciplinary clarification of the term. Unpublished doctoral thesis, Catholic University of America, Washington, DC.

di Pellegrino, G., Fadiga, L., Fogassi, L., Gallese, V., & Rizzolatti, G. (1992). Understanding motor events: a neurophysiological study. *Experimental Brain Research, 91*(1), 176-180.

Dittmann, M. (2003, June). Self-control requires energy that needs to be restored. *American Psychological Association Monitor on Psychology,* 15.

Dodgson, K.V. (2003, Summer/Fall). Homosexuality: A review of recent medical research papers. *The InSpiriter,* vol. 7, no. 4 & 5, p. 1, 6.

Doherty, W.J. (1995). *Soul searching: Why psychotherapy must promote moral responsibility.* New York: Basic Books.

Dörner, G. (1972). *Sexualhormonabhangige gehirndifferenzierung und sexualitat.* New York: Springer-Verlag.

Dörner, G. (1976). *Hormones and brain differentiation.* Amsterdam: Elsevier/North-Holland Biomedical Press.

Dörner, G. (1977). Hormone dependent differentiation, maturation and function of the brain and sexual behavior. *Endokrinologie, 69,* 306-320.

Dörner, G., Geier, T., Ahrens, L., et al. (1980). Prenatal stress as possible aetiogenetic factor of homosexuality among human males. *Endokrinologie, 75*(3), 365-368.

Eagly, A.H. (1987). *Sex differences in social behavior: A social-role interpretation.* Hillsdale, NJ: Erlbaum.

Eagly, A.H. (1995, March). The science and politics of comparing women and men. *American Psychologist, 50*(3), 158.

Eagly, A.H. & Karau, S.J. (1991). Gender and the emergence of leaders: A meta-analysis. *Journal of Personality and Social Psychology, 60,* 685-710.

Eagly, A.H. & Steffen, V. (1986). Gender and aggressive behavior: A meta-analytic review of the social psychological literature. *Psychological Bulletin, 100,* 309-330.

Edinger, E.F. (1994). *The eternal drama: The inner meaning of Greek mythology.* Boston, MA: Shambhala Publications.

Edwards, C. (2004). *The shoes of Van Gogh: A spiritual and artistic journey to the ordinary.* New York: Crossroad Pub. Co.

Edwards, K.J. & Hall, T.W. (2003). Illusory spiritual health: The role of defensiveness in understanding and assessing spiritual health. In T.W. Hall & M.R. McMinn (Eds.)., *Spiritual formation, counseling, and psychotherapy* (pp. 261-275). New York: Nova Science Publishers

Edwards, K.J., Hall, T.W., & Slater, W. (2002, August). The multidimensional structure of spiritual questing. Paper presented at the 110th Annual Convention of the American Psychological Association, Chicago, IL.

Egan, G. (1994). *The skilled helper: A problem-management approach to helping.* Pacific Grove, CA: Brooks/Cole Publishing.

Ehrenberg, M. (2001). The role of women in human evolution. In C.B. Brettell, & C.F. Sargent (Eds.), *Gender in Cross-Cultural Perspective* (pp. 17-22). Upper Saddle River, NJ: Prentice Hall.

Ehrman, B.D. (2002). *Lost Christianities: Christian scriptures and the battles over authentication,* part. 1: The Greek courses (audiotapes). Chantilly, VA: The Teaching Company.

Elkins, D.N. (1998). *Beyond religion: A personal program for building a spiritual life outside the walls of traditional religion* (1st quest ed.). Wheaton, IL: Theosophical Pub. House.

Ellerbe, H. (1995). *The dark side of Christian history.* San Rafael, CA: Morningstar Books.

Ennett, S.T., Tobler, N.S., Ringwalt, C.L., & Flewelling, R.L. (1994, September). How effective is drug abuse resistance education? A meta-analysis of Project DARE outcome evaluations. *American Journal of Public Health, 84*(9), 1394-1401.

Enslin, M.S. (1930). *The ethics of Paul.* New York: Harper.

Erikson, E.H. (1968). *Identity, youth and crisis.* New York: W.W. Norton & Company.

Erikson, E.H. (1969). *Gandhi's truth: On the origins of militant nonviolence.* New York: W.W. Norton & Company.

Esterling, B.A., Antoni, M.H., Fletcher, M.A., Margulies, S., & Schniederman, N. (1994). Emotional disclosure through writing or speaking modulates latent Epstein-Barr virus antibody titers. *Journal of Consulting and Clinical Psychology, 62,* 130-140.

Fadiga, L., Fogassi, L., Pavesi, G., & Rizzolatti, G. (1995, June). Motor facilitation during action observation: A magnetic stimulation study. *Journal of Neurophysiology, 73(6),* 2608-2611.

Falbo, T. & Peplau, L.A. (1980). Power strategies in intimate relationships. *Journal of Personality and Social Psychology, 38,* 618-628.

Fazel, R. (1999). Pastoral societies. In H. Tierney (Ed.), *Women's studies encyclopedia* (pp. 1046-1048). Westport ,CT: Greenwood Press.

Felder, L. (2004, March-April). Case studies. *Psychotherapy Networker, vol. 28 p. 86-87.*

Festinger, L.(1957). *A theory of cognitive dissonance.* Stanford, CA: Stanford University Press.

Figley, C.R. (1995). *Compassion fatigue: Coping with secondary traumatic stress disorder in those who treat the traumatized.* New York: Brunner/Mazel.

Fine, M. & Gordon, S.M. (1989). Feminist transformations of/despite psychology. In M. Crawford & M. Gentry (Eds.) (1995), *Talking difference: On gender and language* (pp.178-185). Thousand Oaks, CA: Sage Publications.

Fishbane, (1999). Honor thy father and thy mother: Intergenerational spirituality and Jewish tradition. In F. Walsh (Ed.), *Spiritual resources in family therapy* (pp. 136-156). New York: Guilford Press.

Fisher, J.D. & Fisher, W.A. (1992). Changing AIDS risk behavior. *Psychological Bulletin, 111*(e), 455-474.

Folkman, S., Chesney, M.A., and Christopher-Richards, A. (1994) Stress and coping in caregiving partners of men with AIDS. *Psychiatric Clinics of North American, 17*(1), 35-53.

Folkman, S. & Lazarus, R. (1985). If it changes it must be a process: Study of emotion and coping during three stages of a college examination. *Personality and Social Psychology, 48* (1), 150-170.

Folkman, S. & Lazarus, R. (1988). *Manual for ways of coping questionnaire.* Palo Alto, CA: Consulting Psychologists Press.

Ford, C.S. & Beach, F.A. (1951). *Patterns of sexual behavior.* New York: Harper & Row.

Forssell, S.L. (2006, fall). Male couple communication about outside sexual activity. *Division 44 Newsletter,* 23-24.

Foucault, M.l (1996). Friendship as a way of life. *Faucault Live: Interviews 1961-1984.* New York: Semiotext(e).

Foushee, M.C. (1984). Dyads and triads at 35,000 feet. *American Psychologist, 39,* 885-893.

Fowler, J.W. (1974). Faith, liberation, and human development: Three lectures. *Foundation, 79,* 1-33.

Fowler, J.W. (1976). Stages in faith: The structural-developmental approach. In T.C. Hennessy (Ed.), *Values and Moral Development* (pp.). New York: Paulist Press.

Fowler, J.W. (1981). *Stages of faith: The psychology of human development and the quest for meaning.* San Francisco, CA: Harper & Row.

Fowler, J.W. & Keen, S. (1978). *Life maps: Conversations on the journey of faith.* Waco, TX: Word Books, J. Berryman (Ed.).

Fowler, J.W. & Vergote, A. (1980). *Toward moral and religious maturity.* Morristown, NJ: Silver Burdett.

Francis, M.E. & Pennebaker, J.W. (1992). Putting stress into words: The impact of writing on psychological, absentee and self-reported emotional well being measures. *American Journal of Health Promotion, 6,* 280-287.

Friedan, B. (1964). *The feminine mystique.* New York: Dell.

Friedman, T.L. (1999). *The lexus and the olive tree.* New York: Farrar, Straus & Giroux.

Fromm, E.(1956). *The art of loving.* New York: Harper & Row.

Fukyama, M.A. (2000, spring). Integrating spirituality into marriage and family counseling. *The Family Digest, 12*(4), 1, 7-9.

Furushima, R.Y. (1983). Faith development theory: A cross-cultural research project in Hawaii. Doctoral dissertation, Columbia University Teachers College, New York, NY. Ann Arbor, MI: University Microfilms International.

Galinsky, A.D., Stone, J., & Cooper, J. (2000). The reinstatement of dissonance and psychological discomfort following failed affirmations. *European Journal of Social Psychology, 30,* 123-147.

Gallese, V. (2005, October 5). The mind's mirror. Interview by Lea Winerman. *American Psychological Association Monitor on Psychology 6*(9), 48-50.

Gallese, V., Fadiga, L., Fogassi, L., & Rizzolatti, G. (1996, April). Action recognition in the premotor cortex. *Brain: A Journal of Neurology*, Part 2, 593-609.

Garbarino, J. (1999) *Lost boys: Why our sons turn violent and how we can save them.* New York: Free Press.

Gendlin, E.T. (1962). *Experiencing and the creation of meaning: A philosophical and psychological approach to the subjective.* New York: Free Press of Glencoe.

Gendlin, E.T. (1970). A theory of personality change. In J.T. Hart & T.M. Tomlinson (Eds.), *New Directions in Client-Centered Therapy* (pp. 129-173). Boston, MA: Houghton-Mifflin.

Gendlin, E.T. (1978). *Focusing.* New York: Everest House.

Gibbs, J.C. (1991). Toward an integration of Kohlberg's and Hoffman's moral development theories. *Human Development, 34*(2), 88-104.

Gielen, U.P., Ahmed, R.A., & Avellani, J. (1992). The development of moral reasoning and perceptions of parental behavior in students from Kuwait. *Moral Education Forum, 17*(3), 20-37.

Gielen, U.P. & Markoulis, D.C. (1994). Preference for principled moral reasoning: A developmental and cross-cultural perspective. In L.L. Adler & U.P. Gielen (Eds.), *Cross-cultural topics in psychology* (2nd ed., pp. 81-101). Westport, CT: Paeger.

Gilligan, C. (1982). *In a different voice.* Cambridge, MA: Harvard University Press.

Gilligan, C. & Wiggins, G. (1987). The origins of morality in early childhood relationships. In J. Kagan & S. Lamb (Eds.), *The emergence of morality in young children* (pp. 227-305). Chicago, IL: University of Chicago Press.

Glasser, W. (1976). *Positive addiction.* New York: Harper & Row.

Gooren, L., Fliers, E., & Courtney, K. (1990). Biological determinants of sexual orientation. In J. Bancroft (Ed.), *Annual review of sex research* (Vol. 1, pp. 175-196). Mt. Vernon, IA: Society for the Scientific Study of Sex.

Goulding, R.A. & Schwartz, R.C. (1995). *The mosaic mind: Empowering the tormented selves of child abuse survivors.* New York: W.W. Norton & Company.

Gray, J. (1992). *Men are from Mars, women are from Venus.* New York: Harper Collins Publishers.

Green, R. (1972). Homosexuality as a mental illness. *International Journal of Psychiatry, 10*(1), 77-98.

Greenberg, M.A. & Stone, A.A. (1992). Emotional disclosure about traumas and its relation to health: Effects of previous disclosure and trauma severity. *Journal of Personality and Social Psychology, 63,* 75-84.

Greenberg, M.A., Wortman, C.B., & Stone, A.A. (1996). Emotional expression and physical health: Revising traumatic memories or fostering self-regulation? *Journal of Personality and Social Psychology, 71,* 588-602.

Griffith, J.L. & Griffith, M.E. (2001). *Encountering the sacred in psychotherapy.* New York: The Guilford Press.

Griffith, M.E. (1999). Opening therapy to conversations with a personal God. In F. Walsh (Ed.), *Spiritual resources in family therapy* (pp.). New York: Guilford Press. Pp. 209-222.

Griffon, D.R. & Smith, H. (1989). *Primordial truth and postmodern theology.* Albany, NY: State University of New York Press.

Grof, S. (1988). *The adventure of self-discovery.* Albany, NY: State University of New York Press.

Grof, C. & Grof, S. (1990). *The stormy search for the self.* Los Angeles: J.P. Tarcher.

Guerrero, M.M.J. (2003). "Pastoral colonialism" and indigenism: Implications for native feminist spirituality and native womanism. *Hypatia, 118*(2), 58-67.

Guillaumo, A. (1956). *Islam.* Baltimore, MD: Penguin.

Haddock, D. (2005, May). Commencement speech, Hampshire College, Amherst, Massachusetts.

Hanh, T.N. (1976). *The miracle of mindfulness.* Boston, MA: Beacon.

Hahn, T.N. (1995) *Living Buddha, living Christ.* New York: Riverhead Books.

Haldeman, D.C. (1999, December). The pseudo-science of sexual orientation conversion therapy. *Angles: The Policy Journal of the Institute for Gay and Lesbian Strategic Studies, 4*(1), 1-4.

Hallowell, A. (1934). Culture and mental disease. *Journal of Abnormal and Social Psychology, 29,* 1-9.

Hallsal, P. (1998). Review of *Christianity, Social Tolerance and Homosexuality* by John Boswell. Retrieved October 2, 2007, from http://www.fordham.edu/halsall/pwh/index-bos.html.

Halpern, D.F. (1992). Sex differences in cognitive abilities (2nd ed.). Hinsdale, NJ: Earlbaum.

Hamilton, W. (1965a, spring). The death of God theology. *Christian Scholar, 46,* 27-48.

Hamilton, W. (1965b, December 13). Radicalism and the death of God. *Christianity and Crisis, 25,* 271-273.

Hammond, P.B. (1971). *An introduction to cultural and social anthropology.* New York: Macmillan.

Hansen, W.B & McNeal Jr., R.B. (1997, April). How D.A.R.E works: An examination of program effects on mediating variables. *Health Education and Behavior, 24*(2), 165-179.

Harshbarger, S. (2002, May-June). A moment of triumph. *Sojourners*, vol. 31, 18.

Hassan, S. (1990). *Combatting cult mind control.* Rochester, VT: Park Street Press.

Helfaer, P.M. (1972). *The psychology of religious doubt.* Boston, MA: Beacon Press.

Helminiak, D.A. (2000). *What the Bible really says about homosexuality.* Tajique, NM: Alamo Square Press.

Helwig, C.C., Tisak, M.S., & Turiel, E. (1990). Children's social reasoning in context: Reply to Gabennesch. *Child Development, 61,* 2068-2078.

Herbert, D. (1995). *Lincoln.* New York: Audioworks.

Herdt, G. (1992). Culture, history, and life course of gay men. In G. Herdt (Ed.), *Gay culture in America: Essays from the field* (pp. 3-21). Boston, MA: Beacon Press.

Hiebert, B., Uhlemann, M.R., Marshall, A., & Lee, D.Y. (1998, April). The relationship between self-talk, anxiety, and counseling skill. *Canadian Journal of Counselling, 32*(2),163-171.

Hilgard, E. & Atkinson, R.C. (1967). *Introduction to psychology* (4th ed.). New York: Harcourt, Brace & World.

Hinterkopf, E. (1998) *Integrating spirituality in counseling: A manual for using the experiential focusing method.* Alexandria, VA: American Counseling Association.

Hoffman, M. (1977). Homosexuality. In F. Beech (Ed.), Human sexuality in four perspectives (pp. 164-189). Baltimore, MD: John Hopkins University Press.

Hoffman, M.L. (1983). Affective and cognitive processes in moral internalization. In E.T. Higgins, D.N. Ruble, & W.W. Hartup (Eds.), *Social cognition and social development: A sociocultural perspective* (pp. 236-274). Cambridge: Cambridge University Press.

Hofling, C.K., Brotzman, E., Dalrymple, S., Graves, N., & Pierce, C.M. (1966). An experimental study in nurse-physician relationships. *Journal of Nervous and Mental Disease, 143,* 171-180.

Hooker, E. (1957). The adjustment of the male overt homosexual. *Journal of Projective Techiniques, 21,* 17-31.

Hooker, E.A. (1972). Homosexuality. In *U.S. Task Force on Homosexuality, Homosexuality: Final Report and Background Papers.* Rockville MD: National Institute of Mental Health.

Houston, P. (1994). *Marriage differences among young adult Asian Indian women.* Unpublished masters thesis, Governors State University, University Park, Illinois.

Howell, K.J. (1997). *Facets of faith and science.* Lanham, MD: University Press of America.

Hyde, J.S. (1984). How large are gender differences in aggression? A developmental meta-analysis. *Developmental Psychology, 20,* 722-736.

Hyde, J.S. (1986). Gender differences in aggression. In J. S. Hyde & M. C. Linn (Eds.), *The psychology of gender: Advances through meta-analysis* (pp. 51-66). Baltimore, MD: Johns Hopkins University Press.

Hyde, J.S., Fennema, E., & Lamon, S.J. (1990). Gender differences in mathematics performance: A meta-analysis. *Psychological Bulletin, 107,* 139-155.

Hyde, J.S. & Frost, L.A. (1993). Meta-analysis in the psychology of women. In F.L. Denmark & M.A. Paludi (Eds.), *Psychology of women: A handbook of issues and theories.* Westport, CT: Greenwood Press.

Hyde, J.S. & Linn, M.C. (1988). Gender differences in verbal ability: A meta-analysis. *Psychological Bulletin, 104,* 53-69.

Hyde, J.S. & Plant, E.A. (1995, March). Magnitude of psychological gender differences: Another side to the story. *American Psychologist, 50*(3), 159-161.

Jarski, R., Gjerde, C., Bratton, B., Brown, D., & Matthes, S. (1985). A comparison of four empathy instruments in simulated patient-medical student interactions. *Journal of Medical Education, 60,* 545-551.

Jaspers, K. (1949). Vom Ursprung and Ziel der Geschichte [About the Origin and Goal of History]. M. Bullock, trans. *The Origin and Goal of History* (1953). New Haven, CT: Yale University Press.

Jeffers, R. (2000). Fire on the hills. In T. Hunt (Ed.), *The collected poetry of Robinson Jeffers: Poetry 1903-1920, Prose, and Unpublished Writings* (Vol. 4, pp. 58-59). Palo Alto, CA: Stanford University Press.

Jenson, L.A. (1996). *Different habits, different hearts: Orthodoxy and progressivism in the United States and India.* Unpublished doctoral dissertaion, University of Chicago, Chicago, Illinois.

Jepson, C. & Chaiken, S. (1990). Chronic issue-specific fear inhibits systematic processing of persuasive communications. *Journal of Social Behavior and Personality, 5,* 61-84.

Johnson, S. (2004). *Mind wide open: Your brain and the neuroscience of everyday life.* New York: Scribner.

Jones, J.I. (1996, fall). The myth of the A.D.D. Child. *Educational Leadership, 53, 87.*

Jones, W.H., Chernovetz, O.C., & Hansson, R.O. (1978). The enigma of androgyny: Differential implications for males and females. *Journal of Counseling and Clinical Psychology, 46,* 298-313.

Kamen-Siegel, L., Rodin, J., Seligman, M.E.P., & Dwyer, J. (1991). Explanatory style and cell-mediated immunity. *Health Psychology, 10,* 229-235.

Keen, S. (1983). *The passionate life: Stages of loving.* San Francisco, CA: Harper & Row.

Keen, S. (1994). *Hymns to an unknown God: Awakening the spirit in everyday life.* New York: Bantam Books.

Keeney, B. (1994). *Shaking out the spirits: A psychotherapists entry into the healing mysteries of global shamanism.* Barrytown, NY: Station Hill Press, Inc.

Keeney, B. (March 13, 2002). Profiles of healing. Presentation given at Governors State University, University Park, Illinois.

Kelley, J.E., Lumley, M.A., & Leisen, J.C.C. (1997, July). Health effects of emotional disclosure in rheumatoid arthritis patients. *Health Psychology, 16*(4), 331-340.

Kelter, P. (2001, June 22). Should spirituality be part of social work? [Letter to the editor}. *The Chronical of Higher Education.*

Keniston, K. (1968). *Young radicals.* New York: Harcourt, Brace & World.

Kenrick, D.T., Neuberg, S.L., & Cialdini, R.B. (1999). *Social psychology: Unraveling the mystery.* Boston, MA: Allyn and Bacon.

Keough, K.A., Garcia, J., & Steele, C.M. (1997). Reducing stress and illness by affirming the self. Unpublished manuscript. University of Texas, Austin, Texas.

Kessler, G. (2007, January). Rice highlights opportunities after setbacks on Mideast trip. *Washington Post,* p. A14. Retrieved December 4, 2007, from: http://www.washingtonpost.com/wp-dyn/content/article/2007/01/18/AR2007011801881.html.

Kierkegaard, S. (1938). *Purity of heart is to will one thing.* New York: Harper & Row.

Killen, P.O. (2005, August 29). *Newsweek,* p. 50.

King, C.S. (1996, March 7). Presentation given at the Prevention Summit, HIV Prevention Community Planning Co-Chairs meeting, Atlanta, Georgia. *Windy City Times,* April. http://www.windycitymediagroup.com.

King Jr., M.L. (1968, April 3). I've been to the mountaintop. Speech in support of the striking sanitation workers at Mason Temple in Memphis, Tennessee. Atlanta, GA: Intellectual Properties Management.

King Jr., M.L. (2001, May-June). A witness to truth. *UU World: The Journal of the Unitarian-Universalist Association,*

Kinzel, A., & Nanson, J. (2000, July). Education and debriefing: Strategies for preventing crises in crisis-line volunteers. *Crisis, 21*(3), 126-134.

Kluckhohn, R. (Ed.) (1964). *Collected essays of Clyde Kluckhohn: Culture and behavior.* New York: The Free Press of Glencoe.

Kohlberg, L. (1969). Stage and sequence: The cognitive developmental approach to socialization. In D.A. Goslin (Ed.), *Handbook of socialization theory* (pp. 347-480). Chicago, IL: Rand McNally.

Kornfield, J. (1993). *A path with heart: A guide through the perils and promises of spiritual life.* New York: Bantam Books

Kornfield, J. (1999). Introduction. In M. Borg (Ed.), *Jesus and Buddha: The parallel sayings.* Berkeley, CA: Seastone.

Kottler, J., Carlson, J., & Keeney, B. (2004, July-August). Bringing the mystery home. *Psychotherapy Networker,*

Kraepelin, E. (1923) *Textbook of psychiatry* (8th ed.). New York: Macmillan.

Kramer, J., & Alstad, D. (1993). *The guru papers: Masks of authoritarian power.* Berkeley, CA: Frog Ltd (North Atlantic Books).

Kushner, H.S. (1983). *When bad things happen to good people.* New York: Avon Books.

Kushner, T. (1992). *Angels in America.* New York: Theatre Communications Group.

Lady Gryphon (2005). Rise of the phoenix. Retrived October 2, 2007, from: http://www.mythicalrealm.com/creatures/phoenix.html.

Laing, R.D. & Esterson, A. (1999). *Sanity, madness, and the family: Families of schizophrenics.* New York: Routledge.

Lance, H.D. (1989, June). The Bible and homosexuality. *American Baptist Quarterly, 8*(2), 140-151.

Lance, H.D. (1992, November 24). The anthropological context of Genesis 19 and Judges 19. Presentation given at the Society of Biblical Literature, San Francisco, CA.

Lance, H.D. (1992). *When Jesus changed his mind.* Sermon preached in First Baptist Church, Ithaca, New York.

Lawrence, D.H. (1964). Phoenix. In V. De Sola Pinto & F.W. Roberts (Eds.), *The Complete Poems of D.H. Lawrence* (p.728). New York: Viking Penguin.

Lawrence, J. (1987). Verbal processing of the Defining Issues Test by principled and non-principled moral reasoners. *Journal of Moral Education,16*(2), 117-130.

Layton, M. (2004, March-April). Case studies: Commentary. *Psychotherapy Networker,*

Lerner, M.J. (1980). *The belief in a just world: A fundamental delusion. Perspectives in social psychology.* New York: Plenum Press.

Lerner, M.L (2005). *The left hand of God: Taking back out country from the religious right.* San Francisco, CA: Harper Books.

Levant, R.F. & Pollack, W.S. (1995). *A new psychology of men.* New York: Basic Books.

Levanthal, H. (1970). Findings and theory in the study of fear communications. In L. Berkowitz (Ed.), *Advances in experimental social psychology* (Vol. 5, pp. 119-186). New York: Academic Press.

Levine, S. (1987). *Healing into life and death.* New York: Anchor Books.

Lifton, R.J. (1961). *History and human survival.* New York: Random House.

Lightdale, J.E. & Prentice, D.A. (1994). Rethinking sex differences in aggression: Aggressive behavior in the absence of social roles. *Personality and Social Psychology Bulletin, 20,* 34-44.

Lincoln, A. (1865). Second inaugural address. In D. Herbert (1995), *Lincoln.* New York: Audioworks.

Linn, M.C. & Hyde, J.S (1975-1976) Gender, mathematics & science. *Educational Research, 18,* 17-19, 22-37.

Linn, M.C. & Peterson, A.C. (1985). Emergency and characterization of sex differences in spatial ability: A meta-analysis. *Child Development, 56,* 1479-1498.

Locke, B.D. & Mahalik, J.R. (2005). Examining masculinity norms, problem drinking, and athletic involvement as predictors of sexual aggression in college men. *Journal of Counseling Psychology, 52*(3), 279-283.

London, P. (1986). *The modes and morals of psychotherapy* (2nd ed.). New York: W.W. Norton & Company.

Lott, B. (2002, February). Cognitive and behavioral distancing from the poor. *American Psychologist, 57*(2), 100-110.

Lovinger, R.L. (1984). *Working with religious issues in psychotherapy.* New York: Jason Aronson.

Lowe, C.M. (1976). *Values orientation in counseling and psychotherapy: The meanings of mental health* (2nd ed.). Cranston, RI: Carroll Press.

Lowen, A. (1975). *Pleasure: A creative approach to life.* New York: Penguin.

Lozoff, B. (2001). *It's a meaningful life, it just takes practice.* New York: Penguin Compass.

Maccoby, E.E. & Jacklin, C.N. (1974). *The psychology of sex differences.* Stanford, CA: Stanford University Press.

MacKenzie, R.A.F. (1968) Job. In R.E. Brown, J.A. Fitzmyer, & R.E. Murphy (Eds.), *The Jerome Biblical commentary* (pp. 511-533). Englewood Cliffs, NJ: Prentice Hall.

MacLeish, A. (1958). *J.B.: A play in verse* (Sentry ed.). Boston, MA: Houghton Mifflin.

Maqsud, M. (1977). Moral reasoning in Nigerian and Pakistani Muslim adolescents. *Journal of Moral Education, 7*(1), 40-49.

Marcia, J.E. (1964) *Determination and construct validity of ego identity status.* Unpublished manuscript.

Marcia, J.E. (1966). Development and validation of ego identity status. *Journal of Personality and Social Psychology, 3,* 551-558.

Marcia, J.E., Waterman, A.S., Matteson, D.R., Archer, S.L., & Orlofsky, J.L. (1993). Ego identity: A handbook for psychosocial research. New York: Springer-Verlag.

Markoulis, D. & Valanides, N. (1997). Antecedent variables for socio-moral reasoning development: Evidence from two cultural settings. *International Journal of Psychology, 32*(5), 301-313.

Markowitz, F. & Ashkenazi, M. (1999). *Sex, sexuality, and the anthropologist.* Urbana, IL: University of Illinois Press.

Marmor, J. (1980). Clinical aspects of homosexuality. In J. Marmor (Ed.) *Homosexual behavior* (pp. 267-279). New York: Basic Books.

Marsella, A.J. (1979) Cross-cultural studies of mental disorders. In A.J. Marsella, R.G. Tharp, & T.P. Ciborowski (Eds.), *Perspectives in Cross-Cultural Psychology* (pp. 233-262).

Maslow, A.H. (1954). *Motivation and personality.* New York: Harper & Row.

Maslow, A.H. (1964). *Religions, values, and peak experiences* (2nd ed.). New York: The Viking Press.

Maslow, A. (1968). *Toward a psychology of being.* New York: D. Van Nostrand.

Maslow, A. (1971). *The farther reaches of human nature.* New York: Viking Press.

Masson, J.M. (1988). *Against therapy: Emotional tyranny and the myth of psychological healing.* New York: Atheneum.

Masters, M.S. & Sanders, B. (1993). Is gender difference in mental rotation disappearing? *Behavior Genetics, 23,* 337-341.

Masters, W.H., Johnson, V., & Kolodny, R.C. (1982). *Human sexuality.* Boston, MA: Little Brown and Co.

Matteson, D.R. (1974) Changes in attitudes toward authority figures with the move to college: Three experiments. *Developmental Psychology, 10,* 3.

Matteson, D.R. (1975). *Adolescence today: Sex roles and the search for identity.* Homewood, IL: Dorsey-Irwin Press.

Matteson, D.R (1977a). Exploration and commitment: Sex differences and methodological problems in the use of the identity status categories. *Journal of Youth and Adolescence, 6,* 353-379.

Matteson, D.R. (1977b). Stereotypes of gay men. Unpublished lecture, Alternative Lifestyles seminar, Governors State University, University Park, Illinois.

Matteson, D.R. (1991, winter). Attempting to change sex role attitudes in adolescents: Explorations of reverse effects. *Adolescence, 26*(104), 885-898.

Matteson, D.R. (1993a). Differences within and between genders: A Challenge to the Theory. In J. E. Marcia, A.S. Waterman, S.L. Archer, & J.L. Orlofsky (Eds.), *Ego identity: A handbook for psychosocial research* (pp. 69-110). New York: Springer-Verlag.

Matteson, D.R. (1993b). Interviews and interviewing. In J.E. Marcia, A.S. Waterman, D.R. Matteson, S.L. Archer, & J.L. Orlofsky (Eds.), *Ego identity: A handbook for psychosocial research* (pp. 137-155). New York: Springer-Verlag.

Matteson, D.R. (1997). Bisexual and homosexual behavior and HIV risk among Chinese-, Filipino-, and Korean-American men. *Journal of Sex Research, 34*(1), 93-104.

Matteson, D.R. (1998). *Is modernity possible without alienation? Marriage choices of Indian and Indian-American women.* Unpublished manuscript.

Maugans, J. (2002, October 13). Light beyond enlightenment. A sermon given at Union University Church, Alfred, New York.

McAdams, D.P., Diamond, A., de St. Aubin, E., & Mansfield, E. (1997). Stories of commitment: The psychosocial construction of generative lives. *Journal of Personality and Social Psychology, 72,* 678-694.

McCorkle, A. (1996). Hidden in the present. In L. Zirker (Ed.), *Finding a way: Essays on spiritual practice* (pp. 77-91). Rutland, VT: Charles El. Tuttle Co., Inc.

McElroy, S. (1983, autumn). Child raising In non-violent cultures: Creating a culture that chooses non-violence with intention. *The Foundations of Peace, 4,* 37.

McIntosh, P. (1988, July-August) White privilege: Unpacking the invisible knapsack. Peace and Freedom. The Women's International League for Peace and Freedom. Philadelphia, PA.

McMullen, E. (2004). Music and language: A developmental comparison. *Music Perception, 21*(3), 289-312.

Mead, M. (1935). *Sex and temperament in three primitive societies.* New York: William Morrow.

Mead, M. (1953). *Growing up in New Guinea.* New York: Mentor.

Meyer-Bahlburg, H.F.L. (1982). Hormones and psychosexual differentiation: Implications for the management of intersexuality, homosexuality and transsexuality. *Clinics in Endocrinology and Metabolism, 11,* 681-701.

Milgram, S. (1963). Behavioral study of obedience. *Journal of Abnormal and Social Psychology, 67,* 371-378.

Milgram, S. (1965). Some conditions of obedience and disobedience to authority. *Human Relations, 18,* 57-76.

Milgram, S. (1974). *Obedience to authority: An experimental view.* New York: Harper & Row.

Milgram, S., Sabini, J., & Silver, M. (1992). *The individual in the social world: Essays and experiments.* New York: McGraw-Hill.

Milhaven, J.G. (1974). Conjugal sexual love and contemporary moral theology. *Theological Studies,* 35(4), pp. 203-211.

Miller, D.L. (1989) *Hells and holy ghosts: A theopoetics of Christian belief.* Nashville, TN: Abingdon Press.

Miller, R.J. (Ed.) (1994). *The complete gospels.* San Francisco, CA: Harper.

Mischey, E.J. (1981). Faith, identity, and morality in late adolescence. *Character Potential: A Record of Research, 9,* 175-185.

Mohr, J.J. & Weiner, J.L. (2006, fall). Client sexual orientation and psychotherapists' clinical perceptions. *Division 44 Newsletter,* 21-22.

Moon, Y.L. (1985, April). A review of cross-cultural studies on moral judgment development using the Defining Issues Test. Paper presented at AERA annual meeting, Chicago, Illinois.

Moore, T. (1997). *Mystic clouds and natural spirituality.* Newport, Gwent, UK: Orion Press Ltd.

Moyne, J. & Barks, C. (1984). *Open secret: Versions of Rumi.* New York: Threshold Books.

Myers, D.G. (1990). *Social psychology* (3rd ed.). New York: McGraw-Hill.

Nader, R. (2000). A paraphrase of a statement made in a presidential election campaign speech.

Narain, L.A., Arya, A., & Dube, D.N. (1986). *Khajuraho: Temples of ecstasy.* New Delhi, India: Lustra Press Pvt. Ltd.

Near, H. (1979) Singing for our lives. *Lifeline extended,* album with R. Gilbert, Appleseed Recordings. Words and music by H. Near, Hereford Music (ASCAP).

Neitzche, F. (1887). The gay science. In Neitzche, F. (1974). *The madman,* W. Kaufmann, trans. New York: Vintage.

Nelson, F.B. (1999). The life if Dietrich Bonhoeffer. In J.W. de Gruchy (Ed.), *The Cambridge Companion to Dietrich Bonhoeffer* (pp. 22-50). Cambridge, UK: Cambridge University Press.

Nelson, J.B. (1978). *Embodiment: An approach to sexuality and Christian theology.* Minneapolis, MN: Augsburg Publishing House.

Newcomb, T.M. (Ed.) (1957). Personality & social change; attitude formation in a student community. New York, Holt, Rinehart

Nieto, D.S. (1996). Who is the male homosexual? A computer-mediated exploratory study of gay male bulletin board system (BBS) users in New York City. *Journal of Homosexuality, 30*(4), 97-124.

Nimmons, D. (2002). *The soul beneath the skin: The unseen hearts and habits of gay men.* New York: St. Martin's Press.

Nissinen, M. (1998). *Homoeroticism in the biblical world: A historical perspective.* K. Stjerna, trans. Minneapolis, MN: Fortress Press.

Nooneman, A. & Holcomb, G. (2002, August 25). Faith development of undergraduates: Helps and hindrances. Presentation at the American Psychological Association, Chicago, Illinois.

O'Hanlon, B. (March 8-11, 2002). Getting Clear About Spirituality in Therapy. Workshop given at the Institute for the Advancement of Human Behavior, Portola Valley, California.

Ochsenfeld, G. (2001, August). Spirituality and nonordinary states of consciousness. Presentation given at Governors State University, University Park, Illinois.

Ochsner, K.N. & Lieberman, M.D. (2001, September). The emergence of social cognitive neuroscience. *American Psychologist, 56*(9), 717-734.

Oliver, M. (1994). *Dream work.* New York: Atlantic Monthly Press.

Oliver, M.B. & Hyde, J.S. (1993). Gender differences in sexuality: A meta-analysis. *Psychological Bulletin, 114*(1), 29-51.

Oltmanns, T.F. & Emery, R.E. (2001). *Abnormal psychology.* Upper Saddle River, NJ: Prentice Hall.

Orlofsky, J.L., Marcia, J.E., & Lester, I.M. (1973). Ego identity status and the intimacy versus isolation crisis of young adulthood. *Journal of Personality and Social Psychology, 27,* 211-219.

Otto, R. (1970). *The idea of the holy: An inquiry into the non-rational factor in the idea of the divine, and its relation to the rational.* J.W. Harvey, trans. New York: Oxford University Press.

Parks, S. (1980). Faith development and imagination in the context of higher education. Unpublished doctoral dissertation, Harvard Divinity School, Cambridge, Massachusetts.

Peale, N.V. (1952) *The power of positive thinking.* New York: Prentice-Hall.

Peale, N.V. & Peale, R.S. (2000). *Discovering the power of positive thinking.* Pawling, NY: Peale Center for Christian Living.

Peers, E.A. (1958). Introduction. In St. John of the Cross, *Ascent of Mount Carmel* (3rd rev. ed.). E.A. Peers (Ed.), trans. New York: Image Books.

Pellegrini, A.D., & Horvat, M. (1995, January-February). A developmental contextualist critique of attention deficit hyperactivity disorder. *Educational Researcher,* 13-19.

Pennebaker, J.W. & Beall, S.K. (1986). Confronting a traumatic event: Toward an understanding of inhibition and disease. *Journal of Abnormal Psychology, 95,* 274-281.

Pennebaker, J.W., Barger, S.D., & Tiebout, J. (1989). Disclosure of traumas and health among Holocaust survivors. *Psychosomatic Medicine, 51,* 577-589.

Pennebaker, J.W., Colder, M., & Sharp, L.K. (1990). Accelerating the coping process. *Journal of Personality and Social Psychology, 58,* 528-537.

Pennebaker, J.W., Kiecolt-Glaser, J.K., & Glaser, R. (1988). Disclosure of traumas and immune function: Health implications for psychotherapy. *Journal of Consulting and Clinical Psychology, 56,* 239-245.

Perls, F. (1973a). *Gestalt dream analysis: A session with four college students.* Video recording. Gouldsboro, ME: The Gestalt Journal Press.

Perls, F. (1973b). *The gestalt approach & eye witness to therapy.* Palo Alto, CA: Science & Behavior Books.

Petrie, K.J., Booth, RJ., Pennebaker, J.W., Davison, K.P., & Thomas, M.G. (1995). Disclosure of trauma and immune response to a hepatitis B vaccination program. *Journal of Consulting and Clinical Psychology, 63,* 787-792.

Pfeiffer, S.I. & Stocking, V.B. (2000). Vulnerabilities of academically gifted students. *Special Services in the Schools, 16,* 83-93.

Philpot, V.D. & Bamburg, J.W. (1996, August). Rehearsal of positive self-statements and restructured negative self-statements to increase self esteem and decrease depression. *Psychological Reports, 79*(1), 83-91.

Phipps, W.E. (1975). *Recovering biblical sensuousness.* Philadelphia, PA: Westminster.

Piaget, J. (1965). *The moral judgment of the child.* M. Gabian, trans. New York: Harcourt, Brace & World, Free Press.

Plant, E.A., Hyde, J.S., Keltner, D., & Devine, P.G. (2000). The gender stereotyping of emotions. *Psychology of Women Quarterly, 24,* 81-92.

Povinelli, D. (August 24-28, 2001). Chimpanzees, children and the evolution of the human capacity for explanation. Presentation at the American Psychological Association Annual Convention, San Francisco CA.

Powell, L.H., Shahabi, L., & Thoresen, C.E. (2003). Religion and spirituality: Linkages to physical health. *American Psychologist, 58*(1), 36-52.

Prectel, M. (1998). *The secrets of the talking jaguar: Memoirs from the living heart of a Mayan village.* New York: Penguin Group.

Prescott, J.W. (1977). Phylogenetic and ontogenetic aspects of human affectional development. In R. Gemme & C.C. Wheeler (Eds.), *Progress in sexology: Selected papers from the Proceedings of the 1976 International Congress of Sexology* (p.19-23). New York: Plenum Press.

Prilleltensky, I. (1997, May). Values, assumptions, and practices: Assessing the moral implications of psychological discourse and action. *American Psychologist, 52*(5), 517-535.

Rapp, C. (1997). Ritual brotherhood in Byzantium. *Tradition, 52,* 285-326.

Ratzinger, J. (2004, August 1). Vatican document on gender differences. *St. Louis Post Dispatch,* p. B2

Raven, B.H. (1999). Reflections on interpersonal influence and social power in experimental social psychology. In A. Rodrigues & R.V. Levine (Eds.), *Reflections on 100 years of experimental-social psychology* (p. 121). New York: Basic Books.

Rea, B.D. (2001, spring). Finding our balance: The investigation and clinical application of intuition. *Psychotherapy, 38*(1), 97-106.

Reed, M.B. & Aspinwall, L.G. (1998, June). Self-affirmation reduces biased processing of health-risk information. *Motivation and Emotion, 22*(2), 99-132.

Regehr, C., Goldberg, G., & Hughes, J. (2002, October). Exposure to human tragedy, empathy, and trauma in ambulance paramedics. *American Journal of Orthopsychiatry, 72*(4), 505-513.

Rest, J., Narvaez, D., Bebeau, M.J., & Thoma, S.J. (1999). *Postconventional moral thinking: A neo-Kohlbergian approach.* Mahwah, NJ: Lawrence Erlbaum Associates.

Rodgers, R. & Hammerstein, O. (1949). You've got to be carefully taught. *South Pacific*. Words and music by R. Rodgers and O. Hammerstein. New York: Williamson Music.

Roetz, H. (1996). Kohlberg and Chinese moral philosophy. *World Psychology, 2*(3-4), 335-363.

Rogers, C. (1961). *On becoming a person: A therapist's view of psychotherapy.* Boston, MA: Houghton-Mifflin.

Rogers, C. (1965). *client-centered therapy: Its current practice, implications, and theory.* Boston, MA: Houghton Mifflin.

Rogers Jr., E.R. (1999). *Sexuality and the Christian body: Their way into the triune God.* Malden, MA: Blackwell Publishing.

Rohr, R. (2005, March). Beyond "certitudes and order": the Vaticans management problem. *Sojourners.* Retrieved from and available at: http://www.sojo.net/index.cfm?action=magazine.article&issue=soj0503&article=050310b.

Rokeach, M. (1960). *The open and closed mind.* New York: Basic Books.

Rokeach, M. (1970). Faith, hope, bigotry. *Psychology Today, 3*(11), 33-37ff.

Roland, A. (1996). Culture, comparativity, and psychoanalysis: Reply to commentary. *Psychoanalytic Dialogues, 6*(4), 489-495.

Roland, A. (1988). *In search of self in India and Japan: Toward a cross-cultural psychology.* Princeton, NJ: Princeton University Press.

Rotter, J. (1971, June). External control and internal control. *Psychology Today, 41*(47), 58-59.

Rotter, J.B., Chance, J.E., & Phares, E.J. (1972). *Applications of a social learning theory of personality.* New York: Holt, Rinehart & Winston.

Russell, B. (1968). *Authority and the individual.* New York: AMS Press.

Sagan, C. (1997). *Demon haunted world: Science as a candle in the dark.* New York: Ballantine Books.

Sagan, C. & Druyan, A. (1992). *Shadows of forgotten ancestors: A search for who we are.* New York: Random House.

Salais, D. & Fischer, R.B. (1995). Sexual preference and altruism. *Journal of Homosexuality, 28,* 185-196.

Samuel, V.J. & Dollinger, S.J. (1989). Self focused attention and the recognition of psychological implications. *The Journal of Psychology, 123*(6), 623-625.

Sanford, N. (Ed.) (1962). *The American college: A psychological interpretation of the higher learning.* New York: John Wiley & Sons

Schauben, L.J. & Frazier, P.A. (1995). Vicarious trauma: The effects on female counselors of working with sexual violence survivors. *Psychology of Women Quarterly, 19,* 49-64.

Schneider, S.L. (2001, March). In search of realistic optimism: Meaning, knowledge, and warm fuzziness. *American Psychologist, 56*(3), 250-263.

Schwartz, R. (1995). *Internal family systems therapy.* New York: Guilford Press.
Schwartz, R.C. (2002). Couples counseling with Dr. Richard Schwartz. In J. Carlson and D. Kjos (Eds.), *Family therapy with the experts.* Three videocassettes. Boston, MA: Allyn and Bacon.
Schwartzer, R. & Wicklund, R.A. (1991). *Anxiety and self-focused attention.* New York: Harwood Academic Publishers.
Scroggs, R. (1983) *The New Testament and homosexuality: The contextual background for contemporary debate.* Philadelphia, PA: Fortress Press.
Seeman, T.E., Dubin, L.F., and Seeman, M. (2003). Religiosity/spirituality and health. *American Psychologist, 58*(1), 5-63.
Seligman, M.E.P., Steen, T.A., Park, N., & Peterson, C. (2005, July-August). Positive psychology progress: Empirical validation of interventions. *American Psychologist, 60*(5), 410-421.
Sennett, R. (1981). *Authority.* New York: Vintage Books
Shafer, B.F. (1978). *The church and homosexuality.* New York: United Presbyterian Church in U.S.A.
Sharp, J.W. (2005, June). On the trail of Kokopelli. Retrieved from www.desertusa.com/mag00/apr/stories/trail_kok.html.
Shaw, B. (1994, July 18) A Groom of one's own? *The New Republic,* 33-41.
Shidlo, A., Schroeder, M., & Drescher, J. (Eds.) (2001). *Sexual conversion therapy: Ethical, clinical, and research perspectives.* Binghamton, NY: The Haworth Medical Press.
Shweder, R.A., Mahapatra, M., & Miller, J.G. (1987). Culture and moral development. In J. Kagan & S. Lamb (Eds.), *The emergence of morality in young children* (pp. 1-83). Chicago, IL: University of Chicago Press.
Shweder, R.A., Mahapatra, M., & Miller, J.G. (1990). Culture and moral development. In J. Stigler, R.A. Shweder, & G. Herdt (Eds.), *Cultural psychology: Essays on comparative human development* (pp. 73-112). New York: Cambridge University Press.
Siegel, D.J. (2002, September). *The developing mind: Toward a neurobiology of interpersonal experience.* New York: Guilford Press.
Siegler, R.S. (1997). Concepts and methods for studying cognitive change. In E. Amsel & K.A. Renninger (Eds.), *Change and development: Issues of theory, method, and application* (pp. 77-98). Mahwah, NH: Lawrence Erlbaum Associates.
Silone, I. (1963). *Bread and wine.* New York: Signet (New American Library).
Silone, I. (1968). *Emergency exit: World perspectives.* New York: Evanston.
Silverman, I. & Eals, M. (1992). Sex differences in spatial abilities: Evolutionary theory and data. In J. Barkow, L. Cosmides, & J. Tooby (Eds.), *The adapted mind: Evolutionary psychology and the generation of culture* (pp. 539-549). New York: Oxford University Press.
Simkin, J.S. & Obern, V. (1980). *In the now.* Video recording. Corona del Mar, CA: Psychological & Educational Films.

Simon, L., Greenberg, J., & Brehm, J. (1995). Trivialization: The forgotten mode of dissonance reduction. *Journal of Personality & Social Psychology, 68*(2), 247-260.

Simon, W. & Gagnon, J. (1969) Psychosexual development. *Transaction, 6,* 15-16.

Skoyles, J.R. (2000). The singing origin theory of speech. Paper presented at the third annual Conference on the Evolution of Language, April 3-6, Paris, France.

Slater, W., Hall, T.W., Edwards, K.J. (2003). Measuring religion and spirituality: Where are we and where are we going? In T.W. Hall & M.R. McMinn (Eds.), *Spiritual formation, counseling, and psychotherapy* (pp. 235-260). Hauppauge, NY: Nova Science Publishers, Inc.

Snarey, J. (1985). The cross-cultural universality of social-moral development. *Psychological Bulletin, 97*(2), 202-232.

Snarey, J. & Keljo, K. (1991). In a Gemeinschaft voice: The cross-cultural expansion of moral development theory. In W.M. Kurtines & J.L. Gewirtz (Eds.), *Handbook of moral behavior and development* (Vol. 1: Theory, pp. 395-424). Hillsdale, NJ: Lawrence Earlbaum Associates.

Solzhenitsyn, A.I. (1973). *The Gulag Archipelago, 1918-1956.* New York: Harper and Row.

Soulforce (2005). 4 step journey: Step 2. Retrieved from http://www.soulforce .org/article/568.

Spera, S.P., Buhrfeind, E.D., & Pennebaker, J.W. (1994). Expressive writing and coping with job loss. *Academy of Management Journal, 37,* 722-733.

Sponsel, L.E. (2000). Do anthropologists need religion, and vice versa? Adventures and dangers in Spiritual ecology. In C.L. Crumley, (Ed.), *New directions in anthropology & environment* (pp. 177-200). Walnut Creek, CA: Altamira Press.

Squier, R. (1990). A model of empathic understanding and adherence to treatment regimes in practitioner-patient relationships. *Social Science Medicine, 30,* 325-339.

Starr, M. (2005, August). A garden of righteousness. *Sojourners,* 34(8), 36.

Steele, C.M. (1988). The psychology of self-affirmation: Sustaining the integrity of the self. In L. Berkowitz (Ed.), *Advances in experimental social psychology* (Vol. 21, pp. 261-302). Hillsdale, NJ: Erlbaum.

Steele, C.M., Spencer, S.J. & Lynch, M. (1993). Dissonance and affirmational resources: Resilience against self-image threats. *Journal of Personality and Social Psychology, 64,* 885-896.

Stein, P.J. & Hoffman, S. (1978). Sports and male role strain. *Journal of Social Issues, 34*(1), 136-150.

Stevens, W. (1950). *The auroras of autumn.* New York: Knopf.

Strup, H.H. & Hadley, S.M. (1977). A tripartite model of mental health and therapeutic outcomes. *American Psychologist, 32,* 187-196.

Sue, D., Sue, D.W., & Sue, S. (2000). *Understanding abnormal behavior* (6th ed.). Boston, MA: Houghton Mifflin.

Swinging both ways (2001, December 19). *Windy City Times,* p. 9.

Szasz, T.S. (1961). *The myth of mental illness: Foundations of a theory of personal conduct.* New York: Harper & Row.

Taylor, A. (1983). Conceptions of masculinity and femininity as a basis for stereotypes of male and female homosexuals. *Journal of Homosexuality, 9*(1), 37-53.

Tennen, H., Affleck, G., Armeli, S., & Carney, M.A. (2000, June). A daily process approach to coping: Linking theory, research, and practice. *American Psychologist, 55*(6), 626-636.

Tennyson, A.L. (1885). The ancient sage. *Tiresias, and other poems.* Retrieved October 4, 2007, from http://whitewolf.newcastle.edu.au/words/authors/T/TennysonAlfred/verse/tiresias/ancientsage.html.

Tesser A., Chen, N., Collins, J.C., Cornell, D., & Beach, S.R.H. (1997). Confluence of self-defense mechanisms: On integrating the self-zoo. Unpublished manuscript, University of Georgia, Athens, Georgia.

Thoma, S.J. (1994). Moral judgment and moral action. In J. Rest & D. Narvaez (Eds.), *Moral development in the professions: Psychology and applied ethics* (pp. 199-211). Hillsdale, NJ: Lawrence Erlbaum Associates.

Thomas, J.R. & French, K.E. (1985). Gender differences across age in motor performance: A meta-analysis. *Psychological Bulletin, 98,* 260-282.

Tillich, P. (1955). *The shaking of the foundations.* New York: Charles Scribner's Sons.

Tillich, P. (1958). *Dynamics of faith.* New York: Harper Torchbook.

Tisak, M. (1995). Domains of social reasoning and beyond. In R. Vista (Ed.), *Annals of child development* (Vol. 11, pp. 95-130). London, UK: Jessica Kingsley.

Tonnies, F. (1957). *Community and society: Gemeinschaft und gesellschaft.* C.P. Loomis (Ed.), trans. East Lansing, MI: Michigan State Unviersity Press.

Turiel, E. (1978). Social regulation and the domain of social concepts. *New Directions for Child Development, 1,* 45-74.

Turiel, E. (1983). *The development of social knowledge: Morality and convention.* Cambridge, UK: Cambridge University Press.

Turner, H.A., Catania, J.A., & Gagnon, J. (1994). The prevalence of informal caregiving to persons with AIDS in the United States: Caregiver characteristics and their implications. *Social Science and Medicine, 38*(11), 1543-1552.

United Nations Population Fund Report (2001, August). "The State of World Population 2001" www.unfpa.org/swp/2001/english/index.html

Vaneechouette, M. & Skoyles, J.R. (1998). The memetic origin of language: Modern humans as musical primates. *Journal of Mimetics: Evolutionary Models of Information Transmission, 2*(2), 129-169.

Ventura, M. (2003). The experience of soul. *Psychotherapy Networker, vol. 27* 52-57, 63.

Ventura, M. (2004, January-February). The question of marriage. *Psychotherapy Networker, vol 28,* 62-65.

Ventura, M. (2005, June 4). Untitled. Presentation at the 31st annual Great Mother Conference, Lake Nebagamon, Wisconsin.

Voltaire, F-M.A. (1946). *Candide [Optimism].* New York: Appleton-Century-Crofts, Inc.

Wagstaff, G. (1982). Attitudes to rape: The "just world" strikes again? *Bulletin of the British Psychological Society, 35,* 277-279.

Walster, E., Aaronson, V., Abrahams, D., & Rottman, L. (1966). The importance of physical attractiveness in dating behavior. *Journal of Personality and Social Psychology, 4,* 508-516.

Washburn, M. (1994). *Transpersonal psychology in psychoanalytic perspective.* Albany, NY: State University of New York Press.

Washburn, M. (1995). *The ego and the dynamic ground: A transpersonal theory of human development* (2nd ed.). Albany, NY: State University of New York Press.

Watanabe-Hammond, S. (1987). The many faces of Paul and Dora. *The Family Networker, vol. 9,* 54, 87-91.

Watanabe-Hammond, S. (1988). Blueprints from the past: A character work perspective on siblings and personality formation. In M.D. Kahn, & K.G. Lewis (Eds.), *Siblings in therapy: Life span and clinical issues* (pp. 356-378). New York: W.W. Norton & Company.

Watanabe-Hammond, S. (1990). Family dances and the rhythms of intimacy. *Contemporary Family Therapy, 12*(4), 327-338.

Waterman, A.S. (1981, July). Individualism and interdependence. *American Psychologist, 36*(7), 762-773.

Waterman, A.S. (Ed.) (1985). *Identity and adolescence: Processes and contents.* San Francisco, CA: Jossey-Bass.

Watt, J. (2002, May). *Letter in the crow: A publication of the Great Mother/New Father Conferences.* West Newton, MA: Jon Parsons.

Watts, W.A., Lynch, S., & Whittaker, D. (1969). Alienation and activism in today's college-age youth: Socialization patterns and current family relationships. *Journal of Counseling Psychology, 16,* 1-7.

Watzlavick, Beavin, Helmick, & Jackson, D.D. (1967). *Pragmatics of hHuman communication.* W.W. Norton & Company.

Webb, J.T (2000, August 7). Mis-diagnosis and dual diagnosis of gifted children: Gifted and LD, ADHD, OCD, oppositional defiant disorder. Symposium Cutting edge minds: What it means to be exceptional. Paper presented at the American Psychological Association Annual Convention, Washington, DC.

Welwood, J. (2000). *Toward a psychology of awakening.* Boston, MA: Shambhala Publications.

Wenkelman, M. (1997). Altered states of consciousness and religious behavior. In S.D. Glazier (Ed.), *Anthropology of religion: A handbook* (pp.). Westport, CT: Glennwood Press.

Weston, R.T. (1993). Cherish your doubts. *Singing the Living Tradition,* Unitarian Universalist Association Hymnal. Boston, MA: Beacon Press. Hymn no. 650.

Wheeler, K. & Barrett, A. (1994). Review and synthesis of selected nursing studies on teaching empathy and implications for nursing research and education. *Nursing Outlook, 42,* 230-236.

Where we stand on faith (2005, August 29). Newsweek/Beliefnet poll. *Newsweek,* 48-49.

White, M. (n.d.). What the Bible says—and doesn't say—about homosexulity. Retrieved October 4, 2007, from http://www.soulforce.org/article/homosexuality-bible-gay-christian.

Whitman, F.L., Diamond, M., & Martin, J. (1993). Homosexual orientation in twins: A report on 61 pairs and three triplet sets. *Archives of Sexual Behavior, 22,* 193.

Wicker, B., Keysers, C., Plailly, J., Royet, J.P., Gallese, V., & Rizzolatti, G. (2003, October 20). Both of us disgusted in my insula: The common neural basis of seeing and feeling disgust. *Neuron, 40*(3), 655-664.

Wiesel, E. (1977). Art and culture after the Holocaust. In E. Fleischner (Ed.), *Auschwitz: Beginning of a new era? Reflections on the Holocaust* (pp. 403-415). New York: KTAV Publishing House, Inc.

Wilber, K. (1990). Two patterns of transcendence: A reply to Washburn. *Journal of Humanistic Psychology 30,* 113-136.

Wilber, K. (1999). Spirituality and developmental lines: Are there stages? *Journal of Transpersonal Psychology, 31*(1), 1-10.

Wilber, K. (2000). *Integral psychology: Consciousness, spirit, psychology, therapy* (1st pbk ed.). Boston, MA: Shambhala Publications.

Wilson, E.O. (1998, April). The biological basis of morality. *Atlantic Monthly,* 53-70.

Winerman, L. (2005, October 5). The mind's mirror. *American Psychological Association Monitor on Psychology, 6*(9), 48-50.

Wink, W. (Ed.) (1999). *Homosexuality and the Christian faith: Questions of conscience for the churches.* Minneapolis, MN: Fortress Press.

Wolkstein, D. (1988). *Inanna.* Video recording. Adapted from D. Wolkstein & S.N. Kramer (1983). *Inanna, queen of heaven and earth: Her stories and hymns from Sumer.* New York: Harper & Row.

Wood, W. & Rhodes, N. (1992). Sex difference in interaction style in task groups. In C. L. Ridgeway (Ed.), *Gender, interaction, and inequality* (pp. 97-121). New York: Springer-Verlag.

World Health Organization. (1958). Constitution of World Health Organization. Annex I. In *The first ten years of the W.H.O.* Geneva, Switz.: World Health Organization.

Wylie, M.S. & Simon, R. (2002, September-October). Discoveries for the black box: How the neuroscience revolution can change your practice. *Psychotherapy Networker, 26*(5), 28, 29, 31.

Zillmann, D. (1984) *Connections between sex and aggression.* Hillsdale, NJ: Lawrence Erlbaum Associates.

Zinnbauer, B.J., Pargament, K., Cole, R., Mark, S., Butter, E.M., Belavich, T.G., Hipp, K.M., Scott, A.B., & Kadar, J.L. (1997). Religion and spirituality: Unfuzzing the fuzzy. *Journal for the Scientific Study of Religion, 36*(4), 549-564.

Zorn, E. (2001, October 13). Secular tenets are much better than "nothing." *Chicago Tribune*. Section 1, p 9.

Zuckerman, M. (1983). Sensation seeking in homosexual and heterosexual males. *Archives of Sexual Behavior, 12*(4), 347-356

Index

B

C

H

I

J

N

Q

R

S

W

Y

Z